The Intellectual Property Holding Company

Many companies that have become household names have avoided billions in taxes by "parking" their valuable intellectual property (IP) assets in holding companies located in tax-favored jurisdictions. In the United States, for example, many domestic companies have moved their IP to tax-favored states such as Delaware or Nevada, while multinational companies have done the same by setting up foreign subsidiaries in places like Ireland, Singapore, Switzerland, and the Netherlands. In this illuminating work, tax scholar Jeffrey Maine teams up with intellectual property expert Xuan-Thao Nguyen to explain how the use of these IP holding companies has become economically unjustified and socially unacceptable, and how numerous calls for change have been made. This book should be read by anyone interested in how corporations – including Gore-Tex, Victoria's Secret, Sherwin-Williams, Toys-R-Us, Apple, Microsoft, and Uber – have avoided tax liability with IP holding companies and how different constituencies are working to stop them.

JEFFREY A. MAINE is Maine Law Foundation Professor of Law at the University of Maine School of Law. An expert on tax law, he has published seven books and numerous articles in the field. Professor Maine focuses his current research on the intersection of taxation and intellectual property, and has co-authored with Xuan-Thao Nguyen a treatise and a law school textbook on the tax treatment of intellectual property. Formerly a practicing attorney at Holland & Knight, Professor Maine has more than twenty years of experience in teaching, including positions at six law schools.

XUAN-THAO NGUYEN is the Gerald L. Bepko Chair in Law and Director at the Center for Intellectual Property & Innovation, Indiana University McKinney School of Law. She is a senior consultant for the World Bank Group IFC. She won the prestigious 2016 Grant Gilmore Award for her publications on the intersection of intellectual property and commercial laws. She has published ten books and more than thirty law review articles on intellectual property, taxation of intellectual property, and commercial law. Her works are cited by the Federal Circuit, the Third Circuit, the Ninth Circuit, federal district courts, and state tax courts.

Cambridge Intellectual Property and Information Law

As its economic potential has rapidly expanded, intellectual property has become a subject of front-rank legal importance. *Cambridge Intellectual Property and Information Law* is a series of monograph studies of major current issues in intellectual property. Each volume contains a mix of international, European, comparative and national law, making this a highly significant series for practitioners, judges and academic researchers in many countries.

Series editors

Lionel Bently
Herchel Smith Professor of Intellectual Property Law, University of Cambridge

Graeme Dinwoodie
Professor of Intellectual Property and Information Technology Law, University of Oxford

Advisory editors

William R. Cornish, *Emeritus Herchel Smith Professor of Intellectual Property Law, University of Cambridge*

François Dessemontet, *Professor of Law, University of Lausanne*

Jane C. Ginsburg, *Morton L. Janklow Professor of Literary and Artistic Property Law, Columbia Law School*

Paul Goldstein, *Professor of Law, Stanford University*

The Rt Hon. Sir Robin Jacob, *Hugh Laddie Professor of Intellectual Property, University College, London*

Ansgar Ohly, *Professor of Intellectual Property Law, Ludwig Maximilian University of Munich, Germany*

A list of books in the series can be found at the end of this volume.

The Intellectual Property Holding Company

Tax Use and Abuse from Victoria's Secret to Apple

Jeffrey A. Maine
University of Maine School of Law

Xuan-Thao Nguyen
Indiana University Robert H. McKinney School of Law

CAMBRIDGE
UNIVERSITY PRESS

CAMBRIDGE
UNIVERSITY PRESS

University Printing House, Cambridge CB2 8BS, United Kingdom

One Liberty Plaza, 20th Floor, New York, NY 10006, USA

477 Williamstown Road, Port Melbourne, VIC 3207, Australia

314–321, 3rd Floor, Plot 3, Splendor Forum, Jasola District Centre, New Delhi – 110025, India

79 Anson Road, #06–04/06, Singapore 079906

Cambridge University Press is part of the University of Cambridge.

It furthers the University's mission by disseminating knowledge in the pursuit of education, learning, and research at the highest international levels of excellence.

www.cambridge.org
Information on this title: www.cambridge.org/9781107128262
DOI: 10.1017/9781316414606

First published 2017

Printed in the United States of America by Sheridan Books, Inc.

A catalogue record for this publication is available from the British Library.

Library of Congress Cataloging-in-Publication Data
Names: Maine, Jeffrey A., author. | Nguyen, Xuan-Thao N., author.
Title: The intellectual property holding company : tax use and abuse from Victoria's Secret to Apple / Jeffrey A. Maine, University of Maine School of Law; Xuan-Thao Nguyen, Indiana University Robert H. McKinney School of Law.
Description: Cambridge, United Kingdom ; New York, NY, USA : Cambridge University Press, 2017. | Series: Cambridge intellectual property and information law
Identifiers: LCCN 2017029642 | ISBN 9781107128262 (hardback)
Subjects: LCSH: License agreements – Taxation – Law and legislation – United States. | Corporations – Taxation – Law and legislation – United States. | Holding companies – Taxation – Law and legislation – United States.
Classification: LCC KF6428.I5 M349 2017 | DDC 343.7306/7–dc23
LC record available at https://lccn.loc.gov/2017029642

ISBN 978-1-107-12826-2 Hardback

Contents

v

Tables and Figures

1   Introduction

The laws of taxation are comparable to the rules of a complex game, such as poker.[1] Like poker, "playing" tax is about winning, or at least keeping, money. The seriousness of either game depends on the size of the stakes and whether the player can afford to lose. It is, after all, only money. But there remains one crucial difference: unlike poker, one cannot fold or opt out of the tax game. We are all obliged to play.

The players in the tax game are the government and the taxpayer. The government has one great advantage in that it writes the rules. However, the government must also (at least in democratic states) answer ultimately to the taxpayer, thus constraining its authoritarian tendencies. Moreover, it is very hard to write rules that contain no loopholes. Lawyers, accountants, and business people often display great ingenuity in exploiting this inherent difficulty. In the end, the game of tax is probably an even contest. Most taxpayers agree that the government is entitled to a reasonable share of financial support in exchange for the services that it provides. However, most taxpayers also agree that the government should obtain those revenues from someone else. Thus, the game is hard fought and never ending.[2]

The game of tax has never been more serious than it is today. Faced with structural budget deficits, many national (and sub-national) governments have become aware of tax minimization strategies that lead to an erosion of their tax revenue bases. Much of this undesirable taxpayer behavior can be linked to the lack of updated tax systems to deal with the rise of intellectual property's role in a rapidly changing global economy. Early systems of taxation did not specifically focus on intellectual

---

[1] *See* John A. Miller & Jeffrey A. Maine, *The Fundamentals of Federal Taxation* 4 (Durham, NC: Carolina Academic Press, 2017).

[2] The game was best described by Louis XIV's Finance Minister John-Baptiste Colbert: "The art of taxation consists in so plucking the goose as to obtain the largest possible amount of feathers with the smallest possible amount of hissing." William Sharp McKechnie, *The State & the Individual: An Introduction to Political Science, with Special Reference to Socialistic and Individualistic Theories* (James MacLehose & Sons, 1896), 77.

property, which was of no particular consequence at a time when tangible, physical property was the driving engine of commerce. As intellectual property's role in the world economy has increased,[3] however, these antiquated tax systems (and their interactions with other tax systems) have created incentives for taxpayers with a lot of intellectual property to avoid taxes.[4]

In recent years, governments have struggled with how to write equitable and efficient tax rules governing emerging intellectual property assets – such as rules that will appropriately incentivize intellectual property development in their jurisdictions, or rules that will ensure their fair and appropriate share of tax revenues from intellectual property. Taxpayers, on the other hand, have attempted, within the letter of the law, to structure their intellectual property transactions to maximize tax benefits and create more value from their intellectual property.[5] For example, tax considerations can be important drivers in deciding how to structure an intellectual property license, or acquire intellectual property, or draft pleadings in an intellectual property lawsuit to achieve optimal results. Tax considerations are also often a key factor in deciding where to locate a firm's intellectual property assets.

Some of the most popular tax planning strategies involve "parking" intellectual property in holding subsidiaries located in tax-favored jurisdictions. In the United States, for example, many domestic companies operating in multiple states have reduced their overall *state tax burden* by moving their intellectual property assets to holding companies located in tax-favored states, such as Delaware or Nevada. Likewise, many US companies with foreign operations have reduced their *US and foreign*

---

[3] In 2012, the US Commerce Department released its comprehensive report on intellectual property. In the United States alone, intellectual property intensive industries support at least 40 million jobs. Intellectual property contributes more than $5 trillion to the US gross domestic product (GDP), or 34.8 percent of the GDP. "Intellectual Property and the U.S. Economy," U.S. Patent and Trademark Office, accessed November 3, 2016, www.uspto.gov/learning-and-resources/ip-motion/intellectual-property-and-us-economy.

[4] Joy Hail, "An Overview of the OECD Action Plan on BEPS," *Taxes: The Tax Magazine* 94 (2016): 47 (noting that the rise and increasing importance of intellectual property have highlighted how out of step traditional tax policies have become). "Apple Should Repay Ireland 13bn Euros, European Commission Rules," *BBC News*, August 30, 2016, www.bbc.com/news/business-37220799 ("Individual governments appear impotent in their attempts to apply their tax laws to multinationals like Apple. They have systems designed to deal with the movement and sale of physical goods, systems that are useless when companies derive their profits from the sale of services and the exploitation of intellectual property").

[5] *See* Alina Macovei & Marc Rasch, "Tax and the Strategic Management of Intangibles," *Intellectual Asset Management* (March/April 2011): 23–28, available at www.iam-media.com/Magazine/Issue/46/Features/Taxand-the-strategic-management-of-intangibles.

tax burdens by transferring their intellectual property assets and operations to controlled foreign subsidiaries in low- (or zero-) tax countries, such as Ireland, Singapore, Switzerland, and the Netherlands, as well as sandy tax havens like Bermuda and the Cayman Islands. This book closely examines these tax minimization strategies – specifically the use of *domestic* and *foreign* IP Holding Companies. Interestingly, the two companies – Apple and Victoria's Secret – that are in the title of this book and subject to further examination in later chapters, formed their key IP Holding Companies in the same year decades ago.

Use of Domestic Intellectual Property Holding Companies

Corporations are utilized for a variety of reasons. Corporations can, for example, protect owners from legal liabilities and provide businesses greater access to financing through capital markets. But corporations can also be used for more questionable purposes – most notably the avoidance of taxes. Leaked documents from a Panamanian law firm reveal how corporate entities in certain US states have been used by some of the world's richest individuals to hide cash and avoid taxes.[6]

The use of corporate entities in certain US states to hold intellectual property is particularly pervasive. Victoria's Secret, Dow, Honeywell, Limited Stores, Lane Bryant, Express, Sherwin Williams, Toys-R-Us, and Abercrombie & Fitch are all examples of US corporations that shift intellectual property assets to wholly owned subsidiary companies located in tax-favored states, but that turnaround and license back the right to use that same intellectual property.[7]

Delaware is a particularly attractive jurisdiction for domestic US subsidiaries. In fact, different companies form an astonishing 600 to 800 subsidiaries annually in Delaware. And the practice is not confined to a specific sector of the economy. In the retail and apparel industry, the notables include Victoria's Secret, Gap, Limited Stores, Lane Bryant, Express, Abercrombie & Fitch, Talbots, H.D. Lee Company, Wrangler Clothing, Spring Industries, and Nordstrom NIHC – all companies that transfer valuable trademarks to Delaware holding subsidiaries. Countless

---

[6] "What Are the Panama Papers?," *The New York Times*, April 4, 2016, www.nytimes.com /2016/04/05/world/panama-papers-explainer.html?_r=0.

[7] Dow Chemical Company, for example, executed an agreement between Dow and its wholly owned Delaware subsidiary, Dow Global Technologies, wherein all of Dow's patents were contributed to its subsidiary for tax shelter purposes, according to Edward Valenzuela, Dow's former Manager of Tax Economics, who was responsible for the finances of the tax shelter and calculation of royalties paid by Dow to its subsidiary.

others, in industries ranging from home improvements to department stores, transfer their intellectual property assets to wholly owned subsidiaries in Delaware. And Fortune 500 Companies, ranging from Stanley Black & Decker to Home Depot to Walmart to Chevron, are organized under the laws of Delaware and have formed IP Holding Companies in the same state.

This begs the question, why are companies attracted to Delaware? After all, it is a small state not known for its natural resources, a technical workforce of Silicon Valley caliber, or sales force. Certainly, Victoria's Secret does not need to set up its subsidiary in Delaware to hold its valuable brand in order to market and sell lingerie. Not only does Delaware have a limited population, it has within its borders only four out of the total 1,060 Victoria's Secret stores in the United States. Likewise, technologically, Honeywell does not need to locate its patents in Delaware in order to manufacture aerospace products, control technologies, turbo chargers, and performance materials. Neither do Sherwin-Williams nor Dow Chemical need their patents to be held in Delaware for manufacturing, marketing, and distribution of their products. These companies, and the vast IP Holding Companies formed in Delaware, are there primarily for the benefit of saving taxes.

Indeed, state tax savings can be great. Victoria's Secret, which had previously transferred its trademarks to its IP Holding Company, turned around and paid to its subsidiary $698,500,000 in 2015 in royalties for the right to use the trademarks. The subsidiary pays no state taxes on the royalty income received while the parent company enjoys a tax deduction for the royalty payments paid to the subsidiary. Nordstrom's IP Holding Company received $197,802,386 in 2002 and $212,284,273 in 2003 from royalty income for the licensing of its parked trademarks in Delaware back to the parent and affiliate companies. Gore, the maker of Gore-Tex products, assigned patents to its subsidiary and then licensed the right to use the patents from the same subsidiary; the subsidiary received $231,000,000 in 2015 in royalty payments from Gore but paid no state income tax on the royalty income because it is a Delaware holding company. And that's not all. As Gore is the subsidiary's sole shareholder, it also receives dividends and gains access to cheap loans from the subsidiary. These are merely three examples among the countless US corporations avoiding state taxes by parking their valuable intellectual property in Delaware. The total sum each year in state taxation escaped through this web-like scheme is in the hundreds of billions of dollars. And because companies are avoiding state income taxes by shifting their intellectual property assets to Delaware, other states are negatively impacted.

How is it possible for corporations to escape paying state income taxes, so easily, on billions of dollars of intellectual property-related income? At least two possible explanations are available. First, despite the fact that the United States is a homogenous country with one federal government and an integrated economy, it functions at the state level as if it were fifty different nations. Each state can do whatever it wants with respect to taxation as long as it does not offend the US Constitution. Delaware is known as the epicenter for incorporation. It has boasted for years about its friendly corporate laws and the sophistication of its judiciary system for corporations. While no one was paying attention in the early 1980s, Delaware took an unprecedented step toward *acquiring* intellectual property assets. The State crafted a gift to corporations of all sizes to encourage the relocation of their intellectual property assets to Delaware. The nickname, "The First State," is apt for Delaware as it leads other states in capturing intellectual property assets and related income. Nevada and Michigan are also attempting to acquire a piece of the intellectual-property-relocation pie. However, they are nowhere near Delaware in terms of sophistication, tradition, and history of corporation friendliness.

Second, intellectual property has become significantly important to both large and small corporations. The major revisions of laws relating to patents, copyrights, and trademarks provide corporations the legal basis for creation, protection, enforcement, and commercialization. As exploding technological developments coincide with major revisions to expand the scope of intellectual property law, corporations are acquiring more intellectual property than ever before through in-house creation and acquisitions. Along with these major revisions leading to the time when Delaware began to capture the relocation of intellectual property, corporations embraced licensing as the new mode of commercialization. The licensing intellectual property model allows corporations to not only use the intellectual property in the operation of business, but also avoid paying taxes on the income generated from that use. Significantly, the assignment to and license back of intellectual property can be implemented with ease as no physical or visible activities occur due to the intangible nature of intellectual property assets that would otherwise attract unwarranted attention. The transfer of ownership of intellectual property can be done easily, allowing the shifting of intellectual property from one state with an income tax to a different state without income tax with great ease.

Moreover, intellectual property income shifting to Delaware occurs without attracting much attention. Delaware quietly continues to keep corporations happy as its laws do not allow the public to investigate, review, examine, inspect, or merely look at any filings or activities of IP Holding Companies.[8] Similarly, Delaware laws protect companies by requiring little public disclosure. As *Bloomberg* reported, Delaware lures corporations to set up shell companies to escape tax, and it stands out for its "emphasis on privacy" to become the birthplace of "corporate secrecy" and the "world's most secretive jurisdiction."[9] In fact, Delaware has, in using these methods, created a template for use by offshore tax havens, from Singapore to Luxembourg and the Cayman Islands to Panama!

Much of Congress's scrutiny and public outcry has not been directed at Delaware. It instead pours toward faraway, distant shores as described below. Perhaps it is easier to express anger and distaste toward other nations and exotic locales rather than toward the small, quiet state located next door to the nation's capital. But we cannot ignore that intellectual property income shifting occurs on a very large scale here in the United States, and that Delaware is at the center of the domestic intellectual property tax minimization strategies. So, as nations struggle to deal with intellectual property income shifting by multinational companies, US states must address intellectual property income shifting by multistate entities. Granted there are no Panama Papers to provide a peek into Delaware's corporate secrecy, but that does not mean Delaware should be ignored. Chapter 2 puts a focus on Delaware to examine how that state has become the "domestic" tax haven. Chapter 3 explores how corporations, over the last several decades, have structured their intellectual property ownership to avoid paying state income taxes.

Years before Congress held its hearings on international tax havens and how certain US multinational corporations relocate intellectual property offshore to avoid paying federal taxes, some states attempted to rectify the problems caused by domestic tax havens. They made efforts to assert that they had jurisdiction to tax the out-of-state IP Holding Company. They encountered strong resistance from the out-of-state IP Holding Company claiming that it had no property or payroll within the jurisdiction for tax purposes and that state taxation of such company's income was unconstitutional.

The constitutional challenges forced some states to seek different solutions. They went after the parent companies within their own state by refusing to allow these companies to deduct royalty payments and other related expenses made to controlled out-of-state subsidiaries. They also

---

[8] Delaware declined, after numerous requests, to provide the authors with information on its IP Holding Companies.

[9] David Kocieniewski, "Delaware's $1 Billion Incorporation Machine," *Bloomberg*, April 27, 2016, available at www.bloomberg.com/news/articles/2016–04–27/delaware-s-1-billion-opacity-industry-gives-u-s-onshore-haven.

declined to recognize the legitimacy of the transfer-and-license-back transactions between the parent company and its wholly owned subsidiary under judicially crafted, common law doctrines, such as the sham transaction doctrine. Some states amended their laws to impose mandatory combined reporting of related companies. Other states insisted on "add-back" of the royalty payments increasing taxation of the parent company. None of these approaches offered a perfect solution as each has its own associated problems.

All in all, very few states have aggressively gone after out-of-state IP Holding Companies or their in-state affiliates. Not only do the costs and enormous time commitment of prolonged litigation serve as additional deterrents, uncertainty itself prevents some states from mounting their challenges against IP Holding Companies.

Despite the efforts employed by these few states, popular media glosses over the issue and the public shows no interest. No outrage, disgust, or cry of unfairness across the populace has materialized. Attention is aroused, of course, by tax lawyers and tax consultants regarding crafting new strategies for their clients. One jurist in a tax case involving an IP Holding Company aptly described the game of tax:

> Once upon a time, before the advent of the shot clock, some basketball teams employed a maneuver known as the "four corners offense." This strategy involved a series of passes among team members that seemingly did not advance the ultimate purpose of putting the ball in the hoop, but had the separate purpose of depriving the opposing team of possession of the ball. In a somewhat analogous enterprise, corporate tax consultants devised a strategy that involved a series of transactions passing licensing rights between related corporations and that was motivated by a desire, not to directly enhance corporate profits, but to keep a portion of those profits out of the hands of state tax collectors.[10]

The massive amount of income generated from the licensing of intellectual property cannot be ignored, and some states are determined to obtain their fair share of the apportioned sum for state tax purposes. Maryland made headline news when it was embroiled in a battle with Gore Enterprise Holdings, Inc., the IP Holding Company of all things Gore-Tex. Litigation lasted for eight years after the state issued an assessment of almost $27 million in tax, interest, and penalties against the company. Massachusetts, New Jersey, and New York are in active pursuit of their fair share of IP Holding Company licensing income through legislative and judicial means. Chapter 4 details different approaches states have adopted to push back against taxpayers involved in the scheme. Chapter 5 considers alternative solutions to the problem.

---

[10] *NIHC, Inc. v. Comptroller of the Treasury*, 439 Md. 668, 669–70 (Md. App. Ct. 2014).

The Multistate Tax Commission has advocated adopting a common approach, and a number of states have joined efforts to accomplish this. But, unsurprisingly, Delaware views this joint effort as a direct threat to its sovereign interests. Delaware's favorable tax treatment for IP Holding Companies is the product of its own policy choice to become super competitive in the national marketplace. The *New York Times* reported that in 2011 alone Delaware had collected $860 million in taxes and fees from absentee corporate residents. Delaware's tax policy, however, allows corporations to escape the taxes paid to other states, resulting in the staggering amount of $9.5 billion tax savings over the past decade.

While some states criticize Delaware, others take the "if you can't beat 'em, join 'em" approach. Nevada, Wyoming, Michigan, and Oregon have embraced and imitated Delaware by remaking their states to become the new friendly jurisdictions for corporations. These states want IP Holding Companies to be easily formed without much disclosure, and they will exempt income from the investment and licensing of intellectual property from state taxation. Both Nevada and Wyoming do not impose a corporation income tax. And Oregon has attempted to fashion itself as the "Delaware of the West."

We can certainly debate the soundness of state responses to IP Holding Companies – which have been either to fight the practice of multistate firms or to adopt the Delaware-type tax model. But any debate must consider "fairness" issues that stem from the domestic IP Holding Company structure. Is the current system fair to companies that operate in only one state? Is the system fair to companies that operate in multiple states but that rely solely on brick-and-mortar operations? Is the system fair for states that have been short-changed of revenues, but that could certainly use those revenues for essential government services? Similar issues of fairness are echoed in connection with the use of foreign IP Holding Companies by multinational firms.

Use of Foreign Intellectual Property Holding Companies

Recent studies reveal that the vast majority of the largest, publicly traded corporations in the United States maintain an astonishing number of subsidiary companies in tax haven jurisdictions.[11] The use of foreign subsidiaries is particularly pervasive among large multinational

---

[11] According to a recent study by a tax advocacy group, at least 358 companies (almost 72 percent of the Fortune 500) maintained at least 7,622 subsidiaries in tax haven jurisdictions. *See* "Offshore Shell Games 2015: The Use of Offshore Tax Havens by Fortune 500 Companies," *Citizens for Tax Justice*, 2, October 5, 2015, http://ctj.org/pdf/offshoreshell2015.pdf [hereinafter Offshore Shell Games 2015] (looking at 2013 10-K

companies that rely on intellectual property. Large established public companies, such as Apple, Microsoft, Google, and Facebook, have carefully set up complicated webs of offshore subsidiaries. The same goes for smaller and younger private companies. It was reported that Uber, for example, which was founded only six years ago, has already set up seventy-five subsidiaries around the world.[12]

Why do US multinational companies set up elaborate foreign subsidiary structures? Apple, for example, does not really need its principle foreign subsidiaries in Ireland to sell iPhones and iPads to non-US customers. Similarly, Microsoft technically does not need its main foreign subsidiary companies in Ireland, Puerto Rico, and Singapore to sell Windows around the world. Statistical, as well as anecdotal, evidence reveals the most likely motivation: The use of foreign subsidiaries in low-tax or no-tax jurisdictions is saving these US multinationals a staggering amount of taxes.[13]

Foreign subsidiaries allow US multinationals to avoid US taxes on foreign income (and sometimes US-source income). *The New York Times* reported that Apple has been able to sidestep billions of dollars in taxes with its intellectual property income-shifting techniques.[14] *Bloomberg* reported that Google too has been able to save billions in taxes to achieve an overall tax rate of 2.4 percent.[15] The use of foreign subsidiaries also permits

reports filed with the Securities and Exchange Commission and using the list of tax havens from the Government Accountability Office). For an earlier study, *see* U.S. Government Accountability Office, *Large U.S. Corporations and Federal Contractors with Subsidiaries in Jurisdictions Listed as Tax Havens or Financial Privacy Jurisdictions*, GAO-09–157 (December 2008), 4, *available at* www.gao.gov/assets/290/284522.pdf.

[12] Brian O'Keefe and Marty Jones, "How Uber Plays the Tax Shell Game," *Fortune*, October 22, 2015, http://fortune.com/2015/10/22/uber-tax-shell/.

[13] Harry Grubert, "Foreign Taxes and the Growing Share of US Multinational Company Income Abroad: Profits, Not Sales Are Being Globalized," *National Tax Journal* 65 (2012): 247–81, *available at* www.ntanet.org/NTJ/65/2/ntj-v65n02p247-81-foreign-taxes-growing-share.pdf?v=%CE%B1&r=032797049889688346 (providing evidence that US multinationals are avoiding corporate income tax by shifting reported income to low-tax jurisdictions).

[14] *See* Landon Thomas Jr. and Eric Pfanner, "Even Before Apple Tax Breaks, Ireland's Policy Had Its Critics," *The New York Times*, May 21, 2013, www.nytimes.com/2013/05/22/business/global/ireland-defends-attractive-tax-rates.html; Charles Duhigg and David Kocieniewski, "How Apple Sidesteps Billions in Taxes," *The New York Times*, April 28, 2012, www.nytimes.com/2012/04/29/business/apples-tax-strategy-aims-at-low-tax-states-and-nations.html.

[15] *See* Jesse Druker, "'Dutch Sandwich' Saves Google Billions in Taxes: Internet Giant Uses Complex Structure to Keep Its Overseas Tax Rate at 2.4 percent," *Bloomberg Businessweek*, October 22, 2010, www.nbcnews.com/id/39784907/ns/business-us_business/t/dutch-sandwich-saves-google-billions-taxes/; Jesse Drucker, "Google 2.4 percent Rate Shows How $60 Billion Is Lost to Tax Loopholes," *Bloomberg News*, October 21, 2010, www.bloomberg.com/news/2010–10-21/google-2-4-rate-shows-how-60-billion-u-s-revenue-lost-to-tax-loopholes.html.

US multinationals to avoid foreign taxes on foreign income. The BBC reported that Facebook (a US multinational) paid only 4,327 pounds in corporate tax in the United Kingdom in 2014, despite Britain being one of the company's largest markets outside the United States.[16]

These results are achievable for many reasons, as explored more fully in Chapter 6. For starters, despite the fact that the world economy has become more interconnected, nations' tax policies differ greatly. As examples, countries impose different corporate income tax rates and offer different incentives for the development and exploitation of intellectual property assets. And some countries have aggressively utilized tax policies to encourage multinationals to relocate their intellectual property assets and related income (and sometimes their residency) to their jurisdictions.

Further, the mobility and intangibility of intellectual property make it relatively easy for multinationals with huge portfolios of intellectual property (e.g., technology and pharmaceutical companies) to shift intellectual property assets and the profits they generate to tax-favored jurisdictions. In some cases, multinationals transfer outright ownership of intellectual property to their controlled subsidiaries. In other cases, they transfer only the economic rights through license arrangements and joint research and development agreements.[17] Regardless, through the manipulation of intercompany prices, multinationals can easily shift intellectual property income from high-tax to low-tax countries saving billions in taxes – a luxury not available to those firms whose value lies mostly in their tangible, physical assets, and whose profits are more linked to brick-and-mortar operations.

Increasingly, nations are using tax policies to draw technological innovation into their borders – not for any global cause, such as increased worldwide welfare, but for self-interests, such as the increased well-being of their own citizens. Research and development activity, with its own positive spillover effects, can lead to technological advances. These advances then can lead to economic growth, meaning increased tax revenues for a country. And, as intellectual property increasingly becomes the dominant source of value in the world economy, more and more multinationals are taking advantage of nations' favorable tax policies to

[16] Kamal Ahmed, "Facebook to Pay Millions of Pounds More in UK Tax," *BBC News*, March 4, 2016, www.bbc.com/news/business-35724308.

[17] A transfer need not be made to each country where it conducts business; a transfer can be of economic rights to one country only, one that offers a very low rate. As seen in Chapter 7, this is often achieved through a cost sharing agreement between a multinational and a foreign subsidiary. Lee Sheppard, "How Does Apple Avoid Taxes?," *Forbes*, May 28, 2013, www.forbes.com/sites/leesheppard/2013/05/28/how-does-apple-avoid-taxes/#34f845a2d6f7.

minimize domestic and foreign taxes. Tax minimization permits multinationals to derive more value from their intellectual property and, thus, better compete with other firms.

We can debate, as a policy matter, whether this level of competition among nations and among firms is desirable or harmful.[18] But we cannot deny, as a practical matter, the desire of multinationals to minimize taxes and their tendencies to engage in creative intellectual property tax maneuvering.[19] Some countries have a compliant tax culture. In Japan, for example, many companies consider paying taxes a matter of loyalty and, thus, do not engage in aggressive tax-planning techniques.[20] This, of course, is the exception rather than the rule, and in most countries there seems to be a public disdain for taxes. Generally, taxes have never been popular; indeed, resistance to paying them has existed since the earliest days of Greece, Rome, and beyond.[21] This resentment may stem from the very nature of the beast. First, taxes are compulsory levies and people generally do not like being told what to do.[22] Second, taxes are unrequited – that is, they are collected for the general welfare and not in return for any specific benefit received. And it is no shock that most people will fight anything that prevents them from pursuing their own self-interests.[23] Despite their compulsory and unrequited nature, taxes

---

[18] For a summary of tax competition literature, *see* John Douglas Wilson & David E. Wildasin, "Capital Tax Competition: Bane or Boon," *Journal of Public Economics* 88 (2004): 1065–91, *available at* http://davidwildasin.us/pub/Wilson-Wildasin-Capital-Tax -Competition.pdf.

[19] *See* Robert S. Peck et al., "Tort Reform 1999: Building Without a Foundation," *Florida State University Law Review* 27 (2000): 427 (recognizing the "general public's disdain for taxes"). *See also* Mark L. Ascher, "But I Thought the Earth Belonged to the Living, Dead Hands: A Social History of Wills, Trusts, and Inheritance Law," *Texas Law Review* 89 (2011): 1168 (footnotes omitted) (observing that the fact "[t]hat Californians in the 1980s voted to repeal a death tax that only a tiny portion of them could ever even have hoped to pay surely says considerably more about our collective resentment of taxes and our widely shared suspicions that both government and government spending are thoroughly out of control than about our attitude toward wealth").

[20] *See* Rosanne Altshuler, Stephen Shay, & Eric Toder, "Lessons the United States Can Learn from Other Countries' Territorial Systems for Taxing Income of Multinational Corporations," 24–25, 34–35 (Tax Policy Center: Urban Institute & Brookings Institution, January 21, 2015), *available at* www.taxpolicycenter.org/sites/default/files/al fresco/publication-pdfs/2000077-lessons-the-us-can-learn-from-other-countries.pdf.

[21] For a timeline of taxes (including taxes in Ancient Egypt, Great Britain, The Roman Empire, Greece, and Medieval Serfs), and how they were received, *see* "Why We've Always Hated Taxes," *Top Accounting Degrees*, accessed November 3, 2016, www.topaccountingdegrees .org/hate-taxes/. *See also* Jack A. Goldstone, "Taxes as Punishment," *NewPopulationBomb*, http://newpopulationbomb.com/2012/08/16/taxes-as-punishment/.

[22] An early, classic example of this proposition can be found in the *Iliad*, in which Achilles's conflict with Agamemnon stemmed from his disdain for being told what to do.

[23] *See* Charles S. Jacobs, "Don't Read This: The Big Mistake Managers Make," *Psychology Today Blog*, May 29, 2013, www.psychologytoday.com/blog/management-rewired/201 305/dont-read.

may be viewed by some as a form of punishment – a penalty for success.[24] In one study, "[t]he participants 'portray[ed] taxation as a threat to the moral order because they believe[d] taxes deprive[d] deserving hardworking middle class people of dignity, while rewarding others who are undeserving (both rich and poor).'"[25] Creators of intellectual property, in particular, may view taxes as violating the moral and constitutional principle that innovation should be rewarded and not punished.

When corporate entities become the subject of taxation, additional objections might be raised. As a policy matter, it can be debated whether taxes should even be imposed on corporate entities. Corporations are not natural persons, it may be argued, so any corporate income is more appropriately taxed to the individual shareholders.[26] Even if a natural entity theory of corporate personality or some other theory supports an entity-level tax on corporate profits, some may argue that such tax is harmful and should be reduced or eliminated. In the United States, corporate income is actually taxed twice – at both the entity level (when earned) and shareholder level (if and when distributed in the form of a dividend). In many other countries, however, corporate income is taxed only once, often through a dividend exemption system or credit imputation system. US multinationals complain that they are at a competitive disadvantage in relation to non-US companies that are taxed more favorably on their foreign profits. Indeed, the Tax Foundation released its 2016 International Tax Competitiveness Index showing the United States has the fifth least competitive tax system in the Organization for Economic Cooperation and Development (OECD).[27] Eliminating the corporate income tax would create a more level playing field between American and foreign companies with respect to foreign income, and could cause dramatic increases in investment in the United States, translating into more jobs, higher productivity, and higher wages.[28]

---

[24] *See* Goldstone, *supra* note 21.

[25] *See* Jenna Bryner, "Why Americans Hate Paying Taxes," *LiveScience*, May 23, 2012, www.livescience.com/20518-paying-taxes-moral-principles.html.

[26] *See* Benjamin H. Harris, "Corporate Tax Incidents and Its Implications for Progressivity," (Tax Policy Center: Urban Institute & Brookings Institution, November 23, 2009), *available at* www.taxpolicycenter.org/publications/corporate-tax-incidence-and-its-implications-progressivity.

[27] Colby Pastre, "2016 International Tax Competitiveness Index," *Tax Foundation*, October 5, 2016, http://taxfoundation.org/article/2016-international-tax-competitiveness-index-0. Only Greece, Portugal, Italy, and France have less competitive tax codes according to the report.

[28] *See* James Pethokoukis, "Why Corporations Shouldn't Pay Any Taxes – Zero, Zilch, Nada," *The Week*, August 4, 2014, http://theweek.com/articles/444861/why-corporations-shouldnt-pay-taxes–zero-zilch-nada; *but see* "Fact Sheet: Why We Need

Chapter 7 examines specific intellectual holding company structures used by US-based multinational companies. These companies defend their tax minimization techniques as in the best interest of their stakeholders.[29] Corporate governors generally owe a fiduciary duty to maximize corporate profits for the benefit of shareholders.[30] In recent congressional hearings, Apple defended its intellectual property tax strategies as actually serving its shareholders. As an example, Apple noted that it "serves its shareholders" by keeping foreign profits offshore (instead of repatriating them to the United States as taxable dividends), "where they can be deployed efficiently to fund international operations at a lower cost."[31] Nontax, business purposes are commonly proffered to legitimize techniques that also happen to minimize taxes. According to Apple, its primary offshore holding subsidiary "performs centralized cash and investment management of Apple's foreign, post-tax income" and "permits Apple to mitigate legal and financial risk by providing consolidated, efficient control of its global flow of funds."[32]

US multinationals also defend their techniques as perfectly legal.[33] From their perspective, there is nothing unlawful about moving intellectual property to tax-favored jurisdictions to save taxes. And this is true. In fact, when examining Apple's use of foreign subsidiaries, investigators and members of Congress made clear that they were not accusing Apple

---

the Corporate Income Tax," Citizens for Tax Justice, June 10, 2013, http://ctj.org/ctjreports/2013/06/fact_sheet_why_we_need_the_corporate_income_tax.php#.VtsqI8Z4XNV (listing three big problems with repealing the corporate income tax).

[29] *But see* Reuven S. Avi-Yonah, "Corporate Taxation and Corporate Social Responsibility," *NYU Journal of Law & Business* 11 (2014): 2, 26, *available at* http://repository.law.umich.edu/cgi/viewcontent.cgi?article=2406&context=articles.

[30] For one of the most cited and most famous articulation of the thesis that the exclusive goal of the corporation is shareholder wealth maximization, *see* Milton Friedman, "A Friedman Doctrine – The Social Responsibility of Business Is to Increase Its Profits," *The New York Times*, September 13, 1970, 32–33, 122–26. For argument that corporations are not legally required to engage in highly aggressive tax strategies to minimize their corporate taxes, *see* Eric C. Chaffee & Karie Davis-Nozemack, "Corporate Tax Avoidance and Honoring the Fiduciary Duties Owed to Corporation and Its Stockholders," *Boston College L. Rev.* 59 (forthcoming 2017).

[31] Testimony of Apple Inc. Before the Permanent Subcommittee on Investigations, US Senate, May 21, 2013, 2, *available at* www.apple.com/pr/pdf/Apple_Testimony_to_PSI.pdf [hereinafter Testimony of Apple, Inc.].

[32] *Ibid.* at 3.

[33] *See, e.g.*, "Statement of William J. Sample, Corporate Vice President, Worldwide Tax, Microsoft Corporation Before the Permanent Subcommittee on Investigations of the US Senate Committee on Homeland Security and Government Affairs," Homeland Security & Governmental Affairs Permanent Subcommittee on Investigations, September 20, 2012, 6, *available at* www.hsgac.senate.gov/subcommittees/investigations/hearings/offshore-profit-shifting-and-the-us-tax-code; Testimony of Apple Inc. Before the Permanent Subcommittee on Investigations, US Senate, May 21, 2013, 10, *available at* www.apple.com/pr/pdf/Apple_Testimony_to_PSI.pdf

of breaking any laws. The strategies fostered by Apple and many other multinational firms represent lawful tax planning.

It is often difficult, however, to draw a distinction between lawful tax planning and abusive tax sheltering.[34] The mantra of the tax planner is found in an old opinion of Judge Learned Hand in which he wrote:

[A] transaction, otherwise within an exception of the tax law, does not lose its immunity, because it is actuated by a desire to avoid, or, if one choose, to evade taxation. Any one may so arrange his affairs that his taxes shall be as low as possible; he is not bound to choose that pattern which will best pay the Treasury; there is not even a patriotic duty to increase one's taxes.[35]

The taxing authority's typical response to Judge Hand's dictum is to assert that rules must be applied to achieve their intended purposes and that usually the government did not intend the result the planner is seeking. Techniques used by multinationals to minimize taxes on foreign intellectual property income may pass muster under current tax laws, but the purposes of the laws are clearly being circumvented. When taxpayers design their intellectual property transactions to their tax advantage in ways unanticipated by the government, government response is warranted.

Government attention to intellectual property income shifting is growing – and, for good reason. There is plenty of evidence that the practice has recently resulted in significant erosion of domestic tax bases.[36] Although it is difficult to gauge the precise magnitude of income shifting,[37] various

---

[34] *See* Allison Christians, "Avoidance, Evasion, and Taxpayer Morality," *Washington University Journal of Law & Policy* 44 (2014), *available at* http://openscholarship.wustl .edu/cgi/viewcontent.cgi?article=1831&context=law_journal_law_policy; *see also* Internal Revenue Manual 9.1.3.3.2.1 (2008), *available at* www.irs.gov/irm/part9/irm_09–001-0 03.html ("The distinction between avoidance and evasion is fine, yet definite. One who avoids tax does not conceal or misrepresent. He/she shapes events to reduce or eliminate tax liability and, upon the happening of the events, makes a complete disclosure. Evasion, on the other hand, involves deceit, subterfuge, camouflage, concealment, some attempt to color or obscure events or to make things seem other than they are").

[35] Helvering v. Gregory, 69 F.2d 809, 810 (2d Cir. 1934).

[36] For US government estimates, *see* Joint Committee on Taxation, "Estimates of Federal Tax Expenditures for Fiscal Years 2014–2018," *JCX-97–14* (August 5, 2014), 22, *available at* https://www.jct.gov/publications.html?func=startdown&id=4663 (estimating the tax expenditure (costs of deferral) at $83.4 billion for 2014); Office of Management and Budget, *Fiscal Year 2016: Analytical Perspectives of the US Government*, Washington, DC: US Government Printing Office, 2015, 228, *available at* www.whitehouse.gov/sites/default/files/omb/budget/fy2016/assets/spec.pdf (estimating the tax expenditure at $61.7 billion for 2014).

[37] For example, one researcher shows that estimates range from 2 percent to 30 percent of corporate profits being shifted out of high-tax countries – a broad range, illustrating the degree of uncertainty regarding the magnitude of income shifting. Erik Cederwall, "Reconciling the Profit-Shifting Debate," *Tax Notes* 150 (2016): 713; OECD, "BEPS

studies show that income shifting from the United States to low-tax jurisdictions drains more than $100 billion in corporate revenue from the United States every year.[38] It is estimated that US multinationals have now accumulated nearly $2.6 trillion in earnings of foreign subsidiaries held offshore – up from $2.3 trillion in 2014.[39] And by at least one estimate, US multinationals would collectively owe an estimated $620 billion in US taxes if they repatriated the funds in the form of dividends.[40]

The chart below provides one economist's estimates of US revenue loss due to income shifting.

Base erosion due to profit shifting is real, it is large, and it is consequential.[41] Less tax revenue means cuts in vital government

Action 11: Improving the Analysis of BEPS (Base Erosion and Profit Shifting Public Discussion Draft)," 25 (OECD, April 16, 2015), available at www.oecd.org/ctp/tax-policy/discussion-draft-action-11-data-analysis.pdf [hereinafter BEPS Action 11] (concluding that "significant limitations" of available data "can only provide general indications of the scale and economic impact of base erosion and profit shifting").

[38] Kimberly A. Clausing, "The Effect of Profit Shifting on the Corporate Tax Base in the United States and Beyond," June 17, 2016, *available at* https://papers.ssrn.com/sol3/papers.cfm?abstract_id=2685442. *See also* Gabriel Zucman, "Taxing Across Borders: Tracking Personal Wealth and Corporate Profits," *Journal of Economic Perspectives* 28 (2014): 121–48 (putting the figure at about $130 billion annually); Joint Committee on Taxation, "Estimates of Federal Tax Expenditures for Fiscal Years 2015–2019," *JCX-141R-15* (December 7, 2015), *available at* www.jct.gov/publications.html?func=selec t&id=5 (estimating the loss for FY 2016 to be $108.6 billion). In large tax havens, profits relative to GDP have risen dramatically in recent years, from 2004 to 2010: Ireland (7.6 percent to 41.9 percent); Luxembourg (18.2 percent to 127 percent); the Netherlands (4.6 percent to 17.1 percent); and Switzerland (3.5 percent to 12.3 percent). A pronounced increase has also been seen in the sandy tax havens. *See* Jane G. Gravelle, *Tax Havens: International Tax Evasion and Avoidance*, (CRS Report No. R40623) (Washington, DC: Congressional Research Services, 2015), www.fas.org/sgp/crs/misc/R40623.pdf [hereinafter CRS Report No. R40623].

[39] Press Release, "Brady, Neal Highlight Another Reason for Pro-Growth Tax Reform: Joint Committee on Taxation Estimates Even More Foreign Earnings from US Companies Stranded Overseas," September 29, 2016, *available at* http://waysand means.house.gov/brady-neal-highlight-another-reason-pro-growth-tax-reform/ (providing two estimates, one based on the most recent tax return data and the other based on financial statement data from Audit Analytics). For earlier estimates, *see* "Untaxed Foreign Earnings Top $2.3 Trillion in 2014," *Audit Analytics*, April 30, 2015, www .auditanalytics.com/blog/untazxed-foreing-earnings-top-2-3-trillion-in-2014/. *See* Edward D. Kleinbard, "Why Corporate Tax Reform Can Happen," *Tax Notes* 146 (2015): 91, *available at* https://papers.ssrn.com/sol3/papers.cfm?abstract_id=2563358; Maxwell Murphy, "Indefinitely Reinvested Foreign Earnings on the Rise," *The Wall Street Journal*, May 7, 2013, http://blogs.wsj.com/cfo/2013/05/07/indefinitely-reinvested-foreign-earnings-on-the-rise/. These funds are often held in US financial institutions, and, thus, are available to US capital markets; but US multinational corporations are constrained in their use of these funds as discussed in later chapters.

[40] David Alexander, "Big US Firms Hold $2.1 Trillion Overseas to Avoid Taxes: Study," *Reuters*, October 6, 2015, www.reuters.com/article/2015/10/06/us-usa-tax-offshore-idUSKCN0S008U20151006.

[41] *See, e.g.*, J Jane Gravelle, "Policy Options to Address Corporate Profit Shifting: Carrots or Sticks?," *New York University School of Law Colloquium on Tax Policy and Public*

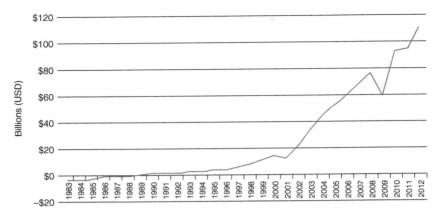

Figure 1.1 Estimates of Revenue Loss Due to Income Shifting
Source: Kimberly A. Clausing, "The Effect of Profit Shifting on the
Corporate Tax Base in the United States and Beyond," *Tax Notes*
(January 25, 2016)

services, increased budget deficits, and higher tax burdens on other
taxpayers, including individuals and smaller businesses. It has been estimated, for example, that small business owners each would have had to
pay $3,244 in additional taxes in 2014 if they had been obligated to pick
up the full tab for offshore tax avoidance by multinational companies.[42]
Beyond their negative revenue effects, tax laws that permit intellectual
property income shifting provide US multinational companies with significant and unfair competitive advantages over smaller US companies
that cannot use overseas operations and offshore tax gimmicks to lower
their effective corporate rate.[43] Such laws also create harmful economic

Finance, April. 26, 2016, *available at* www.law.nyu.edu/sites/default/files/upload_docu
ments/Jane%20Gravelle.pdf [hereinafter Carrots or Sticks] (showing the magnitude of
income shifting by US multinationals to no-tax or low-tax countries); CRS Report No.
R40623, *supra* note 38 (showing low ratios of profits relative to GDP in high-tax
countries, but higher ratios in low-tax countries, such as Ireland, Luxembourg, the
Netherlands, and Switzerland).

[42] Dan Smith & Jaimie Woo, "Picking up the Tab 2015: Small Businesses Pay the Price for
Offshore Tax Havens," US PIRG, April 14, 2015, www.uspirg.org/reports/usp/picking-
tab-2015-small-businesses-pay-price-offshore-tax-havens.

[43] These concerns have been raised by many, including members of Congress. *See* Hearing
Before the Permanent Subcommittee on Investigations, Offshore Profit Shifting and the
US Tax Code – Part II (Apple Inc.), 1-10, May 21, 2013, *available at* www.gpo.gov/fdsys/
pkg/CHRG-113shrg81657/pdf/CHRG-113shrg81657.pdf [hereinafter Senate Apple
Hearing] (citing Opening Statement of Senator Carl Levin [D-Mich.] and Opening
Statement of Senator John McCain).

distortions. For example, under the current system US firms are incentivized to invest and grow business activities abroad rather than in the United States, thus devoting substantial resources to tax planning rather than productive investment.[44]

Base erosion due to profit shifting is not merely a US concern but is also a large problem in many other countries that do not have low tax rates. There is statistical and anecdotal evidence that foreign-based multinationals engage in the same income-shifting strategies as US-based multinationals.[45] Although it is not as easy to estimate the global scale of corporate tax base erosion due to income shifting because of a lack of publicly available survey data, economic studies estimate that for the global market, including the United States, revenue losses may exceed $280 billion per year.[46] The OECD recently found the annual net tax revenue loss to be up to $240 billion.[47] And developed countries

[44] These concerns have been raised by many, including the former Obama administration. *See* The White House & Department of the Treasury, "The President's Framework for Business Tax Reform: An Update," 11, April 2016, *available at* www .treasury.gov/resource-center/tax-policy/Documents/The-Presidents-Framework-for-Business-Tax-Reform-An-Update-04-04-2016.pdf [hereinafter President Obama's Framework]. *But see* Cederwall, *supra* note 37 (arguing ways that the US Treasury and citizens actually gain from profit shifting) (citing Shaun P. Mahaffy, "The Case for Tax: A Comparative Approach to Innovation Policy," *Yale Law Journal* 123 (2013): 827–59; Noam Noked, "Integrated Tax Policy Approach to Designing Research & Development Tax Benefits," *Virginia Tax Review* 34 (2014): 152.

[45] *See* Altshuler et al., *supra* note 20, at 36 ("Anecdotal evidence suggests that foreign-based multinationals may be engaging in similar transactions and perhaps even to a greater degree.").

[46] Clausing, "The Effect of Profit Shifting on the Corporate Tax Base in the United States and Beyond," *supra* note 38. For earlier consistent findings, *see* Tim Dowd, Paul Landefeld, & Anne Moore, "Profit Shifting of US Multinationals" (Joint Committee on Taxation, January 6, 2016), *available at* https://papers.ssrn.com/sol3/papers.cfm?abstrac t_id=2711968; *Measuring and Monitoring BEPS: Action 11 – 2015 Final Report* (Paris: OECD Publishing, 2015), *available at* www.oecd.org/ctp/measuring-and-monitoring-beps-action-11-2015-final-report-9789264241343-en.htm; Ernesto Crivelli, Michael Keen, & Ruud A. de Mooij, "Base Erosion, profit Shifting, and Developing Countries," Oxford University Centre for Business Taxation Working Paper No. 15/118 (May 29, 2015), *available at* www.imf.org/external/pubs/cat/longres.aspx?sk=42973.0; Ruud A. de Mooij & Sjef Ederveen, "Taxation and Foreign Direct Investment: A Synthesis of Empirical Research," *International Tax and Public Finance* 10 (2003): 673–93, *available at* http://link.springer.com/article/10.1023/A:1026329920854; Ruud A. de Mooij, "Will Corporate Income Taxation Survive?," *Economist* 153 (2005): 277–301.

[47] *Measuring and Monitoring BEPS: Action 11 – 2015 Final Report*, *supra* note 46. But, according to the OECD, corporate tax revenue as a percentage of total taxes collected has remained relatively unchanged for the past forty years in both the United States and OECD countries. BEPS Action 11, *supra* note 37, at 61. *See also* Reuven S. Avi-Yonah, "Three Steps Forward, One Step Back?: Reflections on 'Google Taxes,' BEPS, and the DBCT," University of Michigan Public Law and Legal Theory Research Paper Series Paper No. 516 (May 24, 2016), *available at* https://papers.ssrn.com/sol3/papers.cfm?ab stract_id=2783858 (noting this number represents a relatively small portion of total global corporate income tax; moreover, "overall OECD revenue data do not indicate

are not alone; base erosion is a large problem in developing countries as well.[48]

In addition to being economically unjustified, base erosion due to income shifting has become socially unacceptable. In recent years, there has been a growing level of public outrage at the tax avoidance techniques used by large multinational companies. Public resentment has been particularly pronounced in Europe, and it appears that, under heavy criticism and global pressure, some companies are changing their strategies. In 2012, for instance, protests in Britain led Starbucks to agree voluntarily to pay an extra 16 million pounds in British taxes above what it would normally have had to pay.[49] In 2016, Facebook announced steps so that its advertising revenues initiated in Britain will now be taxed in Britain – that is, UK sales made by its UK teams will be booked in the UK, not in Ireland as was the previous practice.[50] Although public attention has been noticeable in Europe, it also has caught on in the United States.[51]

While public opinion can cause multinationals to voluntarily change their behavior, public opinion can also pressure governments to take action.[52] In the United States, a number of US multinational companies, such as Apple, Caterpillar, and Microsoft have come under scrutiny and have been the subject of high-profile congressional hearings. And, members of US Congress from both parties have put forth various legislative proposals. Across the pond, European governments have also begun taking measures to limit intellectual property income shifting. In the

that BEPS has had a significant impact on CIT revenue, since those have held steady at 8–10 percent of total revenue since the 1980s (i.e., before BEPS became a significant issue").

[48] Mark P. Keightley & Jeffrey M. Stupak, *Corporate Tax Base Erosion and Profit Shifting (BEPS): An Examination of the Data* (CRS Report No. R44013) (Washington, DC: Congressional Research Service, 2015).

[49] Allison Christians, "How Starbuck Lost Its Social License – and Paid £20 Million to Get it Back," *Tax Notes International* 71 (2013): 637, *available at* https://papers.ssrn.com/so l3/papers.cfm?abstract_id=2308921; Floyd Norris, "Apple's Move Keeps Profit Out of Reach of Taxes," *The New York Times*, May 2, 2013, www.nytimes.com/2013/05/03/bu siness/how-apple-and-other-corporations-move-profit-to-avoid-taxes.html?_r=0.

[50] Some commentators suggest that "[t]here is simply not enough public outrage to produce serious pressure." Leonid Bershidsky, "Lets Just Give Up On Taxing Big Corporations," *Bloomberg View*, October 8, 2015, www.bloombergview.com/articles/ 2015-10-08/multinationals-don-t-pay-taxes-but-citizens-don-t-object.

[51] *See* Manal S. Corwin, "Sense and Sensibility: The Policy and Politics of BEPS," *Tax Notes* (2014): 137, *available at* https://kpmg-us-inst.adobecqms.net/content/dam/kpmg/ taxwatch/pdf/2014/beps-corwin-tillinghast-tn-100614.pdf (noting the topic has been the featured cover story of many reputable magazines and the subject of a recent documentary film).

[52] *But see Ibid.* (noting public pressure can impact behavior of legislatures in undesirable ways: "Unilateral actions designed to look good to the relevant political constituency can wreak havoc on a coordinated international tax system and threaten to unravel that system in ways that are undesirable for government and business").

most significant development, the OECD in 2015 delivered a number of recommendations on how to deal with income shifting, with many dealing specifically with intellectual property income shifting.

In tackling the problem of multinationals shifting their valuable intellectual property to controlled subsidiaries, some fundamental questions must be addressed. For example, what is an appropriate amount of taxes that a multinational company that relies on intellectual property should pay to society?[53] In 2012, Apple claims to have paid $6 billion in US federal taxes. Is that too much considering Apple supports hundreds of thousands of high-paying jobs in the United States, creates innovative products that improve the lives of millions of Americans, and could have hired more Americans and developed more revolutionary products if it had paid less in taxes?[54] Or, is that not enough considering the benefits it gains from being a US resident – including reliable rule of law, strong intellectual property protections, an educated and skilled workforce, publicly provided infrastructure that allows it to flourish, and access to a thriving, sophisticated consumer market?

Another fundamental question is what should be a fair and appropriate split of tax revenues among nations? It is often argued that intellectual property profits should be linked to where economic activity occurs. But does that mean intellectual property income should be taxed in the jurisdiction in which research and development took place? In the country in which key employees reside or in which goods were manufactured? In the country in which sales took place? And how does one even determine the amount of income from the sale of a product that is attributable to intellectual property?

This book seeks to provide an understanding of the complex issues involved in designing appropriate international tax policies to combat base erosion caused by intellectual property income shifting. Chapter 8 looks at previous government efforts and existing government barriers and explains why they are not working. Chapter 9 explores alternative approaches to limit intellectual property income shifting. The subject is extremely timely as international intellectual property income shifting is a bigger problem today than ever before, and there is evidence that it is

---

[53] Corwin, supra note 51, at 136 (noting "it is more difficult to achieve consensus around what is the right or 'moral' amount of worldwide tax a corporation operating across multiple sovereign jurisdictions should pay under the international rules that are in place today").

[54] "Apples estimates it has created or supported approximately 600,000 jobs in the [United States], including [] 50,000 jobs for Apple employees and approximately 550,000 jobs at other companies in fields such as engineering, manufacturing, logistics and software development." Testimony of Apple Inc., supra note 31, at 1–2.

rapidly accelerating.[55] With recent global attention to the shifting of profits offshore, the process of international tax reform is just beginning.

It should be noted at the outset that this book focuses on intellectual property income shifting, specifically, rather than profit shifting, more generally, since many profit shifting techniques have been effective for multinationals whose profits depend primarily on their valuable intellectual property capital. Many of the biggest multinationals are able to avoid taxes by manipulating their intellectual property – for example, by easily transferring economic rights to their intellectual property to controlled foreign subsidiaries located in tax haven jurisdictions. A study by the Congressional Research Service suggested that "half the difference between profitability in low-tax and high-tax countries, which could arise from artificial income shifting, was due to transfers of intellectual property (or intangibles)."[56] Another study found transfer pricing of intellectual property to account for seventy-two percent of profit shifting.[57] And a Treasury Department study found the potential for improper income shifting was "most acute with respect to cost sharing arrangements involving intangible property."[58]

This book focuses attention on the techniques of US-based multinationals, although both US-based and foreign-based multinationals engage in intellectual property income shifting. It has been suggested that US multinationals, particularly those in the high-tech and pharmaceutical sectors, have a large share of their capital in the form of intellectual property and have been more aggressive than foreign multinationals in shifting their intellectual property offshore to low-tax jurisdictions.[59] Thus, the strategies of US technology giants, such as Apple, Microsoft,

---

[55] For example, one study showed that foreign earnings accumulated offshore has increased 400 percent over a recent ten-year period. *See* Senate Apple Hearing, *supra* note 43, at 2 (Opening Statement of Senator Carl Levin [D-Mich.]).

[56] CRS Report No. R40623, *supra* note 38 (citing Harry Grubert, "Intangible Income, Intercompany Transactions, Income Shifting and the Choice of Locations," *National Tax Journal* 56 (2003): 221–42).

[57] Jost H. Heckemeyer & Michael Overesch, "Multinationals' Profit Response to Tax Differentials: Effect Size and Shifting Channels," Centre for European Economic Research, Discussion Paper No. 13-045 (July 2013), *available at* http://ftp.zew.de/pub/zew-docs/dp/dp13045.pdf. *See also* Harry Grubert, "Intangible Income, Intercompany Transactions, Income Shifting, and the Choice of Location," *National Tax Journal* 56 (2003): 221–42 (estimating that transfer pricing accounts for approximately half of income shifting).

[58] Joint Committee on Taxation, "Present Law and Background Related to Possible Income Shifting and Transfer Pricing," *JCX-37-10* (July 20, 2010), 7, *available at* https://www.jct.gov/publications.html?func=startdown&id=3692 (citing US Department of the Treasury, "Report to the Congress on Earnings Stripping, Transfer Pricing and US Income Tax Treaties," November 2007).

[59] Altshuler et al., *supra* note 20, at 36.

and Uber, are examined closely. These are some of the world's leading multinationals with valuable intellectual property assets. They are global household names and part of our cultural conversation. But they also, according to some, happen to be the most egregious offenders among US corporations trying to avoid taxes, and their techniques are staples of international tax avoidance.[60] Although general and country-specific legislative frameworks are provided throughout the book, US tax laws and the laws of popular low-tax jurisdictions, such as Ireland and the Netherlands, are more heavily emphasized.

******

This book is divided into two major parts. The first part (Chapters 2–5) is devoted to the use of domestic IP Holding Companies by US companies that operate in multiple US states. The second part (Chapters 6–9) focuses on use of foreign IP Holding Companies by multinational companies that have global operations, with a greater emphasis on US-based multinationals. Chapter 10 contains some final thoughts.

Efforts to reduce intellectual property income shifting may take time. History reveals a familiar cycle. Policymakers modify tax laws to protect their revenue bases and limit undesirable income shifting; but tax planners, often steps ahead, alter tax strategies within new laws to continue avoiding them.[61] Presently, however, governments (both national and subnational) seem committed to meaningful tax reform. The mere volume of economic studies, academic and practice literature, government hearings, and reports suggest that plenty of people are passionate enough about the subject that meaningful change might be within reach.[62]

Steve Jobs once said that "people with passion can change the world for the better."[63] That inspirational statement from the creator of Apple, one

---

[60] *See* Danny Yadron, Kate Linebaugh, & Jessica E. Lessin, "Apple Avoided Taxes on Overseas Billions, Senate Panel Finds," *The Wall Street Journal*, May 20, 2013, www.wsj .com/articles/SB10001424127887324787004578495250424727708 (noting Senator John McCain described Apple as the "most egregious offender" among US corporations trying to avoid tax bills).

[61] *See* Stephen C. Loomis, "The Double Irish-Sandwich: Reforming Overseas Tax Haven," *St. Mary's Law Journal* 43 (2012): 829 ("The result is a system of laws that resembles a leaky dyke – Congress plugs one leak only to create another").

[62] Corwin, *supra* note 51, at 136–37 (noting "the current environment, if properly navigated, could present a unique opportunity to make progress on issues that have been stalled for many years now" and suggesting "that it is possible to capitalize on the public engagement and the political will for change, to steer and shape outcomes towards more sensible polity results").

[63] *See* "Steve Jobs: Apple's Core Value," *Speeches*, accessed November 3, 2016, www .speeches.io/steve-jobs-apples-core-value/.

of the multinational, multistate corporations whose strategies are high-lighted in this book, hints at the power of valuable intellectual property and their creators in the twenty-first century. But the statement could also be applied to foreshadow that change is coming with respect to the tax practices of multistate and multinational companies. Apple and other corporate players in the game of tax play with a high level of energy and sophistication. But policy makers are now coming to the table with similar energy and a sense of political urgency such that sensible policy results may emerge for the first time. In this game, unlike the game of poker, we must realize that the two sides need each other. Governments rely on businesses to create jobs and drive economic growth; and multistate and multinational companies need governments for reliable legal systems, an educated workforce, and infrastructure that enable them to get their goods to market.[64] Folding is not an option. There is too much at stake.

---

[64] "A World of Robber Barons," *Economist*, February 22, 2014, www.economist.com/news/special-report/21596667-relationship-between-business-and-government-becoming-increasingly-antagonistic.

2   The Delaware Gift to Corporations
Tracing the Roots of the Domestic IP Holding Company

On December 7, 1787, Delaware became the first state to ratify the Constitution. From Sussex, Kent, and New Castle counties, a group of thirty deputies representing the people of Delaware proudly subscribed their names to ratify the Constitution.[1] With enormous pride in its significant contribution to the establishment of the new nation, Delaware adopted "Liberty and Independence" for its state motto and claims the fitting nickname "The First State."

The First State is small in both size and population, standing 49th in size and 45th in population among the fifty sister states. Despite its diminutive size and sparse density, Delaware enjoys an enviable and powerful stature as the nation's epicenter of all things related to corporation. Business entities in all sectors gravitate to Delaware as the favorite jurisdiction for incorporation. Sixty-four percent of Fortune 500 companies were incorporated in Delaware, making it the leading jurisdiction for publicly traded companies to incorporate. Companies with headquarters in their home states also favor Delaware as the jurisdiction for out-of-state incorporation. Internationally, Delaware is the chosen destination for multinational companies. Overall, Delaware has more than one million entities incorporated in the state and more corporate entities than people.[2]

Delaware has consciously designed itself to capture the corporate preeminence for the state's interests.[3] Delaware distinguishes itself from other states by offering business entities the "complete package of incorporation services" that includes "modern and flexible" corporate laws, "highly-respected" judiciary and legal communities, "business-

---

[1] "Ratification of the Constitution by the State of Delaware; December 7, 1787," accessed May 21, 2016, http://avalon.law.yale.edu/18th_century/ratde.asp.

[2] Leslie Wayne, "How Delaware Thrives as a Corporate Tax Haven," *New York Times*, June 30, 2012, www.nytimes.com/2012/07/01/business/how-delaware-thrives-as-a-corpo rate-tax-haven.html.; www.youtube.com/watch?v=TUYBlJDKApE.

[3] William E. Kirk, III, "A Case Study in Legislative Opportunism: How Delaware Used the Federal-State System to Attain Corporate Preeminence," *Journal of Corporation Law* 10 (1984): 235.

friendly" government, and a "customer service-oriented" Division of Corporations.[4]

The "modern and flexible" corporate laws refer to Delaware's General Corporation Law, which controls more than one million corporations, including more than half of the most powerful companies in the United States. The General Corporation Law provisions govern the internal affairs of the corporation, the duties of the managers or directors and officers of the corporation, and the relationship between the owners or stockholders and the managers. The Division of Corporation in the Delaware Secretary of State's Office handles the filing of corporation documents.

Delaware enacted the General Corporation Law in 1899 with many attractive features. For example, the law provides stockholders and corporations enormous flexibility in governing their affairs. It imposes very few mandatory provisions, and such provisions concern only the most important matters relating to protecting shareholders, for instance, the right to elect directors and to vote on specific major transactions. There are no limits on a corporation's ability to engage in merger activity. Overall, the law pays deference to the business judgment of directors who act loyally and carefully.[5] Under Delaware's "business judgment rule," as long as the majority of the directors who have no conflicting interest with the corporation makes business decisions relating to issues such as the corporation's plans, strategies, and hiring and firing of executive officers with due care and in good faith, the decisions will enjoy a presumption and will not be second-guessed by a court.

Most importantly, the Delaware Constitution requires a two-thirds majority in the Delaware Senate *and* a two-thirds majority of the House of the General Assembly to make any changes to the Delaware General Corporation Law. This requirement ensures the stability of the law and prevents it from being frequently changed by the legislative branch. Also, the interpretation of corporate law is in the province of the Delaware Court of Chancery and the Delaware Supreme Court; both are renowned nationwide for their deep knowledge of corporate law and practices in rendering decisions that form a body of extensive case law relied on by

---

[4] "Why Incorporate in Delaware?," State of Delaware, accessed May 21, 2016, http://corp law.delaware.gov/eng/index.shtml.

[5] "About Delaware's General Corporation Law," State of Delaware, accessed May 21, 2016, http://corplaw.delaware.gov/eng/statute.shtml; "Title 8, Chapter 1. General Corporation Law," State of Delaware, accessed May 21, 2016, http://delcode.delaware .gov/title8/c001/sc04/index.shtml (providing 8 Del. C. 1953, § 141); "The Delaware Way: Deference to the Business Judgment of Directors Who Act Loyally and Carefully," State of Delaware, accessed May 21, 2016, http://corplaw.delaware.gov/eng/delaware_way .shtml.

corporations in business planning. The Delaware Court of Chancery is unique; it was created by the Delaware Constitution in 1792, and has remained true to its fundamental purpose of providing relief where remedy at law is inadequate. The Court is often the arbiter of corporate takeover fights.[6] Consequently, Delaware corporation laws enjoy the stability that many other states' corporation laws lack. Delaware proudly brags about the consistency, predictability, stability, and quality as the key features of its corporate laws, positioning Delaware to continue to maintain its advantage over other states.[7]

With its pre-eminence in the corporate law area, Delaware continues to distinguish itself from other states by amending the law in areas that are favorable to corporations. A notable area is taxation. Delaware desires to attract more business entities to the state by providing tax exemptions to both domestic and foreign companies from Delaware corporate income taxation.

The State of Delaware has crafted a gift to corporations: Delaware corporations with intellectual property assets don't have to pay state income tax if the corporations confine their activities to the maintenance and management of patents, trademarks, and similar types of intangible assets, and the collection and distribution of the income from those assets. Delaware has paved the way for the creation of the Intellectual Property Holding Company ("IP Holding Company") in the last three decades.

Here is a closer look at the statutory detail of Delaware's gift to corporations. Delaware's corporate tax statute, 30 Del. C. § 1902(a), imposes an annual tax rate of 8.7 percent on domestic and foreign corporations' taxable income derived from business activities carried on and property located within Delaware. That tax rate, however, is not applied against the income of tens of thousands of entities, including IP Holding Companies, under the exemption provision.[8]

The statute provides exemptions to fourteen different groups of entities under 30 Del. C. § 1902(b). Understandably, the statute covers entities typically receive tax exemptions. They include fraternities; cemetery corporations; trusts created for religious, charitable, scientific or education purposes, or for the prevention of cruelty to children or animals; not-for-profit business leagues; chambers of commerce; fire

---

[6] "A Short History of the Court of Chancery," Delaware Courts, accessed May 21, 2016, http://courts.delaware.gov/chancery/history.aspx.
[7] "Facts and Myths," State of Delaware, accessed May 21, 2016, http://corplaw.delaware .gov/eng/facts_myths.shtml.
[8] Delaware law authorizes the Department of Finance to require any corporation exempt from tax pursuant to 30 Del. C. § 1902(b) to file information returns setting forth the items of gross income and deductions.

companies; merchants' associations or boards of trade; for profit organizations operated for the promotion of social welfare; pleasure/recreational clubs for non-profit purposes; and homeowners' associations. Embedded in the fourteen groups qualified for tax exemption is the IP Holding Company.

Indeed, the IP Holding Company is buried deep inside the statute as the eighth of the fourteen groups, as seen in subsection 30 Del. C. § 1902(b)(8):

> Corporations whose activities within this State are confined to the maintenance and management of their intangible investments or of the intangible investments of corporations or statutory trusts or business trusts registered as investment companies under the Investment Company Act of 1940, as amended (15 U. S.C. 80a-1 et seq.) and the collection and distribution of the income from such investments or from tangible property physically located outside this State. For purposes of this paragraph, "intangible investments" shall include, without limitation, investments in stocks, bonds, notes and other debt obligations (including debt obligations of affiliated corporations), patents, patent applications, trademarks, trade names and similar types of intangible assets.

That means under this subsection, a Delaware corporation that engages in the maintenance and management of "intangible investments" is exempted from paying the usual 8.7 percent corporate income tax. "Intangible investments" is defined to include the common types of intellectual property assets like patents, patent applications, trademarks, trade names, and "similar types of intangible assets." The catchall phrase "similar types of intangible assets" most likely covers trade secrets and copyrights, the two remaining categories of intellectual property. In other words, a Delaware corporation holding any of the intellectual property assets does not have to pay tax on the income generated from the maintenance and management or investments of the intellectual property.

The origin of Delaware's generous gift to corporations – exempting income generated from intellectual property assets held by IP Holding Company – can be traced to the 1958 amendment to the corporate income tax statute.[9] In 1958, Delaware extended its corporate tax exemptions to corporations whose activities in Delaware are confined to the "maintenance and management of their intangible investments." The 1958 version of 30 Del. C. § 1902(b)'s subsection 8 did not mention any type of intellectual property, as seen below:

---

[9] "Chapter 315 Relating to Corporation Income Tax: An Act to Amend Chapter 19, Title 30, Delaware Code, Relating to Corporation Income Tax," State of Delaware, accessed May 22, 2016, http://delcode.delaware.gov/sessionlaws/ga119/chp315.shtml #TopOfPage.

Corporations whose activities within Delaware are confined to the maintenance and management of their intangible investments and the collection and distribution of the income from such investments or from tangible property physically located outside of Delaware.

That means, as of 1958, businesses could enjoy corporate income tax exemptions on the income generated from the "maintenance and management" of "intangible investments" and "collection and distribution of the income" of intangible investments. Nothing in the statutory provision refer to the assets being patents, copyrights, trade secrets, and trademarks. In other words, intellectual property assets were not explicitly identified as part of "intangible" investments.

One would argue that "intangible investments" include the investment of *intangibles*, namely, intellectual property assets because the term "intangibles" is often used to mean the typical categories within intellectual property, like trademarks, patents, and copyrights. Indeed, a quick glance to Delaware Chapter 19 of Corporate Income Tax reveals that Delaware was aware of patents and copyrights and their power to generate income, as the state included patent and copyright royalties for taxation purposes under the "Computation of taxable income" definition in 30 Del. C. § 1903(b)(2), as newly amended in 1958. This newly amended section specifically included patent and copyrights royalties in the computation of taxable income that a corporation must pay in accordance with the then-required corporate income tax rate of five percent. Delaware then applied an apportionment method to extract the relevant portion of the patent and copyright royalties in the computation of taxable income. The pertinent paragraph provided:

Patent and copyright royalties shall be allocated proportionately to the states in which the product or process protected by the patent is manufactured or used or in which the publication protected by the copyright is produced or printed.[10]

Delaware's allocation and apportionment statute, 30 Del. C. § 1903(b)(2), as noted by the Supreme Court of Delaware, "differs from the apportionment statutes of almost all other states."[11] Specifically, in Delaware a corporation's income generated from several states will be allocated and apportioned as follows: the income is first allocated to the state where the asset is located. Then, the remainder of the income is apportioned to Delaware based on Delaware's percentage of the corporation's total asset values, wages, and gross receipts.[12] In the case of patents, the royalties generated from them will first be allocated to the states in which the

---

[10] http://delcode.delaware.gov/sessionlaws/ga119/chp298.shtml#TopOfPage.
[11] *Director of Revenue v. CNA Holdings, Inc.*, 818 A.2d 953, 956 (Del. 2003).   [12] *Ibid.*

patented products are manufactured or used, and in the case of copyrights, the royalties will first be allocated to the states in which the copyrighted products are produced or printed. The remainder of the income will be apportioned to Delaware based on a percentage.[13]

Delaware's 1958 amendment to include the new 30 Del. C. § 1902(b)(8) exemptions and 30 Del. C. § 1903(b)(2) was purposeful. Delaware was fully aware and mindful of major developments in intellectual property law in the nation after World War II and prepared itself to reap the benefits that would soon be forthcoming. Contextualizing the 1958 exemptions amendment in the framework of intellectual property law development reveals a pathway for the upcoming intersection of Delaware's corporate law and intellectual property law. Indeed, by 1958, Congress had profoundly modernized two areas of intellectual property law: patents and trademarks. Congress lifted copyright law to the modern era later in 1976.

******

With respect to trademark law, Congress completely transformed the then-existing law to reflect the modern experience and practical effects by passing the famous Lanham Act in 1946. For example, prior to the Lanham Act, the old trademark law failed to treat valuable brands that were descriptive, personal names, and geographical names with proper protection as they were not registerable under the federal trademark registration system. The brands had to rely on common law for limited protection. The old law treated these brands erroneously as "trade names," not true trademarks qualified for full and national protection. Consequently, the owners of the brands could not prevent others from using names similar to the brands causing public confusion. As keenly observed by the Senate Committee on Patents on the old trademark law:

There are many reasons why there should be a new trade–mark statute. The present act is substantially the act of February 20, 1905. It has been amended from time to time and supplemented by the act of March 19, 1920, which has also been amended in several particulars. The result is a confused situation. ... Moreover, ideas concerning trade–mark protection have changed in the last 40 years and the statutes have not kept pace with the commercial development. ... Industrialists in this country have been seriously handicapped in securing protection in foreign countries due to our failure to carry out, by statute, our international obligations.[14]

---

[13] *Ibid.*
[14] Senate Committee on Patents, "Providing for the Registration and Protection of Trade – Marks Used in Commerce to Carry Out the Provisions of Certain International Conventions," *United States Senate*, 79th Congress. 2nd Sess., S REP. NO. 1333, at 4–5 (1946), http://ipmall.info/hosted_resources/lipa/trademarks/PreLanhamAct_026_HR_1333.pdf; U.S.C.C.A.N. 1275–1276.

The Lanham Act corrected the inadequacy by permitting federal registration of the valuable brands with proof of secondary meaning. This meant a descriptive trademark could obtain trademark registration, if through extensive use, advertisement, and unsolicited media coverage, the trademark was recognized by the consuming public as a source identifier. The Lanham Act also advanced another significant change related to the use of a trademark, which belonged to another, in false and misleading advertisement. The Lanham Act's potent unfair competition provisions reined in the abusive, deceptive business practices of causing consumer confusion in the marketplace. With the passing of the Lanham Act, trademarks finally received national protection of the goodwill embodied in trademarks, in the interest of preventing trade misrepresentation and public deception, as advocated by the Senate Committee:

> There can be no doubt under the recent decisions of the Supreme Court of the constitutionality of a national act giving substantive as distinguished from merely procedural rights in trademarks in commerce over which Congress has plenary power, and when it is considered that the protection of trade–marks is merely protection to goodwill, to prevent diversion of trade through misrepresentation, and the protection of the public against deception, a sound public policy requires that trademarks should receive nationally the greatest protection that can be given them.[15]

Moreover, modern trademark law owes its debt to two individuals. Edward S. Rogers, a member of the American Bar Association Committee on drafting a new trademark statute during 1935–1937, had a meeting with Congressman Fritz Garland Lanham at the request of the then-Commissioner of Patents. Rogers provided Congressman Lanham with a draft of the new trademark statute, which became H.R. 9041 on January 19, 1938. Congressman Lanham came from Fort Worth, Texas. He championed the bill through a long period of eight years, including the intervening years of World War II, to the day that the bill became law on July 5, 1946. Remarkably, the Lanham Act, in its totality, is "a self-contained statutory device to deal with all kinds of trademark infringement and unfair competition."[16]

In post-World War II America, Congress proceeded next to tackle the antiquated patent system, which had been identified earlier in 1938 by President Franklin D. Roosevelt as a cause of the economic malaise. The patent trouble persisted into the 1940s, as evidenced by the Supreme Court's notably antipatent decision and the Antitrust Division

---

[15] Senate Committee on Patents, *supra* note 14, at 5–6; U.S.C.C.A.N. at 1277.
[16] *NuPulse, Inc. v. Schlueter Co.*, 853 F.2d 545, 549, 7 U.S.P.Q.2d 1633, 1636 (7th Cir. 1988).

of the Department of Justice's hostility to alleged patent abuses. In addition, some areas of then-patent law existed only in judicial decisions and Patent Office practice, not in the patent statute. One individual who is often credited for lifting patent law out of darkness in this period is Judge Giles S. Rich.[17] He was instrumental in drafting substantive changes to patent law and working with the respective Congressional committee on patent law codification. The end result of Judge Rich's and others' efforts was a single, proposed "Patent Code" that pulled together existing statutes, judicial decisions, Patent Office practice, new provisions on contributory infringement, and a non-obviousness requirement for patentability.[18] On July 4, 1952, the Patent Code, presented merely as a "codification" bill to distract unwanted attention, sailed through both houses of Congress on consent calendars, without floor debate, as the houses relied on unanimous recommendations of their respective committees.[19]

The new patent law of 1952 included a very important aspect of patents: patents once granted by the Patent Office must be presumed valid. The new patent law provided substantive changes in patentability, infringement, and many other areas. Also, the clarification of provisions in the new patent law on patentability requirements along with explicit definitions helped the Patent Office in issuing Office Actions with statutory-based reasoning. In other words, the new patent law of 1952 shaped the entire patent system both procedurally and substantively, paving the way for more patents to be granted based on technological innovations soon to be discovered in the coming decades.

In the copyright law area, the first major revision to the federal copyright law was the codification of copyright law that led to the Copyright Act of 1909. After the major overhaul of patent law in 1952, Congress turned its attention to a potential, comprehensive revision of the copyright law by funding studies of important copyright provisions in the later 1950s. The Register of Copyright issued a report on the studies in 1961. With many different stakeholders, including authors, composers, book and music publishers, motion picture studios, and other interest groups, the revision process understandably took a long period of time and finally culminated with the Copyright Act of 1976, bringing copyright law to modern time. As observed by then-Register of Copyrights, Barbara Ringer, the new Copyright Act of 1976 made fundamental changes:

[17] George E. Frost, "Judge Rich and the 1952 Patent Code – A Retrospective," *Journal of the Patent & Trademark Office Society* 76 (1994): 343–47.
[18] *Ibid.* at 346, 352.
[19] Neil A. Smith, "Remembrances and Memorial: Judge Giles S. Rich, 1904–1999," *Berkeley Technology Law Journal* 14 (1999): 912.

The New Act is rather a completely new copyright statute, intended to deal with a whole range of problems undreamed of by the drafters of the 1909 Act. Even more important, the new statute makes a number of fundamental changes in the American copyright system, including some so profound that they may mark a shift in direction for the very philosophy of copyright itself. Properly designated, the New Act is not a "general revision," but is as radical a departure as was our first copyright statute, in 1790.[20]

With the 1946 Lanham Act, the 1952 Patent Act, and the 1976 Copyright Act, the United States transformed all three key areas of intellectual property law necessary for the nation that was experiencing a tremendous economic growth after World War II and continuous technological changes. The modernization of intellectual property law was a recognition that intellectual property assets were becoming important corporate assets to businesses. For instance, the computer industry began to explode in the late 1970s and soon desktops appeared everywhere in the 1980s. Software's rapid development profoundly changed daily activities as software was imbedded in the operation of common devices from the garage opener to the television remote control. Computer hardware and software impact how content from movies and music to photographs and text are being created and disseminated.

In the biotech area, DNA recombinant technology revolutionized the world, enhancing plants' resistant to diseases; increasing crop yields; altering plants, animals, and microbes for human use and consumption; advancing medicines and improving treatments in cancer; and finding cures for diseases. As innovations occur, new and better products and services become available in the marketplace.

Also, around the same time, private label products began to compete with established brands, changing the way consumers shop from retail stores to supermarkets. Trademarks, brands, and logos increasingly functioned as shorthand signals on which consumers and businesses relied in making purchase choices for new products and services. Patents, copyrights, and trademarks collided and intertwined in the marketplace, as patented and copyrighted products and services were designed, manufactured, and marketed to consumers and businesses in association with words, phrases, colors, and logos that capture attention, imagination, and emotion.

Corporations soon came to recognize the importance of intellectual property assets. They innovate new products based on their latest patents. They partner with university and research institutions to exploit new

---

[20] Barbara Ringer, "First Thoughts on the Copyright Act of 1976," *New York Law School Law Review* 22 (1977): 479.

discovery. They roll out the latest creative content protected by copyrights. They market their products and services with strategic trademarks, cultivating loyalty with marketing campaigns. They expand their market share through licensing and franchising. If they don't have the capacity to make the products, they license the intellectual property to others to have the products made. If they don't have the expertise to market and bring the products to end users, they license the intellectual property to distributors and vendors who will bring the products to the masses. They form new business alliances with the use of intellectual property assets. If they need capital and have valuable intellectual property assets, they leverage the assets to obtain financing, whether through equity financing or secured financing.

******

The rise of intellectual property as important corporate assets caught Delaware Legislature's attention. Again, to maintain its pre-eminence in business law and the center of all things corporate, Delaware decided to take the lead. On August 13, 1984, the General Assembly of the State of Delaware adopted a new amendment to its corporate income tax exemption law, among others. Specifically, Delaware added, at the end of paragraph (8) of subsection (b) corporate income tax exemptions of 30 Del. C. § 1902, the following sentence:

For purposes of this paragraph, "intangible investments" shall include, without limitation, investments in stocks, bonds, notes and other debt obligations (including debt obligations of affiliated corporations), **patents, patent applications, trademarks, trade names and similar types of intangible assets**. (Emphasis added.)

For the first time in history, Delaware explicitly acknowledged that intellectual property assets, including patents, patent applications, trademarks, trade names, and "similar types of intangible assets" are the valuable corporate assets held separately by entities whose activities are for the maintenance and management of the assets, the collection and distribution of the royalties, or passive investment relating to the intellectual property assets. Though copyrights and trade secrets are not listed in the amended provision, the phrase "similar types of intangible assets" is broad enough to include them, as well as other new types of intangible property not yet specified.

The addition of the phrase "patents, patent applications, trademarks, trade names and similar types of intangible assets" in 1984 openly invited and encouraged corporations to create IP Holding Company in

Delaware.[21] The phrase cemented Delaware once again as the center for all things favorable to corporations. The key attractive feature for the creation of the Delaware IP Holding Company is the corporate income tax exemption. If the IP Holding Company owns and receives income from its intellectual property assets through the "maintenance and management" and "the collection and distribution of the income from" intellectual property activities, there is no Delaware corporate tax on the income. Delaware's gift to corporations is permanently etched into its statutory language. Dramatically, Delaware would soon witness the influx of companies forming wholly owned subsidiaries to hold their intellectual property assets.

Corporations with intellectual property portfolios responded to the new gift of corporate income tax exemption handed down by Delaware. The corporate benefits generated from the Delaware gift made an impact beyond the Delaware boundaries, as states across the nation would soon experience, when corporations embraced the assignment and license-back intellectual property scheme.

Specifically, to take advantage of the statutory exemption, a company with intellectual property assets will create a wholly owned subsidiary in Delaware to hold its intellectual property assets. The company will then assign its intellectual property assets to the IP Holding Company in exchange for the IP Holding Company's shares. This type of transaction results in no tax under federal tax law because it is a swap of ownership of the intellectual property assets for ownership of the IP Holding Company's shares. The IP Holding Company, as the new owner of the intellectual property assets, will then license back the intellectual property to its parent and sibling companies for certain royalty payments. After all, the parent and sibling companies still need the intellectual property in order to continue the operation of their businesses. The royalty payments received by the IP Holding Company are the

---

[21] Delaware then added one more amendment to subsection (b)(8) by inserting, after the first appearance of the word "investments," the phrase: "or of the intangible investments of corporations or statutory trusts or business trusts registered as investment companies under the Investment Company Act of 1940, as amended (15 U.S.C. 80a-1 et seq.)." Together, the entire subsection (b)(8) provides:

Corporations whose activities within this State are confined to the maintenance and management of their intangible investments or of the intangible investments of corporations or statutory trusts or business trusts registered as investment companies under the Investment Company Act of 1940, as amended (15 U.S.C. 80a-1 et seq.) and the collection and distribution of the income from such investments or from tangible property physically located outside this State. For purposes of this paragraph, "intangible investments" shall include, without limitation, investments in stocks, bonds, notes and other debt obligations (including debt obligations of affiliated corporations), patents, patent applications, trademarks, trade names and similar types of intangible assets.

corporate income exempted from Delaware corporation taxation. As the parent and sibling companies make the royalty payments to the IP Holding Company, they can deduct the payments as business expenses to offset taxable income. The IP Holding Company, having an accumulation of royalty payments, can lend the money back to the parent whenever the parent needs the cash. On the loans, the parent can deduct its interest payments. Often the loans are generously unsecured, and in some instances the parent never pays back! With the royalty cash piling up, the IP Holding Company can invest the money and decide whether to distribute dividends to the parent. With the dividends received the parent does not have to pay tax!

In sum, Delaware's gift of corporate income tax exemption provides multiple layers of benefits to companies with intellectual property portfolios.

Illustratively, Syms, Inc. was among the early companies that readily accepted the Delaware gift. Syms was an off-price retail company that sold brand name clothes at a discount. The company was founded by Sy Syms in 1959. The company used the trademark "Syms" and the slogan "An Educated Consumer is Our Best Customer" in connection with its own brands of clothing. In early 1986, Irv Yacht of Coventry Financial Corporation presented the idea of a Delaware IP Holding Company for tax savings in a letter to Richard Diamond, CFO of Syms, Inc. Yacht promised a method of saving state taxes based on Coventry's program of reducing Syms's state income taxes by reorganizing the business activities of Syms. Specifically, Yacht proposed that Syms form a Delaware subsidiary, transfer the Syms trademarks to that subsidiary, and then execute a license agreement to allow Syms to continue to use the trademarks as it had before the transfer. Yacht outlined that Syms would pay a large royalty to the subsidiary in order to generate a large deduction as business expenses for Syms while the subsidiary would not have to pay any state tax on the royalty income because under Delaware law, IP Holding Company is exempt from income tax. Yacht demanded payment of 25 percent of the tax savings realized in the first year under the Coventry plan. In the subsequent four years, the payments would decrease in percentage.

Richard Diamond liked the Coventry plan, but was leery of the potential risk of a tax audit. Diamond knew that other corporations had already attempted to adopt similar schemes as outlined in the Coventry plan, but many failed to carry out the scheme properly. He and others, however, recognized that only New York State was the most sophisticated state in terms of tax audits, and other states were still in the dark. These states, besides New York, "w[ould] not even realize the impact" of the Delaware

IP Holding Company transactions.[22] Diamond, nevertheless, wanted to minimize his company's risk, just in case the tax savings promised by Yacht did not occur, and insisted that Syms hold part of the payments to Coventry in escrow.

Syms proceeded with the Coventry plan and incorporated SYL as its IP Holding Company in Delaware in December 1986. SYL and then Syms executed a trademark license agreement on December 18, 1986. And Syms transferred its trademarks from Syms to SYL on December 19, 1986. With these documents in place, Syms paid SYL a 4 percent royalty on the annual net sales from October 1, 1986, to the end of December, 1986, despite the fact that the transfer and license-back trademarks did not occur until later! Syms paid $2.8 million in royalty payments to SYL in 1986. In subsequent years, Syms increased the royalty payments from $10 million in 1987 to $12.7 million in 1991. That meant, in accordance with the Coventry plan, the more Syms paid to SYL, the more Syms could deduct and the more tax-free income SYL would enjoy on the royalty payments received.

Under the Coventry plan, SYL's board of directors and officers were Sy Syms, his daughter, Richard Diamond, Edward Jones, and two others. Jones was a partner in Gunnip & Company, a Delaware accounting firm.[23] Jones did not do much for SYL, except for lending his name and claiming to serve as a part-time employee for SYL in exchange for $1,200 - per year. To ensure SYL's nexus or contact requirement with Delaware, Syms paid a third party who specialized in providing "nexus services." Syms paid a total of $2,400 per year to Gunnip & Company for maintaining SYL's nexus with Delaware, with $1,200 of the total amount set aside for Edward Jones. Today, Irv Yacht is CFO for Benefitvision, Inc., touting thirty-five years of experience in financial and operational management. Gunnip & Company continues to thrive in its service of "highly personalized and comprehensive accounting, tax, and business consulting," as indicated on its website.

Around the same time Delaware made its amendment to expand its definition of "intangibles," many notable companies began to form their IP Holding Companies in Delaware: Gore-Tex in 1983; the Limited Stores, Lane Bryant, and Victoria's Secret in 1981–1982; and Lee and Wrangler in the 1980s, among others. Lee and Wrangler are subsidiaries of Vanity Fair Corporation (VF). The parent company segregated the "Lee" and "Wrangler" trademarks into respective Delaware IP Holding Companies and arranged for the license back of the trademarks to various

[22] *Syms Corp. v. Commissioner of Revenue*, 436 Mass. 505, 508 (Mass. 2002).
[23] *Ibid.* at 762 n.4.

VF operating companies, including VFJ Ventures, Inc. (VFJ). The benefits for VF are enormous: for example, in the tax year of 2001, VFJ paid Lee $36 million and Wrangler $66 million in royalties, and VFJ then deducted $102 million! The royalty income received by Lee and Wrangler for that tax year was exempt from tax in Delaware. VF tracked the state tax savings of the VFJ-Lee-Wrangler structure and noted that the structure generated a state tax benefit of more than $6 million in 2001.

Soon, corporations with intellectual property assets including patents, trademarks, and copyrights, embraced the Delaware gift by moving their intellectual property assets from parents to newly created IP Holding Company entities in Delaware. The layer of benefits attracts companies in different sectors across the nation to create IP Holding Companies in Delaware. They are: Home Depot, Stanley Works, Gore Industries, Mallinckrodt Medical, Honeywell, Gap, Victoria's Secret, Abercrombie, Lanco, Sherwin-Williams, Syms, American Greetings, Staples, ConAgra, Kimberly-Clark, Wal-Mart, TJX, Talbots, Nordstrom, Spring Industries, Toys "R" Us, and Tyson Foods, among others.[24] The Attorney General of Alabama noted that by the late 1990s, the rate of new IP Holding Company forming in Delaware was 600 to 800 per year.[25]

The ease of creating and maintaining an IP Holding Company for the handsome benefits provided under Delaware's corporate income tax exemption statute is due in part to expedient services provided by businesses specialized in this niche. Services regarding IP Holding Company formation and activities are readily available in Delaware for small fees. The specialty services companies offer a one-stop shopping approach with a single goal of protecting an IP Holding Company's corporate

---

[24] *NIHC, Inc. v. Comptroller of the Treasury*, 97 A.3d 1092 (Md. App. Ct. 2014); *Staples, Inc. v. Comptroller of the Treasury*, 2015 WL 3799558 (Md. Tax Ct. 2015); *ConAgra Brands, Inc. v. Comptroller of the Treasury*, 2015 WL 854140 (Md. Tax Ct. 2015); *Ex parte VFJ Ventures, Inc.*, 8 So.3d 983 (Ala. 2008) (Lee and Wrangler jeans); *Kimberly-Clark Corporation & Kimberly-Clark Global Sales, Inc. v. Commissioner of Revenue*, 2011 WL 383865 (Mass. App. Tax Bd. 2011); *In the Matter of the Protest of Wal-Mart Stores, Inc.*, 2006 WL 2038698 (N.M. Tax Rev. Dept. 2006); *The TJX Companies*, Inc. v. Commissioner of Revenue, 2009 WL 2359585 (Mass. App. Tax Bd. 2009); *The Talbots*, Inc. v. Commissioner of Revenue, 2009 WL 3162121 (Mass. App. Tax Bd. 2009); *Cambridge Brands, Inc. v. Commissioner of Revenue*, 2003 WL 21665241 (Mass. App. Tax Bd. 2003) (Tootsie Rolls); *Spring Licensing Group, Inc. v. Director, Division of Taxation*, 2015 WL 5011439 (N.J. Tax Ct. 2015) (one of the world's largest producers of home furnishings and specialty fabrics). The Wall Street Journal also provided a list of companies with IP Holding Company. Glenn R. Simpson, "A Tax Maneuver in Delaware Puts Squeeze on Other States," *WSJ*, August 9, 2002, www.wsj .com/articles/SB1028846669582427320.

[25] Brief in Opposition, *VFJ Ventures, Inc., v. Surtees*, 2009 WL 829572, at *3 (March 25, 2009).

income tax exemption by helping the IP Holding Company to create "as much nexus in Delaware as possible by establishing each holding company as a valid corporation controlled and managed in Delaware."[26] That means the services company will assist the IP Holding Company with the leasing of office space, furniture, equipment, and an office phone with a Delaware number. The IP Holding Company will have an address for "corporate stationery, correspondence, filing of payroll and tax returns, and storage of corporate holdings and records." The services company will set up "Delaware bank accounts, through which income is collected and disbursed for all [IP Holding Company] operations, dividends, and loans."[27] The services company will also assist the IP Holding Company with hiring a part-time Delaware employee or independent contractor "with the education and experience to manage a DHC" successfully in order to overcome any scrutiny relating to whether the operation of the IP Holding Company is separate from the parent company.[28] Often, the services company recommends that the Delaware employee or independent contractor should also "serve on the Board of Directors" of the IP Holding Company.[29]

The cost to corporations is miniscule for having a Delaware IP Holding Company. For example, Gore-Enterprise Holdings, the Delaware IP Holding Company with the patent portfolio that includes patents relating to the Gore-Tex technology, paid zero expense for salary and only $1,583 in annual rent while it received $16,973,458 in patent royalty income from the parent company W.L. Gore.[30] The annual service fees charged by a third-party company to ensure that the IP Holding Company meets Delaware's nexus requirements are less than $2,000.

Thousands of Delaware IP Holding Companies share the same office space and address. The *New York Times* reported that 1209 North Orange Street is a favorite of companies with intellectual property portfolios to reap the no corporate tax benefits. The address houses Dillard's, KFC, and "nearly two-thirds of the Fortune 500" tax-exempt subsidiaries![31]

In addition, 1105 N. Market Street in Wilmington, Delaware, has been known as the home of 700 corporate headquarters.[32] The same address is also

---

[26] "Maintaining a Delaware Holding Company," Advantage Delaware LLC, accessed May 22, 2016, www.advantage-de.com/services/de-holding-co-mgmt/maintaing-dhc/.

[27] *Ibid.*   [28] *Ibid.*   [29] *Ibid.*

[30] *W.L. Gore & Associates, Inc. v. Comptroller of the Treasury,* 2010 WL 5927989, at *3 (Md. Tax Ct. November 9, 2010).

[31] Lynnley Browning, *Critics Call Delaware a Tax Haven, New York Times,* May 29, 2009, www.nytimes.com/2009/05/30/business/30delaware.html.

[32] Michael Mazerov, "Closing Three Common Corporate Income Tax Loopholes Could Raise Additional Revenue for Many States" 7–8 (Center on Budget & Policy Priorities 2002), available at www.cbpp.org/4-9-02sfp.pdf.

Figure 2.1 American International Building in Wilmington, Delaware
Source: Erik Hille and Xuan-Thao Nguyen

home for IP holding companies, such as Reed Elsevier Intellectual Property
Management Services; IP Group Inc.; Intellectual Property Holding Co.;
Limited Brands; SMG Brands; GFC Brands; Worldwide Brand; Tyson

Holding company; AWI Licensing Co.; Barloworld; Nabisco Brands; AMEI Technologies Inc.; Ellwood Group Investment Corp.; Bristol IP Co.; Wyndham IP Corporation; Blue Leaf IP Inc.; Insignia IP Inc.; Tinwood Media Intellectual Property Holding Company, Inc.; TMI Holding Inc.; Huck Patents Inc.; Orkin Expansion Inc.; Limco Inc.; Signal Investment & Mgt Co.; and Tristrata Technology Inc., just to name a few.

The building at 1105 N. Market Street is now called the American International Building, replacing the old name "Wilmington Tower," which succeeded the original name "American Life Insurance Company Building." The famed architect, I. M. Pei designed the building with twenty-two stories, and the construction was completed in 1971. The modern-brutalist architecture is emphasized with heavy, block-like concrete forms, which intersect at ninety-degree angles without angles or curves. Its unassuming façade shelters the most valuable corporate assets today: Intellectual Property.

You Cannot Take Delaware's Gift Away

The attraction to form an IP Holding Company in Delaware rests on a proposition percolated by lawyers that other states cannot impose corporate income tax or franchise tax on the IP Holding Company because the entity does not have a physical presence in those states. Tax lawyers in the 1980s, asserting this proposition, relied on their reading of two decisions from the United States Supreme Court, *National Bellas Hess, Inc. v. Department of Revenue of Illinois* in 1967 and *Quill Corp. v. North Dakota* in 1992.[33]

In the first decision, National Bellas Hess was a mail order company incorporated in Delaware and licensed to do business in Missouri. The company had neither offices, distribution centers, warehouses, sales representatives, agents, property, nor a phone listing in the State of Illinois. The company also did not advertise its merchandise for sale in newspapers, on billboards, or by radio or television in Illinois. The company, instead, had all contacts in Illinois via United States mail or common carrier, as the company mailed semiannually its catalogues to customers in Illinois and the rest of the country. All correspondence relating to orders for merchandise with Illinois customers were conducted via mail or common carrier. The company processed orders in Missouri. The State of Illinois asserted that the company's business was sufficient as a "retailer maintaining a place of business in Illinois" for the purpose of

---

[33] Glenn R. Simpson, "A Tax Maneuver in Delaware Puts Squeeze on Other States," *The Wall Street Journal*, August 9, 2002, accessed May 23, 2016, www.wsj.com/articles/SB1028846669582427320.

collecting use tax from consumers who purchased the company's merchandise for use in Illinois. The company challenged Illinois' tax ruling as violating the Due Process Clause of the Fourteenth Amendment and causing undue burden on interstate commerce. The U.S. Supreme Court agreed with the company, holding that Illinois had no power to impose the duty of use tax collection and payment upon a seller whose only connection with customers in Illinois was by mail or common carrier.[34] Simply, the company's business in Illinois lacked the requisite minimum contacts with the state. In reaching its decision, the Court relied on both the Due Process Clause and the Commerce Clause.

Subsequently, mail order business flourished. As seen, twenty-five years later, the Supreme Court of North Dakota in *Quill Corp. v. North Dakota*, which is factually similar to *National Bellas Hess*, declined to follow the decision because "the tremendous social, economic, commercial, and legal innovations" between 1967 and 1992 have rendered the holding obsolete.[35] The Court held that the Commerce Clause requires "substantial nexus" physical presence whereas the Due Process only requires "minimum contacts" with the jurisdiction. With respect to sales or use tax for purchases made by in-state customers, a taxpayer must have a physical presence in a state in order to collect such taxes.

In *Quill Corp. v. North Dakota*, Quill was also a Delaware corporation with offices and warehouses only in three states: California, Georgia, and Illinois. The company had no employees or agents in North Dakota. It owned no tangible property in that state. Its mail order business sold office equipment and supplies. It solicited orders through catalogs, flyers, advertisements in national periodicals, and via telephone calls. After it filled orders, it delivered merchandise to customers in North Dakota by mail or common carrier from locations outside North Dakota. Under North Dakota's relevant tax statute, the company's business qualified as a "retailer maintaining a place of business" in North Dakota. The company was required to collect use tax from North Dakota customers and remit it to the state. Upon appeal, the U.S. Supreme Court rejected North Dakota Supreme Court's conclusion to overturn *National Bellas Hess*, and clarified constitutional concerns under the Due Process Clause from the Commerce Clause relating to state authority on imposing sales and use taxation on out-of-state business. The nexus requirement under the Due Process

---

[34] *National Bellas Hess, Inc. v. Department of Revenue of Illinois*, 386 U.S. 753, 760 (1967).
[35] *Quill Corp. v. North Dakota*, 504 U.S. 298, 301 (1992).

Clause requires "minimum contacts" with the taxing state and Commerce Clause "substantial nexus." Consequently, a state may satisfy the Due Process requirement when a corporation has the "minimum contacts" with the state, but fail the Commerce Clause requirement due to the corporation's lack of "substantial nexus" with the state. The majority affirmed that *National Bellas Hess* stands for the proposition that an out-of-state vendor "whose only contacts with the taxing state are by mail or common carrier lacks the 'substantial nexus' required by the Commerce Clause."[36] In other words, physical presence is required in order for a state to require an out-of-state business to collect use tax from customers.

Numerous states, in their efforts to stave off the onslaught of Delaware IP Holding Companies and their lawyers' arguments, have consistently pointed out that both *National Bella Hess* and *Quill* are confined to sales and use taxes. That means the physical presence requirement for substantial nexus must be met only when states impose sales and use taxes on out-of-state companies. The taxes at issue that involved Delaware IP Holding Companies are corporate income taxes and franchise taxes. Both *Bella Hess* and *Quill* are, therefore, not controlling authorities. States have asserted that they satisfy the Commerce Clause's requirement through "economic nexus" without having the Delaware IP Holding Company's physical presence within the state. Further, the Supreme Court has denied certiorari numerous times when the issue of whether its precedents on the physical presence requirement for substantial nexus extend to state taxes beyond sales and use taxes.[37]

While many states have advanced the argument that state taxation in *National Bellas Hess* and *Quill* are limited to sales and use taxes, some attorneys strongly disagree. The attorneys have staked the position that the cases "stand for the proposition that if a company has no physical presence, they should not be taxed at all."[38] That means income from an out-of-state Delaware Intellectual Property Holding Company is out of reach of state taxing authority. One of the leading tax attorneys in the nation who asserted such a position is Paul H. Frankel. He had represented many companies, arguing that states cannot reach IP Holding Company's royalty income because the IP Holding Company has no physical presence within the taxing states.

The name "Paul Frankel" is synonymous with the tax avoidance transactions with respect to IP Holding Company. Frankel was an influential tax lawyer, a recipient of numerous awards for his tax work on behalf of

---

[36] *Ibid.* at 311. [37] This topic is addressed further in Chapter 4.
[38] Simpson, *supra* note 33.

corporate clients. He was with Morrison & Foerster in the Local and Tax Group. In many major tax cases involving IP Holding Company's, the name "Paul Frankel" appears in the attorneys list. In the early years of Delaware's creation of the gift to corporations, Paul Frankel was there defending corporations against state tax authority. Toys "R" Us, The Gap, Sherwin-Williams, Wendy's, Whirlpool, KFC, Syms Corp., Kmart Properties Inc., Caterpillar, Limited Stores, Lanco, A & F Trademark, Inc., Caciqueco, Inc., Expressco, Inc., Lernco, Inc., Limco Investments, Inc., Limtoo, Inc., Structureco, Inc., and V. Secret Stores, Inc. are among Frankel's clients. With resources from corporations, Frankel led the fight all the way to state supreme courts across the country.

The fame that Frankel had garnered and the attention from corporate clients that he had basked, along with the enormous state tax savings that he has culled for his clients, are quite impressive, and are vastly different from his early days working for the IRS Regional Counsel's Office, where he litigated cases against *pro se* taxpayers including one that involved a deficiency of a mere $237.13.

The combination of the two Supreme Court decisions and the Delaware statute of corporate tax exemption paves the way for the growth of formation and maintenance of IP Holding Company entities in Delaware. Desiring a share of the bounty, other states have attempted to follow Delaware with similar tax exemption incentives to encourage companies to create IP Holding Company in those states, notably, Michigan, Nevada, and Vermont.

Michigan does not impose tax on an IP Holding Company's income generated from royalties. The Michigan Single Business Tax (SBT) imposes taxes only on those who *pay* royalties. The receivers of royalties are not subject to tax.[39] In other words, Michigan's SBT is a value-added, consumption tax. Dow Global Technologies, Inc. (Dow), Whirlpool Properties, Inc. (Whirlpool), AutoZone Parts (AutoZone), Kmart Properties, Inc. (Kmart), and H-D Michigan (Harley-Davidson) are among the IP Holding Companies located in Michigan.[40]

Illustratively, Whirlpool Properties, Inc. was incorporated in the State of Michigan to hold and manage their brands. Whirlpool licenses its

---

[39] *See Zenith Data Systems Corp. v. Michigan Dept. of Treasury*, 1994 WL 191804, at *3 (Mich. Tax Tribunal May 7, 1994) (imposing no tax on licensor of software who received royalties from licensees); *Mobil Oil Corp. v. Dept. of Treasury*, 373 N.W.2d 730, 742–43 (Mich. 1985).

[40] *Dow Chemical Co. v. Nova Chemicals Corp. (Canada)*, 458 Fed.Appx. 910 (Fed. Cir. 2012); *Whirlpool Props., Inc. v. Director, Division. of Taxation*, 208 N.J. 141, 26 A.3d 446 (2011).

intellectual property mostly to the parent company, Whirlpool Corporation, a New Jersey company. The royalty payments received by Whirlpool Properties are not subject to Michigan's SBT. Further, because the parent company is not a Michigan taxpayer, it does not pay SBT to Michigan. Whirlpool Properties also avoided filing any tax returns in New Jersey.[41]

Likewise, according to a plan developed by Price Waterhouse, entitled "Utilization of an Investment Holding Company to Minimize State and Local Income Taxes," Kmart Corporation assigned its trademarks to Kmart Properties, Inc. (KPI), a wholly owned Michigan subsidiary of Kmart, in October 1991. KPI received well-known trademarks and phrases, such as "At Home with Martha Stewart" and "Blue Light Special," among the assigned trademarks. The marks were valued between $2,734,100,000 and $4,101,200,000 by an independent appraiser. KPI then licensed the trademarks back to Kmart for the exclusive right to use the trademarks in the United States and its territories. Kmart made royalty payments based on 1.1 percent of Kmart's gross sales throughout the United States. KPI had a total of five employees transferred from Kmart Corporation. The New Mexico Taxation and Revenue Department noted that the creation of KPI dramatically affected Kmart Corporation's tax liability within New Mexico. Because New Mexico income tax laws allow Kmart Corporation to deduct as business expense the royalty payments made to KPI, that means Kmart Corporation can deduct significantly and pay no tax liability in some years. Being a Michigan company, KPI does not incur any tax liability on royalty incomes received from Kmart Corporation under Michigan law. Effectively, "income formerly attributed to Kmart Corporation's operations in New Mexico and taxed in New Mexico, was shifted to KPI, a corporation with no formal operations in the state, which paid no state income taxes on that income."[42]

Vermont wanted to attract companies to relocate to Vermont. Vermont adopted 32 V.S.A. Section 5837, tracking some of Delaware's statutory language and providing corporations that are qualified as an investment holding company to pay only $75 minimum tax as long as the investment holding company's activities are confined to the maintenance and management of their intangible investments. The term "intangible investments" includes "patents, patent applications, copyrights, trademarks, tradenames and similar types of intangible assets." Assume, for instance,

---

[41] *Whirlpool Properties, Inc.*, 208 N.J. at 155–6.
[42] *Kmart Properties, Inc. v. N.M. Taxation & Revenue Dept.*, 131 P.3d 27, 31 (N.M. App. Ct. 2001), reversed by 139 N.M. 172 (N.M. 2005).

a company holds a patent portfolio relating to the use of catheters in treating patients suffering from atherosclerosis by removing plaques of cholesterol, lipids, and other cellular debris from the inner walls of the arteries. The company licenses the patents to others in exchange for royalty payments. The company also enforces its patents through asserting infringement litigation against others. The company would be deemed as an investment holding company under Vermont statute. The company's activities would be ruled by the Vermont Department of Taxes as "investment" because patent "litigation to protect the value of the patents and recover lost income and damages would be within the scope of the litigation would be income from the investment."[43] In 2003 Vermont repealed the statute as part of its tax reform. Vermont, however, provides corporate income tax exemption to self-insurance company, a model for tax sheltering as discussed later in this chapter.[44]

States such as Nevada, Texas, Washington, and Wyoming are without corporate income tax. Some companies have gravitated to Nevada to form their wholly owned subsidiaries to hold intellectual property assets. The *New York Times* reported that Cisco, Harley-Davidson, Microsoft, Apple, and other companies have established Nevada subsidiaries to avoid taxes in other states.[45] According to the *Times* report, Apple created its Nevada subsidiary in 2006 and named it Braeburn Capital.[46] The ironic name Braeburn, a variety of apples with a complex taste of sweetness and tartness, avoids state corporate income tax while it manages billions of cash and other "liquid" assets.[47]

Here is a closer look into Nevada with the TJX Companies' tax avoidance transactions.[48] Around 1988, Joseph Donovan, a state tax partner with Coopers & Lybrand approached Alfred Appel, head of TJX's tax department, with a proposal to minimize state tax with the transfer of TJX's trademarks to a holding company subsidiary. In September 1992 Appel sent a letter to his boss, Dick Lesser, that the tax department's plan

---

[43] Vermont Department of Taxes Ruling 95–09, accessed November 8, 2016, http://tax.vermont.gov/sites/tax/files/documents/95–09.pdf.

[44] Michael Mazerov, "State Corporate Tax Shelters and the Need for 'Combined Reporting'" 2, Center on Budget and Policy Priorities (October 26, 2007), *available at* www.cbpp.org/sites/default/files/atoms/files/10–26-07sfp.pdf.

[45] Charles Duhigg & David Kocieniewski, *How Apple Sidesteps Billions in Taxes*, New York *Times*, April 28, 2012, www.nytimes.com/2012/04/29/business/apples-tax-strategy-aims-at-low-tax-states-and-nations.html.

[46] *Ibid.*

[47] Mazerov, *supra* note 44, at 3; Sean Farrell, "Apple's Burden: A Mountain of Money It Can't Really Use," *The Guardian*, September 6, 2014, www.theguardian.com/technology/2014/sep/07/apple-iphone-6-cash-pile-tax-avoidance-us.

[48] *The TJX Companies, Inc. v. Commissioner of Revenue*, 2007 WL 2331003 (Mass. App. Tax. Bd. April 3, 2009).

with Coopers & Lybrand would save the company $1–1.5 million in state income tax through the transfer and license-back scheme, and that the royalties charged to the other operating corporations within the TJX structure would be deemed as tax-free income in Nevada and enable the corporations to claim tax royalty deductions to further reduce its state tax liability. Moreover, Coopers & Lybrand crafted a list of purported business reasons for the scheme, and the TJX Board of Directors subsequently adopted these purposes for the transfer of the trademarks to the Nevada IP Holding Company.

Prior to implementing the transfer and license-back trademarks transaction, TJX had already incorporated NBC Fourth Realty Corp. in Nevada as a wholly owned subsidiary to lease certain real property to NBC Nevada Merchants, Inc., another wholly owned subsidiary of TJX, for warehouse and distribution center services. Coopers & Lybrand's plan called for the transfer of TJX's trademarks to NBC Fourth Realty. Cleverly, the name NBC Fourth Realty Corp., without a hint of trademarks or brands, would surely not attract unwanted attention.

Internally, TJX did not hide its tax avoidance purpose, as seen in the Checklist provided by Coopers & Lybrand to TJX for the repurposing of NBC Fourth Realty:

[NBC] was chosen as the company to hold and manage the intangibles because of its location in Nevada and its ownership of realty in Nevada. The real property will provide substance in Nevada for the corporation. In order to show that the actual management of the intangibles takes place in Nevada, at least one full-time employee will have to be hired by [NBC] to perform the necessary tasks which will consist mostly of bookkeeping. NBC Nevada Merchants, Inc. was not chosen because it has employees who regularly travel to Massachusetts to make reports to employees of TJOC. Since one of the purposes in establishing intangibles holding company [sic] in Nevada is to isolate the activities of managing the intangibles in a state which imposes no income tax, a corporation whose employees regularly make trips to other states would be directly contrary to the goal of isolating the activities in Nevada.[49]

On November 22, 1992, NBC Fourth Realty licensed back the trademarks, including "T.J. Maxx," "The Maxx for the Minimum," "Get the Maxx for the Minimum," and "Never the Same Place Twice," to TJX in exchange for royalties equal to two percent of sales. TJX also adopted similar transfer and license-back trademark schemes for its other clothing businesses operated as second-tier wholly owned subsidiaries. For instance, Chadwick's, a catalog mail-order business for off-price women's career and casual apparel, was incorporated in Massachusetts and had

---

[49] *Ibid.* at *7.

a distribution center also located in Massachusetts. TJX caused CDM Corp. to be incorporated in Nevada on November 25, 1992, and caused the trademarks from Chadwick's to be transferred to CDM Corp. As anticipated, CDM then licensed the trademarks back to Chadwick's pursuant to a license agreement between the parties effective on December 13, 1992.

Three years later, TJX acquired Marshalls of Roseville, Minnesota, Inc., the parent company of a group of Marshalls off-price apparel retail chain. TJX followed the same policy of a transfer and license-back trademarks scheme. It incorporated the wholly owned subsidiary Marshalls of Nevada, Inc. or MNV in Nevada to hold the transferred trademarks from Marshalls of Roseville. MNV then licensed the trademarks to operating Marshalls stores in exchange of royalties equal to 1.75 percent of sales.

TJX, however, continued to retain control over the trademarks even though the Nevada subsidiaries, NBC Fourth Realty, CDM, and MNV, are the owners of the trademarks. TJX also retained control of the Nevada subsidiaries' investment of the royalties TJX operating companies paid to the subsidiaries for the use of the trademarks. The loans and interest earned on such loans made by the subsidiaries to the parent company were never repaid.

Nevada continues to attract corporations to its soil without much scrutiny. Not surprising, Microsoft Licensing GP, a wholly owned subsidiary of Microsoft Corporation, manages and supports Microsoft product licensing agreements and delivery of products in North America and South America.[50] The subsidiary was incorporated in 1997 and is located at 6100 Neil Road, Reno, NV 89511. Microsoft Corporation and Microsoft Licensing GP brought breach of patent license agreement against others.[51] According to a Microsoft's annual report to the Securities and Exchange Commission, the Company has eleven subsidiaries in Nevada, most likely some of them are for tax avoidance purposes.[52]

******

In addition to the State of Delaware's gift to corporations with intellectual property assets, there are different tax planning strategies utilized by

---

[50] www.wilmette.com/assets/1/documents/MS_Enterprise.pdf; http://openmeetings.baldwincountyal.gov/sirepub/agdocs.aspx?doctype=agenda&itemid=529777.; "Schedule to Exhibit 10.19: Bsquare Corporation Form 10-K for the Annual Period Ended December 31, 2010," accessed May 23, 2016, www.sec.gov/Archives/edgar/data/1054721/000119312511070073/dex1019.html.

[51] Complaint, *Microsoft Technology Licensing, LLC v. Kyocera Corporation*, 2015 WL 1041506 (W.D. Wash. 2015).

[52] Mazerov, *supra* note 44, at 3.

multistate corporations to avoid paying corporate income tax and franchise tax. One of the tax planning strategies is the self-insurance scheme that exploits a loophole in "captive insurance company" structure.[53] This strategy illustrates the cat-and-mouse chase between states and multistate taxpayers in that states, unfortunately, are several steps behind. This strategy ultimately provides multistate corporations with similar results of avoiding state tax on the royalty income received from the licensing of intellectual property by an IP Holding Company to its parent.

In the self-insurance scheme, the parent corporation will create a wholly owned insurance company in a particular jurisdiction with the purpose of furnishing insurance to the company's affiliates. As a captive insurance company, its income enjoys state corporate income tax exemption.[54] The parent corporation will assign its intellectual property ownership to an IP Holding Company. The ownership of the IP Holding Company will then be assigned to the insurance company. With the ownership of the IP Holding Company, the insurance company can satisfy the capitalization requirements under the jurisdiction's insurance law. The insurance company will then receive substantial income from the royalty payments that the IP Holding Company licenses to its parent corporation and affiliates. As the self-insurance company, the royalty income will not be required to be included in a combined report with the parent corporation and affiliates doing business in a state that typically requires a combined tax report by unitary businesses. Consequently, the royalty income is not subject to state income tax.

The fast food hamburger franchise, Wendy's, is a perfect illustration of the self-insurance scheme.[55] Wendy's International, Inc. (Wendy's) is an Ohio corporation with its domicile in that state and is the parent company

---

[53] Vermon's "captive insurance company" is thriving business, as described below:

A captive insurance company is a closely held insurance company whose insurance business is primarily supplied by and controlled by owners, and in which the original insureds are the principal beneficiaries. The insureds have direct involvement and influence over the company's major operations, including underwriting, claims and management policy and investments. There are currently 4,000 captives licensed worldwide that service their parents' risk financing needs. In Vermont, that figure is 1,000, the most captives of any other state.

Vermont's captive owners represent a wide range of industries including multinational corporations, associations, banks, municipalities, transportation and airline companies, power producers, public housing authorities, higher education institutions, telecommunications suppliers, shipping companies, insurance companies and manufacturers, among others. http://www.vermontcaptive.com/laws-regulations/faqs.html

[54] Mazerov, *supra* note 44, at 2.

[55] *Wendy's International, Inc. v. Hamer*, 996 N.E.2d 1250 (Ill. Ct. App. 2013); Brief of Defendants-Appellees, *Wendy's International, Inc. v. Hamer*, 2012 WL 3569799 (Ill. Ct. App. 2012).

of a host of affiliate corporations in the fast food restaurant business across the nation. After an extensive feasibility study in 2001, Wendy's formed a wholly owned subsidiary, Scioto Insurance Company ("Scioto") in the State of Vermont as a "captive insurance company" that would insure all the affiliated corporations for a wide range of liability, including auto liability and collision, general and excess liability, property, crime, business interruption, and worker's compensation. Wendy's claimed that it established Scioto to reduce risks and insurance expenses. Wendy's then had to capitalize Scioto as required by Vermont insurance law. One of Wendy's affiliates, Markdel, contributed $250,000 in cash to Scioto. Further, Wendy's assigned its entire ownership of Oldemark, LLC to Scioto.

Oldemark was the holding company for Wendy's intellectual property and received substantial income from licensing of the intellectual property to Wendy's. In turn, Wendy's then sublicensed the intellectual property to affiliates and some unrelated third parties. Wendy's paid Oldemark a three percent royalty rate for the use of the intellectual property. The transfer of the ownership of Oldemark to Scioto facilitated the indirect ownership of the intellectual property to Scioto and positioned Scioto as sufficiently capitalized to meet the potential insurance claims of its affiliates. Indeed, on October 15, 2001, Vermont granted Scioto a certificate of authority to transact business in Vermont and Scioto was in good standing for self-insurance purposes. In 2007, Vermont audited Scioto's status as an insurance company and ruled again that it met all the regulatory and financial requirements.

The value of Wendy's trademarks in 2001 was almost one billion dollars. With the ownership of Wendy's intellectual property, including the trademarks, most of Scioto's income came from the licensing of the intellectual property back to Wendy's and affiliates.

From 2001 to 2006, royalty income represented 72 percent to 88 percent of Scioto's total income. Scioto frequently made loans to its affiliates and earned interest income. During the period from 2001 to 2006, Scioto earned from 54 percent to 99 percent of the interest income from intercompany transactions.

When Wendy's International filed its federal consolidated income tax returns for the tax years in issue from 2001 to 2006, it included Scioto in the federal tax returns. For state tax filing, for example, in Illinois, Wendy's Illinois unitary business group did not include Scioto's apportionment income. A "unitary business group" means a group of businesses related through common ownership whose business activities are integrated with, dependent upon, and contribute to each other. A taxpayer corporation operating as a part of an Illinois unitary business

Table 2.1 *2001 to 2006 tax years Scioto's income breakdown*

	12/31/2001	12/31/2002	12/31/2003	12/31/2004	12/31/2005	12/31/2006
Premiums	18,156,759	25,059,030	14,960,726	18,304,358	19,526,916	19,240,927
Royalty Income	47,157,394	207,384,178	217,620,152	234,470,739	231,413,458	327,546,586
Interest Income	108,757	5,453,833	13,772,406	18,228,723	27,658,079	42,566,583
Total	65,422,910	237,897,091	246,353,284	271,003,820	278,598,453	389,354,096

group is treated as a single taxpayer and must apportion its income to Illinois together with the income of the members of its unitary business group through a unitary combined return. Apportionment is intended to assign the amount of income to Illinois that is proportional to the amount of income producing activities in Illinois.

The Illinois Department of Revenue audited Wendy's combined income tax returns and concluded that Scioto was not a true insurance company because the majority of Scioto's income came from intellectual property royalties, not premiums and investments; there was no actual shifting or distribution of risk; and Scioto was not regulated by many states in which it wrote premiums. The Department concluded that Scioto's apportionment income must be combined in Wendy's Illinois tax returns. The Department issued two notices of deficiencies for corporate income and replacement tax, penalty, and interest in the total amount of $2.5 million. Wendy's and the Department then fought their tax battle in court.

The Department lost. Simply, it turned out that Scioto was deemed as an insurance company under the Illinois Income Tax Act and therefore its apportioned income was not required to be combined with Wendy's. Because Illinois did not provide a statutory definition of insurance company, the court followed the available definition for insurance company under federal law. Relevant federal regulation that defines an insurance company emphasizes "the character of the business actually done" by the company. Though Scioto's income from insurance premiums was significantly smaller compared to its royalty and interest income, Scioto's character as licensed by the State of Vermont as an insurance company dictated the finding that Scioto is an insurance company under Illinois law. Scioto's only business was to furnish insurance to Wendy's and other affiliates. Accordingly, Scioto was found to be an insurance company in Illinois. Its income was therefore not required to be combined with Wendy's in Illinois. In other words, Scioto's apportioned income was not subject to Illinois income tax.

What about Scioto's ownership of Oldemark? Interestingly, Wendy's argued that Scioto itself did not engage in the business of licensing intellectual property. The licensing of the intellectual property belonged to Oldemark. The ownership of Oldemark by Scioto was for the purpose of enabling Scioto to have sufficient capitalization as required by Vermont insurance law. This reasoning led to the conclusion that the character of Scioto's business was insurance. Again, Scioto avoided Illinois income tax on royalty income.[56]

---

[56] *Wendy's International, Inc.*, 996 N.E.2d at 1255.

The self-insurance scheme also allows Scioto to escape corporate income tax in Oklahoma. The taxing authority in Oklahoma also lost in its battle against Wendy's and Scioto. Wendy's was allowed to deduct the royalty payments made to Oldemark/Scioto. Scioto was not required to pay corporate income tax on the royalty payments received from Wendy's. All of this was possible because the Oklahoma Supreme Court recognized that Scioto is an insurance company with income derived from the licensing of the intellectual property pursuant to a license agreement. The payments made by Wendy's were deemed as a bona fide obligation. The royalty payments received by Scioto were viewed as a source of income for Scioto's insurance business, and none of these transactions were deemed to occur in Oklahoma. Therefore, Oklahoma could not reach Scioto's royalty payments received from Wendy's for sales within Oklahoma.

This type of self-insurance company, with ownership of IP Holding Company to avoid state income tax, is another state indirect gift to multistate corporations with clever tax planning. As the dissenting justices Gurich and Taylor of the Oklahoma Supreme Court explained, in the self-insurance scheme an IP Holding Company, like Oldemark, is "a disregarded entity for tax purposes" because the insurance company, Scioto, is the sole member of the IP Holding Company. Therefore all income of the IP Holding Company is "attributable to Scioto." The "practical effect" of the self-insurance scheme is the "elimination of state income tax liability" on the royalty income emanating from sales within the state.[57] Unsurprisingly, the attorney for Wendy's in this case was none other than Paul H. Frankel.

******

California, the home of many technology companies, has a special state gift to software companies. A brief detour on software is necessary before scrutinizing California's special gift.

Software is everywhere. It is imbedded in computers, cell phones, remote controls, thermostats, and endless equipment and electronic products. Software is code written by programmers to make a program run. Using a particular programming language, the programmer writes instructions or source code of the software that enables the computer to perform the tasks and users to interact with the computer. The source code is human-readable, but cannot be executed directly by a computer. The source code must be translated by a compiler into object code in order to be executed by a computer.

---

[57] *Scioto Insurance Co. v. Oklahoma Tax Commission*, 279 P.3d 782, 784 (Okla. 2012).

Software can be systems software, which includes operating system and utilities that enable computers to function. Software can be applications software, which includes programs like word processors, power points, spreadsheets, and database management systems that do the tasks with ease for users. Computers need software, otherwise, they would be useless.

Software enjoys a wide range of intellectual property protection. The name of the software can be protected under trademark law if the software is licensed and distributed in association with the name. Certain software functions may receive patent protection if the functions satisfy statutory patentability requirements. With recent Supreme Court rulings narrowing patent protection for software, trade secret is often invoked to protect software source code. If the software source code has independent market value and is kept in secrecy, the software may be an ideal candidate for trade secret protection. Typically, software is protected under copyright law. Copyright protects software's source code, object code, and graphical user interface. That means the copyright owner has the exclusive right to make copies, distribute the copies, prepare derivative works based on the original copyrighted software, publicly perform the software, and publicly display the software.

Utilizing copyright law for software, holders of the copyrights employ the business model of licensing the software. Software companies have several channels to distribute their software copies. The companies, after research and development of the software, can license their software directly to end users pursuant to an end-user license agreement (EULA). Often, companies license the software to original equipment manufacturers (OEMs), granting them the right to copy the software into their computer systems before selling those computer systems with the preinstalled software.

Licenses are what software companies sell to purchasers. Because purchasers buy a license or the right to use the software, they don't have the right to resell the software to others without permission of the software company. In other words, the "first sale" doctrine, the right to transfer to others the copy of the copyrighted work after purchase, under Copyright law is not available to purchasers of software copies. Software companies can apply price discrimination to sell software licenses at different price points to different groups of purchasers. The companies can charge higher prices to businesses and lower prices to students for the same software copies. With licensing as the business model, the software industry is well established and influential. Global packaged software, for example, Microsoft Office is a bundle of Microsoft Excel, Word, Access, and others; its revenue for 2015 was $430 billion. Gartner expects enterprise software to reach $380 billion in 2017.

Let's turn back to state taxation. California and many other states impose a franchise tax on corporations doing business in the state based on the corporation's net income derived from or attributable to sources within the state. The standard apportionment formula or SAF is typically used to determine a corporation's franchise tax liability among states. In California, for example, the SAF is based on three factors: property, payroll, and sales. Each of the three factors, say, property, is expressed as a fraction where the denominator consists of the value of all of the corporation's property worldwide and the numerator consists of the property based in California.

With respect to a software company in California, what is the company's franchise tax liability? Let's take Microsoft as an example. For the tax year of 1995 alone, Microsoft reported $1.65 billion in software royalties and $2.5 billion for tax year 1996. For the licensing of software to OEMs with billing addresses in California, Microsoft received $235 million in 1995 and $407 million in 1996. Applying the SAF, a quick answer for 1995 would be the fraction where the denominator would be $1.65 billion and the numerator $235 million; 1996 would be the fraction where the denominator would be $2.5 billion and the numerator $407 million. In 2002, the California Franchise Tax Board calculated and assessed against Microsoft for a total of $4.7 million in franchise tax liability for the tax year of 1995 and $21.8 million in franchise tax liability for the tax year of 1996, inclusive of penalty.

In reality, Microsoft did not face such franchise tax liability for receiving large sums of royalty payments from OEMs with addresses in California. Here is why.

Under California law, only a sale of *tangible* personal property is treated as a *sale in* California for purposes of computing a corporation's tax liability if the property is shipped to a purchaser within the state. Whereas, the sale of intangible property is treated as a California sale *only* if a greater proportion of the property's "income-producing activity," as measured by its "costs of performance," is performed in California rather than in any other state. Microsoft argued, and the court agreed, that the licensing of the software to OEMs for "the right to install and replicate" Microsoft software is "an intangible property right" and the license of the software to California OEMs does not constitute a California sale under California statute. Therefore, the computation of the "sales" factor in the SAF for Microsoft's franchise tax liability cannot include the royalty income payments Microsoft obtained from the OEMs! That means the numerator is zero![58]

---

[58] *Microsoft Corp. v. Franchise Tax Board*, 212 Cal. App. 4th 78, 95, 150 Cal.Rptr.3d 770, 782 (Cal. App. Ct. 2012).

Essentially, California and other states with similar laws have given software companies a special gift. Software companies face no franchise tax liability when they license and receive royalties from the licensing of the software to OEMs. With this special gift, software companies can enjoy licensing as the business model without paying state franchise tax on the licensing royalty payments received from OEMs in state. Arguably, with California's special gift, there is no need for software companies to form an IP Holding Company for the assignment and license back with respect to the copyrights of software between related entities.

3　The Domestic IP Holding Company's Structure and Phantom

On the surface, the Delaware IP Holding Company statute seems benign. Corporations whose activities in Delaware are confined to the maintenance, management, and investment of patents, copyrights, trademarks, and other intellectual property assets are exempt from paying corporate income tax with the current rate at 8.7 percent. With this statute, Delaware opens its arms to corporations to create IP Holding Companies with ease. That means an IP Holding Company in Delaware will typically own a portfolio of patents, trademarks, and/or copyrights and will maintain the intellectual property assets by keeping the rights in force. The IP Holding Company will protect and enforce various intellectual property rights in proceedings at the United States Patent and Trademark Office and in courts across the nation. These activities, given how valuable the IP assets truly are, would require that someone with expertise and authority make decisions relating to both offensive and defensive use of intellectual property. Also, the maintenance and management of intellectual property assets often cover enforcement of the intellectual property rights through litigation. That means large sums of cost. Essentially, the maintenance and management activities alone do not fully enable the company to enjoy the maximum benefits of the exemption from paying corporate tax in Delaware. The critical activities must be the commercialization of the intellectual property assets that would generate income exempted from paying Delaware corporate income tax. The tax-free attraction, coupled with the reliable and favorable Delaware corporate law, and the sophistication of the courts, serves as a magnet to lure thousands of holding companies to become incorporated in Delaware.

The Delaware IP Holding Company statute, however, means much more to corporations. It offers a generous loophole that corporations have exploited. In the last three decades, companies from a wide range of industries have devised a scheme that extracts benefits beyond what Delaware statute designs. The companies use the Delaware statute to shift income and avoid paying taxes in other states. The companies have cleverly created an assignment and license-back intellectual property scheme among related entities to avoid state taxation on vast amounts of income generated from the intellectual property assets. To do so, the companies must first understand their intellectual property assets.

As companies in the United States spend significant resources and efforts to create, develop, and acquire intellectual property assets over the years, they appreciate how vital the intellectual property assets have become in the operation of their business and to the fierce competition in the marketplace. Companies typically have greater awareness of federal tax treatments of intellectual property development, acquisition, transfer, and licensing, as many of the federal tax provisions related to intellectual property assets came into existence in the 1950s.[1] On the state tax side, most states did not pay attention to intellectual property as the laws relating to patents and copyrights are federal, as dictated by the Constitution.

When Delaware amended its passive holding company statute to include intellectual property in the definition of "intangible investments" in 1984, companies with large intellectual property portfolios began to pay careful attention. Tax accounting firms immediately captured the opportunity opened up by the Delaware IP Holding Company statute and approached corporations with proposed plans of how to reduce state tax liability with the intellectual property assets. The state tax savings are enormous. The tax lawyers and the intellectual property lawyers for corporations also give their blessing for the scheme.

Companies with famous brands like Victoria's Secret, Sherwin-Williams, and Toys "R" Us, or innovative technology like Gore-Tex embraced the scheme to construct the structure and create the phantom, reaping the maximum benefits, including avoidance of state taxation. A closer look at each of these companies in four different sectors of the economy reveals what they all have in common.

Victoria's Secret

Victoria's Secret dominates the intimate apparel industry with a staggering revenue of $12.6 billion for the fiscal year ending January 31, 2016.[2] The much-anticipated annual Victoria's Secret fashion show, featuring "angels" with fake wings and minimalist body coverage, is no ordinary event, considering the cost at $12 million compared to the meager $200,000 to $1 million a typical fashion show incurs. As supermodels

---

[1] Jeffrey A. Maine & Xuan-Thao Nguyen, *Intellectual Property Taxation* (Bloomberg BNA 2015).

[2] Zak Stambor, "Victorias Secret Direct Sales Grow Little in 2016", Digital Commerce 360, last modified February 23, 2017, www.digitalcommerce360.com/2017/02/23/victorias-secret-direct-sales-grow-little-2016/.

are transformed into sensual angels that land on the hour-long television extravaganza wearing underwear available for sale across shopping malls nationwide, Victoria's Secret merges fantasy with reality. The fashion show moves the underwear from being a basic product into a different lifestyle, enticing the public to gain access to the sexy and fun experience with intimate apparel. The show airs in 185 countries, resulting in brand awareness and increased revenue. In the United States alone, more than nine million viewers watched the show on television in 2015.

The fashion show is an example of how Victoria's Secret creates demand for its bras and panties at high prices. In addition, it markets its products by distributing the well-known VICTORIA'S SECRET Catalogue, in addition to having a strong online presence with the highly successful website, www.victoriassecret.com. With more than 1,000 retail stores spreading across the United States, Victoria's Secret provides easy access to the intimates with fantasy.

Remarkably, Victoria's Secret's store sales grow despite shopping malls encountering traffic decrease. In 2014, each Victoria's Secret store in the United States sold an average of $5.06 million of products, compared to $4.96 million the year before. Women, not men, are the shoppers for Victoria's Secret products. In fact, 99 percent of Victoria's Secret shoppers are women, as they all want the lifestyle exulted by the supermodels.[3]

Within the corporate web of companies, Victoria's Secret is a wholly owned subsidiary of L Brands, Inc., located in Ohio, a far cry from the world of lace and satin, of leggy supermodels wrapped in angels' wings. Knowing where it stands in the intimate apparel sector, Victoria's Secret touts to the world that it is an "acknowledged innovator" and "category leader in the women's apparel industry."[4] It owns the famous "VICTORIA'S SECRET" trademark in connection with women's apparel, including intimate apparel and beauty products.

Indisputably, Victoria's Secret basks in an enviable and dominant presence in the lingerie market, occupying 41 percent of the $13.2 billion market in 2014.[5] For almost five decades, Victoria's Secret has successfully transformed a common and basic product into specialty lingerie for women under the helm of the billionaire Les Wexner, the longest reigning CEO of the parent L Brands, which was known as Limited Brands until 2013. The enduring success of Victoria's Secret led Wexner to either sell

---

[3] Natalie Robehmed, "The Victoria's Secret Fashion Show: A $50 Million Catwalk," *Forbes*, last modified November 10, 2015, www.forbes.com/sites/natalierobehmed/2015/11/10/the-victorias-secret-fashion-show-a-50-million-catwalk/#4a6ead784d2e.

[4] *Ibid.*

[5] Claire Zillman, "The Longest-Serving Fortune 500 CEO is a Bra Salesman," *Forbes*, last modified June 5, 2015, http://fortune.com/2015/06/05/leslie-wexner-l-brands/.

or spin off other brands like Abercrombie & Fitch, Limited Too, Lane Bryant, Lerner, Express, and the Limited Stores, in order to concentrate and capture the Victoria's Secret magic without much competition. Wexner did not mastermind the idea of specialty lingerie for women. Selling lots of lingerie, however, did make him a billionaire.

The origin of Victoria's Secret does not begin in Ohio but has a humble genesis in San Francisco. Versions of the genesis have been narrated in print and cinema. They all start with Roy Larson Raymond wanting to purchase lingerie for his wife. Like many men facing the uncomfortable task associated with buying lingerie, he was embarrassed to venture into the intimate space. He decided to change that as part of his MBA project at Stanford; he combined a $40,000 bank loan and $40,000 from relatives to form the Victoria's Secret Partnership.[6] The company listed the address of 1560 Waller Street, in the Haight-Asbury neighborhood, San Francisco, California, on its trademark application to the United States Trademark Office. The partnership adopted the trademark Victoria's Secret and began its first use of the name in connection with women's lingerie on June 12, 1977. Raymond was clever in selecting the name, evoking propriety exemplified by the sexually repressed Victorian era while unveiling the secrets lying beneath the façade. The name plays with history and toys with imagination. The partnership sought federal trademark protection by filing a trademark registration application on February 21, 1978.[7]

To further elicit the appropriate feel of the Victorian period, Raymond carefully considered the font type and overall appearance of the phrase "Victoria's Secret." He selected an ornate border with laurel leaves and branches, Edwardian script for the words, and filed another trademark registration application on March 28, 1980.[8]

Raymond's idea for Victoria's Secret to be a safe space for men to purchase lingerie caught attention. Revenue increased to $4 million in 1982 with six stores in California. But Raymond was not good at business and soon fell into financial trouble. He was at the edge of bankruptcy when Les Wexner stumbled into a Victoria's Secret store. Raymond sold

---

[6] "Obituaries: Roy Raymond, 47; Began Victoria's Secret," *The New York Times,* last modified September 2, 1993, www.nytimes.com/1993/09/02/obituaries/roy-raymond-47-began-victoria-s-secret.html.

[7] "Victoria's Secret Trademark Registration (February 21, 1978)," US Patent & Trademark Office, accessed June 12, 2016, http://tmsearch.uspto.gov/bin/showfield?f=doc&state=4801:hdavll.2.233.

[8] "Victoria's Secret Trademark Registration (March 28, 1980)," US Patent & Trademark Office, accessed June 12, 2016, http://tmsearch.uspto.gov/bin/showfield?f=doc&state=4801:hdavll.2.232.

Figure 3.1 Victoria's Secret Former Logo
Source: USPTO

the Victoria's Secret stores to Wexner's The Limited for $1 million in 1982.[9]

The company that Raymond founded now became Victoria's Secret Inc., a California corporation with an office located at 15 Wisconsin Street, San Francisco, having ownership of the stores and the Victoria's Secret trademarks. The new Victoria's Secret company was also a subsidiary of The Limited. Though Raymond started the lingerie specialty stores, he missed the boat; Wexner saw and later understood that in the lingerie market women are the powerful buyers, not men. He has expanded the business, profited handsomely, and continued to serve as the CEO of L Brands for the last fifty-three years. In 2015, Fortune named him the longest-serving Fortune 500 CEO.[10]

Wexner grew up in a family of retail business and hated the business when he was young. His father opened a women's clothing store and named it "Leslie" after him. His parents worked hard for the business but without much success. Wexner went to law school after college but often found himself drawing designs for stores and storefronts. He soon found that law had a lack of creativity and was so unbearably boring that he dropped out of law school. He returned home to assist his parents with their stores so they could soon take a vacation that they had long postponed and much craved. They went to Miami for a week while the young

---

[9] Stories about Raymond's business demise and his subsequent suicide two years after the sale to Wexner were reported in the news and later written into the film script of the 2010 movie The Social Network. See Naomi Barr, "'Happy Ending, Right?' The founder of Victoria's Secret had a genius idea. But he couldn't see just how far it could go." Slate, last modified October 30, 2013, www.slate.com/articles/business/when_big_businesses_ were_small/2013/10/victoria_s_secret_founding_roy_raymond_had_a_great_idea_but_ les_wexner_was.html; "Obituaries: Roy Raymond, 47; Began Victoria's Secret," supra note 6.

[10] Zillman, supra note 5.

Wexner managed the store by himself. Quickly, with his knowledge of accounting, he discovered that among different categories of clothes in his father's store, only the skirts, sweaters, shirts, and blouses that were known to be the "sportswear separates" categories were profitable, and the losing categories were dresses and coats. His father didn't believe him, a young man without retail experience, and refused to change the direction of the store from general to niche-focused on sportswear. Wexner was determined to prove that he was right about profitability in retail stores specialization.[11]

Wexner also observed in the late 1950s and early 1960s that the idea of specialization was shaping many industries across the United States. In medicine, many of his doctor friends were becoming specialists. In the practice of law, lawyers also were becoming specialists like tax lawyers. Specialization in retail, he believed, would be the way for him to compete against giant department stores. Based on what he experienced at his parents' store, he wanted his stores to be limited in the sense of specialization, focusing only on women's sportswear separates. He called it Leslie's Limited.[12]

On August 10, 1963, he opened his first store in Columbus, Ohio, and by January 1964, the store sold more items and made more money than his father could in an entire year. The store tripled its revenue in the second year, and Wexner opened his second store in 1964. After opening a total of six stores, Wexner imagined the unthinkable of going public. Indeed, The Limited went public with an intrastate offering to limit potential shareholders to Ohio residents. The Limited expanded and had stores in San Francisco, too.[13]

Wexner traveled to San Francisco to visit his Limited stores and that is when he stumbled into a Victoria's Secret store owned by Raymond. Fascinated by the specialty retail of sexy, not erotic, lingerie, Wexner wanted to learn more from the very guarded Raymond. Six months after their first encounter, Raymond called Wexner to inform him that he was about to declare bankruptcy but desired to sell his Victoria's Secret stores to Wexner instead of going bankrupt. Sensing a potential opportunity, on the same day of the telephone call, Wexner flew to San Francisco and negotiated the purchase within twenty-four hours in 1982. Victoria's Secret became a subsidiary of The Limited, which was later known as Limited Brands and then L Brands.

---

[11] Carlyle Adler, "Les Wexner Limited Brands," *CNN Money*, last modified September 1, 2003, http://money.cnn.com/magazines/fsb/fsb_archive/2003/09/01/350795/.
[12] *Ibid.*   [13] *Ibid.*

With the acquisition of Victoria's Secret from Raymond in 1982, Wexner expanded his knowledge and understanding about women's lingerie and later transformed his Ohio company from an apparel-based specialty retailer to a niche market of women's intimates that make customers "feel sexy, sophisticated and forever young."[14] The two women, beside Wexner, who propelled Victoria's Secret's transformation are Cynthia Fedus and Grace Nichols. In 1984, Fedus began at The Limited as a production manager and a year later she moved to Victoria's Secret. Within two years, in 1987, she became president of Victoria's Secret Catalogues Division. She understood that women were powerful purchasers of the products and responded to indulgence in their lingerie. Women did not like the earlier catalogues with pages of models appearing with men in provocative poses. Fedus changed this and broadened the appeal by offering romantic, feminine image with a touch of sensuality in the catalogues, and aspiration bordering fantasy. She also removed the men from the pages. A touch of the English myth of refined, elegance, and class became part of the tantalizing image of Victoria's Secret that was strategically created by including a London address on the cover page with prices listed in both British pounds and US dollars. Fedus worked in Manhattan with dozens of helpers. Under her watchful eye, the photo shoots done in Manhattan for the catalogues and the revenue based on catalogue sales exploded with the assistance of thousands of workers in Ohio, standing by ready to take orders and ship them across the country.[15]

Wexner ran Victoria's Secret by separating it into two divisions. While Fedus was in charge of the catalogues division, Grace Nichols tended to the stores division. In an article published about Nichols, the *New York Times* called her the grand dame of Victoria's Secret. She was known as the company fixer with extensive experience in retail before she joined Limited in 1986 and became Executive Vice President of Victoria's Secret Stores from 1988 to 1992, then President from 1992 until she retired in 2007. Overall, she spent more than twenty years with Limited.[16] She

---

[14] Benjamin Snyder, "7 Surprising Facts about the Victoria's Secret Business," *Fortune*, last modified December 2, 2014, http://fortune.com/2014/12/02/7-surprising-facts-about-the-victorias-secret-business/.

[15] James Morgan, "Frisky Business," *The Washington Post*, last modified September 8, 1991, www.washingtonpost.com/archive/lifestyle/magazine/1991/09/08/frisky-business/966d63 0b-4d59-4925-8ddd-ef60e41931dd/; "The Palm Beach Post, Thursday, January 6, 1994," available at www.newspapers.com/newspage/133031557/; "Executive Changes," *The New York Times*, last modified January 10, 1991, www.nytimes.com/1991/01/10/business/executive-changes-011891.html.

[16] "Grace A. Nichols's Executive Bio," *Equilar Atlas*, accessed June 12, 2016, http://people .equilar.com/bio/grace-nichols-the-men-s/salary/5567#.VxsBw_krJhE; Stephanie Strom, "Grace Nichols; When Victoria's Secret Faltered, She Was Quick to Fix It," *The New*

constantly visited Victoria's Secret stores and kept a close watch on quality and fashion trends. She worked with Wexner on repositioning the Victoria's Secret brand with a higher level of sophistication, quality, and aspiration. That translated into higher prices for each Victoria's Secret bra. Revenue at each of the Victoria's Secret stores grew, and the total number of stores expanded under her leadership.[17]

The road to success in women's intimates was full of learning experiences for Wexner. Wexner's empire once included the Limited Stores, Lane Bryant, Express, Abercrombie & Fitch, Structure, Henri Bendel, and Express, in addition to Victoria's Secret and Bath & Body Works.[18] Victoria's Secret climbed rapidly in sales, as it faced no real competitors in the women's intimate niche, while other L Brands companies faced stiff competition. In the 1990s, The Limited Inc. experienced earnings decline and began to spinoff Victoria's Secret in 1995, and Abercrombie & Fitch and Limited Too in 1998. Wexner sold off Lane Bryant in 2001. By May 2002, Wexner decided to focus on a few brands. The Limited Inc. changed its name to Limited Brands, reflecting Wexner's new direction to transform from a collection of specialty retailers to a family of brands. Wexner decided to shed many more unprofitable businesses and concentrate on women's intimates. He bought back Victoria's Secret and Bath & Body Works from Intimate Brands in 2002. Thereafter, from 2007 to 2010, he began divestitures of Express to affiliates of Golden Gate Capital, and Limited Stores to affiliates of Sun Capital. As part of the divestitures of Limited Stores, Wexner changed the parent company's name from Limited Brands to L Brands in 2013.

Victoria's Secret is now L Brand's crown jewel; it is one of two flagship brands of L Brands, with almost 1,000 stores located throughout the United States. L Brands operates the Victoria's Secret business, including distribution and shipping facilities, from offices in the Columbus, Ohio, area.[19]

York Times, last modified November 21, 1993, www.nytimes.com/1993/11/21/business/profile-grace-nichols-when-victoria-s-secret-faltered-she-was-quick-to-fix-it.html?pagewanted=all; Michael J. Silverstein, Neil Fiske, & John Butman, *Trading Up: Why Consumers Want New Luxury Goods–and How Companies Create Them* (New York: Penguin Group 2005), Chapter 7.

[17] "Grace A. Nichols's Executive Bio," *supra* note 16; Strom, *supra* note 16.

[18] Zillman, *supra* note 5.

[19] L Brands, Inc., 2015 10K Statement, March 20, 2015, p. 13, L Brands SEC Filings, http://phx.corporate-ir.net/phoenix.zhtml?c=94854&p=irol-SECText&TEXT=aHR0cDovL2FwaS50ZW5rd2l6YXJkLmNvbS9maWxpbmcueG1sP2lwYWdlPTEwMTYyNDUzJkRTRVE9MCZTRVE9MCZTUURFU0M9U0VDVElPTl9FTlRJUkUmc3Vic2lkPTU3#s107A1997891F561EFB1EA1B06B6AF0B4.

Victoria's Secret's Tax Strategy

Back in 1980 and before The Limited's acquisition of Victoria's Secret from Raymond, The Limited devised its tax scheme with the assistance of Stanley Schwartz and Frank Colucci, its then general counsel and trademark counsel, respectively.[20] The Limited, which was founded in Columbus, Ohio, in 1963, grew rapidly along with the specialty retailing industry nationwide as the country experienced and preferred new trends in shopping for apparel.[21] The Limited seized the moment by offering "private label" for its clothes sold under the trademark "The Limited," instead of purchasing nationally branded goods from New York for distribution in its stores.[22] The use of its own private label was so successful that soon the private label became the brand in its own right in the mind of the consuming public. In other words, The Limited witnessed first-hand how its homegrown trademark had transformed into an important corporate asset to its apparel business and possessed value apart from the operation of the business. With the rising success, The Limited would soon prepare to go public and wanted to separate the trademarks away from the company.[23]

The Limited formed Limco Investments, Inc. (Limco), a Delaware company on December 19, 1980, and caused the Limited Stores, Inc. to transfer The Limited's trademarks to the new company.[24] The parent company, in exchange for the assignment of the trademark to Limco, received 100 shares of Limco's common stock, par value $1.00 on January 29, 1981. The transaction was a nontaxable event under the Internal Revenue Code section 351.[25] Limco had no employees, as it outsourced its services to others.[26] Limco outsourced administrative and accounting services to Gunnip & Company; legal counsel to Morris, Nichols & Tunnell; and financial and banking services to Wilmington Trust Company. For all the trademark matters, Limco relied on Frank Colucci, the same trademark counsel for the parent company.[27] Colucci represented both the parent company and the subsidiary, handling the same trademarks before and after the transfer of the trademark ownership. Immediately after the transfer of the trademarks from the parent to the subsidiary in exchange for the common stock, Limco licensed the trademarks back to the parent for the use of the trademarks in connection with The Limited's apparel in exchange for a royalty rate of 5 percent of

---

[20] *In the Matter of the Petition of Express*, 1995 WL 561501, at *3 (N.Y. Div. Tax. App. September 14, 1995).

[21] "Heritage," L Brands, accessed June 12, 2016, www.lb.com/our_company/about_us/timeline.aspx.

[22] *Express*, 1995 WL 561501, at *2.   [23] *Ibid.* at *3.   [24] *Ibid.*   [25] *Ibid.*   [26] *Ibid.* at *4.

[27] *Ibid.*

gross sales.[28] Colucci then drafted the licensing agreement between Limco and The Limited.[29]

The Limited was then listed on the New York Stock Exchange on June 10, 1982.[30] It went public without the ownership of its very own name and brands! The lawyers proffered that the reasons for transferring the trademarks to the subsidiary were purely business, such as to shield the trademarks from potential takeover of The Limited by raiders and to enhance the management of trademarks by centralizing the trademarks with Limco, the Delaware IP Holding Company.

In addition, Limco made numerous loans to The Limited and related companies.[31] On paper, these loans included standard provisions and clauses seen in formal written promissory notes or revolving line of credit agreements. The loans, however, were not secured by any assets of the related companies. Also, the loans were rarely paid back.

The success of the trademark assignment and license-back scheme led to the adoption of the scheme for other companies owned by The Limited. For example, Lane Bryant, a subsidiary of The Limited, assigned its trademark to Lanco, a wholly owned Delaware IP Holding Company. Lanco then licensed the trademark back to Lane Bryant as of January 5, 1983, for use in connection with the specialty apparel offered for sale nationwide by Lane Bryant stores. The royalty rate for the use of the Lane Bryant trademark was 5.5 percent of gross sale.[32] The same entities that performed services for Limco also performed services for Lanco. The same trademark counsel, Frank Colucci, rendered similar trademark licensing work for both Limco and Lanco.

The same month that The Limited achieved its momentous accomplishment of being listed on the New York Stock Exchange, Wexner bought Victoria's Secret from Raymond and moved the company's headquarters from San Francisco to Columbus, Ohio.[33] The same scheme of assignment and licensing back the trademarks was adopted for Victoria's Secret.

On November 1, 1983, the new IP Holding Company was incorporated in Delaware and was called V Secret. Following the existing structure in Wexner's empire, Victoria's Secret transferred its prized assets, the

---

[28] The royalty rate was later changed to 6 percent of gross sale for "The Limited" trademark and 5.5 percent for the "Limited Express" trademark, after the parent company retained Valtec Associates, a valuation company to determine the fair market value for the royalty rate. *Ibid.* at *7.

[29] *Ibid.* at *6.   [30] "Heritage," *supra* note 21.   [31] *Express*, 1995 WL 561501, at *11.

[32] *Ibid.* at *8.

[33] Dan Alexander, "Victoria's Other Secret: The Low-Key Billionaire Behind The Lingerie Giant," *Forbes*, last modified September 30, 2014, www.forbes.com/sites/danalexander/2014/09/30/victorias-other-secret-the-low-key-billionaire-behind-the-lingerie-giant/.

trademarks, to V Secret in exchange for 100 shares of V Secret's common stock, on the same date V Secret was formed. The transaction was a nonrecognition transfer under Internal Revenue Code section 351, resulting in no federal tax being owed by either party.[34] Again, the same people and entities that provided the services for Limco and The Limited, and Lanco and Lane Bryant, now also extended similar services to V Secret and Victoria's Secret.[35]

Upon the creation of the structure, V Secret licensed the trademarks that it received from Victoria's Secret back to Victoria's Secret for use in connection with the sales and marketing of products under the Victoria's Secret brand. Frank Colucci again served as trademark counsel and drafted the license agreement between Victoria's Secret and V Secret. The parties entered into the license agreement on January 1, 1987, immediately after the Assignment of Trademarks signed by the parties with the effective date as of December 31, 1986.[36] The royalty rate for the use of the trademark Victoria's Secret was 5.5 percent of gross sales. The duration of the trademark license agreement was five years with an automatic renewal right. Moreover, under the assignment and license-back scheme, there was no limit on the geographical scope for the use of the licensed trademark. This worldwide license was similar to the assignment and license-back structure for the other L Brands companies.[37] V Secret also made similar unsecured loans to its parent company, Victoria's Secret.[38]

By 1986, The Limited Inc. of Wexner's empire had IP Holding Companies, Limco, Lanco, Expressco, and V Secret for the four corresponding parent companies, Limited Stores, Lane Bryant, Express, and Victoria's Secret. The four IP Holding Companies all shared the same office space in Wilmington, Delaware; received trademarks from their respective parent companies; licensed the trademarks back to their respective parent companies; and made unsecured loans to their respective parent companies. All of the intercompany loans, except two made during 1985 were not paid![39] The four IP Holding Companies had no employees and outsourced all services to the same persons. Frank Colucci performed all matters related to the trademarks owned by the four IP Holding Companies, ranging from registration to infringement litigation; however, none of the companies paid trademark services fees.[40]

In the early days, V Secret Inc. acted as a Delaware corporation and had a Delaware address, along with the other IP Holding Companies: Limco, Lanco, and Expressco. They maintained their address initially

[34] *Express*, 1995 WL 561501, at *4.   [35] *Ibid.* at *5.   [36] *Ibid.* at *8–9.   [37] *Ibid.* at *9.
[38] *Ibid.* at *11.   [39] *Ibid.*   [40] *Ibid.* at *12–14.

on Concord Pike, then later on Foulk Road, Wilmington, Delaware.[41] A search in the United States Patent & Trademark Office's database confirms that in 1987 V Secret, Inc. was indeed located at a similar address and the attorney of record was Frank Colucci. By 1994, V Secret, Inc. became V Secret Catalogue, Inc. with a new address on 1105 North Market Street, Wilmington, Delaware 19801, but the same Frank Colucci was the attorney of record. V Secret Catalogue then assigned all of its trademarks to Victoria's Secret Stores Brand Management, Inc., a Delaware wholly owned subsidiary of L Brands, Inc.[42] The IP Holding Company then listed its address as Four Limited Parkway, Reynoldsburg, Ohio 43068.[43] Interestingly, it is located in the same building with Victoria's Secret in the L Brands' Reynoldsburg campus.[44]

We look back at the journey of the famous trademark "Victoria's Secret." It was originally created by Roy Raymond, assigned to Victoria's Secret, Inc., then to the Delaware IP Holding Company V Secret Inc., and then to its subsequent reincarnated form called V Secret Catalogue, Inc., and at the end to Victoria's Secret Stores Brand Management, Inc., a Delaware corporation with an office in Ohio.[45] The attorney listed from 1982 to 2005 for all the transactions was none other than Frank Colucci.

Just imagine this picture: the sweetheart assignment and license-back arrangement allows Victoria's Secret's Delaware IP Holding Company to receive 5.5 percent of the 2015 $12.7 billion sales.[46] That means $698,500,000 of royalty income generated from the use of the trademarks. The IP Holding Company does not have to pay Delaware state tax on this income. Meanwhile, other states cannot reach the apportionment of the royalty income based on the goods sold under the trademarks in their states.[47] Related companies, as licensees of the trademarks, then deducted the royalty payments as business expenses.

---

[41] *Ibid.* at *15.
[42] "Victoria's Secret Underware Trademark Registration (March 17, 1994)," US Patent & Trademark Office, accessed June 12, 2016, http://tmsearch.uspto.gov/bin/gate.exe?f=doc&state=4807:jgpzgl.7.228.
[43] *Ibid.*
[44] Complaint, *Victoria's Secret Stores Brand Management, Inc. v. Cafepress Inc.*, 2:14-cv-02586-GLF-EPD (S.D. Ohio December 11, 2014) *available at* http://digitalcommons.law.scu.edu/cgi/viewcontent.cgi?article=1885&context=historical; "Trademark Assignment Abstract of Title," US Patent & Trademark Office, accessed June 12, 2016, http://assignments.uspto.gov/assignments/q?db=tm&sno=73159253.
[45] "Trademark Assignment Abstract of Title," *supra* note 44.
[46] "Investor Overview," L Brands, accessed June 13, 2016, http://investors.lb.com/phoenix.zhtml?c=94854&p=irol-irHome.
[47] Glenn R. Simpson, "A Tax Maneuver in Delaware Puts Squeeze on Other States," *The Wall Street Journal*, last modified August 9, 2002, www.wsj.com/articles/SB1028846669582427320.

Gore-Tex

A Gore-Tex jacket for the cold weather is ubiquitous. The technology and the name reverberate awe, as captured in Seinfeld's *The Dinner Party* episode where outside it was "scary cold" and George entered Jerry's apartment wearing a new Gore-Tex jacket, which became Jerry's substitute for the definition of "scary cold" to Elaine's inquiry. George bragged about how his father got a deal from a friend for the Gore-Tex jacket and encountered Jerry's tease: "You like saying Gore-Tex, don't you?"[48]

Gore-Tex's famous waterproof technology is legendary as the company always delivers the promise to keep customers dry. Indeed, a quick browse online will reveal loyal fans who are willing to pay for the expensive products and then profess their love for Gore-Tex online.[49] Gore-Tex waterproof prompted a parody t-shirt "Keep Calm and Love Gore-Tex" emblazoned in big letters below a proportionally small crown that conjures images of England and wet rain. The t-shirt is offered for twenty dollars on Amazon.[50]

What most Gore-Tex jacket, glove, and shoe aficionados may not know is that Gore-Tex is much more. It has over 1,000 products in a wide range of markets. Its medical products have been implanted in millions of patients. The Company is the number one maker in the industrial and electronic niches for products that reduce air pollution and help the renewable energy process. The Company made Glide dental floss, the first dental floss in the world with the ability to resist shredding. The Company invented Elixir guitar strings that are better and have a much longer durability life.[51] It is of no surprise when *Fast Company* magazine, founded by Alan Webber and Bill Taylor, two former Harvard Business Review editors with a focus on creative business and innovation, selected Gore-Tex as the most innovative company in 2004. Gore-Tex beat all tech companies in the Silicon Valley and all old and new companies before and after the arrival of the Internet.[52] The Company has also

---

[48] "Seinfeld – The Dinner Party," *YouTube* video, 0:42, February 25, 2010, www.youtube.com/watch?v=lt6KRKHpKhY.

[49] "I love Gore Tex . . . a lot. I've just ridden home from work in what can only be described as Monsoon type weather. It is pissing it down. I was dripping wet on the outside, but snuggly warm and dry on the inside. Expensive yes, but worth every penny on days like today." "I Love Gore Tex . . . a lot Post," *MCN Forum*, accessed June 12, 2016, https://forum.motorcyclenews.com/topic/64676/i-love-gore-tex-a-lot/3.

[50] "Keep Calm and Love Gore-Tex Parody T Shirt," Amazon, accessed June 12, 2016, www.amazon.com/Keep-Calm-Gore-Tex-Parody-Shirt/dp/B00WX9FT8E.

[51] Alan Deutschman, "The Fabric of Creativity," *Fast Company*, last modified December 1, 2004, www.fastcompany.com/51733/fabric-creativity.

[52] *Ibid.*

earned many accolades for management innovation and distributed leadership. It is the darling case study for business schools.[53]

The Gore-Tex Way

The company producing all things Gore-Tex is the venerable W.L. Gore & Associate. It is one of the 200 largest privately held companies in the United States with annual sales worldwide of more than $3 billion. The innovative management structure is known to nurture many profound breakthroughs in "a wide range of unexpected areas allowing the Company to enjoy a double-digit growth rate."[54] It encourages collaborations among talents and teams, leading to new discoveries and niche market dominants, ranging from dental floss and guitar strings to fuel cells. The Company built its enviable presence with the initial discovery of a versatile new polymer, expanded polytetrafluoroethylene (or ePTFE), and subsequent developments of new applications of the fluropolymer in medical, fabric, and industrial markets. Gore-Tex boasts that virtually all of the Company's products, from electronic signal transmission, laminates, medical implants, fabric, membrane, filtration, and sealant to fibers, for examples, can all be traced to the polymer.

Gore-Tex is an iconic and popular brand. Its memorable advertisements in the 1990s and motto "We test inside our labs and outside in your world" popularized the brand.[55] Gore-Tex's brand strength evokes envy, as customers look for the Gore-Tex on clothing and shoes as the primary importance when they shop and attach secondary importance to the actual manufacturer. In branding parlance, the Gore-Tex brand occupies the stage 2 (breakthrough) and acquires a "brand personality" of being excellent in quality.[56] The Company employed a path-breaking marketing strategy, moving from a silent component manufacturer of laminated fabric to having direct communication with customers, with tags "Gore-Tex: Guaranteed to Keep You Dry" on clothing carried on others' labels. The strategy allowed imitators like Intel to later adopt with its "Intel Inside" campaign. The Company also initiated viral marketing by giving thousands of free samples of Glide dental floss and Elixir guitar strings directly to consumers for the purpose of creating demand and, thereby,

---

[53] Gary Hamel, "Innovation Democracy: W.L. Gore's Original Management Model," *Management Innovation Exchange*, last modified September 23, 2010, www.managementexchange.com/story/innovation-democracy-wl-gores-original-management-model.

[54] *Ibid.*

[55] Philip Kotler & Waldemar Pfoertsch, *Ingredient Branding: Making the Invisible Visible* (New York: Springer, 2010), 127.

[56] *Ibid.*

later capturing the market.[57] The Company's viral marketing strategy was later adopted by many.

The Company started in the basement of founders Wilbert L. and Genevieve Gore's home in 1958. The couple pulled their savings from the bank, combined with the sale of their car, and turned their house into an operating Company. Thirteen of the sixteen people who were working for the Company at the beginning lived and worked in the Gore's house. At that time, the Company's business focused on making Teflon-coated electrical wires.

In 1969, the Company's opportunity arrived at an unexpected moment. Robert Gore, the son of Wilbert and Genevieve, was trying really hard to stretch Teflon rods to a thinner plumbers' tape. The conventional wisdom of stretching Teflon was "breakage could be avoided only by slowing the stretch rate or by decreasing the crystallinity."[58] One day, after having followed the conventional wisdom without success, a frustrated Robert reached into the oven to pull out a hot Teflon rod and rapidly stretched it.[59] Contrary to conventional wisdom, it worked. The rod could be stretched and expanded. Robert Gore demonstrated his discovery, later at trial in a patent infringement case, "by heating two Teflon 6C rods at about 285 degrees Celsius for five minutes, stretching one slowly and stretching the other quickly. The slowly stretched rod fractured. The quickly stretched rod stretched about five or six feet and did not break."[60]

More than that, it could be stretched and expanded into a strong, porous, versatile material – what is later called Gore-Tex – the ultimate waterproof, breathable film that can be found in all of the Company's products.[61] Robert Gore's discovery also marked a new beginning of experimental innovation for the Company to later encourage employees to take 10 percent of their working time to tinker, ponder, explore, and work on initiatives of their own imagination.[62]

Robert Gore filed his patent application, No. 39753, on May 21, 1970. The application never matured to patent. A new application was filed on July 3, 1973, claiming priority over the earlier-filed application. The new application was subsequently granted patent 3,953,566 on April 27, 1976, with the title "Process for Producing Porous Products" ("the '566 patent").

---

[57] Deutschman, *supra* note 51.

[58] *W.L. Gore & Associates, Inc. v. Garlock, Inc.*, 721 F.2d 1540, 1545 (Fed. Cir. 1983).

[59] Debbie M. Price, "Gore-tex Style," *Baltimore Sun*, last modified April 20, 1987, http://articles.baltimoresun.com/1997-04-20/business/7901010531_1_gore-tex-robert-gore-gore-associates/2.

[60] *W.L. Gore & Associates Inc. v. International Medical Prosthetics Research Associates Inc.*, 1990 WL 10072467, at *8 n.7 (D. Ariz. May 10, 1990).

[61] *Garlock, Inc.*, 721 F.2d at 1545.   [62] Hamel, *supra* note 53.

Another application for "Porous Products and Process Therefor" was filed on June 21, 1977, and granted patent 4,187,390 on February 5, 1980 ("the '390 patent"). Both the '566 patent and the '390 patent are related and share the same abstract:

This invention provides a tetrafluoroethylene polymer in a porous form which has an amorphous content exceeding about 5 percent and which has a micro-structure characterized by nodes interconnected by fibrils. The material has high porosity and high strength. It can be used to produce all kinds of shaped articles such as films, tubes, rods, and continuous filaments. Laminations can be employed and impregnation and bonding can readily be used to produce a large variety of articles. Compressed articles of very high strength can also be produced from these porous forms.[63]

The delay between Robert Gore's discovery in 1969 and the two patents granted nearly ten years later in 1976 and 1977 was due in part to questions raised by a 1967 patent issued in Japan to Sumitomo Electric Industries. In late 1979 and early 1980, the Company brought two law suits against Garlock, Inc. for infringement of the two patents. Garlock moved for invalidity of the patents on the ground that the patented invention was obvious and anticipated by Sumitomo. The district court ruled in favor of Garlock in 1982. The Company appealed to the Federal Circuit while two other competitors exploited the opportunity opened up by the patents being declared invalid. C.R. Bard began to use Gore's material for its vascular grafts and Tetratec "started coating fabrics with the same razor-thin membrane."[64] The year 1982 was "a very, very long year" for the Company,[65] and the litigation was a "hard fought and bitterly contested" case with five weeks of trial, thirty-five witnesses, over 300 exhibits, and a record on appeal consisting of 2,000 pages![66]

The Court of Appeals for the Federal Circuit reversed, crediting Robert Gore's inventions "filled a long sought yet unfilled need" and "enjoyed prompt and remarkable commercial success due to their merits."[67] The Company then sued both C.R. Bard and Tetratec with successful

---

[63] "Process for Producing Porous Products Patent," US Patent & Trademark Office, accessed June 12, 2016, http://patft.uspto.gov/netacgi/nph-Parser?Sect1=PTO1&Sect2=HITOFF&d=PALL&p=1&u=%2Fnetahtml%2FPTO%2Fsrchnum.htm&r=1&f=G&l=50&s1=3953566.PN.&OS=PN/3953566&RS=PN/3953566; "Porous Products and Process Therefor Patent," US Patent & Trademark Office, accessed June 12, 2016, http://patft.uspto.gov/netacgi/nph-Parser?Sect1=PTO1&Sect2=HITOFF&d=PALL&p=1&u=%2Fnetahtml%2FPTO%2Fsrchnum.htm&r=1&f=G&l=50&s1=4187390.PN.&OS=PN/4187390&RS=PN/4187390.
[64] "Gore-Tex Success a Fabrication? – Miracle Cloth Resists Downpour of Lawsuits," *Wilmington News Journal*, last modified November 4, 1992, http://community.seattletimes.nwsource.com/archive/?date=19921104&slug=1522699.
[65] *Ibid.*   [66] *Garlock, Inc.*, 721 F.2d at 1547.   [67] *Ibid.* at 1545.

settlements. In 1984, the Company brought another patent infringement action against International Medical Prosthetics Research Associates Inc., or IMPRA, an Arizona Company, for making vascular grafts from Teflon material.[68]

Robert Gore, the former president and CEO of the Company, was inducted into the National Inventors Hall of Fame in 2006 for the invention of Gore-Tex.

Gore-Tex, Innovation, and Tax

A little more than half a century after Robert Gore's eureka moment, the Company has strategically capitalized on its breakthrough discovery. It now has more than 10,000 employees who are called "associates" and is privately owned by members of the Gore family and associates.[69] Proud of its unique management style where associates work in teams without bosses, the Company believes that its working environment is conducive to innovation.[70] The Company's three stage review process called "Real, Win, Worth" evaluates new ideas advanced by associates. Central to "Worth" is whether a particular idea can be protectable under the patent system in order for the idea to have a sustained advantage.[71] Translating innovation into patents, the Company claims that it has been granted more than 2,000 patents worldwide in electronics, medical devices, and polymer processing, among other areas.[72]

The Company was incorporated in 1959 with headquarters in Newark, Delaware. Over the years, it has grown into a specialty manufacturing

---

[68] "Gore-Tex Success A Fabrication? – Miracle Cloth Resists Downpour of Lawsuits," *supra* note 63; *International Medical Prosthetics Research Associates Inc.*, 1990 WL 10072467, at 1. IMPRA challenged the validity of the '390 patent, alleging that the patent was a "rigorous duplication" of the Sumitomo patent. *Ibid.* at 1. The patent was held in invalid. *Ibid.* at 34–35.

[69] "WL Gore & Associates," *Forbes*, accessed June 12, 2016, www.forbes.com/companies/wl-gore-associates/.

[70] The company's management style is seen as a lattice structure. As observed by Lucien Rhodes, the company's "lattice contains no titles, no orders, and no bosses. Associates, as all Gore employees are called, are allowed to identify an area where they feel they will be able to make their best contribution. Then, they are encouraged to maximize their individual accomplishments ...." Lucien Rhodes, "The Un-manager," *Inc. com*, last modified August 1, 1982, www.inc.com/magazine/19820801/5178.html. Gore's management for innovation has been noted by Gary Hamel & Bill Breen. Gary Hamel & Bill Breen, *The Future of Management* (Massachusetts: Harvard Business School Publishing: 2007), 87 ("Gore is as flat as the proverbial pancake. There are no management layers and there is no organizational chart. Few people have titles and no one has a boss ... [T]he core operating units at Gore are small, self-managing teams, all of which share two common goals: 'to make money and have fun'").

[71] Hamel, *supra* note 53.

[72] "Gore at a Glance," *Gore*, accessed June 12, 2016, www.gore.com/about/the-gore-story.

company with numerous manufacturing facilities in the United States, notably, in Maryland, New Jersey, Pennsylvania, Arizona, California, and in Europe and Asia.[73] It has many facilities and prefers to keep each of its plants around 200 associates, small enough to encourage lattice structure of management and encourage interactions that lead to innovations. The Company's technology, which is protected by patents, allows the Company to command high prices and attract followers from different industries. Maximizing its success, in 1983, the Company began to set up a scheme to exploit both patent management and taxation.

Ian Campbell, current general counsel for W.L. Gore, recommended the creation of a Delaware IP Holding Company to Robert Gore in 1983. The Company created Gore Enterprise Holding (GEH), a Delaware wholly owned subsidiary, to manage W.L. Gore and Associates' patents. Although business reasons are often articulated by the Company for the creation of GEH, the organizing minutes noted that state tax savings was a reason for the creation of GEH.

Consistent with the Company's intension, GEH was a passive, non-operational entity.[74] GEH had neither employees nor related expenses until much later in the 1990s when it eventually hired an employee to manage patent paper work.[75]

For new inventions that lead to new filings for patent protection, GEH has no Gore associates working in teams in pursuit of innovations. GEH depends on the Company's employees who have novel ideas and reduce the ideas to practice ripe for patent protection. Without the Company and its employees, GEH has neither patent applications to file for protection nor patents granted by the US Patent Office to own. Shifting the ownership of patents from the Company into GEH, the scheme manifests through the immediate license back of the patents to the Company for its use in the daily business of making and selling products based on the patents.

The original license agreement between the parties reveals that GEH grants to W.L. Gore a *perpetual* license to all the patents, including then-existing patents and subsequently acquired patents.[76] The subsequently acquired patents can only be in existence after the Company's employees have conducted their research, resulting in the invention of new products

---

[73] Brief and Appendix of Petitioners, *Gore Enterprise Holdings, Inc. v. Comptroller of the Treasury*, 2013 WL 4397802, at *6 (Md. Ct. App. June 25, 2013).

[74] Brief of Appellant, *Comptroller of the Treasury v. Gore Enterprise Holdings, Inc.*, 2012 WL 4122950, at *5 (Md. Ct. App. June 15, 2012).

[75] *Ibid.* at *5–6.

[76] Perpetual license of patents is not permitted under patent law because the patent term is limited for twenty years from date of application.

and processes. GEH does not have to compensate these employees for their work; the Company's payroll system takes care of them. GEH benefits from this scheme without much effort. All it needs to do is simply have its name listed as the assignee on patent applications for all inventions conceived by the Company's employees. In fact, approval for whether to file a patent application is conducted by the Company's employee, not by GEH. Important persons whose names appear on patent information lists are the Company's employees because the information is "important in making business and marketing decisions" to the Company, not GEH.[77]

After new patents are granted, they will then be included in the list of patents, subject to the original patent license agreement between the Company and GEH. Royalty payments under the original patent license agreement were dependent on the Company profits.[78] In 1999, the parties amended the original patent license agreement and changed the royalty to a rate of 7.5 percent of the sales of all products manufactured by the Company.[79]

[Gore] shall pay to [Holdings] a royalty at the rate of 7 ½ per centum of the sales prices of all products manufactured, by [Gore] in the United States and sold by [Gore] for use, disposition or consumption in the United States or any of its territories and possessions or in any foreign country; provided, however, that [Gore's] obligations for royalty payments for any calendar year shall not exceed an amount equal to the Net Income from operations of [Gore] for that year.[80]

Recently, GEH touts that its patent portfolio includes 800 US patents and 3,500 foreign patents. That is a very impressive portfolio for a company with only one employee.

As a non-operating company, GEH simply cannot do the work associated with patent procurements. The work would typically entail having a patent policy related to an employee's invention disclosure, gathering information necessary for drafting of the patent applications, filing patent applications, and prosecuting pending patent applications, among others.

GEH depends on the Company for the daily operation because it has no capability. Pursuant to service agreements entered by GEH and the Company, GEH depends on the Company for office space, corporate services, and legal services, in order to exist.[81] The 1995 "Legal Services

---

[77] *Ibid.* at *10.   [78] *Ibid.* at *9.

[79] *Gore Enterprise Holdings, Inc. v. Comptroller of Treasury*, 437 Md. 492,500 (Md. Ct. App. 2014).

[80] Respondent's Brief, *Gore Enterprise Holdings v. Director of Revenue*, 2002 WL 32946540, at *9 (Mo. July 22, 2002).

[81] Brief of Appellant, *Gore Enterprise Holdings, Inc.*, 2012 WL 4122950, at *9.

Consulting Agreement" signed by GEH and the Company shows that the Company's attorneys are doing all of the following tasks for GEH:

- Prosecution of patent applications, domestic and foreign.
- Conduct or manage litigation or defense of patents against infringement.
- Provide advice with respect to utilization of outside counsel.
- Counsel, conduct, or manage applications to foreign patents and applications.
- Counsel with respect to patent infringement, domestic and foreign.
- Counsel with respect to interferences with pending patents.
- Counsel with respect to licensing negotiations and activities.[82]

In the earlier years, from the beginning of GEH's creation in 1983 until 1995, GEH didn't pay the Company for its rental of the Company's office space. In 1995, GEH hired its one and only employee who functions as a patent administrator. The scope of the patent administrator's work is simple, compared to the important, substantive tasks performed by the Company's attorneys as listed in the legal services agreement between GEH and the Company.[83]

Based on the Company's $3.08 billion sales of Gore-Tex products in the fiscal year ending March 31, 2015, the royalty rate of 7.5 percent of sales should yield a very large sum for GEH.[84] A look at an older tax year is instructive. GEH's 1996 tax return indicates a zero expense for salary; $1,583 for rent; and "$16,973,458 in royalty income received from W.L. Gore."[85] Pursuant to the license agreement entered by GEH and W.L. Gore, the royalty payments based on the $3.08 billion of sales would be $231,000,000.

The handsome amount is not subject to state taxation as the Company further structures its scheme by creating Future Value, Inc. (FVI), another Delaware company, solely for the purpose of managing the Company's excess capital. The creation of FVI allows GEH to transfer all of its investment securities to FVI in exchange for all of FVI's shares. This transfer did not result in tax to either of the companies. Moreover, the Company, as the sole shareholder of GEH when GEH declared a dividend in the form of the FVI stock, immediately became the sole owner

[82] *Gore Enterprise Holdings, Inc.*, 437 Md. at 500.   [83] *Ibid.* at 501.

[84] "#43 WL Gore & Associates," *supra* note 69.

[85] *W.L. Gore & Associates, Inc. v. Comptroller of the Treasury*, 2010 WL 5927989, at *2 (Md. Tax Ct. November 9, 2010). Although GEH receives some of its income from third-party royalty transactions, "the evidence also indicates that post-1996 third-party royalties were not a separate business but were directly connected to W.L. Gore operations. Returns further show that most of the expenses of GEH were for services performed by W.L. Gore for GEH or for ordinary business fees required to maintain patents." *Ibid.*

of FVI.[86] Whenever the Company needs cash, FVI is there to supply the cash by extending a line of credit.

Stringing the pieces together, there is a circular flow. The circle begins with the Company. The Company's employees through research and development invent new products and processes. GEH files patent applications, procures patents in its name, and licenses the patents back to the Company for its marketing and sales force to exploit the patents. The large majority of GEH's revenue comes from the royalties paid by the Company. FVI serves as a "depository for assets built up through royalties" GEH received from the Company. GEH declares a dividend to the Company, the sole shareholder of GEH. FVI extends loans to the Company, the sole shareholder of FVI.[87] Unsurprisingly, GEH, FVI, and the Company all have common employees, directors, and officers.[88]

Sherwin-Williams

What are cool places to visit in Cleveland? According to Cool Cleveland, a trip to the Sherwin-Williams Center for Excellence, the museum of the Sherwin-Williams Company, is a must. It is located in the lobby of the Company's downtown corporate headquarters in Cleveland, Ohio. The museum carefully curates the Company's history of innovation in the coatings industry, prominently highlighting the first patent obtained by Henry Sherwin himself back in 1877 for a sealable can of paint. The Company proudly asserts that it now has a patent portfolio of more than 500 patents and its material and chemical inventions have continued to revolutionize the coatings industry.[89]

The Sherwin-Williams Company proudly traces its origin to 1866, one year after the Civil War, when Henry Sherwin used his savings to purchase a partnership in the Truman Dunham Company of Ohio, a business concern distributing pigments and painting supplies. When the partnership dissolved four years later, Sherwin invited Edward Williams to form a partnership for a new paint business, the Sherwin Williams & Company. The partnership was later changed into a new corporation called the Sherwin-Williams Company.

The Company today is a publicly traded Fortune 500 company. With staggering sales of $10 billion per year in architectural coatings; industrial finishes and associated supplies; coatings for original equipment

---

[86] *Gore Enterprise Holdings, Inc.*, 437 Md. at 501.

[87] *Ibid.* at 516; Brief of Appellant, *Gore Enterprise Holdings, Inc.*, 2012 WL 4122950, at *9–11.

[88] *W.L. Gore & Associates, Inc. v. Comptroller of the Treasury*, 2010 WL 5927989, at *5.

[89] "Welcome to the Center of Excellence," The Sherwin-Williams Company, accessed June 12, 2016, http://excellence.sherwin.com/.

Figure 3.2 Sherman-Williams Former Logo
Source: USPTO

manufacturers; special purpose coatings for the automotive aftermarket, industrial maintenance and traffic paint markets; and paints and related products to independent dealers, mass merchandisers and home improvement centers, the Company's coatings are everywhere.

Sherwin-Williams Within Reach

Henry Sherwin's motto "What is worth doing is worth doing well" serves as the guiding inspiration for the Company. The Company wants its coatings products everywhere, literally covering the earth. Its iconic logo "Cover the Earth," which first appeared in 1893, shows SWP red paint being poured across the planet's surfaces and seas, with gigantic droplets stubbornly ignoring gravitational force to continue their dripping power into the solar system, leaving viewers to wonder which planets these drips would reach next.[90] It is a surrealist dream of corporate desire, predating the surrealism arts movement by almost four decades! From the Company's perspective, the logo represents its desire to protect and beautify surfaces, history, and heritage of the past 150 years to provide the best products that meet the most stringent environmental regulations.[91] The Company was listed on the New York Stock

---

[90] David Griner, "Now Its Sherwin-Williams' Turn for a Much-Needed New Logo, Right? Or Is the Earth-Smothering Icon Actually Brilliant?" *Adweek*, last modified September 3, 2015, www.adweek.com/adfreak/now-its-sherwin-williams-turn-much-needed-new-logo-right-166701.

[91] *Ibid.*

Exchange in 1964. Soon, due to criticism, the Company replaced the "Cover the Earth" logo with a new identity, but the hiatus did not last long. In 1979, when John G. Breen became the new President and CEO, he brought the surrealist, yet iconic, logo back.[92]

The Company developed its own products and brands, along with aggressive acquisitions of other product lines and facilities, to become one of the largest manufacturers of paints and varnishes. The Company's products are available under brands such as Sherwin-Williams, Dutch Boy, Krylon, Minwax, Thompson's, and Water Seal, among others. Strategically, when it comes to selling products, the Company employs two different approaches: the Sherwin-Williams branded products are available exclusively through a network of more than 4,000 Company-operated stores, and the other brands are available through a network of third-party distributors and stores. To increase its visibility and eliminate middlemen, the Company maps its Sherwin-Williams stores with care to ensure that more than 90 percent of the US population can reach the stores within an easy driving distance of a fifty-mile radius.

In addition to the US operations, Sherwin-Williams has expanded its reach to Canada, Latin America, South America, Europe, and Asia/ Pacific regions. Together, the Company's products are available in more than 100 countries worldwide. Globally, the Company is third in the development, manufacture, and sale of paint, coatings, and related products. In the United States, Sherwin-Williams boasts of its rank as the largest corporation and the leader in the industry.

Sherwin-Williams Coatings with Tax

John G. Breen was brought in to refocus the Company when it faced looming bankruptcy in 1979. He hired a new management team and implemented a decentralization corporate culture to turn domestic divisions in the Company into profit centers. Divisions gained autonomy in operational decision making and were accountable for their own results. Divisions were charged for any working capital and fixed assets provided by the Company. Breen rapidly reshaped the Company, staved off take-over attempts, and raised the Company's value. For the next twenty years, Breen guided the Company through focused acquisitions and witnessed the Company's value increase forty-one times from $108 million to $4.4 billion. Breen retired as CEO in 1999.[93]

---

[92] "Timeline," The Sherwin-Williams Company, accessed June 13, 2016, http://excellence .sherwin.com/history_timeline.html.

[93] Steve Minter, "IW Manufacturing Hall of Fame 2013 Inductee: John Breen Former Chairman and CEO, Sherwin Williams," *Industry Week*, last modified November 5,

Under the decentralized operating autonomy, however, the divisions faced some confusion relating to the management of trademarks that were used by more than one division. Understanding the value of trademarks in the marketplace, the Company decided to focus on a way to centralize the management of trademarks in mid-1990.

The Company's intellectual property attorneys, tax planning manager, Chief Financial Officer, and General Counsel held meetings to discuss the idea of forming trademark holding companies in Delaware. The Company engaged the assistance of Donald Puglisi of Puglisi & Associates, Inc. and a Commissioner of Delaware's Public Service Commission for his service relating to the creation and management of trademark holding companies. In the fall of 1990, the Company proceeded with the assignment and license-back trademarks scheme.

On January 31, 1991, the Company caused the incorporation of Sherwin-Williams Investment Management Company (SWIMC) and Dupli-Color Investment Management Company (DIMC) in Delaware. Their corporate activities are confined to "the maintenance and management of their respective intangible investments and the collection and distribution of the income from such investment or from tangible property physically located outside of Delaware."[94] On the same date, the Company assigned the trademarks associated with non-aerosol products to the SWIMC and trademarks associated with aerosol products to DIMC. The Company exchanged the trademarks for 100 percent of SWIMC's shares and 85 percent of DIMC's shares. The remaining 15 percent of DIMC's shares was owned by Dupli-Color Products Company, a wholly owned subsidiary of the Company.

The Company already had amassed a large trademark portfolio as of 1991. About 95 percent of the Company products were sold in the United States. That meant the trademarks associated with the Company's products were also from the United States. The Company promptly assigned all of the US trademarks and pending registrations related to non-aerosol products to SWIMC. A list of 420 trademarks changed hands from the Company to SWIMC, in exchange for 1,000 shares of SWIMC stock, par value $0.01. In addition to shifting the trademark assets to SWIMC, the Company also transferred $50,000 to SWIMC as part of its contribution. Likewise, the Company assigned a portfolio of 120 trademarks relating to aerosol products along with $42,500 to DIMC in exchange for 850 DIMC shares, par value $0.01.

2013, www.industryweek.com/iw-manufacturing-hall-fame/iw-manufacturing-hall-fame-2013-inductee-john-breen.
[94] *In the Matter of the Petition of the Sherwin-Williams Co.*, 2003 WL 21368741, at *9 (N.Y. Tax. App. Trib. June 5, 2003).

The Company hired American Appraisal Associates (AAA), the largest appraiser in the United States, to conduct a valuation of the trademarks before the assignment and license-back scheme. AAA estimated that the fair market value of Sherwin-Williams' US trademarks was a staggering amount of $328 million as of 1991.

To arrive at the fair market value for the trademarks in 1991, AAA first determined the royalty rates for the trademarks by finding comparable royalties for use of similar marks on similar products in similar markets. AAA essentially adopted the "relief from royalty approach" method by identifying the arm's-length royalty rates that a holder of comparable trademarks would charge to an unrelated licensee for the use of the trademarks. Then, AAA applied the royalty rates to the projected sales to determine the expected royalties that the holder of the trademarks would have to pay if the holder did not own the trademarks. The amount would then be discounted to arrive at the present value.[95] Specifically, upon determining the royalty rates for each of the product industry provisions, AAA applied the royalty rates to ten-year projections of sale of the products. The discount rate of 20 percent was used to derive the present value of the trademarks. AAA determined the 20 percent discount rate by using a combined method of Arbitrage Pricing Theory and the Capital Asset Pricing Method.

Moreover, AAA noted that trademarks have unlimited life because as long as they are in use, they have value and are protected under Trademark Law. To ascertain the value of the marks beyond the ten-year period, AAA took the product or industry division's final year's "royalty savings as a result of owning a trademark and capitalized it at the discount rate less the stabilized growth rate that varied by division, but was either 4 percent or 5 percent."[96] Combining the figures, AAA estimated that $328 million was the fair market value of Sherwin-Williams' US trademarks as of the date of transfer from Sherwin-Williams to SWIMC and DIMC.

The next day, February 1, 1991, following the transfer, both SWIMC and DIMC entered into license agreements with Sherwin-Williams to use the same trademarks that they had just received from Sherwin-Williams. SWIMC and DIMC granted to Sherwin-Williams the right to use the trademarks in connection with the manufacture, distribution, and sale of products and services in the entire United States. In other words, nothing had changed in substance with respect to the usage of the trademarks in daily practice. Sherwin-Williams encountered no disruption with its usage of all the trademarks.

[95] *Ibid.* at *13–15.   [96] *Ibid.* at *15.

Under the trademark license agreements, Sherwin-Williams agrees to pay SWIMC and DIMC in accordance with the royalty rates based upon sales conducted by individual divisions: Automotive, 4.5 percent; Specialty Products, 4.0 percent; Stores, 2.5 percent; Consumer, 2.5 percent; and Chemical Coatings, 1.0 percent.[97] These royalty rates were provided by AAA per Sherwin-Williams' request before the actual assignment and license-back schemes between Sherwin-Williams and SWIMC and DIMC.

The week before the transactions, Sherwin-Williams' Board of Directors held a meeting on January 23, 1991, articulating business reasons for forming SWIMC and DIMC to hold and manage the Company's trademarks. These business reasons included improving quality control of the trademark usage, increasing efficiency and enhancing the ability to enter into third-party licensing arrangements, as well as increasing overall profitability stemming from Delaware's corporate income tax exemption for investment and trademark holding companies.[98] Contrary to the meeting minutes, after the formation of SWIMC and DIMC, the quality control system didn't change; the Company itself continued to fully engage in the quality control functions of the trademarks.[99] Also, the Company continued to maintain the trademark docketing services; monitor the maintenance reminder system for trademark renewals; identify crucial dates for filing renewal affidavits for the trademarks; and provide registration support, licensing enforcement, and legal interpretations of trademark protection.[100] The Company received payments from SWIMC and DIMC for the services.

Likewise, the minutes of the Board's meeting on January 23, 1991, indicated that the formation of SWIMC and DIMC was for the purpose of licensing the new portfolio of trademarks to a third party. This business purpose was merely on paper, as there was no evidence showing that the two trademark holding companies actively sought licensing opportunities with a third party. Both SWIMC and DIMC had no third-party marketing plan or program because they depended on Sherwin-Williams for potential licensing opportunities.[101] As trademark holding companies, both SWIMC and DIMC simply had neither the experience nor the necessary information to make their own assessments and to select appropriate third-party licensees who "could maintain the brand value proposition associated with the assigned trademarks and, thus, there could be no rational expectation" that SWIMC and DIMC "could increase value and generate benefit by engaging in third-party

---

[97] *Ibid.* at *12.   [98] *Ibid.* at *7.   [99] *Ibid.*   [100] *Ibid.* at *16.   [101] *Ibid.* at *7.

licensing."[102] In other words, both SWIMC and DIMC are owners of the trademarks, without managing, maintaining, controlling, and licensing the trademarks themselves. Sherwin-Williams continues to be the Company doing the work related to management and licensing of the trademarks, as it had performed before the transfer of the trademarks.

Without having any full-time employees or any officers with trademark experience, SWIMC and DIMC were mere shell entities. SWIMC and DIMC received their substantial royalty payments from Sherwin-Williams. The Company then took deductions for the royalty payments and, thereby, understated its income in a particular state. As Delaware companies, both SWIMC and DIMC were exempt from Delaware income taxes.[103]

As expected, SWIMC and DIMC would make loans to Sherwin-Williams, using the royalty payments that Sherwin-Williams had paid them. The arrangement is both convenient and beneficial to Sherwin-Williams. For example, in October 1991, SWIMC made a loan of $7 million at 5.812 percent interest, which was the LIBOR rate plus three-eighths of 1 percent, for ninety days. Sherwin-Williams paid SWIMC the loan amount plus an interest amount of $98,328.13 when the loan was due.[104] The Company could deduct the interest payments, as it could for the trademark royalty payments, further reducing its state tax liability.

Upon formation, both SWIMC and DIMC shared the same office and address in Delaware. Their office had a desk, a chair, and a computer. They subleased the office and paid a small amount of $360 per month for rent in Newark, Delaware, to Puglisi and Associates, Inc. "for the convenience of Dr. Puglisi."[105] A search on the internet for SWIMC today reveals that it is still at the same address at 850 Library Ave., Suite 204, Newark, Delaware 19711. It lists www.swimcinc.com for its web address. A click on the web address takes visitors to a blank page which contains the following information:

For licensing opportunities or information please contact:

Gregory F. Lavelle
Vice President
SWIMC, Inc.
850 Library Avenue, Suite 204-H
Newark, DE 19711

Mr. Lavelle is currently Senator Lavelle, Senate Minority Whip for the State of Delaware. He was also one of the associates who had worked for

---

[102] *Ibid.* at *8. In fact, by the end of the 1991, less than 1/10th of 1 percent of SWIMC's royalty income was generated from third-party sources; SWIMC's royalties came from its license of the trademarks back to the Company.
[103] *Ibid.* at *19.   [104] *Ibid.* at 24.   [105] *Ibid.* at *18.

Donald Puglisi, the mastermind behind the assignment and license-back scheme. Puglisi himself was the President and Treasurer of both SWIMC and DIMC while he was a full-time finance professor at the University of Delaware, and he charged the Company $18,000 per year for his services.[106] SWIMC's address is the same address as listed for Puglisi & Associate.[107]

DIMC subsequently assigned all of its registered trademarks to SWIMC, as Sherwin-Williams decided not to have DIMC as a subsidiary. SWIMC now owns on paper a much larger trademark portfolio.

Toys "R" Us

Charles Lazarus, the founder of Toys "R" Us, returned from World War II after serving as an Army cryptographer[108] and opened Children's Bargain Town in Washington, DC, a baby furniture store in 1948. He was only twenty-five years old. He grew up in a family where business entrepreneurship was important, as his father owned a bicycle shop, and his uncle was in the baby furniture business. The baby furniture store quickly expanded its merchandise to include what the customers wanted with the furniture; they wanted toys. As a keen observer of customer behavior, Lazarus noted that unlike furniture, which rarely breaks or runs out of fashion, toys are fads. Children like certain toys, but not for too long. They like new or different toys. Or their toys break or get lost somewhere. Their parents and relatives would purchase more toys. Lazarus soon discovered that toys are a commodity and his business could be very lucrative.

Toys "R" Us Superstores

The 1950s-postwar period was an exciting time of explosive growth in the United States. During this period, a new mode of grocery shopping was shaping how Americans conducted their purchases. The freedom to walk down the aisles, select whatever items one desires to purchase, and put the

---

[106] *Ibid.* at *5, 10. Puglisi later became a subject of media scrutiny during the sub-primed back Collateralized Debt Obligations (CDOs). His name as a director of 200 CDOs earned him $400,000 in director's fees. *See* Matthew Goldstein, "Special Report: For Some People, CDOs Aren't a Four-Letter Word," *Reuter,* last modified May 27, 2010, www.reuters.com/article/2010/05/27/us-subprime-cdos-directors-idUSTRE64Q2Z C20100527.

[107] *In the Matter of the Petition of the Sherwin-Williams Company,* 2003 WL 21368741, at *18.

[108] Anita Lienert, "For Toys 'R' Us Chief, The Playground Is Global," *Chicago Tribune,* last modified December 19, 1993, http://articles.chicagotribune.com/1993-12-19/business/9312190059_1_toys-r-us-stores-japan-employees-and-customers.

selected items in the cart for purchase in a supermarket is irresistible. The variety of items to choose and the freedom-of-choice experience from supermarkets led Lazarus to revolutionize his own approach to his toy business. He restructured his business, transforming his stores into superstores for toys. He changed his company name from Children's Supermart to Toys "R" Us.[109] He invented the category-killer concept in 1957. By 1966, he had four stores with $12 million in annual sales and sold the company to Interstate Stores, a giant retailing company at that time. He continued the toy operation for Interstate Stores with growth and profits. Interstate, with many unprofitable retailing divisions, soon found itself in bankruptcy. Lazarus restructured Interstate, selling off other retail divisions, and keeping only the toy division.[110] He gave Interstate a new name as it went through bankruptcy; the company was now called Toys "R" Us. His stores were dedicated only to toys. Parents and children can self-serve themselves with aisles of toys, from one category to the next. The self-service superstore kept the price attractive. The business formula was a huge success.[111] Toys "R" Us subsequently became a publicly traded company in 1978.

Lazarus adopted the iconic Toys "R" Us logo, with the letter written backward as though a child had scribbled it, in 1957.[112] The grammatically incorrect phrase displeased some but attracted much attention to his stores. The federal registration for the phrase claims first use in 1960, and the then-applicant was Children's Supermart, Inc. located at 10700 Tucker Street, Beltsville, Maryland. About the beloved mascot giraffe, Lazarus recalled in an interview with the *Chicago Tribune* that he found a stuffed giraffe with big eyelashes in a store in Milan, Italy, and paid $50 for the toy in the early 1950s.[113] In February 1960, he added the giraffe Geoffrey along with the jingle evoking every child's secret desire: "I Don't Want to Grow Up, I'm a Toys "R" Us Kid."[114]

After the company went public, it added new "R" Us stores like Kids "R" Us and Babies "R" Us. Lazarus passed the reins of the company to other executives in 1994. The company faced stiff competition with the arrival of Walmart, Target, and Costco with their own aisles of toys. It is no longer a publicly traded company as of 2005; it is currently being

---

[109] *Ibid.*

[110] "Our History – Annual Report 2002," Toys "R" Us, accessed June 13, 2016, http://m edia.corporate-ir.net/media_files/irol/12/120622/toysrus/ar2002/page0.html.

[111] "History," Toys "R" Us, accessed June 13, 2016, www.toysrusinc.com/about-us/his tory/charles-lazarus/; Paul Klebnikov, "Trouble in Toyland," *Forbes*, last modified June 1, 1998, www.forbes.com/forbes/1998/0601/6111056a.html.

[112] "Our History," *supra* note 110.   [113] Lienert, *supra* note 108.

[114] "Our History," Toys "R" Us, accessed June 13, 2016, www9.toysrus.com/about-us/ history/.

privately held by an investment group that had acquired the company for $6.6 billion.

Toys "R" Us, Inc. ("Toys") is still the largest toy retailer in the world with $12.4 billion net sales and 66,000 employees.[115] Worldwide, Toys "R" Us sells toys and related products in 1,800 stores. In the United States alone, it has 864 Toys "R" Us and Babies "R" Us stores across the entire nation. Outside the United States, it has more than 755 stores, as well as more than 250 licensed stores in thirty-seven countries and territories.[116]

Toys for Tax

In 1984, six years after it became a publicly traded company, some executives had new ideas for the Company's valuable trademarks. 1984 was the same year Delaware amended its law to bestow a gift of no tax liability on the intangible investment of an IP Holding Company. Exploiting Delaware's gift, Toys devised its assignment and license-back scheme for its trademark portfolio in 1984.

Using the beloved mascot Geoffrey, Toys decided that the wholly owned subsidiary would be named "Geoffrey" when it incorporated the new entity in Delaware. Toys assigned its trademark portfolio, inclusive of the iconic trademarks "Toys "R" Us," "Kids "R" Us," and "Geoffrey" character logos, and other valuable trademarks and trade names to Geoffrey, Inc. on August 1, 1984. The valuation of the trademarks held by Geoffrey, Inc. was later conducted by Arthur Andersen & Co. in 1991, and it was at $1.5 billion.[117]

In exchange for the shifting of trademark ownership from Toys to Geoffrey, Toys received Geoffrey stock, as Toys benefited from having to pay no tax on the transaction. With many Toys operating stores in different states across the country, the need to use the trademarks before and after the assignment of the trademarks continued. Toys entered into an exclusive license agreement with Geoffrey that all stores could continue to operate and sell toy products and services under the trademarks.[118] The original trademark license agreement in 1984 covered all states, except

---

[115] "Toys "R" Us, Inc. Reports Results for Full Year and Fourth Quarter of Fiscal 2014," Toys "R" Us, accessed June 13, 2016, www.toysrusinc.com/press-room/releases/finan cial/2015/toysrus-inc.-reports-results-for-full-year-and-fourth-quarter-of/.

[116] "About Us," Toys "R" Us, accessed June 13, 2016, www.toysrusinc.com/about-us.

[117] *Geoffrey, Inc. v. Commissioner of Revenue*, 2007 WL 2122007, at *3 (Mass. App. Tax. Bd. 2007).

[118] *Bridges, Secretary of Department of Revenue, State v. Geoffrey, Inc.*, 984 So.2d 115, 118 (La. Ct. App. 2008).

New York, Texas, Pennsylvania, Massachusetts, and New Jersey.[119] Later, the license arrangement was expanded to cover these states. For example, on May 3, 1992, Geoffrey entered into a license agreement with Toys "R" Us-Mass, Inc., a subsidiary of Toys, to use the trademarks in connection with the sales of toy products at Toys "R" Us stores and Kids "R" Us stores within the State of Massachusetts.

Geoffrey is a shell. Its office space in Delaware is almost nonexistent. Indeed, it leased space for $100 per month from an accounting firm, the same firm that provided bookkeeping services for Geoffrey, for a fee of $150 per month in 1993 and 1994.[120] Geoffrey exists without any full-time employees; it typically has one or more part-time employees. It relies on Toys, Inc. for management, accounting, tax, and treasury services. For instance, Toys Inc. and Geoffrey signed a service agreement dated February 3, 1996, wherein Toys provides assistance to Geoffrey with trademark concerns and licensing issues, as well as investment opportunities and accounting matters. Knowing that trademarks are important in its business, Toys assigned an intellectual property specialist to be in charge of Geoffrey's trademark portfolio. To monitor the use of the trademarks at the retail sales level, Toys assigned regional and district managers at the stores with responsibilities of inspecting and monitoring the proper use of the trademarks by the stores and reporting any irregularities and concerns to appropriate personnel. Toys charged Geoffrey $300,000 annually for the services rendered.[121]

With respect to royalty payments, the original trademark license agreement was set at a remarkably low rate of 1 percent of the net sales by Toys and all of its affiliates, associates, and subsidiary companies of all the products and services rendered under the licensed trademarks. Toys aggregated the sale figures from all stores across the United States to calculate its total net sales figure and then made one royalty payment annually to Geoffrey's account.[122]

The royalty rate was later changed to a higher number, doubling or tripling the original rate. Specifically, the royalty rate for the use of the Toys "R" Us trademarks became 3 percent, and the Kids "R" Us marks 2 percent of Toys' net sales of the products and services, as seen in the licenses covering Oklahoma and Massachusetts.[123] With respect to the trademark Babies "R" Us, there was a little more complex royalty structure with 1 percent of net sales for the first year, 1 ½ percent for the

---

[119] *Geoffrey, Inc. v. South Carolina Tax Commission*, 313 S.C. 15, 17 (S.C. 1993).
[120] *Geoffrey, Inc. v. Oklahoma Tax Commission*, 132 P.3d 632, 634 (Okla. Ct. App. 2006).
[121] *Geoffrey, Inc. v. Commissioner of Revenue*, 453 Mass. 17, 20 (Mass. 2009)
[122] *Ibid.* at 20.
[123] *Oklahoma Tax Commission*, 132 P.3d at 634; *Commissioner of Revenue*, 453 Mass. at 19.

second year, and 2 percent for subsequent years, pursuant to the license agreement between Geoffrey and Toys in the State of Massachusetts. The royalty payments, for Massachusetts alone, for the tax years of 1996–2001, were $33 million that Toys paid to Geoffrey.[124]

Toys then deducted the royalty payments made to Geoffrey from its taxable income. For example, in South Carolina where Toys "R" Us began doing business in 1985, Toys made royalty payments to Geoffrey based on South Carolina net sales of Toys products and services within that state. Toys deducted the royalty payments from its South Carolina taxable income. Geoffrey claimed that, as a Delaware company, it would be exempted pursuant to Delaware's corporate law. Geoffrey would also claim that without personnel, payroll, and property located within South Carolina, it should pay no tax on the royalty income received from Toys for the licensing of the trademarks on toys sold in South Carolina.[125] Likewise, Geoffrey asserted that it has neither property nor personnel located in Massachusetts and should not pay tax on the $33 million royalty payments received from Toys for the use of the trademarks licensed by Geoffrey to Toys during the tax years that Massachusetts conducted audits of the company.

******

Victoria's Secret, Gore-Tex, Sherwin-Williams, Toys "R" Us, and countless other IP Holding Companies provide a glimpse into the secretive world of the domestic tax haven. The domestic tax haven gives birth to corporate transactions to avoid state tax liability.

In a nutshell, a typical structure of transactions for the creation of an IP Holding Company involves a multistate parent company with valuable intellectual property assets. The parent will search for a favorable jurisdiction to form an IP Holding Company. Ideally, the parent wants the jurisdiction to exempt the income received by the IP Holding Company. Upon forming the wholly owned subsidiary in the jurisdiction, the parent will shift the ownership of its valuable intellectual property assets to the subsidiary. Often, the parent does not hire any valuation company to ascertain the true value of the intellectual property assets. There is no need. In return for assigning the ownership of the intellectual property assets to the subsidiary, the parent will typically own all or the majority of the shares in the subsidiary. The transaction is not subject to federal tax.

Ironically, the parent knows that they are still in need of using the intellectual property for the daily operation of the business *after* they

---

[124] *Commissioner of Revenue*, 453 Mass. at 20.
[125] *South Carolina Tax Commission*, 313 S.C. at 17–18.

have no ownership of the intellectual property assets. They would cease to exist in the marketplace if they didn't have the same access to the intellectual property assets. The only way they can use the same trademarks or patents again is to license them back from the IP Holding Company. Conveniently, the IP Holding Company licenses all the intellectual property back to them, allowing them to use, make, market, and sell products and services in connection with the intellectual property.

Without having a full-time employee and without possessing any expertise, the IP Holding Company receives handsome royalty payments from the parent and siblings under the license arrangements. The majority of the royalty payments come from the same source: the parent and sibling companies. Rarely, the royalty payments come from outsiders because the IP Holding Company has neither expertise, relationship, nor personnel to assess potential third-party licensees. The IP Holding Company also has no employee to create innovation for patent protection; it looks to the parent or sibling companies and their employees for the creation of innovation, new patent applications, and new patent procurements. Essentially, the entire assignment and license-back scheme seems to be in form, not substance.

Nothing seemingly changes: the parent and siblings continue to operate their businesses with the intellectual property even though the parent does not own them anymore. But something really has changed: the parent now can deduct all the royalty payments that it pays to the IP Holding Company, reducing the parent's taxable income. The IP Holding Company now is flush with income, and it does not have to pay taxes because it was incorporated in a state with favorable laws allowing exemption for the royalty income. Sitting with handsome cash, the IP Holding Company can invest and make loans to the parent periodically at a favorable rate. The parent does not need to go to outside lenders for those loans, as the convenient and favorable rates are always waiting for the parent at the IP Holding Company. In addition, with regard to the interest payments on the loans, the parent can also benefit by deducting them as expenses. As the sole shareholder of the IP Holding Company, the parent can receive a dividend whenever it wants the IP Holding Company to distribute the dividend to it.

The structure is like a phantom. It is there, and yet it is not there. It is there in the sense that on paper the ownership of the intellectual property assets has changed. On paper, there is a license agreement for the use of the intellectual property assets. In substance, the parent's operation with respect to the intellectual property remains the same. The parent continues to use and manage the intellectual property as though nothing has occurred. On paper, the parent does not own the intellectual property. In substance, it functions as the owner of the intellectual property with full use and control of the intellectual property. On paper, the IP Holding Company has ownership and control of the intellectual property. In substance, the IP Holding Company cannot license the intellectual property to third-party licensees because it does not have the expertise, the skills, and the knowledge of how to select a licensee and monitor selected licensees' behavior with respect to the licensed intellectual property assets. Moreover, it does not have any full-time employees with the necessary skills to conduct all the monitoring, licensing, and enforcing of the intellectual property. It relies on the parent to do all.

In many ways, the IP Holding Company is itself the phantom. It exists, and it does not exist. It is formed in Delaware. It is a mailbox. At most, it may rent an office from an accounting firm for a small, monthly rental fee. It may share that same office with others. In most cases, it has no employees to use the rented office. It is all for show. It does not actually engage in the licensing, controlling, enforcing, and monitoring of the intellectual property; the parent company continues to provide the services as the parent company used to do before shifting the ownership. Without doing anything, it receives money. Lots of money. It receives royalty payments from the parent annually or periodically. The payments are dependent on the net sales. The payments are very large, as they are a percentage of the net sales aggregated from the use of the entire intellectual property portfolio across the nation. The phantom's account continues to accumulate riches coming from the royalty payments. The phantom has no use for the riches; it lives for the parent as it loans back money to the parent. In the circular flow, the phantom and the parent are indistinguishable.

Before the creation of the structure, the parent company uses the intellectual property in the operation of its business, to make and sell products based on the intellectual property that it has either developed in-house or acquired over the years. That is all. By creating the structure, the parent company magically produces and enjoys significant tax benefits. It gets to deduct the "royalty payments," thereby, reducing its taxable income. It gains easy access to loans with favorable interest rates; whenever it needs, it can obtain the loans from the IP Holding Company. It gets to deduct the "interest payments" and, again, reduce its taxable income. It also receives dividends. All of these new gains it now enjoys in addition to having the right to use the same intellectual property in the operation of its business to make and sell products based on the intellectual property!

The structure and the phantom can be utterly simple and deceitful. It can be simple because all it needs is to have the parent company assign its intellectual property assets to a wholly owned subsidiary. The subsidiary then licenses the trademarks back to the parent. The circular flow benefits both the parent and the subsidiary that are actually functioning like one entity.

******

The Roots of Assignment and License Back

The assignment and license-back intellectual property arrangement itself is not new; it has been in existence for at least 170 years. The arrangement can be traced back to 1845 in the famous *Waterman v. MacKenzie* decision by the US Supreme Court, though the assignment and license-back arrangement in that case was not for tax avoidance purposes but for financing reasons. The facts in that case are still resonant today.

In *Waterman v. MacKenzie*, Lewis E. Waterman invented an improvement in fountain pens and obtained a patent for his invention on February 12, 1884. Waterman was born on November 20, 1836, in Decatur, New York. He himself was a life insurance salesman who often faced problems with leaking fountain pens when he tried to seal a deal with a client's signature on an insurance agreement.[126] He sought to address the ink leaking problem for ten years and finally succeeded with his invention.[127] Using the capillary action and producing the appropriate pressure, Waterman's invention controlled the flow of ink in a special way that prevented blots and enhanced the longevity of the pen's usefulness. His invention set his pens apart from all the fountain pens available at that time. He had created the ideal fountain pen and wanted to open a business selling this new type of pen. He filed for patent protection.

Waterman needed money. He found a business partner, Asa L. Shipman, to form "The Ideal Fountain Pen Company" in New York City. Shipman would provide $6,500 in the form of a patent mortgage to Waterman. Under the patent mortgage, Waterman would assign ownership of the patent to Shipman. Waterman would then get the patent back after he repaid the loan. On the one hand, Waterman needed the money for the new business, and on the other hand, his new business needed to

---

[126] Terry Trucco, "Where to Find It; Help for a Vintage Fountain Pen," *The New York Times*, last modified January 17, 1991, www.nytimes.com/1991/01/17/garden/where-to-find-it-help-for-a-vintage-fountain-pen.html.

[127] Waterman died on May 2, 1901 in Brooklyn, New York. *See* "Death List of a Day, Lewis Edson Waterman," *The New York Times*, last modified May 2, 1901, http://query.nyti mes.com/mem/archive-free/pdf?res=9407E4DD1139E733A25751C0A9639C946097 D6CF.

use the patented invention for the manufacturing, marketing, and selling of the pens.

He devised a plan. The day after he obtained the patent, he assigned the patent to his wife, Sarah E. Waterman, on February 13, 1884. Five days before his wife assigned her ownership in the patent for the mortgage to Shipman, she granted Waterman exclusive license for the manufacture and sale of the patented pens. Specifically, in the license agreement between Mr. and Mrs. Waterman, she granted to him "the sole and exclusive right and license to manufacture and sell fountain pen-holders, containing the said patented improvement throughout the United States." In return, he would pay her "the sum of twenty-five cents as a license fee upon every fountain pen-holder so manufactured by him." On his birthday, November 20, 1884, the license agreement was executed, but it was never recorded with the US Patent Office. Five days later, on November 25, 1884, Mrs. Waterman signed the patent mortgage, assigning all of her rights in the patent to Asa L. Shipman.

Waterman's partnership with Shipman ended a few months later. Waterman then formed the L.E. Waterman Company. The Company continues to operate today selling luxury Waterman pens of style and elegance.

Without the assignment to and license back between Waterman and his wife, there would be no Waterman Company today!

Figure 3.3 Waterman's Newspaper Clipping
Source: http://www.vintagepens.com/images/perm/1883_Waterman_
ad.jpg

The assignment and license arrangement accomplished Waterman's dream. He established and built his pen company. With the patent, he had the monopoly in the improvements to manufacture and sell his ideal, practical fountain pens. Through the license agreement he was the only one enjoying the monopoly. With the patent, he assigned the ownership to his wife so they could obtain the necessary capital for the new business. The assignment to her and license back to him didn't hinder what he sought to accomplish but enhanced his business opportunity! Moreover, her subsequent assignment to Asa L. Shipman as a patent mortgage subjects the mortgagee, Shipman, to the earlier-executed exclusive license agreement between her and her husband, Mr. Waterman!

Though the assignment and license back in this case was not for tax avoidance, the benefits and how the arrangement was used became known to all. In subsequent years, companies across the United States embraced the arrangement for a wide range of purposes, including tax avoidance and financing.[128]

---

[128] Xuan-Thao Nguyen, *Financing Innovation: Legal Development of Intellectual Property as Security in Financing, 1845–2014*, 48 Indiana L. Rev. 509 (2015).

4   The Scrutiny from the States

States have discovered the Delaware's IP Holding Company gift to corporations and now feel the impact of the tax scheme involving the assignment and licensing back of intellectual property among affiliated entities. Many states have learned the details of the structure and the phantom through the few audits and reported cases of multistate companies with strong intellectual property presence. In response, states have devised different approaches to combat the scheme and have encountered varying degrees of success. Multistate companies, as expected, have vigorously fought back in court. Some, with the assistance of specialist state tax litigators, are not hesitant to litigate all the way to the state's highest court, costing both sides of the tax battle. In most cases, the taxing authority faces a constitutional challenge to the tax assessment on either the royalty payments received by the IP Holding Company or the deduction of the royalty payments made by the parent or its operating affiliate in the taxing jurisdiction.

There is no uniformity in responses among states in their efforts to address the tax consequences of the IP Holding Company and the assignment and license-back scheme. Roughly speaking, there are four different approaches states have employed to combat the problems relating to the IP Holding Company. First, some states have contended that they have the right to tax the out-of-state IP Holding Company's income because the entity has nexus with the taxing jurisdiction. They tax the IP Holding Company's income. Second, some states have argued that the transactions between the IP Holding Company and the operating affiliate lack economic substance. These states refuse to allow the affiliate to deduct the royalty and interest payments to the IP Holding Company and include the proportion of royalty payments in the affiliate's state income base. Third, some states attempt to avoid the IP Holding Company problems by enacting mandatory combined reporting statutes. Fourth, other states have enacted the so-called "add back" statutes, which legislatively disallow deductions for royalty and interest payments made to related corporations.

A major problem with states employing different approaches is the unpredictability faced by taxpayers. When faced with the same entities involved in the same transactions, one state may rule against the taxpayer while another state may rule in favor of the taxpayer. For example, Gore-Tex received conflicting rulings from Missouri and Maryland tax authorities. Likewise, Sherwin-Williams faced contradictory rulings from Massachusetts and New York.

Creating Economic Nexus to Tax the Out-of-State IP Holding Company

Generally, a state has constitutional authority to impose taxes on income or receipts derived from sources within that state. If a taxpayer has property in that state and generates income from the use of the property, the state can exercise its taxing authority on the income. In the assignment and license-back scheme involving intellectual property, the state faces a knotty issue of whether the state can tax an out-of-state corporation's income generated by the use of intellectual property within the state. The out-of-state IP Holding Company, incorporated in Delaware, for instance, would counter that it owns and manages the intellectual property in Delaware; it does not have any property, employees, or warehouses within the taxing state. In other words, the IP Holding Company claims that it has no physical presence in the state, no substantial nexus with the taxing jurisdiction, and, therefore, the state violates the Commerce Clause of the US Constitution by imposing corporate income taxation against the IP Holding Company.

Despite the potential constitutional challenge, some states have decided to forge ahead against the IP Holding Company. South Carolina took the early lead in imposing taxes on Delaware IP Holding Companies' income based on the IP Holding Company's licensing activity within South Carolina. In 1993, the South Carolina Supreme Court reviewed whether the Tax Commission's decision to tax a Delaware IP Holding Company's income was constitutional in the seminal case, *Geoffrey, Inc. v. South Carolina Tax Commission*.

Recalling the Toys "R" Us scheme, the parent company assigned its trademarks to its wholly owned subsidiary Geoffrey, the Delaware IP Holding Company. Geoffrey received royalty income from payments made by Toys "R" Us for the use of the trademarks in connection with toys and services sold in South Carolina and other states. In addition to licensing the trademarks, Geoffrey also provided to the parent its "merchandising skills, techniques, and 'know-how' in connection with marketing, promotion, advertising, and sale" of toy products to consumers.[1]

---

[1] *Geoffrey, Inc. v. South Carolina Tax Commission*, 437 S.E.2d 13, 15 (S.C. 1993).

Upon payments to Geoffrey, Toys "R" Us then deducted the royalty payments from its South Carolina taxable income. The Tax Commission first disallowed the deduction taken by Toys "R" Us. That strategy did not work, so the Tax Commission abandoned it, and, instead, targeted the royalties paid by Toys "R" Us in South Carolina and received by Geoffrey.

Going after Geoffrey, the Tax Commission argued, was sound under South Carolina's tax statute, S.C. Code Ann. § 12-7-230. The statute provides that an out-of-state corporation's income derived from "transacting, conducting, doing business, or having an income within the jurisdiction of" South Carolina is subject to the then-corporate income tax of 5 percent of a proportion of the corporation's entire net income. On appeal, the South Carolina Supreme Court analyzed whether South Carolina's authority to tax out-of-state corporations like Geoffrey violates the Due Process Clause and the Commerce Clause of the US Constitution.

The state supreme court noted that under the US Supreme Court decision in *Quill Corp. v. North Dakota*, the Due Process Clause requires that there must be a "minimum connection between a state and the person, property or transaction it seeks to tax" and the "income attributed to the state for tax purposes must be rationally related to values connected with the taxing State."[2] This nexus requirement under the Due Process Clause can be satisfied even when the corporation has no physical presence in the taxing state, as long as the corporation has purposefully directed its activity at the state's economic forum.

Geoffrey insisted that it had not purposefully directed its activities toward South Carolina because Geoffrey had entered into the trademark licensing agreement with Toys "R" Us at a time when Toys "R" Us had no stores in South Carolina. Toys "R" Us' subsequent entrance into South Carolina was a unilateral decision that could not create the minimum connection between Geoffrey and South Carolina for tax purposes. The state supreme court, however, did not accept Geoffrey's argument, pointing out that due to the nature of Geoffrey's business of owning, licensing, and managing its trademarks, Geoffrey had anticipated where and how its trademarks would be used when it selected a new licensee and entered into a new trademark agreement. Therefore, Geoffrey had contemplated and purposefully sought the benefits of economic contact with South Carolina and other states that the license agreement covered. Geoffrey had knowledge of and consented to Toys "R" Us's use of Geoffrey's trademarks in connection with Toys "R" Us's products and services in South Carolina. Likewise, if Geoffrey did not want its

[2] *Ibid.* at 18 (quoting *Quill Corp. v. North Dakota*, 504 U.S. 298, 306 [1992]).

trademarks to be used by Toys "R" Us in South Carolina, Geoffrey had both the trademark ownership and the ability to prohibit such use and, therefore, would have no contact with South Carolina.

Accordingly, the state supreme court rejected Geoffrey's claim that it had not purposefully directed its activities toward South Carolina. The court held that through trademark licensing and receiving royalties for trademark use in South Carolina, Geoffrey had the minimum connection with South Carolina as required under the Due Process Clause.

Moreover, the state supreme court ruled that the Due Process nexus was also satisfied by the presence of Geoffrey's intangible property in South Carolina. The court identified the intangible property to include the accounts receivable created by Toys "R" Us in South Carolina for Geoffrey, and the license agreement between Geoffrey and Toys "R" Us, which the trial court deemed to be a franchise in South Carolina. The court found that the intangible property was located in South Carolina for tax purposes, rejecting Geoffrey's argument that the intangible property had its situs at the corporate headquarters in Delaware under the doctrine of *mobilia sequuntur personam*.

Additionally, the court held that the tax imposed on Geoffrey was rationally related to values connected with South Carolina under the second prong of the Due Process test. The court stated that South Carolina had conferred benefits upon Geoffrey by providing an orderly society in which Toys "R" Us could conduct its business of selling toys to its customers and, thereby, allowing Geoffrey to collect income through royalty payments made by Toys "R" Us. The income earned by Geoffrey represented the protection, benefits, and opportunities Geoffrey received from South Carolina. Also, the fact that South Carolina taxed only a portion of Geoffrey's income generated within South Carolina's boundaries was further evidence of rationality.[3]

With respect to the Commerce Clause requirement and whether South Carolina tax violated the Commerce Clause by imposing corporate tax on Geoffrey, the state supreme court acknowledged that the requirement of "substantial nexus" between Geoffrey and South Carolina must be established. The court found that Geoffrey's insistence on physical presence being required under the US Supreme Court's decision in *Bellas Hess* is "misplaced."[4] The court observed that in *Quill Corp. v. North Dakota*,

---

[3] South Carolina apportioned income was determined under the single factor, gross receipts, apportionment formula where gross receipts from royalty payments from South Carolina sales are divided by the total gross receipts from everywhere during the taxable year. *See SC Private Letter Ruling No. 2003–1*, 2003 WL 23335049 (S.C.Tax. Com. March 10, 2003).

[4] *Geoffrey, Inc.*, 437 S.E.2d at 18.

the US Supreme Court revisited the physical presence requirement "and, while reaffirming its vitality as to sales and use taxes, noted that the physical presence requirement had not been extended to other types of taxes."[5] Accordingly, the court rejected Geoffrey's argument that there was no substantial nexus with South Carolina. The court reasoned that the "presence of intangible property alone is sufficient to establish nexus."[6] By licensing its trademarks to Toys "R" Us for use in South Carolina and deriving income from the licensing of the trademarks in South Carolina, Geoffrey had a "substantial nexus" with South Carolina.[7]

The reasoning in *Geoffrey* on "substantial nexus" seems cursory and conclusory, but the strategy pioneered by South Carolina attracted other states' attention. The assertion of "substantial nexus" based on the out-of-state corporation's economic connection vis-à-vis the trademark licensing arrangement and related activities is also called "economic nexus." The economic-based nexus between the out-of-state IP Holding Company and the taxing jurisdiction, in light of the IP Holding Company's lack of physical presence within the taxing jurisdiction, is an aggressive approach. Under the "economic nexus" theory, states assert that the IP Holding Company derives income from the sales of products with the use of the IP Holding Company's intellectual property within the state. Even though the IP Holding Company does not have a physical presence through traditional means of payrolls, offices, employees, or representatives, states insist that the IP Holding Company does have the presence of its intellectual property activities conducted through the IP Holding Company's affiliate within the state. The economic nexus is sufficient to support the taxing authority's decision.

By default, South Carolina leads other states in imposing taxes on the IP Holding Company under the "economic nexus" front. Specifically, South Carolina started the "economic nexus" movement to reach the apportioned royalty income the out-of-state IP Holding Company received from the licensing of trademarks for use in connection with goods and services sold within South Carolina. Some states have embraced the "economic nexus" approach.

For instance, the North Carolina taxing authority, in a case titled *A & F Trademarks, Inc. v. Tolson*, assessed corporate income and franchise taxes against nine Delaware IP Holding Companies including A & F Trademark, Inc.; Caciqueco, Inc.; Expressco, Inc.; Lanco, Inc.; Lernco, Inc.; Limco Investments, Inc.; Limtoo, Inc.; Structureco, Inc.; and V. Secret Stores, Inc.[8] Each of these companies was a wholly owned subsidiary of

---

[5] *Ibid.* at 18, n. 4.   [6] *Ibid.* at 18   [7] *Ibid.*
[8] *A & F Trademarks, Inc. v. Tolson*, 605 S.E.2d 187 (N.C. Ct. App. 2004), cert. denied, 611 S.E.2d 168 (N.C. 2005), cert. denied, 126 S. Ct. 353 (2005).

The Limited, Inc. These companies are owners of known brands: Abercrombie & Fitch, Express, Lane Bryant, Lerner, Limited, Structure, and Victoria's Secret, respectively. The Limited, Inc., the parent company of the nine IP Holding Companies, masterminded the entire scheme by strategically arranging for each company to hold a corresponding known brand.

Indeed, in the typical assignment and license-back scheme, The Limited, Inc. caused the trademarks to be assigned to the nine IP Holding Companies in exchange for ownership of the stock of the subsidiaries. The nine IP Holding Companies then licensed their trademarks to related retail companies in 130 locations throughout North Carolina, at a royalty rate between 5 percent and 6 percent of the gross sales. Collectively, in the taxable year of 1994, their related retail companies paid to the nine IP Holding Companies a staggering $301,067,619 in royalties. The IP Holding Companies also made loans to the related retail companies at market rate interest. The IP Holding Companies received $122,031,344 in interest payments for 1994. These amounts constituted 100 percent of the nine IP Holding Companies' income for that year. The related retail companies then deducted the royalty and interest payments to reduce their tax liability.

The nine IP Holding Companies appealed the assessments in a consolidated proceeding. Following South Carolina's lead in *Geoffrey*, the North Carolina court in *A & F Trademarks* agreed with the state taxing authority that the physical presence requirement in *Quill Corp.* only applies to sales and use taxes, and does not extend to corporate income and franchise tax. There are important distinctions, the court opined, between sales and use taxes and income and franchise taxes that render the physical presence requirement inappropriate as a nexus test.[9] On the one hand, sales and use taxes are typically based on the vendor's activities in the state. On the other hand, income and franchise taxes are based on the use of the taxpayer IP Holding Company's intellectual property in the state by an affiliated licensee, and not on any activity by the taxpayer IP Holding Company in the state.[10] Moreover, the North Carolina court observed that the US Supreme Court had already dictated that the presence of the recipient of income (like the IP Holding Company) from intellectual property in a state is "not essential to the state's income tax on income of a nonresident."[11] The *A & F Trademarks* court concluded:

---

[9] *Ibid.* at 194.   [10] *Ibid.*
[11] *Ibid.* at 194–95 (citing *International Harvester Co. v. Wisconsin Department of Taxation*, 322 U.S. 435, 441–42 [1944] for the proposition that states are entitled to tax a nonresident's income to the extent it is "fairly attributable either to property located in the state or to events or transactions which, occurring there, are subject to state regulation and which are within the protection of the state and entitled to the numerous other benefits which it confers").

Since the tax at issue in this case is not based on the taxpayers' activity in North Carolina, but rather on the taxpayers' receipt of income from the use of the taxpayers' property in this State by a commonly-owned third party, "it would [be] inappropriate and, indeed, anomalous … [to determine] nexus by [the taxpayers'] activities or [their] physical presence" in North Carolina.[12]

Therefore, the *A & F Trademarks* court rejected the physical presence as the *sine qua non* of a state's jurisdiction to tax under the Commerce Clause for purposes of income and franchise taxes.[13] The court held that "where a wholly owned subsidiary licenses trademarks to a related retail company operating stores located within North Carolina, there exists a substantial nexus with the State sufficient to satisfy the Commerce Clause."[14]

The reasoning articulated in *A&F Trademarks* was later adopted by the courts in New Jersey and Oklahoma, finding "economic nexus" against Delaware IP Holding Companies.[15]

Some other states, however, have gone even further by targeting the out-of-state IP Holding Company's income from licensing of trademarks and business methods to independent franchisees who are *not* related companies to the IP Holding Company! For example, KFC Corporation is a Delaware company having its primary business in the ownership and licensing of the KFC trademark and related system. KFC licenses its system to independent franchisees who own and operate 3,400 KFC restaurants throughout the United States. In Iowa, KFC owns no restaurant, has no employees, and has no affiliated franchisees. In 2001, the Iowa Department of Revenue made an assessment for unpaid corporate income taxes, penalties, and interest for 1997, 1998, and 1999 against KFC. The tax case subsequently came up on appeal to the Iowa Supreme Court. The state supreme court had to decide whether the corporate income tax on an out-of-state corporation's income generated from the licensing of the KFC trademark and related system to independent franchisees violated the Commerce Clause of the United States Constitution. The court held that physical presence is not required under the Commerce Clause in order for Iowa to impose corporate income tax on the revenue earned by KFC arising from the use of its intangibles by the independent

---

[12] *Ibid.* at 195.   [13] *Ibid.*   [14] *Ibid.*
[15] *Lanco, Inc. v. Director, Division of Taxation*, 879 A.2d 1234, 1242 (N.J. Super. Ct. App. Div. 2005) ("We are satisfied that the physical presence requirement applicable to use and sales taxes is not applicable to income tax and that the New Jersey Business Corporation Tax may be constitutionally applied to income derived by plaintiff from licensing fees attributable to New Jersey."); *Geoffrey, Inc. v. Oklahoma Tax Commission*, 132 P.3d 632, 640–41 (Okla. Civ. App. 2005) ("The imposition of Oklahoma income tax attributable to royalty earned by Geoffrey under a licensing agreement which based that royalty on the sales generated within the State of Oklahoma by Geoffrey's license does not offend due process or unduly burden interstate commerce.").

franchisees located within Iowa. The court emphasized that the intangibles owned by KFC were used in the fast-food business by franchisees "firmly anchored within the state."[16] Further, Iowa franchisees were required to purchase equipment, supplies, paper goods, and other products from KFC-approved manufacturers and distributors, in compliance with KFC's applicable standards for franchising.[17] The court concluded that by licensing franchises within Iowa, KFC has received "the benefit of an orderly society within the state and, as a result, is subject to the payment of income taxes that otherwise meet the requirements" of the Commerce Clause.[18]

Other states, noting that some states have been successful in reaching the Delaware IP Holding Company's royalty income via economic nexus assertion, have applied similar reasoning in corporate excise tax cases. Massachusetts is an example. In Massachusetts, corporate excise tax is based on both income and net worth.[19]

Massachusetts's pertinent tax statute and related regulation require an out-of-state corporation to file a return in Massachusetts and pay the associated excise tax if the corporation owns property that is held by another entity in Massachusetts under a lease, consignment, or "other arrangement."[20] In 2009, the Massachusetts Supreme Judicial Court interpreted the phrase "other arrangement" to mean the licensing of trademarks from an out-of-state corporation to other entities in Massachusetts.[21] Most importantly, the court focused on the constitutional question of whether the imposition of the corporate excise tax on an out-of-state corporation that does not have a physical presence in Massachusetts violates the Commerce Clause. The court emphasized that the controlling test to decide the constitutional question for taxing the income of an out-of-state IP Holding Company is *Complete Auto Transit, Inc. v. Brady*, not *Quill Corp. v. North Dakota*.[22] That means the correct test to apply in determining whether Massachusetts tax law satisfies the Commerce Clause is the "substantial nexus" test articulated in *Complete Auto Transit* for an income-based tax. The Massachusetts

---

[16] *KFC Corporation v. Iowa Department of Revenue*, 792 N.W.2d 308, 324 (Iowa 2010), cert. denied, 565 U.S. 817 (2011).

[17] *Ibid.* at 311.   [18] *Ibid.* at 328.

[19] *Corporate Excise Tax*, Mass.Gov, accessed August 10, 2016, www.mass.gov/dor/busines ses/current-tax-info/guide-to-employer-tax-obligations/business-income-taxes/corpora tions/corporate-excise-tax.html ("A corporation's total excise is the combination of the property/net worth and net income measures").

[20] *Geoffrey, Inc. v. Commissioner of Revenue*, 453 Mass. 17, 22 (2009) (quoting Mass. Gen. Laws ch. 63, § 39; 830 Mass. Code Regs. § 63.39.1[4][d][1]).

[21] *Ibid.* at 22–23.

[22] *Ibid.* at 18 (quoting *Complete Auto Transit, Inc. v. Brady*, 430 U.S. 274, 279 (1977)); *Quill Corp. v. North Dakota*, 504 U.S. 298, 317–18 (1992).

Supreme Judicial Court rejected the "physical presence" test mandated in *Quill Corp.* because that test is only applicable to sales and use taxes. The rejection is consistent with the majority in *Quill Corp.* that had noted "we have not, in our review of other types of taxes, articulated the same physical-presence requirement . . . established for sales and use taxes."[23]

What is "substantial nexus" from Massachusetts's perspective? The Massachusetts supreme court has declared that "substantial nexus" means a "greater presence, both qualitatively and quantitatively" than the "minimum connection between a State and a taxpayer that would satisfy a due process inquiry."[24] With the "substantial nexus" test as the guiding post, the Massachusetts court applied it to the facts in *Geoffrey, Inc. v. Commissioner,* which involved the same taxpayer and had similar facts to South Carolina's *Geoffrey* case, albeit sixteen years later. The court noted that by purposefully licensing its trademarks for use in connection with toys available at Toys "R" Us, Kids "R" Us, and Baby Superstores, Geoffrey has been able to reap economic benefits from Massachusetts's retail marketplace. The licensing of the trademarks allows Geoffrey to collect significant royalty income from these stores in Massachusetts. As owner and licensor of the trademarks, Geoffrey retained the rights in the trademarks and was afforded the protection of the legal system and access to courts located in Massachusetts. Overall, Geoffrey's business activities in Massachusetts had substantial nexus with that State.[25]

Disallowing the Royalty and Interest Payments Deduction Approach

In scrutinizing the assignment and license-back transactions between the parent company or affiliate and the IP Holding Company, some states have decided to disallow the royalty payments made by the parent company or affiliate to the IP Holding Company. These states assert that the

---

[23] *Quill,* 504 U.S. at 314.

[24] *Capital One Bank v. Commissioner of Revenue,* 453 Mass. 1, 9–16 (2009) (tracing the U.S. Supreme Court's development of "substantial nexus" and "physical presence" tests and holding the out-of-state Capital One and FSB had a substantial nexus with Massachusetts through their branded credit cards issued to Massachusetts residents). On the same date the Supreme Judicial Court of Massachusetts handed down the *Capital One* decision, it issued the *Geoffrey, Inc. v. Commissioner* decision and stated that the holding in *Capital One* is controlling: "In our decision in *Capital One Bank . . .,* released today, we concluded that the constitutionality, under the commerce clause, of the Commonwealth's imposition of an income-based excise on an out-of-State entity is not determined by the 'physical presence' test articulated in *Quill . . .,* but by the 'substantial nexus' test articulated *in Complete Auto Transit . . . .* Our holding in *Capital One* is controlling with respect to Geoffrey's constitutional claim." *Geoffrey, Inc.,* 453 Mass. at 18.

[25] *Geoffrey, Inc.,* 453 Mass. at 24.

assignment and license-back transactions between the parent company and the IP Holding Company are a sham, lacking economic substance or business purpose. The sole reason for the transactions was for tax avoidance.

The sham transaction doctrine allows the state tax authority to disregard transactions that have no economic substance or purpose other than tax avoidance. A viable business entity, within the context of the sham transaction doctrine, must be created for a substantial business purpose or actually engage in substantive business activity. Whether a transaction is a sham under the doctrine is a factual inquiry, and the burden of proof is on the taxpayer in the abatement process.[26]

Massachusetts and Maryland are two leading states in applying the sham transaction doctrine to deny deductions of royalty payments made by the in-state company to the related Delaware IP Holding Company.

For example, as recalled in *Syms v. Commissioner*, the parent company was a New Jersey corporation, founded in 1959, engaging in the business of retail clothing sold at prices lower than those in department stores. The parent company adopted the trademark "Syms" and various logos and slogans to brand its clothing. In 1989, Irv Yacht, a consultant from Coventry Financial Corporation, presented the idea of a trademark holding subsidiary to the parent company. Yacht pitched the idea as a method for saving state taxes, developing a program that would reduce the parent company's income taxes by reorganizing the business activities of the parent company in certain areas. Yacht proposed for the parent company to form an IP Holding Company in Delaware, transfer the trademarks to the IP Holding Company, and then execute a license-back agreement under which the parent company would continue its use of the trademarks as it had before the transaction. Under the license agreement, the parent company would pay a large royalty to the IP Holding Company for the purpose of generating a deduction for the parent company on its state excise taxes. The IP Holding Company, Yacht explained, would not pay any state tax on the royalty income due to a favorable Delaware exemption law. Yacht's fee was 25 percent of the tax savings the parent company realized in the first year, with a declining percentage for the subsequent four years.

The parent company considered Yacht's proposal, recognized the risk of a tax audit, and expressed its concern: "There have been cases when corporations attempted to do this and did not do it properly and thus had problems in various states. It is everyone[']s feeling that New York is the most sophisticated state in terms of tax audit and most other states will

[26] *Syms Corp v. Commissioner of Revenue*, 765 N.E.2d 758, 763 (Mass. 2002).

not even realize the impact of the transactions."[27] The parent company insisted to hold part of Yacht's fee in escrow in case the planned tax savings failed to materialize.

In addition to the tax avoidance concern, the parent company consulted a trademark attorney for advice on whether the assignment and license-back transaction would be deemed valid under trademark law. The parent company received the assurance that the transfer would be valid because "Syms Corp. will own and control the subsidiary. Whether or not the subsidiary is an active entity, its assets (consisting of the trademarks) belong to the parent company. Syms Corp. will, in fact, continue to stand behind the goods and services identified by these marks."[28]

With assurances from both tax and trademark fronts, the parent company adopted Yacht's plan and on December 4, 1986, proceeded with the incorporation of SYL, Inc., the IP Holding Company in Delaware. The IP Holding Company's Board of Directors and officers were Sy Syms, Marcy Syms, Richard Diamond, and Edward Jones, a partner in a Delaware accounting firm. The parent company and the IP Holding Company executed a license agreement on December 18, 1986, wherein the parent company has the right to use the trademarks nationally. The royalty rate was 4 percent of the parent company's annual net sales. The following day, December 19, 1986, the parent company transferred the ownership of the trademarks to the IP Holding Company.

The royalty payments were the only source of income for SYL, the IP Holding Company. Every year during the relevant tax audit period, the parent company made one large royalty payment amount of more than $10 million to the IP Holding Company. Upon holding the royalty sum for a few weeks, the IP Holding Company then gave the money back to the parent with interest (minus expenses) in the form of a tax-free dividend. With regard to the daily operation, the IP Holding Company had only one part-time employee who received $1,200 per year. The part-time employee was Edward Jones, the partner from the Delaware accounting firm. The IP Holding Company had no corporate office, except an address rented from the accounting firm. The accounting firm also rented the same address to hundreds of other corporations that employed a similar transaction pattern relating to their intellectual property assets. Though the parent company assigned the intellectual property to the IP Holding Company, the parent continued to maintain and protect the trademarks, along with their associated goodwill and value. The parent company continued to control and pay for advertising expenses and conducted quality control of the trademarks. In short, all

---

[27] *Ibid.* at 761.   [28] *Ibid.*

activities and personnel who were responsible for the activities remained the same after the transfer of trademark ownership from the parent company to the IP Holding Company.

These facts, the Massachusetts Supreme Judicial Court ruled, supported a finding that the assignment and license-back transaction was a sham, "part of a contrived mechanism by which affiliated entities shifted income, tax free, between themselves in a circular transaction" for their benefit, and could be disregarded pursuant to the sham transaction doctrine.[29] The parent company, therefore, was not allowed to deduct the royalty payments as the payments were not ordinary and necessary expenses to conduct the parent company's business, but were used as a means to avoid tax.

The sham transaction or economic substance doctrine is a long-established, judicially created principle whose roots can be traced back to a 1935 US Supreme Court decision in *Gregory v. Helvering*. In that case, the Court disregarded a transaction which complied with the literal terms of the tax code, where the taxpayer caused the wholly owned corporation to transfer stock to a new corporation which then transferred the stock back to the taxpayer, solely to avoid paying tax on the dividend.[30] The Court subsequently applied the doctrine to later cases. In 1945, in *Commissioner v. Court Holding Co.*, the US Supreme Court disregarded a transaction where the taxpayer transferred its asset in the form of a dividend to two shareholders who immediately assigned the asset to a purchaser who had already negotiated with the taxpayer to purchase the asset. The sole reason for the transaction was for the taxpayer to avoid paying corporate income tax.[31] Likewise, in *Knetsch v. United States*, the Supreme Court disregarded a transaction where the taxpayer paid a "fee for providing the façade of 'loans' " whereby the taxpayers sought to reduce their taxes because "there was nothing of substance to be realized" by the taxpayer from "this transaction beyond a tax deduction."[32] The doctrine represents a judicial effort to effectuate and enforce the statutory purpose of the tax code that tax benefits should not be afforded to transactions that are fictitious or lack economic reality, despite the appearance of literal compliance with relevant tax code provisions. The doctrine allows courts to look behind the formalities of a transaction to ascertain its economic substance.[33]

---

[29] *Ibid.* at 765. *See also Talbots, Inc. v. Commissioner of Revenue*, 944 N.E.2d 610 (Mass. App. Ct. 2011).

[30] *Gregory v. Helvering*, 293 U.S. 465 (1935).

[31] *Commissioner v. Court Holding Co.*, 324 U.S. 331 (1945).

[32] *Knetsch v. United States*, 364 U.S. 361, 366 (1960).

[33] *See Coltec Industries, Inc. v. United States*, 454 F.3d 1340, 1353–57 (Fed. Cir. 2006); *Kearney Partners Fund, LLC v. U.S.*, 803 F.3d 1280, 1295 (11th Cir. 2015) (discussing the economic substance doctrine).

To reduce the confusion in the lexicon of sham transaction and economic substance transaction, in March 2010, Congress provided clarification of the "economic substance doctrine" by codifying the doctrine. The federal statutory definition states that a "transaction shall be treated as having economic substance only if (A) the transaction changes in a meaningful way (apart from Federal income tax effects) the taxpayer's economic position, and (B) the taxpayer has a substantial purpose (apart from Federal income tax effects) for entering into such transaction."[34] Courts continue to embrace the doctrine to stamp out fictitious transactions that facially conform to the tax statute.[35]

In addition to disallowing the royalty payments under the economic substance transaction doctrine, some states have asserted that the royalty payments under the assignment and license-back scheme are not ordinary and necessary expenses. Under tax law, an expense is "ordinary" if it is normal, usual, common, or customary in the business. An expense is "necessary" if it is appropriate and helpful for the development of the business.[36] For example, in the *Syms* case, though the royalty payments were pursuant to a contractual obligation between the parent company and its wholly owned IP Holding Company, that alone does not render the payments to be ordinary business expenses.[37] The payments, in the context of that case, were not common to achieve a business objective, but "instead was created solely for the purpose of effectuating a camouflaged assignment of income."[38] The assignment and license-back transaction between the parent company and the IP Holding Company in that case should have been royalty-free because the parent company continued to control all important aspects of the trademarks and used the trademarks in the operation of its business as though no transfer had ever occurred.

The *Syms* decision was subsequently followed by the lower court in Massachusetts in *Talbots, Inc. v. Commissioner of Revenue*. Similar to other IP Holding Company transactions, The Classics Chicago, Inc. (TCC) was incorporated in Delaware to hold the trademarks assigned by the parent company, Talbots. TCC licensed the trademarks back to Talbots and affiliates in exchange for annual royalty payments. TCC's only source of

---

[34] *See* Health Care and Education Reconciliation Act of 2010, Pub. L. No. 111–152, § 1409, 124 Stat. 1029, 1067–1070 (codified at 26 USC § 7701 [o]).

[35] *CNT Investors, LLC v. CIR*, 144 T.C. 161, 194 (T.C. 2015) ("Despite their lexical imprecision, prior opinions of this Court and other courts form a substantial body of precedent for the application of judicial doctrines to disallow tax results in transactions that, on their face, technically strictly conform to the letter of the Code and the regulations").

[36] *Welch v. Helvering*, 290 U.S. 111, 113–14 (1933).

[37] *Syms Corp v. Commissioner of Revenue*, 765 N.E.2d 758, 765 n.14 (Mass. 2002).

[38] *Ibid.* at 765.

income during the relevant tax period was the royalty and loan interest payments received from Talbots. TCC had no employees. All of TCC's decisions were made by various Talbots employees. TCC contracted two independent contractors for minimal bookkeeping-related services. The Commissioner adjusted Talbots's taxable income for tax years from 1994 to 2001 by disallowing the deduction Talbots had claimed for the royalty payments it made to TCC for the license of the trademarks and interest payments on the loans from TCC. The Commissioner also reattributed to Talbots the royalty and interest income earned by TCC. The Tax Appeal Board affirmed the Commissioner's decision, finding that the transfer and license arrangement between Talbots and TCC was a sham transaction. The Massachusetts Court of Appeals then found that there was sufficient evidence to support the Board's finding of the sham transaction for tax avoidance purposes. Talbots subsequently sought review from the Supreme Judicial Court but was denied.[39]

The Massachusetts tax authority was also successful in *IDC Research, Inc. v. Commissioner.*[40] International Data Group ("IDG") formed IDG Holdings ("Holdings") as a wholly owned subsidiary in Delaware and transferred the ownership of the trademark to Holdings. Despite the transfer of ownership, IDG continued to use the trademark and identification as the trademark's owner. During the relevant tax years, IDG did not identify Holdings as the trademark owner. As to the purported license between IDG and Holdings, there was no written license agreement. Holdings also received royalty payments from IDG's foreign subsidiaries. IDG then withdrew millions of dollars from Holdings' account in the form of loans without typical loan documentation, terms or interest. The Tax Appeal Board found that Holdings did not engage in substantive business activity, but served only as a means for IDG to divert royalty income from Massachusetts to Delaware. The Board affirmed the Commissioner's refusal to abate a portion of the corporate excise taxes assessed to IDG. The Court of Appeals then upheld the Board's finding that the assignment and license arrangement was a sham transaction.

There is a burden on the state tax authority in asserting that the transactions between the Delaware IP Holding Company and the in-state affiliates are indeed a sham. That can be an onerous and factually intensive inquiry. Massachusetts failed to establish sufficient evidence to demonstrate a sham transaction in several cases, including cases concerning

---

[39] *Talbots, Inc. v. Commissioner of Revenue*, 944 N.E.2d 610 (Mass. App. Ct. 2011), cert. denied, 949 N.E.2d 925 (Mass. 2011).

[40] 937 N.E.2d 1266 (Mass. App. Ct. 2010), cert. denied, 942 N.E.2d 183 (Mass. 2011).

Tootsie Roll candy and Sherwin Williams.[41] That means the in-state taxpayer company was able to establish that the assignment and license-back scheme was substantive business activity beyond the creation of tax benefits. The substantive business activities may include the Delaware IP Holding Company's investments and licensing agreements with unrelated third parties.[42] Due to the uncertainty associated with the sham transaction inquiry approach, Massachusetts subsequently adopted a new approach – enacting an "add back" statute in 2003. The "add back" approach has also been adopted by a number of states, as discussed later in this chapter.

Going After the IP Holding Company in a "Separate Reporting State" and Applying the Unitary Business Principle to Apportion the IP Holding Company's Income

In some states, related corporations must file separate tax returns. These states are called "separate reporting states."[43] The separate reporting states, nevertheless, assert that the separate filing requirement does not prevent them from going after the out-of-state IP Holding Company that lacks economic substance and has an interdependent relationship with the in-state affiliates. These states believe that the out-of-state IP Holding Company is required to apportion the income generated from the parent's or affiliate's activities within the state. One of the leading states utilizing this approach is Maryland.

Maryland has focused on the IP Holding Company's lack of real economic substance as a separate business entity and the interdependency of the IP Holding Company with its parent corporation. For example, in *Comptroller v. Gore*, the Maryland taxing authority conducted an audit and noted that W.L. Gore, the Maryland parent company, set out to create wholly owned subsidiaries, GEH and FVI, to effectively address corporate issues and coordinate operational, patent/intellectual property, and human resources within the corporate structure.[44] The parent company created GEH to hold the parent's patents and license the patents perpetually back to the parent. Without the parent company, GEH would have no patents because GEH does not create,

---

[41] *Cambridge Brands, Inc. v. Commissioner of Revenue*, 2003 WL 21665241 (Mass. App. Tax. Bd. July 16, 2003); *Sherwin–Williams Co. v. Commissioner of Revenue*, 778 N.E.2d 504 (Mass. 2002).

[42] *Sherwin-Williams*, 778 N.E.2d at 517 (evidence of "substantive business activity, beyond the creation of tax benefits for Sherwin–Williams was substantial").

[43] Currently, "separate reporting states" include Georgia, Mississippi, Nevada, New Jersey, Oklahoma, South Carolina, Virginia, and Washington.

[44] *Gore Enterprise Holdings, Inc. v. Comptroller of the Treasury*, 87 A.3d 1263 (Md. 2014).

invent, or make any product. GEH relies on the parent's employees as inventors of new processes and products. GEH relies on the parent's employees to prepare the patent applications for filing with the US Patent Office in order to procure future patents. The parent's employees control and determine the patent procurement strategies in connection with the business and marketing decisions driven by the patent portfolio.

Likewise, FVI was created to function as the depositary for the parent by holding the money transferred from GEH, after GEH received royalty payments from the parent company. FVI then funneled the money back to the parent through the form of loans.

The license and service agreements between and among these entities demonstrated that GEH and FVI are dependent on the parent company's business activities to produce their income. GEH and FVI also depended on the parent company for office space, corporate services, and legal services. In other words, GEH and FVI were not capable of operating as separate business entities apart from the parent company. Based on the unitary business relationship with the Maryland parent company, GEH and FVI were deemed to have a substantial nexus with Maryland. GEH and FVI were subject to the apportionment formula for Maryland income tax.

The Comptroller assessed more than $26 million in back taxes, interest, and penalties against GEH for tax years 1996–2003 and $2.6 million against FVI for the same tax period. GEH appealed the Comptroller's assessment, and the case, subsequently, reached the Court of Appeals of Maryland.

The court held that Maryland's authority to tax against GEH satisfies the constitutional requirements under both the Due Process and Commerce Clauses. The Court noted that it had decided several cases involving an IP Holding Company similar to the present case and held that the constitutional requirements for state income taxation against the IP Holding Company were satisfied by virtue of the fact that the IP Holding Company "had no real economic substance as separate business entities."[45] Strikingly, these IP Holding Company subsidiaries had similar characteristics, the court observed:

Neither subsidiary had a full time employee, and the ostensible part time "employees" of each subsidiary were in reality officers or employees of independent "nexus-service" companies. The annual wages paid to these "employees" by

---

[45] *Ibid.* at 1275. The Court relied heavily on its precedent, *Comptroller of the Treasury v. SYL, Inc.*, 375 Md. 78 (2003), for a finding of nexus between Maryland and the IP Holding Company.

the subsidiaries were minuscule. The so-called offices in Delaware were little more than mail drops. The subsidiary corporations did virtually nothing; whatever was done was performed by officers, employees, or counsel of the parent corporations. The testimony indicated that, with respect to the operations of the parents and the protections of the trademarks, nothing changed after the creation of the subsidiaries. Although officers of the parent corporations may have stated that tax avoidance was not the sole reason for the creation of the subsidiaries, the record demonstrates that sheltering income from state taxation was the predominant reason for the creation of [IP Holding Company] Delaware.[46]

Because the IP Holding Company had no real economic substance as a separate business entity, a portion of the IP Holding Company's income can be taxed based upon the parent corporation's Maryland business. In other words, "the basis of a nexus sufficient to justify taxation ... [is] the economic reality of the fact that the parent's business" in Maryland is what produces the IP Holding Company's income.[47] That means the Maryland-taxable entity is subject to report its income under the separate reporting features of Maryland law and the IP Holding Company's apportioned income is also subject to Maryland's taxation.

The court also affirmed Maryland's apportionment formula as constitutional through a justified application of the unitary business principle. Specifically, the court upheld the lower court's reason on the fairness of the apportionment formula:

The tax calculation utilized by the Comptroller was intended to apportion to Maryland only the Delaware Holding Company income connected to the operating transactions of W.L. Gore. Expenses were deducted from the income if the Delaware Holding Company made an affirmative demonstration that the expenses were directly related to the income. GEH made no attempt to allocate Delaware Holding Company expenses to the W.L. Gore connected income. Consequently, GEH's tax liability was calculated by multiplying royalties paid by W.L. Gore times the W.L. Gore apportionment formula. For FVI, the tax is calculated by multiplying interest paid by W.L. Gore times the W.L. Gore apportionment formula. There was no other evidence offered by the Petitioners that this formula method was unfair.[48]

The Court of Appeals also affirmed the Comptroller's use of the apportionment formula under the unitary business principle recognized by the United States Supreme Court in *Container Corp. v. Franchise Tax Board* which has described the unitary business principle as follows:

The unitary business/formula apportionment method is a very different approach to the problem of taxing businesses operating in more than one jurisdiction. It rejects geographical or transactional accounting, and instead calculates the

---

[46] *Ibid.*   [47] *Ibid.* at 1281.   [48] *Ibid.* at 1285.

local tax base by first defining the scope of the "unitary business" of which the taxed enterprise's activities in the taxing jurisdiction form one part, and then apportioning the total income of that "unitary business" between the taxing jurisdiction and the rest of the world on the basis of a formula taking into account objective measures of the corporation's activities within and without the jurisdiction. This Court long ago upheld the constitutionality of the unitary business/formula apportionment method, although subject to certain constraints.[49]

Typically, a unitary business features functional integration, centralized management, and economies of scale. In *Gore*, the Court of Appeals found that both GEH and FVI demonstrated "integration of business functions and personnel, centralized management through the inclusion of [the parent company's] employees on the subsidiaries's boards, and a reliance on [the parent] for everything from furniture to legal services."[50]

In tracing the income of GEH and FVI to Maryland, the Comptroller first looked to Maryland Tax Code, TG 10-402(c), but the methods of allocating income under that provision would have yielded an apportionment factor of zero. The Comptroller then looked to TG 10-402(d), which permits the Comptroller to alter the methods by using the parent's allocation formula. That means the Comptroller allocated GEH's and FVI's income derived directly from the income tax returns of the parent company.[51] Consequently, the Comptroller's "apportionment formula captured [the parent's] expenses in Maryland – expenses that simultaneously constituted income for GEH and FVI. Thus, the formula reflects a reasonable sense of how [GEH's and FVI's] income is generated."[52]

Gore-Tex must not have been happy with the $26 million tax assessment. Moreover, the decision must have been very frustrating to Gore-Tex. Not long ago, the Company received a decision from the Supreme Court of Missouri relating to its assignment and license-back transactions between GEH and the parent company. The tax assessment was reversed because the Missouri Court found that GEH had no Missouri source income![53] In Maryland, Gore-Tex received an opposite result.

Essentially, under *Comptroller v. Gore*, an IP Holding Company must have economic substance as a separate entity from its parent or affiliate in order to avoid nexus with the taxing state and, thereby, taxation of the apportioned income. Armed with the decision from the high court in *Comptroller v. Gore*, Maryland has subsequently pursued tax assessments

---

[49] *Ibid.* (quoting *Container Corp. of America v. Franchise Tax Board*, 463 U.S. 159, 165 [1983]).
[50] *Ibid.* at 1285–86.   [51] *Ibid.* at 1287.   [52] *Ibid.*
[53] *Acme Royalty Company v. Director of Revenue*, 96 S.W.3d 72, 74–75 (Mo. 2002).

against Nordstrom, ConAgra Brands, and Staples.[54] The Comptroller subsequently prevailed in each of these cases.

The prevalent use of an IP Holding Company to avoid paying tax on apportioned income has irritated the Maryland high court. The court illustrated the cat and mouse chase that the state tax authority must pursue against the evasive and sophisticated strategies employed by corporations. Justice Robert N. McDonald took liberty with the basketball maneuver "four corners offense" to describe the Nordstrom tax avoidance strategy:

This case illustrates a variation on that theme [the "four corners offense"]. Nordstrom, Inc. ("Nordstrom") created several subsidiary corporations, including Petitioner NIHC, Inc. ("NIHC"), which then engaged in a series of transactions with Nordstrom and with each other, involving the licensing rights to Nordstrom's trademarks. When the dust settled, the rights to use Nordstrom's trademarks ended up where they had begun – with Nordstrom. But Nordstrom's Maryland taxable income was significantly reduced. NIHC, although it had engaged in no value-creating business activity itself, recognized a significant gain – putatively beyond the reach of Maryland taxation – that was ultimately related to the reduction in Nordstrom's Maryland taxable income. From the perspective of the Respondent Comptroller, the transactions appeared to be an effort to shift income from Nordstrom – where a portion of it would be taxable by Maryland – to subsidiaries that arguably had no nexus to Maryland – where the income would escape Maryland taxation. The Comptroller did not accept that conclusion and issued tax assessments against the subsidiaries' income. The Tax Court concluded, and the Circuit Court and the Court of Special Appeals affirmed, that the subsidiaries, including NIHC, lacked economic substance separate from Nordstrom and, applying a recent decision of this Court, that their income had a nexus with Maryland through Nordstrom's business activities and was therefore taxable by Maryland.[55]

Nordstrom paid its IP Holding Company $197,802,386 for the use of the trademarks in 2002 and $212,284,273 in 2003. Nordstrom then received "loans" from its subsidiary for slightly lesser amounts during the same period. The total assessment against Nordstrom's IP Holding Company was almost two million dollars, which was based on the amount of income shifted from Nordstrom to its IP Holding Company through the trademark transactions. The Court of Appeals upheld the lower tax court's decision because there was "no question" that income recognized by the IP Holding Company from these transactions had a connection to

---

[54] *NIHC, Inc. v. Comptroller of the Treasury*, 97 A.3d 1092 (Md. 2014); *ConAgra Brands, Inc. v. Comptroller of the Treasury*, 2015 WL 854140, at *4–5 (Md. Tax Ct.t February 24, 2015); *Staples, Inc. v. Comptroller of the Treasury*, 2015 WL 3799558, at *3 (Md. Tax Ct. May 28, 2015).
[55] *NIHC, Inc.*, 97 A.3d at 1092–93.

business activities of Nordstrom in Maryland during the taxing period in 2002 and 2003.[56] Most importantly, the court ruled that Maryland's separate reporting requirement does not bar the Comptroller's assessment on the IP Holding Company's income attributable to an IRC 311(b) gain that had been "reported, properly subject to tax, and not previously taxed."[57]

In the case against Staples, the Comptroller assessed taxes, interest, and penalties for the tax years 1999 through 2004 against Staples and its Superstore in the aggregate amount of $14,392,364. For ConAgra Brands, the IP Holding Company incorporated in Nebraska and wholly owned by ConAgra Foods, Inc., the Comptroller issued a total amount of more than $3 million in assessment.

The approach described above employed by Maryland is akin to a "combined reporting" approach utilized by other states. That means the IP Holding Company's apportioned royalty income attributed to the state is combined with the affiliate's income in the state.

Adopting "Combined Reporting" against both the IP Holding Company and the Parent

In recent years, a growing number of states have instituted a major corporate tax reform known as "combined reporting." Under combined reporting, a parent company effectively disregards the legal existence of its related subsidiaries and reports on a combined basis the operations of its related subsidiaries involved in a unitary business. The result is that a parent company and its wholly owned IP Holding Company are effectively treated as a single corporation for state income tax purposes and intercompany transactions, such as royalty payments from a parent company to its IP Holding Company, are eliminated. The mandatory "combined reporting" requirement eliminates the state tax avoidance benefits stemming from the creation of and transactions with the IP Holding Company. This is part of the recognition that a deduction for the royalty payments made to the IP Holding Company for the use of the intellectual property once owned by the parent company is effectively eviscerated by the parallel income to the related IP Holding Company.

New York is one of the states with a combined reporting requirement.[58] In prior cases involving the assignment and licensing back of intellectual

---

[56] *Ibid.* at 1094.   [57] *Ibid.* at 1103–04.

[58] New York has recently made sweeping changes to its corporate franchise tax. *See* "New York State Corporation Tax Reforms of 2014," *Perspective* (Vol. 2014, No. 20):

property, New York's former corporate tax law imposed a franchise tax on all domestic and foreign corporations doing business, employing capital, owning or leasing property, or maintaining an office in New York State. Then the relevant tax statute provided circumstances wherein a corporation must report on a combined basis to properly reflect its franchise tax liability. No combined report was required unless the taxing authority deemed such a report was necessary. Former regulations interpreting the tax statutory provisions provided that a group of corporations may be required to file combined reporting where three conditions are met: (1) the taxpayer corporation owns or controls at least 80 percent of the other corporations which are to be included in the combined report; (2) the group of corporations is engaged in a unitary business; and (3) reporting on a separate basis distorts the activities, business, income, or capital in New York State of the taxpayers. These conditions were aptly referred to as the ownership test, unitary business test, and distortion of income test, respectively.[59]

Typically, if the facts in a particular case meet the ownership test and the unitary business test, the facts would give rise to the rebuttable presumption of distortion of income. The taxpayer opposing combined reporting bears the burden of proving that it engaged in the transaction for valid, nontax business purposes and that the transaction has purpose, substance, or utility apart from its anticipated tax consequences. In other words, the taxpayer must prove the "subjective and objective prongs of the economic substance doctrine or sham transaction analysis."[60] If the taxpayer succeeds in demonstrating that the transaction merits tax respect, the taxpayer must next bear the burden of establishing that the transaction was at arm's length in order to rebut the presumption of distortion.

Notably, the New York tax authority prevailed in its assessment cases against Sherwin-Williams and Talbots.[61] As discussed earlier in connection with Sherwin-Williams, the New York tax authority required Sherwin-Williams to file a combined corporate franchise tax report with its two wholly owned Delaware intellectual property holding companies, SWIMC and DIMC, for the tax year 1991.

12, accessed August 12, 2016, www2.deloitte.com/content/dam/Deloitte/us/Documents/Tax/us-tax-article-new-york-state-corp-tax-reforms-2014.pdf.

[59] See *In the matter of the Petition of Kellwood Company*, 2011 WL 4537050, at *47 (N.Y. Tax. App.Trib. September 22, 2011) (citing New York Tax Law § 209[1], §211.4; 20 NYCRR 6–2.1[a][1], [a][2], [a][3]).

[60] *Ibid.* at *47–48.

[61] *Sherwin-Williams Co. v. Tax Appeals Tribunal*, 12 A.D.3d 112 (N.Y. App. Div. 2004), appeal denied, 4 N.Y.3d 709 (2005); *In the Matter of the Petition of Talbots, Inc.*, 2008 WL 4294963 (N.Y. Tax. App. Trib. September 8, 2008).

Recalling Sherwin-Williams' paint business story, the Ohio Corporation, doing business in New York and nationwide, had created SWIMC to hold and manage 400 domestic trademarks associated with its nonaerosol products, and DIMC for the 120 trademarks related to its aerosol products. SWIMC and DIMC licensed the trademarks back to Sherwin-Williams in exchange for royalty payments based on a percentage of net sales. In Sherwin-Williams's 1991 corporate franchise tax return, it deducted the trademark royalty payments made to the two subsidiaries.

The New York tax authority determined that Sherwin-Williams must file a tax return on a combined basis with SWIMC and DIMC. That meant the deductions for the royalty payments were not allowed. The battle between Sherwin-Williams and the New York tax authority unfolded from 1997 to 2002 with extensive hearings, numerous expert witnesses, almost 150 exhibit submissions, and appeals. In the end, the New York Supreme Court, Appellate Division, ruled that the Tax Tribunal had demonstrated, through the record, ample evidence to support a determination that sufficient intercorporation transactions occurred among Sherwin-Williams and its two IP Holding Companies, SWIMC and DIMC. Next, the Court found that there was substantial evidence to support the conclusion that Sherwin-Williams failed to rebut the presumption of distortion. Though Sherwin-Williams offered that forming SWIMC and DIMC improved quality control oversight of the trademarks, "providing flexibility in preventing hostile takeovers, increasing investment return, affording liability protection, and taking advantage of Delaware's corporate tax exemption for investment management and trademark holding companies," other established facts, however, presented a different reality. Specifically, both SWIMC and DIMC were run by a part-time person with no trademark expertise; the management and control of the trademarks were contracted back to Sherwin-Williams; and the subsidiaries had recycled the royalty payments back as loans to Sherwin-Williams.

The ruling from New York was unsettling to Sherwin-Williams and others because Sherwin-Williams had prevailed in Massachusetts under the same facts.[62] Unfortunately for Sherwin-Williams, the New York court remarked that the Massachusetts decision "does not control because, in addition to being from another jurisdiction, the applicable laws in Massachusetts and New York are not identical."[63]

---

[62] *Sherwin-Williams Co. v. Commissioner of Revenue*, 778 N.E.2d 504 (Mass. 2002).
[63] *Sherwin-Williams Co.*, 12 A.D.3d at 118.

A few years later, New York also required Talbots to file a tax return on a combined basis with The Classics Chicago, Inc., its wholly owned subsidiary IP Holding Company, in the assignment and license-back trademarks transactions.[64] Recalling the Massachusetts approach in its own case against Talbot, Massachusetts disallowed the parent company to deduct the royalty payments paid to the IP Holding Company under the sham doctrine. New York had effectively reached the same result of not allowing Talbots to deduct the royalty payments by requiring Talbots to combine the royalty payments to Talbots's return. Both approaches dictate extensive factual inquiry.

In addition to New York, there are numerous states with a combined reporting requirement.[65] Interestingly, New York's aggressiveness in going after IP Holding Companies is a relatively new departure from its old position. For example, the New York Division of Tax Appeals ruled in favor of Victoria's Secret, Express, Lane Bryant, and The Limited Stores in a consolidated case back in 1995,[66] while North Carolina taxed the royalty income received by nine IP Holding Companies: A & F Trademark, Inc.; Caciqueco, Inc.; Expressco, Inc.; Lanco, Inc.; Lernco, Inc.; Limco Investments, Inc.; Limtoo, Inc.; Structureco, Inc.; and V Secret Stores, Inc.[67]

New York has also made major changes to its corporate tax law, effective January 1, 2015. Under the amended corporate tax law, a corporation is taxable in New York if it derives receipts within New York of over $1 million. Also, a corporation that is part of a unitary group that meets the ownership test and is deriving receipts of less than $1 million but more than $10,000 from activity in New York, will be taxable in New York

---

[64] *In the matter of the Petition of Talbots, Inc.*, 2008 WL 4294963, at *32, 35.

[65] *See, e.g.*, Alaska, Alaska Stat. § 43.20.145(a); Arizona, Ariz. Rev. Stat. Ann. § 43–947; California, Cal. Rev. & Tax. Code § 23362; Colorado, Colo. Rev. Stat. § 39-22-303(11); Hawaii, Haw. Rev. Stat. § 18-235-22-03; Idaho, Idaho Code Ann. § 63-3027(t); Illinois, 35 Ill. Comp. Stat. § 5/502e; Kansas, Kan. Stat. Ann. § 79–32,142(a); Maine, Me. Rev. Stat. Ann. §§ 5220, 5200.4; Massachusetts, Mass. Gen. Law ch. 63, § 32B; Minnesota, Minn. Stat. § 289A.08.3; Montana, Mont. Code Ann. § 15-31-141(1)–(2); Nebraska, Neb. Rev. Stat. §§ 77-2734.01, .05; New Hampshire, N.H. Rev. Stat. Ann. § 77-A:6; North Dakota, N.D. Cent. Code § 57-38-14; Oregon, Or. Rev. Stat. § 317.710(2); Texas, Tex. Tax Code § 171.1014 (eff. 1/1/08); Utah, Utah Code Ann. § 59-7-402; Vermont, Vt. Stat. Ann § 5862; West Virginia, W. Va. Code § 11-24-13a(a). Maryland is considering similar legislation. Out of 44 states with corporate income tax, twenty-four states plus Washington, DC have mandatory combined reporting.

[66] *In the Matter of the Petition of Express*, 1995 WL 561501 (N.Y. Tax App. Div. September 14, 1995).

[67] *A & F Trademarks, Inc. v. Tolson*, 605 S.E.2d 187 (N.C. Ct. App. 2004), cert. denied, 611 S.E.2d 168 (N.C. 2005), cert. denied, 126 S. Ct. 353 (2005).

if the New York receipts of the members of the unitary group who individually exceed $10,000 equal at least $1 million in the aggregate.[68]

In addition, New York has discovered that having the combined reporting requirement was not sufficient to capture the income shifting of royalties among intracompanies related to the assignment and license scheme. It proceeded to pass the first add-back statute in 2003 and then amended that statute ten years later to address royalties between related members.[69]

Enacting the Add-Back Statutes Approach

Look at the confusing approaches thus far! Some states select the approach to tax the out-of-state IP Holding Company directly, but they invariably face a nexus challenge asserted by taxpayers. Other states may wish to use the sham transaction doctrine to target the tax avoidance emanated from transactions between the out-of-state IP Holding Company and in-state affiliates by refusing the deduction of the royalty payments. Some states may impose combined reporting. The cases brought under the sham transaction doctrine are factually intensive and do not always yield satisfactory results to the state tax authority because the taxpayers can sidestep by careful planning of the transactions with documentation to demonstrate business purposes. In addressing these problems, twenty states have enacted "add-back" statutes to require the in-state corporation to "add-back" claimed expense deductions for the royalty and interest payments made by the in-state corporation to the out-of-state IP Holding Company located in Delaware or other jurisdictions free of corporate income taxation. The add-back to income is subject to an apportionment formula.

Essentially, the add-back statutes provide a corrective measure to combat the tax avoidance sum generated when the in-state, operating corporations transfer their intellectual property rights and assets to wholly owned subsidiaries or related entities, and then make royalty payments to those entities for the use of the intellectual property while continuing to incur all the expenses associated with the creation, control, and management of the intellectual property; advertisement; and product development costs. The transactions shift and store income in the IP Holding Company while claiming associated expenses in the in-state operating

---

[68] McKinney's Tax Law § 209(1)(d)(i) (2016).

[69] N.Y. Tax Law § 208(9)(o)(3); Timothy P. Noonan & Elizabeth Pascal, "Changes to New York's Royalty Addback Rules," *State Tax Notes* (September 30, 2013), www.hodgsonruss.com/media/publication/122_09_2013%20Changes%20to%20New%20York_s%20Royalty%20Addback%20Rules.pdf.

corporation and distorting the true picture of the in-state operating corporation's profitability. The imbalance occurs regardless of whether the transactions have or do not have nontax purposes.

Obviously, states that apply the unitary business concept, which combines both the royalty receipts and interest received by the IP Holding Company and the payments made by the in-state affiliates in a single report, do not have to enact an add-back statute.

Alabama, for example, enacted its add-back statute in 2001, effective for all tax years beginning subsequent to December 31, 2000, to balance the shifting of income generated from operating corporations within Alabama to the IP Holding Company.[70] Alabama requires certain adjustments to the federal taxable income amount in order to determine the amount of state taxable income under its add-back statute. The statute restricts the deductibility of certain intangible and interest expenses for the purpose of determining the state taxable income.

In addition to Alabama, there are many other states with variations of add-back statutes.[71] The Multistate Tax Commission drafted a model add-back statute in 2006. Numerous states have now adopted their own version of the add-back statute.[72] The add-back statute, in some states, includes specific exceptions to the add-back requirement. Not all states have identical exceptions.

In a nutshell, Alabama's add-back statute requires that a corporation add back into its taxable income expenses and costs related to intellectual property that are paid to a related member such as an IP Holding Company. An exception to the add-back requirement is available where

---

[70] The Alabama Legislature enacted Act No. 2001–1088, Ala. Acts 2001, which amended § 40–18–35, Ala. Code 1975, to add subsection (b). Subsection (b) of § 40–18–35 is now referred to as Alabama's add-back statute.

[71] Overall, the twenty states are Alabama: Ala. Code § 40-18-35(b), effective 2001; Arkansas, Ark. Code Ann. § 26-51-423(g)(1), effective 2004; Connecticut, Conn. Gen. Stat. § 12-218 (c), effective 1999; District of Columbia: D.C. Code § 47-1803.02, effective 2004; Georgia, Ga. Code Ann. § 48-7-28.3, effective 2006; Illinois, 35 Ill. Comp. Stat. 5/203(a) (2), effective 2005; Indiana, Ind. Code § 6-3-2-20, effective 2006; Kentucky, Ky. Rev. Stat. Ann. § 141.205, effective 2005; Maryland, Md. Code Ann. § 10–3061, effective 2004; Massachusetts, Mass. Gen. Laws Ch. 63, §§ 31I, 31J, 31K, effective 2002; Michigan, Mich. Comp. Laws § 208.9, effective 1975; Mississippi, Miss. Code Ann. § 27-7-17, effective 2001; New Jersey, N.J. Stat. Ann. § 54:10A-4(k)-4.4, effective 2002; New York, N.Y. Tax Law § 208(9)(o), effective 2003, amended 2013; North Carolina, N.C. Gen. Stat. § 105–130.7A(c), effective 2001; Ohio, Ohio Rev. Code Ann. § 5733.042, effective 1999; Oregon, Or. Rev. Stat. § 150-314.295, effective 2005; South Carolina, S.C. Code Ann. § 12-6-1130, effective 2005; Tennessee, Tenn. Code Ann. § 67-4-2006 (b), effective 2004; and Virginia, Va. Code Ann. § 58.1-402(B). *But see* R.I. Gen. Laws § 44-11-11.

[72] Multistate Tax Commission, *MTC.gov*, accessed August 12, 2016, www.mtc.gov/uploadedFiles/Multistate_Tax_Commission/Uniformity/Uniformity_Projects/A_-_Z/Add-Back% 20-%20FINAL%20version.pdf (Rhode Island eliminated intangibles add-back).

the add-back is "unreasonable." The court in Alabama had interpreted "unreasonable" to mean when the tax resulting from the application of the add-back statute has "no fair relation" to or is "out of proportion" to the corporation's activities in Alabama, rather than when the add-back deduction has a business purpose or economic substance.[73]

Illustratively, in *Surtees v. VFJ Ventures, Inc.*, Alabama assessed taxes against VFJ Ventures for $1.02 million, which represented additional corporate income tax owed to the State.[74] VFJ is the manufacturer of jeanswear under the Lee and Wrangler brands. VFJ has a cutting facility and sells its products through two distribution facilities located in Alabama. With 600 employees in Alabama's facilities, VFJ's gross sales were approximately $2.1 billion in 2001, the tax year at issue in the litigation. A portion of the $2.1 billion in sales was attributable to VFJ's activities in Alabama. VFJ is a subsidiary of VF Corporation, the parent holding company comprising hundreds of subsidiaries worldwide with corporate headquarters located in Greensboro, North Carolina. Among VF's subsidiaries are IP Holding Companies created in Delaware to own and manage trademarks.

H.D. Lee Company, Inc. (Lee) and the Wrangler Clothing Corporation (Wrangler) are two subsidiaries among VFJ Ventures's IP Holding Companies, owning and managing the Lee and Wrangler brands, respectively. Both Lee and Wrangler license their trademarks to related corporations: VFJ and other VF subsidiaries for a royalty rate at 5 percent. In the relevant tax year of 2001, 78 percent of Lee's income came from licensing payments with related corporations and 97 percent of Wrangler's income derived from licensing deals with related corporations. In dollar value, VFJ paid $36 million to Lee and $66 million to Wrangler in royalty payments for the use of the trademarks on its products, respectively. VFJ then deducted all of those royalty payments, totaling $102 million, as ordinary and necessary business expenses under the federal tax code, IRC §162, resulting in a reduction in the amount of its federal taxable income. Consequently, the deduction of the royalty payments from the federal taxable income reduced VFJ's tax liability in Alabama, shifted the royalty payments for the use of trademarks in VFJ's operating facilities in Alabama out of the state to Delaware, and ensured that the royalty payments could not be subjected to state taxation. In the end, VFJ's total state-tax savings was approximately $6 million in the tax year of 2001.

---

[73] *Surtees v. VFJ Ventures, Inc.* 8 So.3d 950, 968–69 (Ala. Civ. App. 2008).
[74] *Ibid.* at 960.

Applying the add-back statute, the Alabama tax authority asserted that the royalty payments VFJ made to Lee and Wrangler during the 2001 tax year must be added to VFJ's federal taxable income for the purpose of determining VFJ's taxable income in Alabama. Specifically, Alabama demanded an additional amount of $1,019,899 in state taxes. VFJ challenged the additional portion attributable to the add-back statute. The Court of Appeals upheld the state tax authority's assessment. The Supreme Court of Alabama later affirmed and adopted the Court of Appeals' opinion in its entirety.

Recall the situation in Massachusetts during the time period when the Supreme Judicial Court decided the *Syms* and *Sherwin-Williams* cases under the sham transaction doctrine. The court ruled in favor of *Sherwin-Williams* and against *Syms*. In 2003, four months after the court issued the decisions in Sherwin-Williams, the Massachusetts Legislature enacted G.L. c. 63, §§ 31I and 31J (collectively, the "Add-back Statutes"). Effectively, the Massachusetts add-back statute prevents corporate taxpayers from deducting royalty payments, expenses, and costs paid to the related IP Holding Company or entity. Under Massachusetts law, the deductions become presumptively disallowed and would be "add[ed] back" to the taxpayer's net income unless "(A) the taxpayer establishes by clear and convincing evidence, as determined by the commissioner, that the adjustments are unreasonable; or (B) the taxpayer and the commissioner agree in writing to the application or use of an alternative method of apportionment."[75]

Substantive guidance in determining whether the adjustments are unreasonable is available in the promulgated regulations. Indeed, according to the regulations, the add-back will be considered unreasonable where the taxpayer establishes by clear and convincing evidence that it incurred the interest or intangible expense as a result of a transaction "(1) that was primarily entered into for a valid business purpose and (2) that is supported by economic substance."[76] The taxpayer fails to meet its burden of demonstrating by clear and convincing evidence that a disallowance is unreasonable "unless the taxpayer demonstrates that reduction of tax was not a principal purpose for the transaction."[77] Essentially, under Massachusetts statute and regulations, a presumptively required add-back is unreasonable only where the transaction was primarily for a valid business purpose and had economic substance and tax reduction was not a principal purpose.

---

[75] Mass. Gen. Laws ch. 63, § 31I(c)(i).
[76] 830 Mass. Code Regs. § 63.31.1(4)(a)1.b (2006).   [77] *Ibid.*

After the enactment of the add-back statute, the Massachusetts Court of Appeals considered an appeal on the type of related entity expense deductions governed by the add-back statute in *Kimberly-Clark Corp. v. Commissioner*.[78] Factually, in that case, Kimberly-Clark and Scott decided to merge in 1996. As a result of the merger, the parent companies needed to restructure the ownership and control of their intellectual property to produce significant tax savings. The parent companies created Kimberly-Clark Worldwide (Worldwide) to hold the ownership of the patents. Worldwide then licensed the patents back to the parents and affiliates in exchange for royalty payments. Worldwide did not have any patent license arrangements with any third party. The royalties received by Worldwide were then immediately returned to Kimberly-Clark by way of the cash-management system. The Commissioner applied the Massachusetts add-back statute to add the royalty expenses for the tax year 2002 under G.L. c. 63, § 31I. The Board later affirmed the Commissioner's decision upon finding that Kimberly-Clark failed to demonstrate that the tax reduction was not a principal purpose of the 1996 transactions. The Appellate Court ruled in a case of first impression that the add-back statute provides that a deduction of interest or expenses paid to a related member will only be allowed if the taxpayer establishes by clear and convincing evidence, as determined by the Commissioner, that the adjustments are "unreasonable."[79] The court upheld the Board's finding.

Virginia also enacted its add-back statute in 2004. It then made some modifications on April 1, 2014, that had retroactive effect to tax years beginning on or after January 1, 2004. One of the reasons for the modifications is the court's unfavorable decision to the taxing authority in *Wendy's International Inc. v. Virginia Dept. of Taxation*.

As discussed earlier in Chapter 2 about the self-insurance scheme that the fast food company Wendy's has masterminded, the tax case in Virginia focused on the same Wendy's.[80] The parent company, Wendy's International, Inc., assigned all of its trademarks to Oldemark, a wholly owned subsidiary. Wendy's also formed a wholly owned subsidiary, Scioto Insurance Company, in Vermont as a self-insurance company to reduce its business risks and insurance expenses. To supply capital to Scioto, the parent company Wendy's assigned its ownership of Oldemark, LLC to Scioto. Oldemark then licensed all of Wendy's trademarks back to Wendy's pursuant to a license agreement between

---

[78] *Kimberly-Clark Corp. v. Commissioner of Revenue*, 981 N.E.2d 208 (Mass. App. Ct. 2013).
[79] *Ibid.* at 215.
[80] *Wendy's International, Inc. v. Virginia Department of Taxation*, 84 Va. Cir. 398 (Va. Cir. Ct. 2012).

Oldemark and Wendy's in exchange for a 3 percent royalty rate for the use of the intellectual property. Wendy's, in turn, sublicensed the trademarks to franchisees for use of the trademarks and Wendy's operating systems in exchange for 4 percent of the restaurants' gross sales. Wendy's then added back the royalties paid and deducted them on its federal income tax return.

In 2007, Wendy's sought a refund from the Virginia Department of Taxation. Under Virginia tax law, corporations are required to add back to taxable income "the amount of any intangible expenses and costs directly or indirectly paid, accrued, or incurred to or in connection directly or indirectly with one or more direct or indirect transactions with one or more related members to the extent such expenses and costs were deductible or deducted in computing federal taxable income for Virginia purposes."[81] Virginia's former statute provided exceptions to the add-back statute. One of the exceptions provides that:

[t]he related member derives at least one-third of its gross revenues from the licensing of intangible property to parties who are not related members, and the transaction giving rise to the expenses and costs between the corporation and the related member was made at rates and terms comparable to the rates and terms of agreements that the related member has entered into with parties who are not related members for the licensing of intangible property.[82]

The Commissioner declined the refund request, but the Circuit Court ruled in favor of Wendy's based on the court's interpretation of the exceptions to add-back. Under the plain meaning, the word "derives" does not imply that only the related entity, Oldemark, actually engaged directly in licensing unrelated franchises. Therefore, the word "derives" does not infer that Oldemark received the royalties from direct licensing in order for Wendy's to qualify for the exception of the add-back. Thus, Wendy's is entitled to the exception because "Oldemark derives at least one-third of its gross revenues from unrelated franchises as a result of Wendy's pass through to Oldemark of the same proportion of royalties paid to Wendy's by related and unrelated members. This is at the same rates and terms comparable to license agreements with unrelated franchises."[83]

The attorney who represented Wendy's was, again, Paul H. Frankel of Morrison & Foerster. With the loss, Virginia subsequently "has modified the exception to apply only to the portion of the intangible income received by the related member from 'licensing agreements for which the rates and

---

[81] *Ibid.* at 398.   [82] *Ibid.* at 399 (citing Va. Code § 58.1–402[B][8][a](2)).
[83] *Ibid.* at 400.

terms are comparable to the rates and terms of agreements that the related member has actually entered into with unrelated entities.' "[84] The revision, in effect, reverses the court decision in Wendy's.[85]

New Jersey also enacted its add-back statute in 2002 to "prevent tax avoidance from income shifting amongst members of a corporation by denying an otherwise allowable deduction for expenses paid to a related member" and to "close the loopholes of tax avoidance schemes or mechanisms whereby legitimate New Jersey sourced income escaped tax to the detriment of New Jersey and other small businesses unable to use such corporate shields."[86] The New Jersey tax authority has been aggressive in add-back cases. For example, in *Spring Licensing Group, Inc. v. Director*, the New Jersey tax authority demanded that an out-of-state IP Holding Company file a Corporate Business Tax (CBT) return to report and pay taxes on royalty income received from its parent company doing business in New Jersey, even though the parent company had already added back the deducted royalty payments on the parent company's CBT returns. The lower tax court subsequently upheld the state tax authority's decision because New Jersey is a "separate entity" state and, therefore, "[d]uplication of reporting by corporate family members for an item such as here, as royalty payments, as income for one and a correspondence expense for the other, is not out of the realm of normalcy."[87] Further, the lower tax court noted that the add-back statute addresses concerns of double taxation of the same royalty payments alleged by the IP Holding Company.

---

[84] "State & Local Tax Alert," *GrantThornton* (May 28, 2014): 2–3, accessed August 12, 2016, www.grantthornton.com/~/media/content-page-files/tax/pdfs/SALT-alerts-states-M-W/V A/2014/VA-HB-5001-5-27-14.ashx; "Virginia – Ten Year Retroactive Limitations Place on Addback Exceptions," *Pricewaterhouse Cooper* (April 7, 2014), accessed August 12, 2016, www.pwc.com/us/en/state-local-tax/newsletters/salt-insights/assets/pwc-virginia-ten-year-retroactive-limitations-addback-exceptions.pdf. Craig D. Bell notes that the Appropriations Act for the 2012–2014 biennium added a retroactive interpretation in Virginia Code § 58.1.402(B)(8) for addback requirement exceptions. With regard to these two exceptions, the budget bill states:

Notwithstanding the provisions of section 58.1-402(B)(8), Code of Virginia, for taxable years beginning on and after January 1, 2004:
(ii) The exception in § 58.1-402(B)(8)(a)(2) for a related member deriving at least one-third of its gross revenues from licensing to unrelated parties shall be limited and apply only to the portion of such income derived from licensing agreements for which the rates and terms are comparable to the rates and terms of agreements that the related member has actually entered into with unrelated entities. Craig D. Bell, "Taxation," *Richmond Law Review* 171, 173–74 (2014), *available at* http://lawreview .richmond.edu/wp/wp-content/uploads/2015/01/Bell-491.pdf.

[85] Bell, *supra* note 84, at 174.

[86] *Spring Licensing Group, Inc. v. Director, Division of Taxation*, 2015 WL 5011439, at *1, 8 (N.J. Tax Ct. August 14, 2015).

[87] *Ibid.* at *6.

Across the Hudson River, New York began to embrace add-back by enacting legislation in 2003 to require taxpayers to add back royalty and interest payments to related companies. The former legislation provided several exceptions. Under the conduit exception, no add-back is necessary if the related member paid the royalty during the same year to a nonrelated member at arm's length and for a legitimate business reason. Under the treaty exception, no add-back is required if the member made royalty payments to a related member in a country subject to a treaty with the United States and the payments were taxed at an equal or higher rate than New York. In 2007, New York added a third exception to add-back royalty payments between entities that filed a combined return in New York. Peculiarly, New York statute also created a loophole by allowing a taxpayer who was required to add back royalty payments to deduct the royalty payments it received from a related member.[88] In 2013, New York fixed the loophole and made major changes to its add-back law.

New York's amended add-back law is based on the Multistate Tax Commission's model add-back statute. The law requires royalty payments to be added back except where a taxpayer is included in a combined report with a related member. A related member is defined similarly to the definition under the Internal Revenue Code § 465(b)(3)(C), substituting a fifty percent ownership requirement for New York's previous thirty percent.

The New York add-back statute specifically provides four different exceptions. In addition to the conduit exception and the treaty exception, the two other exceptions include: (a) the related member was subject to tax in New York or another state; the tax base included royalty payments paid by the taxpayer with the aggregate effective rate not less than 80 percent; and the transaction giving rise to the royalty payment between the taxpayer and the related member was for a valid business purpose; and (b) if the taxpayer and the commissioner agree in writing as to the application and use of alternative adjustments. Unlike other states, New York does not include the amorphous, subjective standard of "unreasonableness" exception to the add-back.

With different approaches employed by different states, there is no clear winner. Sadly, the confusion to taxpayers is immeasurable. Much inefficiency and uncertainty await corporations with intellectual property assets to navigate through different approaches in their planning, regardless of whether they intend to avoid state taxation.

---

[88] N.Y. Tax Law § 208(9)(o)3); Noonan & Pascal, *supra* note 69, at 838.

5 Domestic Tax Havens: Exploring Solutions

"Any one may so arrange his affairs that his taxes shall be as low as possible; he is not bound to choose the pattern which will best pay the Treasury; there is not even a patriotic duty to increase one's taxes."[1]   Judge Learned Hand

Benjamin Franklin, a drafter of both the Declaration of Independence and the Constitution, in a letter to the French scientist Jean-Baptiste Le Roy dated November 13, 1789, provided a quick update of major events in the newly founded nation with the barely assembled government along with a keen observation about certainty and taxation: "Our new Constitution is now established, everything seems to promise it will be durable; but, in this world, nothing is certain except death and taxes."[2]

The Framers of the Constitution designed the new nation with a dual government system of shared power between federal and state. They understood the good and evil of taxation and the potential abuse by government of the taxing power. They drafted the Constitution to grant the federal government the power to tax under the Taxing and Spending Clause. As subsequent years can attest, the federal government was reluctant to impose an income tax. Congress had attempted numerous times to pass federal income tax legislation without much success. Not until 1909, did Congress successfully attach a provision for a constitutional amendment on income tax to a tariff bill. The Sixteenth Amendment to impose a federal income tax became a reality, as it was ratified on February 3, 1913.

Under the shared power structure with the federal government, states have the power to impose tax as long as the taxes are not in violation of the state's constitution and the United States Constitution. State taxes must be within the boundaries of the Due Process and Commerce Clauses. The US Supreme Court has interpreted the constitutional requirement to

---

[1] *Helvering v. Gregory*, 69 F.2d 809, 810 (2d Cir. 1934).
[2] Benjamin Franklin, *The Writings of Benjamin Franklin*, vol. 10 (Albert Henry Smith ed., The MacMillan Company, 1907), 68–69, *available at* https://archive.org/details/writingsofbenjam10franuoft.

be that in order for a state to impose on a taxpayer the obligation to collect sales and use taxes on in-state sales, there must be a nexus between the taxpayer and the taxing jurisdiction. The Court has drawn a bright-line physical-presence requirement under the Commerce Clause. On other types of taxes, the Court has explicitly announced that "we have not adopted a similar bright-line, physical-presence requirement."[3] Does it mean that the substantial nexus of the Commerce Clause's physical presence is only for sales and use taxes? Does it mean states can impose income tax and franchise tax on taxpayers without establishing physical presence with the taxing jurisdiction? Does it mean that the Court has deliberately saved the question of the substantial nexus physical-presence requirement for income tax, franchise tax, and excise tax for another day? Is the Court or Congress the appropriate body to address the level of presence for state taxation and the impact on interstate commerce?

Twenty-five years have passed since the Supreme Court's ruling on the physical-presence requirement for substantial nexus under the Commerce Clause in a case centering on an out-of-state mail-order seller's obligation to collect sales and use taxes. Congress has stood by the sideline, showing its lack of interest in states' multijurisdiction taxation. While the Court and Congress are looking away, a cursory glance at what has changed in the United States during the interval of time marked by the Court's last seminal decision reveals that the nation has entered the information age, witnessing tremendous technological and digital revolution epitomized by the internet, cell phones, and computer networking. Central to the revolution is intellectual property, including patents, copyrights, trademarks, and trade secrets.

According to a study conducted by the Multistate Tax Commission, states suffered an estimated loss of $4.8 billion in state revenue for 2001 alone from domestic tax shelters, primarily IP Holding Companies.[4] States facing the rise of the IP Holding Company have attempted to impose an income tax against the out-of-state IP Holding Company without offending the Commerce Clause. The problem faced by these states is that a typical out-of-state IP Holding Company has been structured to neither own property nor have payroll within the taxing jurisdiction. To overcome that problem, some states have invented "economic nexus," asserting that the IP Holding Company has received royalty payments from its affiliates, the operating companies within the taxing

---

[3] *Quill Corp. v. North Dakota*, 504 U.S. 298, 317 (1992).

[4] Report of Multistate Tax Commission, "Corporate Tax Sheltering and the Impact on State Corporate Income Tax Revenues" (July 15, 2003), *available at* www.mtc.gov/uplo adedFiles/Multistate_Tax_Commission/Resources/Studies_and_Reports/Corporate_Ta x_Sheltering/Tax%20Shelter%20Report.pdf.

jurisdiction, from the licensing of the intellectual property to these affiliates-licensees. These states see the direct link: money moving from in-state to out-of-state stemming from the IP license transactions. The monetary sum can reach in the millions of dollars for licensing transactions in each tax year. States become indignant and irritated, as seen in briefs submitted to tax tribunals and courts, watching the shifting of income to the tax haven Delaware.[5] These states know that there is nothing much they can do about Delaware and its tax exemption incentives, as a state has the authority to tax or not to tax corporate income.

One of the few things that states can do is to formulate a consensus in rejecting the constitutional claim of a physical-presence requirement in order to establish a "substantial nexus" for taxing the IP Holding Company's income.[6] With the Great Recession in 2008 and its aftermath, many states have experienced budget problems, and as they are watching their revenues plummet, they have become acutely inventive in multi-jurisdictional taxation. It came as no surprise that some states have fully embraced the "economic nexus" approach for purposes of reaching the out-of-state IP Holding Company's royalty income as a measure to cure states' fiscal problems.

In the fight against domestic tax havens for IP Holding Companies, some states have gone a little too far afield with "economic nexus" as the hook to reel in the income received by the IP Holding Company. For example, in *Griffith v. ConAgra Brands*, the out-of-state licensor received royalty payments for the use of its trademarks by the licensees who did not operate any retail stores in West Virginia.[7] The licensees distribute their seafood products bearing the trademarks directly to unrelated,

---

[5] Brief in Opposition, *Geoffrey, Inc. v. Comm'r of Revenue*, 2009 WL 1486854 (May 22, 2009);

[6] *See KFC Corp. v. Iowa Dep't of Revenue*, 792 N.W.2d 308 (Iowa 2010), *cert. denied*, 132 S. Ct. 97 (2011); *Geoffrey, Inc. v. Comm'r of Revenue*, 899 N.E.2d 87 (Mass. 2009), *cert. denied*, 557 U.S. (2009); *Geoffrey, Inc. v. Okla. Tax Comm'n*, 132 P.3d 632, 638 (Okla. Civ. App. 2006); *Lanco, Inc. v. Dir., Div. of Taxation*, 908 A.2d 176, 177 (N.J. 2006), *cert. denied*, 551 U.S. 1131 (2007); *Tax Comm'r of W. Va. v. MBNA Am. Bank, N.A.*, 640 S. E.2d 226 (W. Va. 2006), *cert. denied sub nom. FIA Card Servs, N.A. v. Tax Comm'r of W. Va.*, 127 S.Ct. 2997 (2007); *A&F Trademark, Inc. v. Tolson*, 605 S.E.2d 187, 195 (N.C. Ct. App. 2004), *cert. denied*, 546 U.S. 821 (2005); *Kmart Props., Inc. v. Taxation & Revenue Dep't*, 131 P.3d 27 (N.M. Ct. App. 2001), *cert. granted*, 40 P.3d 1008 (N.M. 2002), *cert. quashed*, 131 P.3d 22 (N.M. 2005); *Bridges v. Geoffrey, Inc.*, 984 So.2d 115 (La. Ct. App. 2008); *Sec'y, Dep't of Revenue v. Gap (Apparel), Inc.*, 886 So.2d 459, 462 (La. Ct. App. 2004); *Comptroller of the Treasury v. SYL, Inc.*, 825 A.2d 399 (Md. 2003); *Geoffrey, Inc. v. S.C. Tax Comm'n*, 437 S.E.2d 13 (S.C. 1993). *See also General Motors Corp. v. City of Seattle*, 25 P.3d 1022, 1029 (Wash. Ct. App. 2001); *Couchot v. State Lottery Comm'n*, 659 N.E.2d 1225, 1230 (Ohio 1996); *Borden Chems. & Plastics, L.P. v. Zehnder*, 726 N.E.2d 73, 80 (Ill. App. Ct. 2000); *Buehner Block Co. v. Wyoming Dep't of Revenue*, 139 P.3d 1150, 1158 n.6 (Wyo. 2006).

[7] *Griffith v. ConAgra Brands, Inc.*, 728 S.E.2d 74, 81–82 (W. Va. 2012).

third-party wholesalers and retailers in West Virginia. Despite that the facts in this case do not resemble the typical assignment and license-back scheme where the out-of-state IP Holding Company licenses the assigned trademarks that it has received from the parent company to affiliates who operate in-state, the taxing authority of West Virginia made an assessment against the out-of-state licensor. The Supreme Court of West Virginia affirmed the assessment. The problem with the court's decision is that *Griffith v. ConAgra Brands* does not involve the type of transactions that would lend the same level of support for "economic nexus." Unlike the licensees in Victoria's Secret, Toys "R" Us, and *Talbots*, the licensees for the ConAgra Brands have no retail stores within the taxing jurisdiction. Having the trademarks affixed to seafood products available for sale in unaffiliated, third-party grocery stores does not automatically mean the licensees of the trademarks are operating their business within the state. Given the fact that the licensees have no physical presence within the taxing jurisdiction, the licensor of the ConAgra Brands' connection with the taxing jurisdiction is virtually nonexistent. The transactions in ConAgra Brands do not fall into the typical assignment and license-back scheme seen in a tax avoidance scenario.

Another startling example of states asserting "economic nexus" that has gone too far is in the banking-transactions-with-credit cards context wherein the state imposes income tax and franchise tax against the out-of-state taxpayer. In *Tax Commissioner of West Virginia v. MBNA America Bank, N.A.*, the bank was an out-of-state corporation with its principal place of business in Delaware. The bank had neither property nor employees in West Virginia during the relevant tax years.[8] MBNA's business was issuing and servicing Visa and MasterCard credit cards. It promoted its business in West Virginia via mail and telephone solicitation.[9] MBNA's gross receipts attributable to its West Virginia customers were around ten million dollars.[10] But MBNA had no affiliates operating in West Virginia. The West Virginia Supreme Court, nevertheless, held that the physical-presence substantial nexus requirement applies only to use and sales taxes, not to business franchise and corporate income taxes. The state supreme court adopted "significant economic presence" analysis for the substantial nexus requirement.[11] Accordingly, the court affirmed West Virginia's imposition of business franchise and corporate income taxes against MBNA. Six years after the *MBNA* decision, Justice Benjamin of

---

[8] *Tax Comm'r of W. Va. v. MBNA Am. Bank*, 640 S.E.2d 226, 227 (W. Va. 2006).
[9] *Ibid.*   [10] *Ibid.* at 227–28.
[11] *Ibid.* at 234 ("Rather than a physical presence standard, this Court believes that a significant economic presence test is a better indicator of whether substantial nexus exists for Commerce Clause purposes.").

the West Virginia Supreme Court urged his colleagues to overrule the *MBNA* case because the "significant economic presence" test is "amorphous" and "useless in aiding an out-of-state entity in planning for its tax liability arising from its economic contact" with West Virginia.[12] The decision "is not a correct statement of the law" for fear that "MBNA will continue to linger like a dormant virus in our body of law, threatening to erupt into a full-blown infection every time this Court is presented with a tax case like the instant one."[13] Massachusetts has also adopted similar analysis for the imposition of excise tax against out-of-state taxpayers in the banking-transactions-with-credit cards context. These cases represent a new frontier of state taxing power that has rather attenuated constitutional support.[14]

In the intellectual property context, the danger with zealously championing the "economic nexus" approach may lead states to impose income tax on any out-of-state intellectual property owner, patentee, author, and artist for having their intellectual property rights used by a third party who sells, distributes, and markets products or services based on the intellectual property rights in a taxing jurisdiction pursuant to a license, distribution, or publication agreement. The United States Constitution does not permit states to have such broad power to tax out-of-state taxpayers whose only "contact" with the state is the mere presence of the intellectual property vis-à-vis the products or services based on the intellectual property rights. In other words, the out-of-state patentees, authors, and artists will be taxed in violation of the Commerce Clause's substantial nexus requirement because these intellectual property owners and creators have no affiliates operating business within the taxing jurisdiction, own no property, and have no employees in the taxing jurisdiction. These intellectual property owners and creators have the right to enjoy the benefits of their exclusive intellectual property rights via receipts of royalty payments from the licensing of their intellectual property. Their economic contact with the taxing jurisdiction barely exists for state taxation purposes.

Without the direct guidance from the Supreme Court on whether imposing income tax on an out-of-state IP Holding Company that has been receiving royalty payments from in-state affiliates for the use of intellectual property assigned from the parent to the IP Holding Company is constitutionally permissible, states face uncertainty. Taxpayers also face uncertainty in their tax planning as products associated with their intellectual property are being distributed across

---

[12] *Griffith*, 728 S.E.2d at 86.   [13] *Ibid.* at 85, 87.
[14] *Capital One Bank v. Comm'r of Revenue*, 899 N.E.2d 76, 84–87 (Mass. 2009).

multiple jurisdictions. Both sides are understandably frustrated. States believe that IP Holding Company taxpayers are abusing the loophole to avoid paying taxes and that the rigid physical presence requirements are no longer applicable in today's technological advancements. On the other hand, the IP Holding Company taxpayers believe that states are abusing their taxing power by imposing income tax on out-of-state corporations without regard to the Constitution, and extending their reach beyond the limits erected by the Constitution. The losing taxpayers are waiting for the Supreme Court to grant certiorari in the near future. The taxing authorities from one jurisdiction to the next have urged the Court to decline certiorari petitions. So far, the Court has not taken up the invitation. But no one knows for sure when the Supreme Court will accept a certiorari petition on the constitutionality of taxing an out-of-state IP Holding Company's income. The debate has intensified while the wait sees no end.

The US Supreme Court Has Not Spoken; Should Congress Decide?

There is a temptation to suggest that Congress should decide on an appropriate multistate corporations' nexus standard, given the Supreme Court has not spoken on the matter. Certainly, the various nexus standards may have an impact on states' economic activity, job growth, innovation, and, perhaps, the national economy. These matters are best left to Congress for careful consideration of the burdens for multistate corporate taxpayers having a physical presence in multiple states. Congress can, of course, investigate the burdens for taxpayers with intellectual property located in one state while the products and services based on the intellectual property are manufactured, licensed, and distributed in other states through franchises and intercompany arrangements.

Also, any desire of lessening state tax burdens emanated from multistate companies to have uniformity among states that "would require a policy decision based on political and economic considerations that vary from State to State" should be the task appropriate for Congress.[15] Because its role within the three branches of government is to deliberately determine and weigh potential legislations, Congress, "after due consideration is given to the interests of all affected States," makes its decision to act or not act.[16]

Congress, however, has shown no appetite. In the *Quill* decision, the Supreme Court invited Congress to exercise its power to evaluate state

---

[15] *Moorman Mfg. Co. v. Bair*, 437 U.S. 267, 279 (1978).   [16] *Ibid.* at 280.

use tax burdens on interstate commerce. Congress is "free to decide whether, when, and to what extent the States may burden interstate mail-order concerns with a duty to collect use taxes."[17] Twenty-five years later, Congress continues to demure. Consequently, it is highly unlikely that Congress will inject itself on state taxation of income generated from the use of intellectual property in connection with products and services sold in the state.

Add-back as the Solution?

As seen in Chapter 4, the various approaches of denying deductions claimed by the in-state affiliate company, going after the IP Holding Company in a "separate reporting state," and adopting "combined reporting" for both IP Holding Companies and parent companies, are confusing, onerous, and unpredictable. In these approaches, the taxing authority and the taxpayer often litigate about whether the transactions between the parent and the IP Holding Company are shams or lack economic substance. The factually intensive inquiry is costly to both sides and yields little certainty. In some states, the taxing authority and the taxpayer disagree on whether there exists distortion of income. Again, litigation on distortion of income is costly and the outcomes unpredictable.

Abandoning the confusing approaches, states may instead consider enacting the add-back statute on apportioned royalties generating from the licensing of patents, copyrights, trade secrets, trademarks, and similar types of property. States are within their taxing power to require the royalty payments deduction, taken by the parent company, to be added back to the parent's federal taxable income. Because the parent company is an in-state operating company subject to state taxation, the taxing authority avoids the type of constitutional challenge typically asserted by the out-of-state IP Holding Company.

With the add-back statute focused on apportioned intellectual property royalties, a state can carefully design what is best for the state. For instance, the state can provide specific exceptions to the add-back requirements.[18]

---

[17] *Quill Corp. v. North Dakota*, 504 U.S. 298, 318 (1992).

[18] The Pennsylvania General Assembly passed the addback law, 72 Pa. Cons. Stat. §. 7401(3) (1)(t)(1), on July 9, 2013. The law is effective for tax years beginning after December 31, 2014. Pennsylvania's Department of Revenue issued an Information Notice on February 19, 2016 to provide explanations and examples illustrating the new addback statute. *See* "Information Notice Corporation Taxes 2016–1," *Pennsylvania Department of Revenue,* last modified February 19, 2016, www.revenue.pa.gov/GeneralTaxInformation/TaxLawPoli ciesBulletinsNotices/Documents/Informational%20Notices/info_notice_ct_2016–01.pdf.

States may opt to adopt the model add-back statute advocated by the Multistate Tax Commission (MTC).[19] The MTC model statute of requiring the add-back of certain intangible and interest expenses was adopted by the full Commission on August 17, 2006. More than twenty states have enacted versions of the add-back statute. The MTC model statute provides a definition of intangible expenses paid to a related member or party that must be added back. The *intangible expenses* include:

(1) expenses, losses and costs for, related to, or in connection directly or indirectly with the direct or indirect acquisition, use, maintenance or management, ownership, sale, exchange, or any other disposition of intangible property to the extent such amounts are allowed as deductions or costs in determining taxable income before operating loss deductions and special deductions for the taxable year under the Code;

(2) amounts directly or indirectly allowed as deductions under section 163 of the Code for purposes of determining taxable income under the Code to the extent such expenses and costs are directly or indirectly for, related to, or in connection with the expenses, losses, and costs referenced in (1);

(3) losses related to, or incurred in connection directly or indirectly with, factoring transactions or discounting transactions;

(4) royalty, patent, technical, and copyright fees;

(5) licensing fees; and

(6) other similar expenses and costs.[20]

The definition, however, has attracted some criticism. For instance, the catchall category of the intangible expenses (*other similar expenses and costs*) leaves the door open for states to include a wide range of expenses that may narrow the deductibility available for the parent company. Illustratively, Company A needs to use a wide range of software developed by unrelated entities. Company A's parent licenses the software from the unrelated entities, and then subsequently sublicenses the software to Company A. The parent, however, cannot deduct the software license expenses because it has sublicensed the software to its related entity, Company A.

In addition, the MTC model statute defines interest expense as "amounts directly or indirectly allowed as deductions under section 163 for purposes of determining taxable income" under the Tax Code.[21]

---

[19] "Model Statute Requiring the Add-Back of Certain Intangible and Interest Expenses," *MTC.gov*, last modified August 17, 2006, www.mtc.gov/uploadedFiles/Multistate_Ta x_Commission/Uniformity/Uniformity_Projects/A_-_Z/Add-Back%20-%20FINAL%2 0version.pdf.

[20] *Ibid.* at 1.   [21] *Ibid.* at 4.

Some states, including Ohio, have a broader definition of interest expense to include amounts that may be deducted for purposes of determining federal taxable income.[22] Consequently, these states can deny deductibility of any interest expense paid to a related company.[23] This will lead to non-uniformity among the states.

The MTC model provides a definition for a related member or entity. States, however, generally pay attention to affiliates as part of a taxpayer's unitary group or consolidated group. The MTC model provides two common exceptions to the add-back requirements: *subject to tax exception* and *conduit* exception. The *subject to tax exception* means the income received by the related party is subject to tax in the state or another state. The *conduit exception* applies when the related party pays the intangible expense to an unrelated third party. In addition to the two exceptions, at least seven states, Alabama, Connecticut, Illinois, Indiana, Massachusetts, New Jersey, and Ohio have included a third exception, the *unreasonableness exception*. The *unreasonableness exception* to the add-back requirement applies where the corporation establishes that the adjustments are unreasonable.[24]

Based on reported cases, states with add-back statutes have not encountered the same high level of litigation compared to states that impose income tax against the out-of-state IP Holding Company. The *unreasonableness* exception to the add-back requirement, however, seems to be a subjective, amorphous standard, exposing the statute to challenge, as seen in Alabama in *Surtees v. VFJ Ventures*.

Add-back statutes face a number of potential constitutional challenges. Obviously, taxpayers may argue that the add-back statute is a backdoor response to avoid the stringent substantial nexus requirement. States deny the parent or affiliated operating company the deduction of the royalty payments because they could not directly tax income received by the out-of-state IP Holding Company due to the lack of substantial nexus between the IP Holding Company and the taxing jurisdiction. The add-back statutes effectively impose a tax on the IP Holding Company income.[25] Taxpayers may also argue that the add-back statutes discriminate against interstate commerce in violation of the Commerce Clause by

---

[22] Ohio Rev. Code § 5733.042(A)(4).

[23] *See* Michele Borens & Jessica L. Kerner, "20 Years of Ambiguity in Addback Statutes," *State Tax Notes* (October 28, 2013), *available at* www.sutherland.com/portalresource/lo okup/poid/Z1tOl9NPluKPtDNIqLMRV56Pab6TfzcRXncKbDtRr9tObDdEn43E p83!/fileUpload.name=/70st0263.pdf.

[24] Brief of the Multistate Tax Commission as Amicus Curiae in Support of Respondents G. Thomas Surtees and the State of Alabama Department of Revenue, VFJ Ventures, Inc. v. Surtees, 2008 WL 6486437, *10 n.6 (Alabama May 31, 2008).

[25] *Surtees v. VFJ Ventures, Inc.*, 8 So.3d 950, 978–79 (Ala. Civ. App. 2008).

denying a deduction for ordinary business expenses because they are paid to an out-of-state corporation that is located in a state without taxing the payments.[26] Essentially, taxpayers could claim that add-back statutes treat transactions with an out-of-state IP Holding Company differently than transactions with in-state companies. Add-back statutes require that payments made in transactions with an out-of-state IP Holding Company to be added back while royalty payments made in transactions between the operating company and an in-state IP Holding Company are not required to be added back.[27]

Some states may not want to adopt add-back statutes for fear that corporations will quickly design their transactions around the law to avoid royalty payments by calling the payments something else.[28] If the taxing state revises the statute again, the corporations may follow with their own rearrangement. The cat-and-mouse chase will frustrate states and render add-back statutes ineffective.[29] On the other hand, the potential cat-and-mouse chase scenario may be more palatable to multistate corporations with the hopeful belief that their tax planning experts would soon assist them in crafting new ways to avoid add-back. Some states may face litigation on the interpretation of the exceptions to the add-back requirement.[30] Pennsylvania has attempted to minimize potential litigation by providing explanations, discussion of the exceptions, and illustrative examples for its add-back statute.[31]

As expected, Delaware does not sit idly watching twenty or so states that have adopted versions of add-back statutes. As the domestic tax

---

[26] Petition for a Writ of Certiorari, *VFJ Ventures, Inc. v. Surtees*, 2009 WL 180859 (January 21, 2009).

[27] Borens & Kerner, *supra* note 23, at 266.

[28] The Times reported on a new loophole called "embedded royalty" companies, "in which corporations set up Delaware holding companies that license their assets to other Delaware entities. The secondary Delaware entities buy goods or services from other parts of the company, add in the price of the royalty, and sell them back to the operating company, giving it a tax break on the royalty." Lynnley Browning, "Critics Call Delaware a Tax Haven," *New York Times*, May 29, 2009, www.nytimes.com/2009/05/30/business/30delaware.html. Also, corporations may use "embedded royalty" structure to bundle intellectual property and tangible property in intercompany transactions without identifying the intellectual property royalty. Multistate Tax Commission, accessed November 8, 2016, www.mtc.gov/getattachment/The-Commission/Committees/ALAS/ExhibitA.pdf.aspx

[29] Testimony of Professor Richard Pomp, Hearing on H.0784 Before the Vt. House Comm. on Ways and Means, 2003–2004 Leg. Sess. (March 25, 2004).

[30] *Morgan Stanley & Co. v. Dir., Div. of Taxation*, 2014 N.J. Tax LEXIS 23 (N.J. Tax Ct. October 29, 2014) (challenge related to subject to tax and unreasonable exceptions).

[31] "Information Notice Corporation Taxes 2016–1," Pennsylvania Department of Revenue, last modified February 19, 2016, www.revenue.pa.gov/GeneralTaxInformation/TaxLawPoliciesBulletinsNotices/Documents/Informational%20Notices/info_notice_ct_2016–01.pdf.

haven, Delaware is afraid that add-back statutes will render Delaware's gift to a corporation in the form of a tax exemption for an IP Holding Company's income irrelevant. That means Delaware will lose its standing as the domestic tax haven for the IP Holding Company to be incorporated solely for favorable tax treatment. Realizing the danger, Delaware has declared that its "sovereign interests are at the heart" of add-back statutes.[32] Delaware, therefore, has injected itself into the fight by filing a brief in support of taxpayers who filed petition for writ of certiorari to the Supreme Court challenging the constitutionality of the add-back statute.

The arguments advanced by Delaware center on two premises. The first is that the add-back statute "impermissibly interferes with Delaware's corporate tax policy, which is an integral component of Delaware's economic development program" and the second is that Delaware is "constitutionally entitled to devise and implement its corporate tax policies without encroachments from other states."[33] Delaware has chastised add-back statutes as extraterritorial due to disallowance of deduction of the royalty payments, unless the payments themselves are taxed in the related IP Holding Company's home state. Because the home state of the IP Holding Company is Delaware which does not tax on the royalty income, the add-back statute is "triggered, resulting in additional tax liability" for the taxpayer, the licensee of the related IP Holding Company.[34]

Delaware has openly admitted that it purposefully positioned itself as the domestic tax haven by clarifying the scope of corporate income tax exemption for companies with intellectual property assets. Delaware calls these companies "intangibles holding companies."[35] Not only do they not pay Delaware corporate income tax, but they are also exempt from Delaware's annual license fee and gross receipt tax.[36] Delaware believes that these exemptions allow the state to compete with other states in encouraging the IP Holding Company to locate in Delaware. Delaware defends that its policy is "sensible" because the IP Holding Companies provide meaningful employment with competitive compensation to the people of Delaware and create new business in accounting, legal, and specialized administrative support. Most importantly, these employment and business opportunities have minimal impact on Delaware's environment and infrastructure. Overall, the trade-off of not extracting income taxes in exchange for employment and business opportunities has greatly benefited Delaware.[37]

Delaware's tax haven strategy for IP Holding Companies reflects the state's long appreciation for "the evolving nature of the American economy"

---

[32] Brief of the State of Delaware as Amicus Curiae in Support of Petitioner, *VFJ Ventures, Inc. v. Surtees*, 2009 WL 481241, at *1 (February 23, 2009).

[33] *Ibid.* at *2–7.   [34] *Ibid.* at *9–10.   [35] *Ibid.* at *4.

[36] *Ibid.* at *5 (citing 30 Del. Code Ann. § 2301(o).   [37] *Ibid.*

with "the need to develop the emerging technology and intellectual property industries."[38] To make the state even more attractive to corporate taxpayers with respect to intellectual property, Delaware has passed recent legislation to enable Delaware's Court of Chancery to mediate technology disputes.

With all of its efforts relating to intellectual property, Delaware views add-back statutes as a "constitutional assault" on the state's "policy judgments and business development initiatives."[39] Delaware criticizes these statutes as penalizing taxpayers who choose to locate their IP Holding Company subsidiaries in Delaware. Moreover, these statutes are an attempt to "nullify" all the benefits that Delaware has carefully planned and "chosen to grant" in its considered tax policy.[40]

In making these arguments, Delaware perhaps ignores several crucial points. These add-back statutes do not impose a tax on Delaware IP Holding Companies. The statutes address whether to allow deductions to the in-state taxpayer licensees. States have the right to allow or disallow deductions. Deductions are known to be a matter of legislative grace. Disallowing expenses paid by the taxpayer licensee does not automatically amount to a tax on the IP Holding Company, the licensor and recipient of the royalty payments.

The battle between Delaware and other states with add-back statutes will continue, with Delaware currently praying that the United States Supreme Court would soon accept a writ of certiorari petition from a taxpayer related to the Delaware IP Holding Company. The Supreme Court so far has exhibited no interest in a domestic tax haven for the IP Holding Company. All indications suggest that add-back statutes will be a viable option despite the potential problems discussed above.

Including Both Combined Reporting and Add-back in the Solution?

Many advocates have championed the idea of mandatory combined reporting of income as a solution to the IP Holding Company problem.[41]

---

[38] *Ibid.* at *3.   [39] *Ibid.*   [40] *Ibid.*

[41] Richard D. Pomp, "State Tax Reform: Proposals for Wisconsin," 88 *Marq. Law Review* 45 (2004) [hereinafter Pomp, State Tax Reform]; Michael J. McIntyre et al., "Designing a Combined Reporting Regime for a State Corporate Income Tax: A Case Study of Louisiana," 61 *La. L. Rev.* 699 (2001); Charles E. McLure, Jr., "The Nuttiness of State and Local Taxes–and the Nuttiness of Responses Thereto," *State Tax Notes* 851 (September 16, 2002); Lee A. Sheppard, "Self-Inflicted Wounds: What Europe Can Teach the States," *State Tax Notes* 309 (July 26, 2004). *See also* Mark J. Cowan & Clint Kakstys, "A Green Mountain Miracle and the Garden State Grab: Lessons from Vermont and New Jersey on State Corporate Tax Reform," 60 *Tax Lawyer* 351, 363–69 (2007) (praising the virtues of combined reporting).

With combined reporting, related corporations that are part of a "unitary group" are treated as one entity for tax purposes. Many advocates believe that combined reporting will clamp down on the IP Holding Company income-shifting loophole. Others oppose the combined reporting requirement for fear that it may cause income distortions by attributing income to the wrong state due to the calculation averaging the income and apportionment of all the businesses regardless of the real economic activity experienced by the corporation in the state.

The Multistate Tax Commission adopted the model statute for Combined Reporting in August 2006 and later amended it in July 2011.[42] Currently, twenty-five states and the District of Columbia have followed the combined reporting approach.[43] The remaining twenty states with a corporate income tax have not. Some states are not quite enthusiastic about adopting the approach because it is viewed as unfriendly to business. Indeed, businesses do not like the approach due to the complexity and, perhaps, it is more difficult to design around compared to the add-back statutes. The Maryland Chamber of Commerce, for example, has opposed combined reporting based on the belief that the approach "would result in massive shifts in tax liability, complicate tax compliance and make Maryland less competitive."[44]

The administrative costs may also deter states from readily adopting the combined reporting approach. Rhode Island has estimated that it would need to double the current staff of the Division of Taxation's Corporate Tax in order to cope with the additional duties and responsibilities that would arise from combined reporting.[45] Nevertheless, Rhode

---

[42] www.mtc.gov/uploadedFiles/Multistate_Tax_Commission/Uniformity/Uniformity_Pro jects/A_-_Z/Combined%20Reporting%20-%20FINAL%20version.pdf.

[43] The twenty-five states, as of December 2015, are: Alaska, Arizona, California, Colorado, Connecticut, Hawaii, Idaho, Illinois, Kansas, Maine, Massachusetts, Michigan, Minnesota, Montana, Nebraska, New Hampshire, New York, North Dakota, Oregon, Rhode Island, Texas, Utah, Vermont, West Virginia, and Wisconsin. States without corporate income tax are: Nevada, South Dakota, Washington, and Wyoming. The twenty-one states that have not adopted combined reporting are: Alabama, Arkansas, Delaware, Florida, Georgia, Indiana, Iowa, Kentucky, Louisiana, Maryland, Mississippi, Missouri, New Mexico, New Jersey, North Carolina, Ohio, Oklahoma, Pennsylvania, South Carolina, Tennessee, and Virginia. "Closing State Corporate Tax Loopholes: Combined Reporting," Institute for Local Self-Reliance, last modified December 2015, https://ilsr.org/rule/combined-reporting/; "List of Combined Reporting States Grows," *MultiState Insider*, last modified October 7, 2015, www.multistate.com/insi der/2015/10/list-of-combined-reporting-states-grows/.

[44] "Combined Reporting Could Become a Reality in Maryland," *KatzAbosch*, accessed September 24, 2016, https://www.katzabosch.com/news/combined-reporting-could-be come-a-reality-in-maryland/.

[45] "Tax Administrator's Study of Combined Reporting," State of Rhode Island and Providence Plantations Department of Revenue Division of Taxation, last modified March 15, 2014, *available at* www.tax.ri.gov/Tax%20Website/TAX/reports/Rhode%20

Island concluded that the benefits from combined reporting outweigh the administrative costs, and proceeded with the adoption of the combined reporting law applicable to taxable years beginning in 2015.[46]

A more suitable solution, perhaps, is an inclusion of both combined reporting and add-back. Let's take a look at what has happened in New York for a better understanding of this potential solution.

New York, as discussed in Chapter 4, is among the states with a version of combined reporting. Prior to 2007, New York required combined reporting to be filed if three tests were met: (1) stock ownership, (2) a unitary business, and (3) distortion of income. For the distortion of income test, New York's then-existing law provided that the income would be presumed to be distorted when there were substantial inter-corporate transactions among the corporations. Typically, tests (1) and (2) are fairly easy to demonstrate, but test (3) is difficult due to an intensive factual inquiry and battle of the experts. Consequently, the taxpayer and the taxing authority would often engage in a prolonged dispute to ascertain whether the taxpayer's transactions have economic substance. There was no certainty as to which side was going to prevail in this costly fight.

New York had learned the hard way. As mentioned before, in 1995 the New York taxing authority lost in a substantial case against Victoria's Secret, Express, Limited, and Lane Bryant. The Administrative Law Judge (ALJ) in that case ruled that all of the IP Holding Companies were legitimate, and that the transactions between the IP Holding Companies and their affiliates were at arm's length, a transfer pricing concern. In a lengthy finding and opinion of forty-one pages issued by the ALJ, New York lost under the then-existing combined reporting approach! With the devastating loss, New York then had to watch North Carolina's victory in a case that involved the same IP Holding Companies for Victoria's Secret, Express, Limited, and Lane Bryant, in addition to Lerner, Caciqueco, and A&F.[47] Adding salt to the injury that New York had suffered, the North Carolina decision provided the legal reasoning map for both New Jersey and Oklahoma to subsequently adopt in their cases against the IP Holding Company assignment and license-back scheme.

New York then decided to tackle the problem by fixing some of the loopholes in its then-existing law. New York amended its combined

---

Island%20Division%20of%20Taxation%20-%20Study%20on%20Combined%20Reporting%20-%2003-17-14%20FINAL.pdf.

[46] R.I. Gen. Laws § 44-11-4.1.

[47] *A&F Trademark, Inc. v. Tolson*, 605 S.E.2d 187, 195 (N.C. Ct. App. 2004), *cert. denied*, 546 U.S. 821 (2005).

reporting law in 2007 to require taxpayers to meet a control test to file a combined report where there are substantial intercorporate transactions, regardless of the transfer price for the transactions. New York eliminated the transfer pricing emphasis because both the taxpayers and the taxing authority had wasted much resources in litigating arm's-length pricing. In 2013, New York amended the law again by replacing the substantial intercorporate transactions combined reporting approach with "unitary combined reporting." The new law requires that a combined report must be filed by any taxpayer who either owns or controls 50 percent of the stock of the other corporations, or where the taxpayer's 50 percent or more stock is owned or controlled by such other corporations and that the taxpayer is engaged in a unitary business with those corporations. In other words, the new law removes the distortion of income test that was both complex and costly to litigate.[48]

Such changes in the combined reporting law, however, were not sufficient to close off loopholes. New York had passed the add-back statute in 2003 to require the intangible expenses to be added back. New York amended the add-back statute twice in 2007 and 2013 to ensure that its add-back statute and the newly revised combined reporting law work in tandem, clamping down all the loopholes relating to the IP Holding Company income shifting. The latest amendment to the add-back statute reflects New York's decision to follow the Multistate Tax Commission's model add-back statute.

A lesson to learn from New York's experience is that both combined reporting and add-back law may be needed in order to be more effective in addressing income shifting. Indeed, there are a number of states that have both combined reporting and add-back statutes, such as Connecticut, Illinois, Massachusetts, Michigan, New York, Oregon, and Virginia. Even though Maryland has not enacted combined reporting legislation, the courts in that state have effectively ruled for combined reporting results. Maryland also adopted an add-back statute in 2004.

Trying All Three Approaches: Lessons from Massachusetts

In the age of budget crunches and sophisticated tax planners for multi-state corporations, the solution to the assignment and license-back scheme with intellectual property ownership shuffled from the true

---

[48] "Inside New York Tax Reform: Understanding the New Unitary Combination Provisions," PriceWaterhouseCooper, last modified May 22, 2014, www.pwc.com/us/e n/state-local-tax/newsletters/salt-insights/assets/pwc-understanding-new-yorks-new-uni tary-combination-provisions.pdf.

creator to the IP Holding Company without losing the right to use the same intellectual property in the operation of the business, may not be either this approach or that approach. Even the inclusion of both the combined reporting and add-back requirements may not be sufficient to chase the evasive, camouflage royalty income. States may consider adopting a combination of all three approaches: going after the IP Holding Company, requiring combined reporting, and adding back the deduction of intangible payments.

At least one state has done just that, using the combination of all three approaches. Massachusetts is an example of an outlier, as it has pursued the original owner of the intellectual property assets (the parent company in the assignment and license-back scheme) by disallowing deduction of the royalty payments to the IP Holding Company under the sham transaction principle, in addition to adopting its add-back statute in 2003 and combined reporting in 2008. As described in greater detail in Chapter 4, Massachusetts applied the sham transaction or economic substance doctrine to cases where the original owner of the intellectual property assets assigns them to its wholly owned Delaware IP Holding Company and then licenses back the IP assets for use in the business of the parent company. Upon extensive factual inquiry, the transfer of the ownership of the intellectual property was merely in form because all of the activities and personnel involved in the control and management remained unchanged, Massachusetts found that the transaction was a means to avoid paying tax. Massachusetts denied the parent company's deduction of the royalty payments to the Delaware IP Holding Company as ordinary and necessary expenses. Though Massachusetts enjoyed some victory under the sham transaction, it also suffered losses in the early 2000s when the corporate taxpayers appealed their cases all the way to the highest court.

The Massachusetts legislature did not want to continue the uncertainty and the large cost of litigating under the sham transaction doctrine. In 2003, the Massachusetts legislature adopted the add-back statute applicable for taxable years beginning on or after January 1, 2002.[49] With respect to intellectual property, the Legislature intended the taxpayer to add-back to net income related member interest and intangible expense.[50] The statute sets a high bar for the taxpayer who seeks a deduction, as a deduction may be allowed only if the taxpayer can establish by clear and

---

[49] "Directive 99–9: Disallowance or 'Add-back' of the Deduction for Certain State Taxes to Corporate Net Income," *Mass. Gov*, accessed September 24, 2016, www.mass.gov/dor/businesses/help-and-resources/legal-library/directives/directives-by-years/1990–1999-directives/directive-99–9-disallowance-or-add-back-of.html.

[50] Mass. Gen. Laws ch. 63, §§ 31I, 31J, 31K.

convincing evidence that the Commissioner's disallowance of royalty pay-ments and interest expenses paid by the taxpayer to a related member was unreasonable.[51]

Moreover, as recalled in *Kimberly-Clark v. Commissioner of Revenue*, the parent companies created an entity to hold all the patents and the new entity licensed the patents back to the parents and affiliates in exchange for royalty payments. For the 2002 tax year, Kimberly-Clark deducted the royalty payments and did not add them back in compliance with the newly enacted add-back statutes. Kimberly-Clark failed to meet the test for disallowance. In reaching its decision, the Massachusetts Tax Appeal Board concluded that since the passage of the add-back statute, "to avoid add back of the royalty expenses at issue here, a taxpayer must demon-strate, by clear and convincing evidence, the presence of both economic substance and valid business purpose as well as that tax reduction was not a principal purpose of the transaction."[52] In other words, the sham transaction doctrine has been both "modified and strengthened" by the add-back statutes.[53]

Five years later, in 2008, Massachusetts House Bill 4904, "An Act Relative to Tax Fairness and Business Competitiveness," became law. Consequently, combined reporting is the new requirement for taxpayers. Combined reporting ended Massachusetts's separate filing regime wherein each corporation subject to taxation in Massachusetts filed its own separate tax return. Combined reporting would greatly affect multi-jurisdictional taxpayers. In enacting the new law, Massachusetts had estimated that its revenue would increase by $136 million in Fiscal Year 2008 and $226 million in Fiscal Year 2009, as the requirement would close off tax loopholes.[54]

Perhaps what Massachusetts did may be deemed as unnecessary from the perspective of addressing the tax avoidance loopholes in the inter-company licenses and interest expenses relating to intellectual property. The add-back statutory provisions on license and interest expenses have already allowed Massachusetts to eliminate the deductions of the royalty and interest payments between related companies by disallowing the expenses that have been deducted for purposes of computing federal taxable income. The taxpayer must add back the deductions. What good would the combined reporting do then? On the one hand, combined

---

[51] *Kimberly-Clark Corp. v. Comm'r of Revenue*, 981 N.E.2d 208, 219 (Mass. App. Ct. 2013).
[52] *Ibid.*   [53] *Ibid.*
[54] Natasha Varyani, "Combined Reporting in Massachusetts: A Primer on the Controversy," Massachusetts Bar Association, accessed September 26, 2016, www.massbar.org/publications/section-review/2008/v10-n3/combined-reporting-in-massachusetts-a-primer-on-the-controversy.

reporting requires the income of the entire unitary group, but on the other hand, the add-back statute may have very well already collected the same amount of the revenue expected from the adoption of combined reporting. Though that is true in the end results, what Massachusetts has done seems to provide the state ample means to effectively shut down currently identified loopholes.

International Tax Sourcing Rule for IP Holding Company's Income

We often say that there are fifty countries in the United States and each has its own history and government. Each state treats taxpayers from other states as "foreign" individuals and entities. The foreign taxpayers conduct business across state boundaries. Similarly, the United States is a nation of the world of nations and many US companies conduct business abroad while other foreign companies conduct their business within the United States. In thinking about a state's power to tax and about income apportionment, it may be useful to look at U.S. international tax source rules that are used to determine when intellectual property royalties, for example, are either domestic source or foreign source.

According to Section 861(a)(4) of the US Tax Code, royalties from licensing of intellectual property are generally sourced according to where the "patents, copyrights, secret processes and formulas, good will, trademarks, trade brands, franchises, and other like property" are used.[55] That means, if a licensee uses intellectual property in its US trade or business, the royalties are US source income even if the intellectual property was developed overseas and the royalties are paid overseas pursuant to a contract executed overseas.

Consistent with the general sourcing rule, the Service in Revenue Ruling 68–443 held that the source of royalties for use of a trademark is the country in which the products bearing the trademark are ultimately used and where the trademark is protected despite the fact that the initial sale of the trademarked products took place in the United States. In that Ruling, X was a foreign corporation with ownership of its trademark in foreign countries. X entered into a license agreement with Y, a domestic corporation, granting Y the right to use X's foreign trademark on Y's products for subsequent distribution and sales. Pursuant to the license agreement, Y would owe X a royalty based on the sales price of the trademarked products. Y then manufactured the trademarked products in the United States and subsequently sold them to foreign buyers in the

---

[55] 26 U.S.C. § 861(a)(4).

United States for resale and consumption in foreign countries. The initial sale of the trademarked products was deemed as having taken place in the United States. Y could not sell the trademarked products for ultimate consumption in the United States because the ownership of the US trademark for these products was held by Z, an unrelated entity. The Internal Revenue Service framed the issue as "whether, by reason of the initial sale of the products to the foreign buyers in the United States, Y corporation has 'used' the foreign trademark in the United States and the royalties paid by Y to X are income from sources within the United States."[56] The Service ruled that the royalty received by X from Y for the use of the foreign trademark is income from sources outside the United States despite the fact that the initial sale of the trademarked products took place in the United States. The initial sale of the trademarked products to foreign shippers was for their ultimate consumption outside the United States. The Service observed that "[a]lthough the amount of the royalty income is measured by the sales of the trademarked products, the place of sale does not necessarily determine the source of such royalty income."[57]

Conversely, Revenue Ruling 75–254 held that any royalty received by a domestic corporation as the owner of the United States trademarks on its products ultimately used in the United States would be US source income even though the sale of the trademarked products took place outside the United States.[58] In that Ruling, S was a domestic corporation with ownership of the trademark in the United States and foreign countries. S acquired a manufacturing facility in Puerto Rico and began the manufacture, packaging, and sale of proprietary drug products. S sold its trademarked drug products f.o.b. in Puerto Rico to M, a newly formed domestic company and a wholly owned subsidiary of S. M had the right to use S's trademarks in the advertisement and sale of S's drug products in the United States. M was required to pay to S distribution expenses involved in purchasing S's products in Puerto Rico, including warehousing, selling, and delivery to wholesalers and retailers in the United States. M was not required to pay for the license to use the trademarks in the United States. The issue decided by the Service was "whether any portion of the payments received by S on the ultimate use of its products in the United States would be treated as an imputed royalty for the use of S's trademarks in the United States and would thus be considered United States source income."[59] Because the sale of the trademarked drug products in the present case was inclusive of the right to use the trademark on

---

[56] Rev. Rul. 68–443, 1968–2 C.B. 304.   [57] *Ibid.*
[58] Rev. Rul. 75–254, 1975–1 C.B. 243.   [59] *Ibid.*

the resale of the products, there were no imputed royalties for the use of S's trademarks in the United States. Therefore, the gross income received by S for the sale of its trademarked drug products manufactured and sold f.o.b. in Puerto Rico for resale in the United States through its domestic wholly owned corporation is Puerto Rico source income.

Likewise, in Revenue Ruling 80–362, the Service applied the general sourcing rule for patent royalties and held that the royalties are subject to the current tax rate and withholding rule.[60] Similarly, in Revenue Ruling 72–232, the Service held that royalties paid for the use of a foreign copyright for textbooks printed in the United States but sold solely in the foreign country were sourced outside the United States.[61] Again, the source of a royalty based on a copyright is the place where the copyrighted material is consumed and protected by copyright law.

For example, the Tax Court in *Goosen v. Commissioner* applied the sourcing rule that "[r]oyalty income paid for the right to use intangible property generally is sourced where the property is used or is granted the privilege of being used" in deciding "where petitioner's name and likeness were used or would be used to determine the source of petitioner's royalty income."[62] The petitioner in that case was a citizen of South Africa, residing in England, who played golf professionally worldwide.[63] He won the US Open in 2001.[64] He owned the rights to his name and likeness outside the United States. He entered various endorsement agreements with companies for the use of his name and likeness in connection with various products. In the Upper Deck Endorsement Agreement, petitioner granted Upper Deck the right to use petitioner's name and likeness in connection only with video games.[65] The Tax Court found that Upper Deck sold 92 percent of its golf cards inside the United States and 8 percent outside the United States. Because the golf cards were where Upper Deck used the petitioner's name and likeness, the Tax Court held that the golf card sales should be a determining factor in sourcing and, therefore, petitioner's royalty income from Upper Deck is 92 percent US source income.[66]

Applying the United States' international "sourcing" rule to state cases like *Gore-Tex* and *KFC*, Maryland, Iowa, and other states may argue that their tax assessment decisions are consistent and in line with the law and policy well established by the federal government. For example, Maryland may assert that because Gore-Tex patents are used in Maryland, royalties from the licensing of the Gore-Tex patents are, therefore, sourced in

[60] Rev. Rul. 80–362, 1980–2 C.B. 208.   [61] Rev. Rul. 72–232, 1972–1 C.B. 276.
[62] *Goosen v. CIR*, 136 T.C. 547, 563 (T.C. 2011).   [63] *Ibid.* at 565.   [64] *Ibid.*
[65] *Ibid.* at 564–65.   [66] *Ibid.* at 565; *see also Garcia v. CIR*, 140 T.C. 141 (T.C. 2013).

Maryland, regardless of the fact that the patents were developed outside of Maryland, and the royalties were paid outside of Maryland pursuant to a license agreement executed outside of Maryland. Similarly, Iowa may attempt to apply the same "sourcing" rule and argument in its tax assessment against KFC. Iowa can claim that the plain language of the sourcing rule covers "franchises." Therefore, payments from the franchising of the KFC system are sourced in Iowa because the franchise technique, know-how, and trademarks are all used in Iowa and protected by Iowa's law, regardless of the fact that the franchise system was developed outside of Iowa and the payments were made outside of Iowa pursuant to a franchise agreement executed outside of Iowa.

It should be cautioned, however, that looking solely to U.S. source rules as a solution to domestic shifting of intellectual property income would be mistake. As demonstrated in the second half of the book (Chapters 6 through 9), foreign shifting of intellectual property and related income is quite prevalent. Indeed, in the international context many have called for a whole new approach to sourcing global income.

6   Key Incentives to Create Foreign IP Holding Companies

In the first half of this book (Chapters 2–5), we explored the use of *domestic* IP Holding Companies by US corporations that operate in multiple US states. As we saw, many multistate companies reduce their overall state income tax burden by parking certain intellectual property assets in controlled subsidiaries located in states, such as Delaware, with favorable tax regimes for intellectual property. In the second half of this book (Chapters 6–9), we explore the use of *foreign* subsidiaries by multinational corporations that have offshore income. Specifically, we will see how many multinational corporations with large amounts of intellectual property, based in the US and abroad, reduce taxes on their worldwide income by transferring their intellectual property to controlled foreign subsidiaries based in tax-favored countries, such as Ireland or the Netherlands.

Naturally, the tendencies of multistate or multinational companies to shift income from one jurisdiction to another (one state to another or one country to another) are strongest when tax policies differ greatly among those jurisdictions. Uniform tax policies among states or among nations would provide very little "tax" reason to move mobile intellectual property assets and related income across borders.

Income tax policies are generally uniform among individual states within the US. General state and local statutory tax rates on corporate income do not vary greatly (averaging approximately 7.5 percent),[1] and those rates are imposed on a uniform base – federal adjusted gross income with certain modifications made at the state level. Against this backdrop, however, a few states have carved out a special rule for tax exemption on certain intellectual property income. As we saw in earlier chapters, this tax

---

[1] *See* KMPG, "Corporate Tax Rates Table," accessed October 14, 2016, https://home.kpmg.com/xx/en/home/services/tax/tax-tools-and-resources/tax-rates-online/corporate-tax-rates-table.html (noting the top marginal rates at the state and local government level average approximately 7.5 percent). *See also* Kimberly A. Clausing, "Lessons for International Tax Reform from the U.S. State Experience Under Formulary Apportionment," 5, June 29, 2014, *available at* https://papers.ssrn.com/sol3/papers.cfm?abstract_id=2359724 (noting for the average of all states, corporate tax rates have been relatively stable over time, averaging 7.2 percent in 1986, and 6.6 percent in 2012).

exemption has been enough of an incentive for many multistate companies to shift their intellectual property and related income to those states.

In the international context, it is a bit more complicated. Unlike each US state's approach to corporate income taxation, each country's approach has developed in a unique cultural, historical, and economic context. The result is that tax policies among nations are hardly uniform; indeed, they differ greatly. Much more so than tax policies among US states. Some nations have tax laws in place that are highly unattractive to multinational companies with intellectual property. Others have tax laws that were designed deliberately to aggressively attract intellectual property investment and income. Thus, the incentives for global shifting of intellectual property are numerous and extend beyond a country's special tax rate on, or tax exemption of, intellectual property income.

This chapter identifies six key incentives for multinational companies to form separate foreign IP Holding Companies and to engage in global tax reduction efforts. They include: (1) varying statutory corporate tax rates; (2) countries' conflicting bases of jurisdiction to tax (and dividend tax policies); (3) conflicting standards for determining corporate residency; (4) availability of "hybrid entity" structures; (5) countries' competing research and development (R&D) incentives; and (6) so-called "patent boxes." As we will see, these incentives often overlap increasing the tendencies of multinationals to shift intellectual property income offshore. While no attempt is made here to present them in any particular order of importance, we do begin with the impact of tax rate policies, which studies have shown strongly influence the location of intellectual property. We end with the impact of so-called "patent boxes" or "innovation boxes" on intellectual property location choices. Patent boxes are a relatively recent tax tool used by a growing number of countries; they apply a lower tax rate to certain intellectual property income.

Statutory Corporate Tax Rates

In contrast to sandy tax haven countries like Bermuda and the Cayman Islands, most industrialized countries, indeed all advanced countries that comprise the Organization for Economic Cooperation and Development (OECD), levy a national tax on corporate profits.[2] Subnational or local/municipal governments may also levy a tax on corporate profits,

---

[2] *See* Kyle Pomerleau, "Sources of Government Revenue in the OECD, 2014," Tax Foundation (November 12, 2014), http://taxfoundation.org/article/sources-government-revenue-oecd-2014.

Table 6.1 *Combined Corporate Tax Rates for OECD Countries (2016)*[3]

Australia	30%
Austria	25%
Belgium	33.99%
Canada	26.5%
Chile	24%
Czech Republic	19%
Denmark	22%
Estonia	20%
Finland	20%
France	33.3%
Germany	29.72%
Greece	29%
Hungary	19%
Iceland	20%
Ireland	**12.5%**
Israel	25%
Italy	31.4%
Japan	32.26%
Korea	24.2%
Luxembourg	29.22%
Mexico	30%
Netherlands	25%
New Zealand	28%
Norway	25%
Poland	19%
Portugal	21%
Slovak Republic	22%
Slovenia	17%
Spain	25%
Sweden	22%
Switzerland	24%
Turkey	20%
United Kingdom	20%
United States	**40%**

which can increase the overall corporate income tax burden in a given country.[4] The table above shows how countries differ substantially in the

[3] *See* KMPG, "Corporate Tax Rates Table," *supra* note 1 (highlighting the lowest and highest tax rates for 2016).

[4] For example, although Germany's national corporate income tax rate is 15 percent, a solidarity surcharge and municipal taxes bring the overall tax rate for corporations to about 30 percent. Andreas Perdelwitz, "Germany: Corporate Taxation Country Analysis," Sections 1.1.1, 1.1.3 (Amsterdam: International Bureau of Fiscal Documentation,

combined statutory rate (national rate plus average subnational rate, if applicable) at which corporate income is taxed.

Ireland and the United States are highlighted because of their contrasting tax rate policies. On one end of the rate spectrum, Ireland has adopted a very attractive corporate income tax rate to lure investment. In Ireland, the standard corporate income tax rate is only 12.5 percent for active business income – one of the lowest in the world.[5] However, in order to avail itself of the 12.5 percent rate, a company must derive income from a trade that is actively carried on in Ireland.[6] That means real substance including strategic decision making, value added activities, and employees with skills to carry out those activities, must be confined within its borders.

The United States is on the other end of the rate spectrum. It has one of the highest corporate income tax rates in the world. The top marginal federal corporate income tax rate is 35 percent, which applies to both passive and active business income.[7] In addition, state and local governments may impose income taxes, which are deductible in computing federal taxable income, bringing the US rate on corporate income to approximately 40 percent – the highest in the OECD.[8] The high corporate income tax rate, as well as other tax variables, cause the United States

2014). In Switzerland, the federal corporate tax rate is only 8.5 percent, but taxes at the canton or municipality level (determined by negotiation with the local canton) bring the total tax rates up to around 12–24 percent. *See* Bureau of National Affairs, Global Tax Chart Builder (September 25, 2014), *available at* http://taxandaccounting.bna.com/btac/ [hereinafter Global Tax Chart].

[5] KPMG, "Ireland Country Profile," 2, *EU Tax Centre* (March 2013), *available at* www .kpmg.com/Global/en/services/Tax/regional-tax-centers/european-union-tax-centre/Doc uments/eu-country-profiles/2013-ireland.pdf. The tax rate is 25 percent for passive income. To enjoy the lower 12.5 percent rate, an Irish company that holds intellectual property must be engaged in the active development, management, and exploitation of that intellectual property.

[6] *See* "Ireland as a Location for Your Intellectual Property Trading Company," *Arthur Cox*, (April 2015), *available at* www.arthurcox.com/wp-content/uploads/2015/04/Arthur-Cox-Ireland-as-a-location-for-your-IP-Trading-Company-April-20152.pdf; "Ireland's Intellectual Property Tax Regime," *Walkers* (January 2016), *available at* www.walkersglo bal.com/images/Publications/Advisory/2016/01.08.201_Walkers_Ireland_Intellectual_P roperty_Tax_Regime.pdf.

[7] 26 U.S.C. § 11(b). The US corporate rate is the third highest in the world, exceeded only by the United Arab Emirates and Puerto Rico. *See* Tax Foundation, "Corporate Income Tax Rates Around the World," August 18, 2016, *available at* http://taxfoundation.org/ar ticle/corporate-income-tax-rates-around-world-2016.

[8] *See* Scott A. Hodge, "The Countdown is Over: We're #1," Tax Foundation (April 1, 2012), http://taxfoundation.org/article/countdown-over-were-1. *See* KMPG, "Corporate Tax Rates Table," *supra* note 1; KPMG, "Corporate and Indirect Tax Rate Survey 2014," accessed October 18, 2016, *available at* www.kpmg.com/Global/en/IssuesAndInsights/A rticlesPublications/Documents/corporate-indirect-tax-rate-survey-2014.pdf; OECD, Tax Policy Analysis, OECD Tax Database, historical table II.1, accessed October 18, 2016, *available at* https://stats.oecd.org/Index.aspx?DataSetCode=TABLE_II1 [herein-after OECD Historical Table II.1].

to rank among the bottom five countries in terms of international tax competitiveness.[9]

Many OECD countries have lowered their corporate tax rate in recent years in an effort to attract investment. In fact, over the past thirty years, the average top marginal corporate income tax rate in the OECD has dropped from approximately 48 percent to approximately 25 percent.[10] These countries typically pay for rate-lowering corporate tax reforms, at least in part, by scaling back tax preferences and increasing other revenue bases.[11] The United States is an outlier when it comes to rate reduction policies. While many OECD countries have been reducing their corporate rate statutory rates, the United States has maintained the same high corporate tax rate for the past thirty years. Figure 6.1 below compares the statutory corporate tax rates in the United States and OECD countries for 1981–2015.

Generally, the corporate income tax raises little revenue compared to other revenue sources. In OECD countries, it represents on average less than 9 percent of total government revenue.[12] This comes as no surprise as most OECD countries have reduced their corporate tax rates and rely mainly on consumption and social insurance taxes for the bulk of their revenue. What is surprising, however, is the fact that the United States, despite maintaining one of the highest rates in the world and also being the home of many of the most successful global companies, also raises very little revenue from the corporate income tax. As recent as the 1950s, the United States yielded about a third of its receipts from the corporate income tax. Today, that number is less than 10 percent.[13] This begs the

---

[9] Kyle Pomerleau, "International Tax Competitiveness Index 2016," *available at* https://drive.google.com/file/d/0B6586UGJDFOLRzhWUVJmLVVYM1U/view.

[10] *See* OECD Historical Table II.1, *supra* note 8. In The Netherlands, for example, corporate income tax rates decreased from 45–48 percent (1980), to 40–35 percent (1990), to 30–35 percent (2000), to the current rates of 20–25 percent. Statement of Frank M. Schoon, Testimony Before the Committee on Ways and Means United States House of Representatives, Key Elements of the Dutch Corporate Income Tax System, May 24, 2011, available at https://waysandmeans.house.gov/UploadedFiles/Schoontest.pdf.

[11] Alan J. Auerbach, Michael P. Devereux, & Helen Simpson, "Taxing Corporate Income," National Bureau of Economic Research Working Paper 14494 (November 2008), *available at* http://www.nber.org/papers/w14494.pdf.

[12] *See* Pomerleau, *supra* note 2 (providing a chart showing sources of revenue).

[13] OECD, "Tax Policy Analysis, Revenue Statistics Tax Structures Table 6," accessed October 20, 2016, *available at* http://www.oecd.org/tax/tax-policy/table-6-tax-revenue-main-head ings–total-taxation-2013.htm. The United States derives the bulk of its total revenues from its personal income tax (47.2 percent for 2013). *Ibid. See* Mark P. Keightley, *Reasons for the Decline in the Corporate Tax Revenues* (CRS Report No. R42113) (Washington, DC: Congressional Research Service, 2011), 1, *available at* http://economic-legislation.blogspot .com/2011/12/reasons-for-decline-in-corporate-tax.html. *See also* Nancy Folbre, "Tax Havens and Treasure Hunts," The New York Times, April 4, 2011, http://economix.blog s.nytimes.com/2011/04/04/tax-havens-and-treasure-hunts/?_r=0.

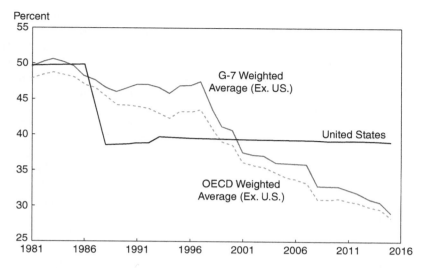

Figure 6.1 Comparison of Statutory Corporate Tax Rates in the United States and OECD Countries, 1981–2015
Prepared by "The President's Framework for Business Tax Reform: An Update," April 14, 2016.
Source: OECD

question: Why has the United States seen a decline in corporate tax revenues over the past half-century?

There are several explanations. One is that corporations subject to tax are eligible for an increasingly wide range of US tax preferences that reduce taxable income. The US tax code is now more than ever cluttered with favorable tax preferences, such as various write-offs and cost recovery deductions (accelerated depreciation and amortization allowances for capitalized expenditures) for business investment.[14] It has been estimated that these corporate tax benefits, excluding international tax provisions, reduce US corporate tax receipts by about 15 percent a year.[15] As a result

---

[14] 26 U.S.C. §§ 176, 168, 179.

[15] *See* Rosanne Altshuler, Stephen Shay, & Eric Toder, "Lessons the United States Can Learn from Other Countries' Territorial Systems for Taxing Income of Multinational Corporations," 7 n.8, (Tax Policy Center: Urban Institute & Brookings Institution, January 21, 2015), *available at* http://www.taxpolicycenter.org/sites/default/files/alfresc o/publication-pdfs/2000077-lessons-the-us-can-learn-from-other-countries.pdf (basing on data reported by U.S. Office of Management and Budget, Analytical Perspectives: Budget of the United States Government, Fiscal Year 2015 (2014) (U.S. Gov't Printing Office), table 14.2, 210–15).

of these benefits, many US corporations today pay no federal income tax at all. Only one-third of all active US corporations had federal income tax liability from 2006 to 2012.[16] However, these typically larger corporations often enjoy an *effective* rate much lower than the statutory rate because of favorable tax preferences. Effective rates vary depending on the year and also vary across industries. One study indicated that the overall average federal tax rate for US corporations was only 23 percent for a recent four-year period, which is well below the federal statutory rate of 35 percent.[17] Other studies suggest that the effective tax rates for US corporations ranged from 12 to 18 percent for a recent period.[18] It should be noted that while effective rates are typically lower than statutory rates, the US average effective rate is still higher, by about six percentage points, than the average effective corporate rate for OECD countries.[19]

A second explanation for the decline is that corporations subject to tax account for much less US business activity than in years past.[20] In 1980, almost 80 percent of net business income was earned by corporations

---

[16] Larger corporations were more likely to owe tax. "Most Large Profitable U.S. Corporations Paid Tax but Effective Tax Rates Differed Significantly," Government Accounting Office, last modified March 17, 2016, http://www.gao.gov/products/GAO-16-363.

[17] "The President's Framework for Business Tax Reform: An Update," April 7, 2016, *available at* https://www.treasury.gov/resource-center/tax-policy/Documents/The-Presidents-Framework-for-Business-Tax-Reform-An-Update-04-04-2016.pdf [hereinafter President Obama's Framework]. For a similar finding, *see* Altshuler et al., *supra* note 15, at 6 n.6 (citing Kevin A. Hassett & Aparna Mathur, "Report Card on Effective Corporate Tax Rates: United States Gets an F," 1 (Tax Policy Outlook, February 2011), American Enterprise Institute [noting that in 2010, the U.S. average effective corporate rate was 74 percent of the statutory rate]).

[18] *See* Damian Paletta, "With Tax Break, Corporate Rate is Lowest in Decades," The Wall Street Journal, February 3, 2012, http://www.wsj.com/articles/SB10001424052970204662204577199492233215330 (citing February 2012 study by Congressional Budget Office finding total corporate federal taxes paid fell to 12.1 percent of profits earned from activities within the United States in FY2011); *see also* Citizens for Tax Justice & Institute on Taxation and Economic Policy, "Corporate Taxpayers & Corporate Tax Dodgers, 2008–2010," November 3, 2011, *available at* http://www.ctj.org/corporatetaxdodgers/CorporateTaxDodgersReport.pdf (finding 280 of the Fortune 500 companies were paying tax at half the 35 percent statutory rate – 18.5 percent in 2009–2010 and 17.3 percent in 2009–2010. Seventy-eight of these companies paid no federal income tax between 2008 and 2010. *See* Hearing Before the Permanent Subcommittee on Investigations, Offshore Profit Shifting and the U.S. Tax Code – Part I (Microsoft & Hewelett-Packard), 12, September 20, 2012, *available at* https://www.gpo.gov/fdsys/pkg/CHRG-112shrg76071/pdf/CHRG-112shrg76071.pdf [hereinafter Microsoft Part I] (providing testimony of Reuven S. Avi-Yonah).

[19] For comparisons, *see* Jane G. Gravelle, "International Corporate Tax Rate Comparisons and Policy Implications," CRS Report $41743, January 6, 2014, *available at* https://www.fas.org/sgp/crs/misc/R41743.pdf.

[20] *See generally* Jason DeBacker & Richard Prisinzano, "The Rise of Partnerships," Tax Notes 147 (2015): 1563.

subject to an entity tax.[21] By 2008, such corporations earned less than 30 percent of total net business income.[22] And today over 60 percent of business income in the United States is earned by pass-through entities that pay no corporate income tax.[23] So-called "S corporations" and a host of other unincorporated entities, such as partnerships and limited liability companies, are not subject to the corporate tax. Instead, their income flows through to the owners who pay tax on their share of the entity's income.[24]

It is easy today to qualify as a pass-through entity and avoid the corporate tax. Since the enactment of subchapter S in 1958, Congress has liberalized the eligibility requirements for S corporation status.[25] And in 1996, the Treasury adopted an elective classification system for unincorporated entities.[26] They need only check a box on a tax form to receive pass-through tax treatment. But some entities, such as publicly traded entities, are mandatorily subject to corporate tax.[27] Most US multinational entities fall into this group.

A third explanation for the erosion of the US corporate tax revenue base is the increasing use of clever tax minimization techniques by multinational companies. One example is the shifting of intellectual property assets and the profits they generate away from the United States and into other countries. Plenty of evidence shows that income shifting is real and is a significant problem for the United States, and that intellectual property accounts for the bulk of it. According to one analysis, income shifting from the United States to other jurisdictions drains as much as $100 billion in corporate revenue from the United States every year.[28] Another study puts the figure at about $130 billion.[29] The Joint

---

[21] Mark P. Keightley, *A Brief Overview of Business Types and Their Tax Treatment* (CRS Report No. R43104) (Washington, DC: Congressional Research Service, 2013), 3.

[22] *Ibid.*

[23] Mark P. Keightley, *A Brief Overview of Business Types and Their Tax Treatment* (CRS Report No. R43104) (Washington, DC: Congressional Research Service, 2013):3.

[24] 26 U.S.C. §§ 701, 702, 704.

[25] *See* Jeffrey A. Maine, "Evaluating Subchapter S in a 'Check-the-Box' World," The Tax Lawyer 51 (1998): 717.

[26] Treas. Reg. § 201.7701-1, -2, -3.   [27] 26 U.S.C. § 7704.

[28] Kimberly A. Clausing, "The Effect of Profit Shifting on the Corporate Tax Base in the United States and Beyond," June 17, 2016, *available at* https://papers.ssrn.com/sol3/papers.cfm?abstract_id=2685442. For an earlier study, *see* Kimberly A. Clausing, "The Revenue Effects of Multinational Firm Income Shifting," Tax Notes (2011): 1560–1566, *available at* https://papers.ssrn.com/sol3/papers.cfm?abstract_id=2488860.

[29] Gabriel Zucman, "Taxing across Borders: Tracking Personal Wealth and Corporate Profits," Journal of Economic Perspectives 28 (2014): 121–48, *available at* http://gabriel-zucman.eu/files/Zucman2014JEP.pdf; *see also* Gabriel Zucman, *The Hidden Wealth of Nations: The Scourge of Tax Havens* (Chicago: University of Chicago Press, 2015).

Committee on Taxation (JCT) itself estimates the loss for FY2016 to be $108.9 billion per year.[30]

Base erosion due to profit shifting is not merely a US concern. Economic studies estimate that for the world as a whole, including the United States, revenue losses may exceed $280 billion per year.[31] The OECD recently found that the annual net tax revenue loss is up to $240 billion.[32] Base erosion is a large problem in developing countries as well.[33]

Searching to uncover the incentives for income shifting, we begin by looking at corporate tax rates of nations. Intuitively, different tax rates should have a lot to do with income shifting. Assume, for example, that a US multinational company, which develops and sells pharmaceuticals, develops a new drug. It earns $10 million from sales in the United States and $10 million from sales in Europe. If both US profits and European profits are taxed at the US rate of 40 percent, the multinational would pay $8 million in taxes ($20 million x .40). If, however, we can structure the transaction so that the European profits are taxed at a foreign country's lower rate – like Ireland's 12.5 percent rate – the multinational would pay only $5,250,000 in taxes ($10 million x .40 and $10 million x .125) for a savings of $2,750,000!

While its seems intuitive that different tax rates among nations would influence where companies choose to locate their intellectual property, the question remains whether any empirical evidence bears this true. A number of economic studies that have looked at the role of corporate tax rates in income shifting have sought to answer the following questions: Is there a negative statistically significant relationship between profits and tax rates? Has the reduction in tax rates abroad increased the incentive to shift income abroad? Unsurprisingly, the studies do find that profits are

---

[30] The Joint Committee on Taxation, "Estimates of Federal Tax Expenditures for Fiscal Years 2015–2019," JCX-141R-15, December 7, 2015, *available at* https://www.jct.gov/publications.html?func-select&id=5.

[31] Clausing, "The Effect of Profit Shifting on the Corporate Tax Base in the United States and Beyond," *supra* note 28. For similar findings, *see* Tim Dowd, Paul Landefeld, & Anne Moore, "Profit Shifting of U.S. Multinationals," (Joint Committee on Taxation, January 6, 2016), *available at* https://papers.ssrn.com/sol3/papers.cfm?abstract_id=2711968; *Measuring and Monitoring BEPS: Action 11 – 2015 Final Report* (OECD Publishing, 2015), *available at* https://www.oecd.org/ctp/measuring-and-monitoring-beps-action-1 1-2015-final-report-9789264241343-en.htm; Ernesto Crivelli, Michael Keen, & Ruud A. de Mooij, "Base Erosion, profit Shifting, and Developing Countries," Oxford University Centre for Business Taxation Working Paper No. 15/118 (May 29, 2015), *available at* https://www.imf.org/external/pubs/cat/longres.aspx?sk=42973.0.

[32] *Measuring and Monitory BEPS: Action 11 Final Report* (Paris: OECD Publishing, 2015).

[33] Mark P. Keightley & Jeffrey M. Stupak, *Corporate Tax Base Erosion and Profit Shifting (BEPS): An Examination of the Data* (CRS Report No. R44013) (Washington, DC: Congressional Research Service, 2015).

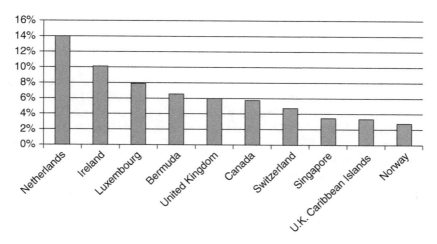

Figure 6.2 Top Gross Income Countries, Affiliates of US Multinational
Firms, 2012 (shown as share of total income)
Source: Kimberly A. Clausing, "The Effect of Profit Shifting on the
Corporate Tax Base in the United States and Beyond," *Tax Notes*
(January 25, 2016)

very sensitive to tax rates. To put it more simply, significant rate differentials encourage income shifting,[34] and most income shifting is done
with respect to the lowest tax rate countries. Indeed the greater the
difference between the domestic and foreign rates, the greater incentive
to shift income abroad.[35] Figure 6.2 above shows the top ten foreign tax

[34] Clausing, "The Effect of Profit Shifting on the Corporate Tax Base in the United
States and Beyond," *supra* note 28. For further evidence that multinationals' decisions
about where to invest are sensitive to tax rates in foreign jurisdictions, *see* Rosanne
Altshuler & Harry Grubert, "Taxpayer Responses to Competitive Tax Policies and
Tax Policy Responses to Competitive Taxpayers: Recent Evidence," Tax Notes
International: Special Reports (2004), *available at* https://ideas.repec.org/p/rut/rutre
s/200406.html; Harry Grubert & John Mutti, "Taxes, Tariffs and Transfer Pricing in
Multinational Corporation Decision Making," *The Review of Economics and Statistics*
73 (1991): 285.

[35] Further evidence of the connection between the lowering of tax rates by foreign countries
and the shifting of profits can be found by comparing the timeline in Figure 6.1 with the
timeline in Figure 1.1 of Chapter 1. Figure 6.1 above reveals that OECD nations
(excluding the United States) began reducing their statutory corporate tax rates in the
late 1990s and early 2000s, while the United States maintained its corporate rate of 40
percent. Figure 1.1 of Chapter 1 interestingly reveals that US revenue loss due to income
shifting began to drastically increase at the same time – late 1990s and early 2000s. And as
one can see from comparing the two charts, the lower the statutory rate of foreign
countries, the greater the US revenue loss due to income shifting.

havens where US multinational companies had foreign affiliate gross profits in the year 2012.[36]

While not all of these ten jurisdictions have low *statutory* rates, as earlier shown in Figure 6.1, they all offer multinationals a very low *effective* tax rate, which is just as appealing. Seven of the locations are tax havens with effective tax rates less than 5 percent: Netherlands, Ireland, Luxembourg, Bermuda, Switzerland, Singapore, and the Caribbean Islands (including the Cayman Islands).[37] These locations produce low effective tax rates for many reasons, for example, favorable tax preferences and even special tax regimes for intellectual property. Some countries may negotiate even lower tax rates to lure foreign business of multinational companies. Apple, for instance, revealed that it was able to negotiate a special corporate tax rate of 2 percent or less with Ireland.[38]

Because of the low effective tax rates, multinationals have an incentive to shift their income to these jurisdictions, and a lot of it. These countries alone account for 50 percent of all foreign income earned by foreign subsidiaries of US multinational companies. Thus, a statistically significant relationship between profits and tax rates exists.[39] Shifting income to these low-tax jurisdictions has effectively lowered the tax bills of many US multinationals. According to US government data, the average tax rate for US controlled foreign subsidiaries declined from 26.0 percent in 1998 to 10.6 percent in 2012.[40] According to a study by Citizens for Tax Justice

---

[36] Gross profits are net income with foreign income tax payments added. Clausing, "The Effect of Profit Shifting on the Corporate Tax Base in the United States and Beyond," *supra* note 28, at 7.

[37] "Effective tax rates are calculated as foreign income taxes paid by all affiliates in a given country relative to their income (net income plus foreign tax payments)." *Ibid.*

[38] Testimony of Apple Inc. Before the Permanent Subcommittee on Investigations, US Senate, May 21, 2013, *available at* www.apple.com/pr/pdf/Apple_Testimony_to_PSI .pdf.

[39] Clausing, "The Effect of Profit Shifting on the Corporate Tax Base in the United States and Beyond," *supra* note 28, at 11. While decisions where to locate income are tax sensitive, decisions where to locate employees, manufacturing, and other economic activity are not. *Ibid.* In other words, there does not appear to be a statistically significant relationship between sales and tax rates or between employees and tax rates. Harry Grubert, "Foreign Taxes and the Growing Share of U.S. Multinational Company Income Abroad: Profits, Not Sales, are Being Globalized," 1, *US Department of Treasury Office of Tax Analysis Working Paper* 103 (February 2012), *available at* www.tr easury.gov/resource-center/tax-policy/tax-analysis/Documents/WP-103.pdf. These low-tax locations, although accounting for half of U.S. multinational foreign income, account for only 5 percent of all U.S. multinational foreign employment. Clausing, "The Effect of Profit Shifting on the Corporate Tax Base in the United States and Beyond," *supra* note 28, at 7–8.

[40] The Joint Committee on Taxation, "Background, Summary, and Implications of the OECD/G20 Base Erosion and Profit Shifting Project," 33, *JCX-139-15*, November 30, 2015, *available at* www.jct.gov/publications.html?func=startdown&id=4853 (citing, in Figure 1 – Average Tax Rate of U.S. CFCs, 1998–2012 [Biennial] – calculations by the

(CTJ), the average tax rate of fifty-seven companies, that publicly disclosed their tax calculations to foreign governments on foreign profits, was 6 percent. For Apple? A mere 2.3 percent.[41]

In addition to encouraging income shifting from a high-tax country to a low-tax country, significant rate differentials put pressure on "transfer pricing," which only further exacerbates the problem. Transfer pricing is a tool used by multinationals to shift profits from high-tax countries to low-tax countries through the pricing of transactions between related affiliates (the licensing of intellectual property from one affiliate to another, or the sale of goods or services from one affiliate to another). Because corporate tax rates vary greatly among countries, foreign subsidiaries of multinationals do not always act at "arm's-length" in order to save taxes. By overpricing or underpricing transactions with foreign affiliates, multinational companies can direct the bulk of their profits from one country to another – from high-tax to low-tax countries and from low-tax to no-tax countries.

Consider Starbucks, which reportedly used transfer pricing to direct the bulk of its United Kingdom profits from the UK to low-tax countries.[42] Starbucks has a foreign subsidiary company in the UK (a high-tax country), as well as subsidiaries in the Netherlands and Switzerland (low-tax countries). The subsidiary in the UK paid a lot for coffee sold to it by the subsidiary in Switzerland, and it paid a lot for the right to use intellectual property to the subsidiary in the Netherlands. Starbucks sets these payments high to maximize the deduction in the United Kingdom and divert income to Switzerland and the Netherlands. Inflated high enough, these payments (deductions in the UK) could result in zero taxes owed to the UK and very low taxes in Switzerland and the Netherlands. Due to the rate differential among these countries, Starbuck's related affiliates are not working at arm's length.

These transfer pricing strategies are quite common. There is evidence of substantial income shifting through transfer pricing,[43] and much of it is

staff of the Joint Committee on Taxation based on data from the Internal Revenue Service [Statistics of Income Division]). "Average tax rates for each CFC are calculated as total cash taxes paid by the CFC to its country of incorporation divided by the sum of its pretax earnings and profits and total cash taxes paid by the CFC to its country of incorporation." *Ibid.*

[41] Citizens for Justice, "Offshore Shell Games 2015: The Use of Offshore Tax Havens by Fortune 500 Companies," *Citizens for Tax Justice*, October 5, 2015, http://ctj.org/ctjreports/2015/10/offshore_shell_games_2015.php#.Vv6bncf6X8s.

[42] Floyd Norris, "Apple's Move Keeps Profit Out of Reach of Taxes," *The New York Times*, last modified May 2, 2013, www.nytimes.com/2013/05/03/business/how-apple-and-other-corporations-move-profit-to-avoid-taxes.html?ref=todayspaper&_r=1.

[43] Testimony of Stephen E. Shay, Deputy Assistant Secretary International Tax Affairs, U.S. Department of Treasury, House Ways and Means Committee, Hearing on Transfer

with respect to transfers of intellectual property between affiliates.[44] The fact that profits may be artificially inflated in low-tax countries (like Switzerland and the Netherlands) and depressed in high-tax countries (like the United States or the United Kingdom) through aggressive transfer pricing in related party transactions is a major government concern. The United States calls it as a "principal tax policy concern" that needs to be addressed.[45] Many high-tax countries have transfer pricing rules to ensure that related affiliates engage in transactions at arm's length and report the proper amount of income. But in reality, it is challenging for countries to stop abusive transfer pricing practices because of the difficulty in monitoring prices, especially for unique and difficult to value assets such as intellectual property. *The Economist* describes these aggressive transfer pricing tax strategies as a "big stick in the corporate treasurer's tax-avoidance armoury."[46]

In sum, the difference between a country's high domestic corporate income tax rate and other countries' low foreign rates provides an incentive for a domestic-based multinational to shift its intellectual property income abroad. Rate differentials also provide an incentive for multinationals to engage in aggressive transfer pricing practices to maximize the tax benefits of income shifting. These incentives only increase as the differences between the domestic rate and foreign rates expand.[47] If the differences become great enough, they may even encourage multinationals to pick up and move their residency to a low-tax

Pricing Issues (July 22, 2010), *available at* www.steptoe.com/resources-detail-7061.html (referencing a 2010 Treasury Study).

[44] A study by the Congressional Research Service suggested that about half the difference between profitability in low-tax and high-tax countries, which could arise from artificial income shifting, was due to transfers of intellectual property (or intangibles) and most of the rest through the allocation of debt. Jane G. Gravelle, *Tax Havens: International Tax Avoidance and Evasion* (CRS Report No. R40623) (Washington, DC: Congressional Research Service, 2015), 10 (citing Harry Grubert, "Intangible Income, Intercompany Transactions, Income Shifting and the Choice of Locations," *National Tax Journal* 56 (2003): 221–42). And a Treasury Department study conducted in 2007 found the potential for improper income shifting was "most acute with respect to cost sharing arrangements involving intangible assets." Joint Committee on Taxation, "Present Law and Background Related to Possible Income Shifting and Transfer Pricing," 6, *JCX-37-10* (July 20, 2010), *available at* www.jct.gov/publications.html?func=startdown&id=3692 [hereinafter JCX-37-10 Report] (citing US Department of the Treasury, "Report to the Congress on Earnings Stripping, Transfer Pricing and U.S. Income Tax Treaties," November 2007).

[45] JCX-37-10 Report, *supra* note, at 5.

[46] Alfredo J. Urquidi, "An Introduction to Transfer Pricing," *New School Economic Review* 3 (2008): 28, *available at* www.newschooljournal.com/files/NSER03/27-45.pdf (citing "Moving Pieces," *The Economist*, February 22, 2007).

[47] Michael J. Graetz & Rachel Doud, "Technological Innovation, International Competition, and the Challenges of International Income Taxation," *Columbia Law Review* 113 (2013): 347.

country.[48] Indeed, the United States has seen a flurry of tax-motivated inversions through mergers with foreign companies.[49]

As noted earlier, many countries have lowered their statutory corporate income tax rate in recent years. The United Kingdom reduced its standard corporate tax rate from 23 percent in 2013 to 21 percent in 2014, and again to 20 percent in 2015.[50] In 2016, it announced that it would cut its corporate tax rate to less than 15 percent, very close to Ireland's low rate of 12.5 percent.[51] There are different motives for rate reduction policies. Some countries may wish simply to increase their share of worldwide corporate tax revenues of multinationals, recognizing the powerful impact low rates can have in income shifting. Others may seek to retain or lure economic activity within their borders, such as research and development (R&D) programs that bring high-value jobs and other attendant benefits.

Ireland has maintained, for the past two decades, the lowest corporate tax rate among the world's most developed countries. It has been key among economic policies to attract investment to Ireland. Ireland seems less motivated by collecting corporate tax revenue than putting people to work, which can increase personal tax revenues. Indeed, as a result of Ireland's low-tax rate, a number of multinational companies have established subsidiaries and put boots on the ground. Apple, for example, chose Ireland instead of a sandy tax haven country for its key offshore subsidiaries. These subsidiaries, according to Apple, employ "nearly 4,000 people engaged in manufacturing, customer service, sales support,

---

[48] Significant rate differentials among countries may affect a multinational company's willingness to locate in a high-tax country following a merger. Harry P. Huizinga & Johannes Voget, "International Taxation and the Direction and Volume of Cross Border M&A," *The Journal of Finance* 64 (2009): 1217. Significant rate differentials may also encourage inversions, which are designed to reduce a multinational's effective tax rate without changing business operations. "Corporate Tactics to Avoid Taxes," *The New York Times*, April 13, 2016, www.nytimes.com/2016/04/14/opinion/corporate-tactics-to-avoid-taxes.html?_r=1. (letter to editor by Avi-Yonah).

[49] *See* Donald J. Marples & Jane G. Gravelle, *Corporate Expatriation, Inversions, and Mergers: Tax Issues* (CRS Report No. R43568) (Washington, DC: Congressional Research Service, 2016). *See also* Diana Furchtgott-Roth, "Free Pfizer! Why Inversions Are Good for the U.S.," *The New York Times*, April 7, 2016, www.nytimes.com/2016/04/08/opinion/free-pfizer-why-inversions-are-good-for-the-us.html?_r=0; "Corporate Tactics to Avoid Taxes," *supra* note 48; Huizinga & Voget, *supra* note 48.

[50] KPMG, "United Kingdom Country Profile," 5, *EU Tax Centre* (March 2013), *available at* www.kpmg.com/Global/en/services/Tax/regional-tax-centers/european-union-tax-centre/Documents/eu-country-profiles/2013-uk.pdf.

[51] "Brexit: George Osborne Pledges to Cut Corporate Tax," *BBC News*, July 4, 2016, www.bbc.com/news/business-36699642. Earlier, in 2010, the UK government announced its effort "to create the most comprehensive corporate tax regime in the G20." *See* Martin A. Sullivan, "The U.K. Patent Box: Extraordinary Complexity," *Tax Notes*, December 12, 2011: 1307.

supply chain and risk management operations and finance support services."[52]

The United States maintains one of the highest corporate income tax rates in the world (40 percent when subnational taxes are considered). As a result, US multinationals benefit from strategies aimed at shifting income offshore. The foreign share of worldwide income of US multinational corporations has risen sharply in recent years,[53] and income shifting has become worse as the difference between the US statutory rate and the rates in foreign countries has increased. The US has acknowledged this phenomenon.[54] Nevertheless, the United States continues to impose its high corporate tax on both domestic and foreign income of resident multinationals.

Bases of Jurisdiction to Tax Cross-Border Income (and Dividend Tax Policies)

Countries adopt different approaches to taxing foreign income of their resident multinational companies, which can induce the shifting of intellectual property income offshore.

Most countries have a *territorial* system of taxation, meaning they collect tax only on income earned within their territorial borders. These countries generally do not seek to tax foreign income earned directly abroad or to tax foreign income earned indirectly abroad through foreign subsidiaries. (Note that no country has a pure territorial system, as countries tax some types of foreign income earned abroad.) Tax exemption is achieved in the latter case by exempting dividend payments received by a domestic multinational company from its foreign subsidiary company. Indeed, territorial systems are often referred to as dividend exemption systems. To illustrate, France has a territorial income tax base.[55] Thus, French resident companies are subject to French corporate income tax on their French source income only. Profits derived from active business carried on overseas and any dividends received from foreign subsidiaries are generally not subject to French corporate income tax. Some countries, such as France, have long-standing territorial systems. Other countries, such as the United Kingdom and Japan, have more

---

[52] Testimony of Apple Inc., *supra* note 38, at 2.   [53] Grubert, *supra* note 39, at 1.

[54] President Obama's Framework, *supra* note 17, at 14. The Trump Administration, in response, has proposed cutting the corporate tax rate from 35 percent to 15 percent.

[55] KPMG, "France Country Profile," 4, *EU Tax Centre* (March 2013), *available at* www .kpmg.com/global/en/services/tax/regional-tax-centers/european-union-tax-centre/docu ments/eu-country-profiles/2013-france.pdf; Bloomberg BNA, Tax and Accounting Center, *Global Tax Guide*, 6, July 31, 2014, *available at* http://taxandaccounting.bna.co m/bta/display/batch_print_display.adp [hereinafter Global Tax Guide].

recently (2009) moved to a territorial approach to international taxation.[56]

The second approach, known as a *worldwide* system, taxes resident companies on their worldwide income. That is, both domestic source income (earned at home) and foreign source income (earned abroad). Issues of double taxation may arise for taxpayers residing in a country that taxes income on a worldwide approach. Because resident companies in these countries are subject to domestic tax on their worldwide income, income earned in a foreign country may be taxable in both the home country as well as in the foreign country. To avoid this problem, countries often create bilateral tax treaties, which credit the taxes paid to one country toward the taxes by another.[57] Legislative relief provides an additional approach to mitigate double taxation. Some countries choose to offer a tax credit for foreign taxes paid, while others offer a tax deduction. The United States is one of few remaining countries with a worldwide approach.[58] Tax credits generally allow US corporations to offset US taxes with the income taxes paid in the foreign country – that is, taxes paid directly to foreign tax authorities or indirectly by foreign subsidiaries on distributed earnings.[59]

It should be pointed out that some countries claim to have a worldwide system, but then exempt most foreign dividends and branch profits from taxation, which makes them effectively territorial systems. Germany subjects a German multinational to tax on its worldwide income, but then exempts foreign subsidiary dividends (and foreign branch income earned in a treaty country), making it a territorial system.[60]

---

[56] *See* Stephanie Berrong, "News Analysis: How Much Would Territoriality Cost?," *Tax Notes Today*, Apr. 20, 2011.

[57] "The OECD Has Developed a Model Treaty Resolving Issues of Double Taxation." *Model Tax Convention on Income and on Capital: Condensed Version 2014* (OECD Publishing, 2014), *available at* http://dx.doi.org/10.1787/mtc_cond-2014-en.

[58] Jason Fichtner & Adam N. Michel, "The OECD's Conquest of the United States: Understanding the Costs and Consequences of the BEPS Project and Tax Harmonization," Mercatus Center George Mason University, March 2016: 20 (noting that in the early 20th century, all but one of the thirty-four OECD countries had a worldwide tax system; today the United States is one of only six countries that still tax worldwide income). Countries that still take a worldwide approach include Chile, Ireland, Mexico, and South Korea.

[59] I.R.C. §§ 901–908. The United States also allows a deduction for foreign income taxes. 26 U.S.C. § 164(a). A taxpayer is not allowed to take both a deduction and a credit for the same foreign income tax, and therefore must choose between the two. 26 U.S.C. § 275 (a)(4).

[60] Altshuler et al., *supra* note 15, at 28 (citing Andreas Perdelwitz, "Germany: Corporate Taxation Country Analysis," Sections 1.1.1, 1.1.3 [Amsterdam: International Bureau of Fiscal Documentation, 2014]). In Japan, 95 percent of foreign subsidiary dividends paid to a Japanese multinational are exempt if the Japanese company owns at least 25 percent of the foreign subsidiary. *Ibid.* at 26.

All countries, whether adopting a territorial or worldwide approach, claim jurisdiction to tax income earned within their borders.[61] Even countries that tax resident companies on their worldwide income also typically tax foreign companies on income earned within their borders. The United States, for instance, taxes foreign companies on their US source income. Subject to some important exceptions addressed in Chapter 8, the United States does not tax foreign companies on their foreign source income even if the foreign company is a wholly owned subsidiary of a US company. Foreign income earned by a foreign subsidiary, however, will be subject to US taxation if, and when, it is repatriated as a dividend to the US parent. Thus, US tax on foreign income of a foreign subsidiary of a US parent can be delayed until the foreign income is realized by the US parent in the form of a dividend. At that point, it will be subject to the 35 percent US corporate tax rate, although a tax credit may be allowed for foreign income taxes paid by foreign subsidiaries on distributed earnings.[62] This delay is commonly known as *deferral*. Deferral is really just the act of delaying the recognition of income and payment of tax until a later date.[63]

With this framework, we begin to see how a worldwide approach to taxation encourages the use of foreign subsidiaries to achieve deferral – for example, the ability of US multinationals to shift income to foreign subsidiaries in low-tax countries to avoid current US taxation of foreign earnings (until brought home in the form of dividends to the US parent) and to increase their current after tax profits.[64] To flesh this out, consider a US multinational company with global sales. US profits earned by the US multinational are clearly subject to current US taxation (taxed when

---

[61] *See* Timothy J. Goodspeed & Ann Dryden Witte, "International Taxation," *in* *Encyclopedia of Law and Economics* 4 (1999): 257, *available at* http://encyclo.findlaw.co m/6080book.pdf. ("All countries claim the right to tax all income generated within that country's border; that is, all countries begin with a source basis for taxation.")

[62] 26 U.S.C. §§ 901, 902, 904. Credits for foreign taxes paid with respect to the distributed earnings as well as excess foreign taxes paid in respect of other foreign income may be sufficient to offset the US tax on the dividend. Microsoft Part I, *supra* note 18, at 10 (providing testimony of Stephen E. Shay). For ways in which US multinationals use excess foreign tax credits against low taxed foreign income, *see* J. Clifton Fleming, Jr., Robert J. Peroni, & Stephen E. Shay, "Reform and Simplification of the U.S. Foreign Tax Credit Rules," *Tax Notes* 101 (2003): 103.

[63] Neal Frankle, "What is Tax Deferral?," *Wealth Pilgrim*, November 18, 2015, www.weal thpilgrim.com/what-is-tax-deferral/.

[64] *See* Office of Tax Policy, U.S. Department of Treasury, "The Deferral of Income Earned through U.S. Controlled Foreign Corporations," 12 (December 2000), *available at* www.treasury.gov/resource-center/tax-policy/Documents/Report-SubpartF-2000.pdf [hereinafter Subpart F Study]. *See also* President Obama's Framework, *supra* note 17, at 11–12 ("Because of deferral, U.S. corporations have a significant opportunity to reduce overall taxes paid by shifting profits to low-tax jurisdictions").

earned). But what about the foreign profits? Current US taxation of the US multinational's foreign income depends really on how foreign operations are conducted. If the foreign income is earned directly by the US multinational (i.e., through branches as opposed to controlled foreign subsidiaries), the foreign income will be subject to current US taxation when earned. If, however, a US multinational sets up foreign subsidiaries for foreign operations, the foreign income of those subsidiaries will not be subject to US taxation when earned. It will only be subject to US taxation if, and when, the subsidiary pays dividends to the US parent.[65]

As is often the case, many US multinationals delay paying themselves dividends to avoid the US tax hit. By delaying payment of taxes, multinationals can enjoy the time value of money by reinvesting the amount of taxes that would have been due at a low foreign tax rate. If payment is deferred long enough, the return on investment eventually exceeds the amount of tax liability, wiping it out.[66] It is thus feasible that foreign income may be retained abroad indefinitely, resulting in US multinationals never paying US taxes on their foreign income.[67] To the extent that US multinationals, who have the resources to do so, purposefully keep income from their foreign subsidiaries overseas, they begin to effectively create a territorial system for themselves. Thus, worldwide taxation is largely to blame for the large sum of foreign profits stashed overseas.[68]

Deferral creates a strong incentive to move intellectual property and related income to low-tax or no-tax jurisdictions.[69] The incentive for multinational companies to shift income abroad is increased when they are able to use deferred earnings for investment in the United States.[70] Technically, US multinationals are not supposed to use deferred earnings for US operations. But, in reality, many find a way.[71]

Worldwide taxation, including the taxation of repatriated foreign earnings, encourages some US multinationals to take more drastic measures and move their tax residence outside the United States.[72] Just as the high US corporate tax rate has been blamed for inversions, the US's taxation of worldwide income provides another incentive to invert to territorial nations.

[65] Altshuler et al., *supra* note 15, at 11.   [66] Subpart F Study, *supra* note 64.
[67] President Obama's Framework, *supra* note 17, at 11–12.
[68] Danny Yadron, Kate Linebaugh, & Jessica E. Lessin, "Apple Avoided Taxes on Overseas Billions, Senate Panel Finds," *The Wall Street Journal*, May 20, 2013, www.wsj.com/art icles/SB10001424127887324787004578495250424727708 (citing Mihir Desai, a professor at Harvard Business School).
[69] Microsoft Part I, *supra* note 18, at 10 (providing testimony of Stephen E. Shay).
[70] *Ibid.*
[71] Hewlett-Packard, for example, used a short-term loan program (a series of back to back to back to back loans) to get between $6 billion and $9 billion of offshore profits to the US in 2010 without paying US taxes.
[72] Altshuler et al., *supra* note 15, at 16.

Consider a US multinational company with sales in the United States, as well as Bermuda, Canada, Ireland, and Mexico. The US multinational will pay 35 percent on income earned in each country. But if that multinational can invert to Canada, which has a territorial system, it will pay 35 percent only on income earned in the United States, but zero percent in Bermuda, 15 percent in Canada, 12.5 percent in Ireland, and 30 percent in Mexico.[73] The United States has seen a recent flurry of tax-motivated inversions through mergers with foreign companies located in low-tax, territorial system countries. The number has risen drastically in the past decade.[74]

As a final point, it should be noted that the dividend tax policy of countries can also contribute to incentives to shift income. The United States uses a "classical" corporate tax system, which imposes double taxation. It first taxes a US multinational company on its worldwide income (domestic income as well as foreign income earned directly or indirectly through foreign subsidiary dividends). It then taxes shareholders of the US multinational company when they receive a dividend distribution regardless of whether the dividends are with respect to domestic or foreign profits, and regardless of the amount of domestic and foreign taxes paid with respect to that income.[75] For individuals, US dividends are taxed at a preferential rate (top 23.8 percent, which includes the 3.8 percent Medicare tax on net investment income, compared with a top ordinary income tax rate of 39.6 percent). But when combined with the corporate tax rate, the rate on distributed corporate income is quite high.[76] This high double taxation adversely affects foreign profits distributed by a US multinational company to its US resident shareholders.

Standards for Determining Corporate Residency

Under the two bases of jurisdiction discussed above (territory and worldwide), countries have developed conflicting rules for determining whether a corporation is a resident or nonresident taxpayer, which can incentivize multinationals to utilize foreign IP Holding Companies. Much is at stake for multinational companies. For example, if a multinational company is deemed to be a resident of the US (which has a worldwide system), it will have to pay tax at the US rate (35 percent) on all of its income, foreign and domestic. In contrast, if a multinational

---

[73] Graetz & Doud, *supra* note 47.   [74] *See* Marples & Gravelle, *supra* note 49.

[75] In the United States, subsidiary loans to or investments in US parent corporations are treated as dividend distributions subject to tax. 26 U.S.C. § 956. But excess foreign tax credits from operations in high-tax countries may be used to avoid taxes on repatriated dividends from low-tax countries.

[76] OECD Historical Table II.1, *supra* note 8.

company decides to be a resident of neighboring Canada (territorial system), it will be taxed at the US rate only on income earned in the United States. For the company residing in Canada, income earned in other countries will be taxed at those countries' lower rates as well.

Some countries determine the residence of a corporation based on its *place of incorporation*. In the United States, for example, the test for determining whether a corporation is a domestic or foreign corporation for US tax purposes is easy because one must look only to where it was created or organized.[77] From the United States' perspective, if a company is incorporated in the United States it is a domestic corporation and its worldwide income is subject to US taxation. If a company is incorporated outside the United States, then it is a foreign corporation and only its US source income, if any, is subject to US taxation.

Another method of determining the residence of a corporation involves looking to *where central management and control is exercised*. Until recently, Ireland applied such a residency test for certain companies. Ireland's general rule is that an Irish-incorporated company is a resident for Irish tax purposes regardless of where it is managed and controlled. Under an important exception, however, an Irish-incorporated company was deemed a resident of the country where it was managed or controlled if the company (1) was controlled by a parent company in an EU or tax-treaty country, like the United States; and (2) was engaged in a trade in Ireland or related to a company that was. Under this exception, a US multinational company could form an IP Holding Company in Ireland, but manage it in Bermuda. Although incorporated in Ireland, such a company would not be viewed by Ireland as an Irish company subject to Irish taxes as long as such company was related to another company (e.g., a second-tier, Irish-incorporated subsidiary) engaged in a trade in Ireland.[78] This exception paved the way for the popular tax planning strategy known as the "Double Irish" structure described more fully in Chapter 7. In 2015, Ireland changed its tax residency rules so that all Irish-registered companies are considered tax residents in Ireland. Even under the new law, however, there is an important treaty-based exception, which can lead to similar results – residency of an Irish-incorporated company will be based on place of management and control.[79]

---

[77] 26 U.S.C. § 7701(a)(3)–(4).

[78] KPMG, "Ireland Country Profile," *supra* note 5, at 2 (noting that an Irish-incorporated company is a resident for tax purposes regardless of where it is managed and controlled, subject to some important exceptions [e.g., companies controlled by an EU or tax treaty country where the company or a related company is engaged in a trade in Ireland]).

[79] *See* Sam Schechner, "Ireland to Close 'Double Irish' Tax Loophole: Change to Come Slowly, Particularly Affecting U.S. Tech Firms Like Google and Facebook," *The Wall Street Journal*, last modified October 14, 2014, www.wsj.com/articles/ireland-to-close-double-irish-tax-loophole-1413295755.

Many countries adopt a broader view of residency by using both a place-of-incorporation test and place-of-management test. Examples include, Switzerland,[80] the United Kingdom,[81] and Australia.[82] Central management and control typically means the highest level of decision making (typically by directors of a company) and not day-to-day control.

These different residency rules can produce a situation in which a company is considered a resident of more than one country. For these cases, most bilateral treaties contain provisions to determine residency. Many provide that a corporation will be considered a resident of the country where the principal place of business is or where effective management is. For example, the Ireland-Malta Treaty provides that if a corporation is a resident of both Ireland and Malta, then it shall be deemed to be a resident of the country in which its place of effective management is situated.[83] This underscores the important role treaties can play if a multinational desires to direct intellectual property profits to a low-tax country. Ireland does not have a treaty with Bermuda, so a new company incorporated in Ireland but doing business in Bermuda would be deemed a tax resident of Ireland under Ireland's updated residency rules and subject to Irish taxes. Ireland does have a treaty with Malta, however, so a company incorporated in Ireland but doing business in Malta can be deemed a Malta corporation not subject to Irish taxes.[84]

---

[80] KPMG, "Switzerland Country Profile," 2, *EU Tax Centre* (March 2013), *available at* www.kpmg.com/Global/en/services/Tax/regional-tax-centers/european-union-tax-cen tre/Documents/eu-country-profiles/2013-switzerland.pdf.

[81] KPMG, "United Kingdom Country Profile," *supra* note 50, at 2. Altshuler et al., *supra* note 15, at 16 (noting the same with Germany).

[82] Tom Toryanik, "Australia: Individual Taxation Country Analysis," Section 1.10.1, (Amsterdam: International Bureau of Fiscal Documentation, 2014).

[83] Convention Between Ireland And Malta For The Avoidance Of Double Taxation And The Prevention Of Fiscal Evasion With Respect To Taxes On Income, Art. 4(3), *available at* www.revenue.ie/en/practitioner/law/double/malta.pdf. See *also* Agreement Between the Government of Ireland and the Government of the Hong Kong Special Administrative Region of The People's Republic of China for the Avoidance of Double Taxation and the Prevention of Fiscal Evasion with Respect to Taxes on Income, Art. 4 (3), *available at* www.revenue.ie/en/practitioner/law/double/hong-kong.pdf.

[84] It could also be noted that treaties often impact whether withholding tax must be withheld on royalty payments. Some countries impose a flat-rate source-based tax (known as withholding tax) on royalty payments to another company. Bilateral treaties, however, often reduce or exempt the withholding tax. In Ireland, for example, patent royalties are generally subject to Irish withholding tax. However, an Irish company does not have to withhold tax on a royalty payment to a foreign company if the foreign company is not an Irish resident but is a resident for tax purposes in another EU Member State or country that has entered into a double taxation agreement with Ireland, which imposes a tax that generally applies to royalties receivable in that territory from outside sources. *See* Authur Cox, *supra* note 6. Article 12(2) of the Ireland-Hong Kong Treaty provides that a royalty withholding tax not to exceed 3 percent may be charged by either country in the event

Sometimes, multinational corporations exploit the disparate residency rules to make income magically disappear. Indeed, it is possible to form a foreign subsidiary that is not, for tax purposes, a resident in any country – meaning no tax returns and no taxes owed to any national government! To illustrate this anomaly, assume, for example, that "High Tax Country" decides whether it can tax a corporation based on place of incorporation, but "Tax Haven Country" decides whether it can tax a corporation based on place of management. Now assume a multinational company incorporates a foreign subsidiary in Tax Haven Country, but the people managing that subsidiary are located in the High Tax Country. High Tax Country would view it as a resident of Tax Haven Country because it was incorporated in Tax Haven Country. Likewise, Tax Haven Country would view it as a resident of the High Tax Country because it was managed in High Tax Country. This situation has been described as "the Holy Grail of tax avoidance" – a foreign IP Holding Company that is not, for tax purposes, a resident in any country – it is neither here nor there.[85] It is an international phantom!

Hybrid Entity Structures

Another loophole that multinational companies exploit for their intellectual property income shifting is the use of so-called hybrid entities. In the 1990s, the US Treasury Department approved a quirky regulation that allows companies to declare what type of entity they are for US tax purposes by simply checking a box on a form. Under the regulations, known as "check-the-box" regulations, US multinational companies can actually declare controlled foreign subsidiaries as "disregarded" for US tax purposes – that is, as though they do not exist under US tax law.[86] The result is the creation of *hybrid entities*.

How are hybrid entities treated in other countries? Although a "checked" foreign IP Holding Company of a US parent is disregarded as a separate entity by the United States, it is treated as a corporation by foreign countries. Thus, a low-tax foreign country would recognize payments made to and from the subsidiary, whereas the United States would not. In short, other countries respect the subsidiary as a true company.

that royalties arise in one country and the beneficial owner of the royalties is a resident of the other country.

[85] *See* Statement of Senator Carl Levin (D-Mich). Before U.S. Senate Permanent Subcommittee on Investigations on Offshore Profit Shifting and the U.S. Tax Code – Part 2 (Apple Inc.), May 21, 2013, *available at* www.gpo.gov/fdsys/pkg/CHRG-113shrg81657/pdf/CHRG-113shrg81657.pdf.

[86] Certain specific organizations in various countries are always de facto corporations. *See* Treas. Reg. § 301.7701–2(b)(8) (listing foreign entities always classified as corporations).

The United States treats it as a phantom. Multinationals have been able to utilize hybrid entities to achieve favorable tax outcomes. An example would be a company with tax deductions in foreign countries (lower taxes paid to foreign countries), and no corresponding income in the United States (no increased taxes paid to the United States).

To understand how hybrid entities can achieve tax savings, one must understand something about the US antideferral rules known as the controlled foreign corporation ("CFC") rules.[87] Under these rules, royalties received by a controlled foreign subsidiary of a US parent company are subject to current US taxation even if they haven't been paid out as dividends to the US parent. But, if those payments are being received by a "checked" foreign subsidiary that is disregarded for US tax purposes (a phantom), then those royalty receipts are disregarded for US tax purposes and not subject to current US taxation under the CFC rules. Thus, the payment could produce a deduction in a foreign country that recognizes the paying company as an entity and allows a deduction for payment made by that entity, while there would still be no corresponding income inclusion in the United States since the CFC rules were purposefully avoided by checking a box on a form. We take a closer look at these rules in Chapter 8, and see there how Apple, Uber, and others utilize check-the-box to avoid them.

Research and Development (R&D) Incentives

We have seen how the general tax policies of a nation (e.g., having a low corporate income tax rate) can attract intellectual property and income that flows therefrom. In addition to the incentives described above, many countries offer additional bonuses for multinationals to move their intellectual property and its related income to their jurisdictions.

Intellectual property is targeted for special treatment for obvious reasons. Economists generally agree that intellectual property development is important to economic growth and building national wealth.[88] And they believe that government support of intellectual property development is

---

[87] Cynthia Ram Sweitzer, "Analyzing Subpart F in light of Check-the-Box," *Akron Tax Journal* 20 (2005): 1.

[88] Graetz & Doud, *supra* note 47, at 348 (citing, e.g., Robert M. Solow, "Technical Change and the Aggregate Production Function," *The Review of Economics and Statistics* 39 (1957): 320; Joseph F. Brodley, "The Economic Goals of Antitrust, Efficiency, Consumer Welfare, and Technological Progress," *New York University Law Review* 62 (1987): 1026; Herbert Hovenkamp, "Restraints on Innovation," *Cardozo Law Review* 29 (2007): 253.

important.[89] Governments support intellectual property development in a variety of ways, such as legal protections for intellectual property, grants, direct loans, and loan guarantees, and various tax incentives. These tax incentives generally fall within one of two categories: (1) those on the development side of intellectual property, such as tax deductions and credits for qualified research spending; and (2) those on the income side of intellectual property, such as a low effective rate on income from intellectual property.[90] Both of these incentives reduce the effective tax rate on intellectual property income. And a combination of the two – a current deduction for research expenses that contribute to low-taxed income – is a powerful incentive to shift income.

We start by looking first at the front end of the intellectual property life cycle (i.e., the development side of intellectual property). Many countries provide a tax deduction, a tax credit, or a combination of the two for spending on qualified R&D.[91] Tax deductions are historically justified as a means to tax only the net income of a taxpayer, whereas tax credits are typically driven from political judgments to subsidize or encourage certain activities. But today, both deductions and credits are used to deliberately attempt to drive economic decision making and promote socially desirable activities. For R&D, both are generally designed to encourage private spending that would not otherwise occur in the market. It is generally thought that R&D produces positive spillover effects, such as attracting engineers, scientists, and other high-value workers as well as luring capital essential for intellectual property.[92] Countries adopt R&D deductions and credits to reduce market failures in the innovation sector, although some commentators have suggested special tax incentives are inappropriate.[93]

[89] Graetz & Doud, *supra* note 47, at 349 (citing Charles I. Jones & John C. Williams, "Measuring the Social Return to R&D," *The Quarterly Journal of Economics* 113 (1998): 1133; OECD, "Tax Incentives for Research and Development: Trends and Issues," 6, (2002), *available at* www.oecd.org/sti/inno/2498389.pdf; Office of Tax Policy, U.S. Department of the Treasury, "Investing in U.S. Competitiveness: The Benefits of Enhancing the Research and Experimentation (R&E) Tax Credit," 1 (2011), *available at* www.treasury.gov/resource-center/tax-policy/Documents/Report-Investing-in-US-Comp etitiveness-2011.pdf.

[90] Some countries offer employment tax incentives for R&D employees. *See* Graetz & Doud, *supra* note 47, at 354 (describing Netherlands' special payroll tax deduction, Belgium's partial withholding tax exemption for wages paid to certain R&D workers, and Hungary's tax credit for salary costs related to research activities).

[91] Some countries, like Bulgaria, Luxembourg, and Poland, offer no special tax regimes for companies that conduct research and development activities. *See* Global Tax Chart, *supra* note 4.

[92] Graetz & Doud, *supra* note 47, at 406 (article in Part II.D. summarizes data on benefits of R&D tax incentives).

[93] *See* David Hasen, "Taxation and Innovation – A Sectorial Approach" (March 11, 2016), *available at* https://papers.ssrn.com/sol3/papers.cfm?abstract_id=2746681. *See also* Graetz & Doud, *supra* note 47, at 406 (arguing "R&D tax incentives are inevitably

Before delving into specific deductions and credits for R&D, it should be noted that tax deductions and credits differ in one important way. Tax deductions reduce income before the tax rate is applied, whereas tax credits reduce tax liability dollar for dollar. Thus, a credit is worth more to a taxpayer since a deduction only reduces tax liability in proportion to the taxpayer's top marginal tax rate. For this reason, tax credits may be a more powerful tool in incentivizing R&D activity within a country's borders.

With respect to tax deductions, many countries allow R&D costs to be immediately expensed as opposed to being capitalized and amortized over time. An immediate deduction for R&D costs serves dual functions. It encourages investment in research and reduces the uncertainties regarding timing for claiming research and development deductions. The designs of R&D deductions vary amongst countries. The United States, for instance, has a 100 percent deduction for costs qualifying as research or experimental expenditures.[94] Some countries, in contrast, offer enhanced deductions greater than 100 percent for qualifying research expenditures.[95] The United Kingdom, for example, provides an enhanced deduction of up to 130 percent for large companies.[96] In Singapore, for years 2011 to 2018, expenditures for R&D and certain other qualifying activities (up to a certain expenditure cap) can qualify for 400 percent write-off allowances (with expenditures exceeding the cap eligible for a 100 percent write-off allowances).[97]

overbroad, rewarding spending that would have occurred without the tax break, and subsidizing R&D that produces little or no positive spillover"). For additional thoughts about tax-subsidized research, see Martin A. Sullivan, "Will International Tax Reform Slow U.S. Technology Development?," *Tax Notes* 141 (2013): 459, *available at* http:// taxprof.typepad.com/files/141tn0459.pdf.

[94] 26 U.S.C. § 174 (enacted in 1954). Research or experimental expenditures are broadly defined in the regulations as "expenditures incurred in connection with the taxpayer's trade or business which represent research and development costs in the experimental or laboratory sense," and generally include all "costs incident to the development or improvement of a product." Treas. Reg. § 1.174–2(a)(1). Expenditures are incurred in the experimental or laboratory sense if they are incurred in activities "intended to discover information that would eliminate uncertainty concerning the development or improvement of a product." Treas. Reg. 1.174–2(a)(1).

[95] Some countries were early to adopt enhanced deductions for R&D, such as Austria which adopted a 125 percent deduction in 1988. *See* Graetz & Doud, *supra* note 47 (summarizing countries that have offered super deductions for R&D, like Austria, Hungary, the United Kingdom, Denmark, and Czech Republic).

[96] KPMG, "United Kingdom Country Profile," *supra* note 50, at 5; PricewaterhouseCoopers "Global Research & Development Incentives Group," *PricewaterhouseCoopers* (November 1, 2012): 23, *available at* www.pwc.com/gx/en/tax/as sets/pwc-global-research-development-incentives-group-november-2012-pdf.pdf.

[97] "Writing-Down Allowances for Intellectual Property Rights," Inland Revenue Authority of Singapore, accessed October 20, 2016, www.iras.gov.sg/irashome/Businesses/Comp anies/Working-out-Corporate-Income-Taxes/Claiming-Allowances/Writing-Down-All owances-for-Intellectual-Property-Rights/.

Many countries offer a tax credit for qualified research spending.[98] The credit amount varies from country to country. In the United States, the R&D tax credit percentage is 20 percent.[99]

Countries have manipulated their deductions and credits to attract multinational companies with large R&D activities. For example, in some countries, like the United States, the R&D credit is *incremental* (that is, it is a percentage of qualified research spending above a base amount, which can be thought of as a company's normal level of R&D investment).[100] An incremental credit is not as beneficial because it only applies if a multinational is increasing its R&D over time. In most countries, however, like the United Kingdom, the R&D credit is *volume based*, meaning the tax credit depends simply on the volume or amount of annual qualified R&D expenditures.[101] Some countries, such as Ireland and France, have moved from a purely incremental credit to one that is volume based in order to make their credit more attractive to multinational companies with large R&D activities.[102]

Multinational companies with large R&D arms look to other design features. For example, in some countries, like the United States, the same

---

[98] The United States enacted its research credit in 1981. France enacted its credit two years later in 1983. *See* Benoit Mulkay & Jacques Mairesse, *Financing R&D Through Tax Credit in France* 3 (May 2008), 1, http://zinc.zew.de/pub/zew-docs/veranstaltungen/inno vationpatenting2008/papers/MulkayMairesse.pdf. Some other countries adopted their credits much later, for example, Hungary, 2003 and Ireland, 2004. Eduard Sporken & Edwin Gommers revised by Csaba László, Tamás Mlinárik, & Zsófia Pongrácz, "Tax Treatment of R&D Expenses in Hungary," *International Transfer Pricing Journal* 14 (2007): 24–25. Eduard Sporken & Edwin Gommers revised by Tom Maguire, "Tax Treatment of R&D Expenses in Ireland," *International Transfer Pricing Journal* 14 (2007): 27–28.

[99] 26 U.S.C. § 41.

[100] 26 U.S.C. § 41(a)(1). The term qualified research is defined as research eligible for tax deduction under section 174. *See also* 26 U.S.C. § 41(d) (providing additional requirements as well).

[101] *See, e.g.*, Tax Reform Options: Incentives for Innovation: Hearing Before the Senate Committee On Finance, 112th Congress 57 (September 20, 2011), *available at* www .finance.senate.gov/imo/media/doc/76378.pdf (prepared testimony of Dirk Pilat, Head, Structural Policy Division, OECD Directorate for Since, Technology, and Industry), *available at* www.finance.senate.gov/imo/media/doc/OECD%20SFC%20Hearing%20 testimony%209%2020%2011.pdf. "Looking to the Future: Life after the 'Double Irish,' " *International Tax Review*, February 24, 2015, www.internationaltaxreview.co m/Article/3430276/Looking-to-the-future-Life-after-the-Double-Irish.html.

[102] "Looking to the Future: Life after the 'Double Irish,' " *supra* note 101. Patrick Eparvier, "Monitoring and Analysis of Policies and Public Financing Instruments Conducive to Higher Levels of R&D Investment – The 'POLICY MIX' Project – Country Review FRANCE," 19, March 2007, *available at* http://ec.europa.eu/invest-in-research/pdf/do wnload_en/france.pdf; PricewaterhouseCoopers, *supra* note 96, at 13; Eduard Sporken & Edwin Gommers revised by Alan Katiya, Nathalie Cordier-Deltour, & Vincent Berger, "Tax Treatment of R&D Expenses in France," *International Transfer Pricing Journal* 14 (2007): 14–18.

research dollar cannot qualify for both current tax deduction and tax credit.[103] But in more tax-friendly countries, like Ireland, it is possible.[104] In some countries, the R&D tax credit is not allowed for capital expenditures on buildings or structures used in carrying on research and development activities. For other friendlier jurisdictions, the credit is permitted but subject to limitation. For some the credit is not refundable, but in others it is.

An interesting thing about all of these front-ended tax incentives is that they generally are not conditioned on profits remaining in, and taxed by, the country that provided the tax incentive. Thus, through the use of creative tax planning strategies, profits attributable to R&D in the United States do not have to stay in the United States. As will be seen in Chapter 7, many US multinational entities conduct the vast amount of research in the United States and claim credits for R&D spending, but the vast amount of worldwide profits attributable to that research is not taxed in the United States. As an example, Microsoft spent over $7.8 billion (out of a total R&D budget of $9.1 billion) on R&D in the United States and received $200 million in US tax credits.[105] Much of their profit attributable to the research conducted in the United States, however, was located in low-tax foreign countries.[106]

Patent Boxes

We now turn to tax incentives on the *income side* of intellectual property. Many countries in recent years have enacted back-ended tax incentives called "innovation boxes" or "patent boxes" to encourage multinational companies to move their intellectual property and innovation activities within their borders. Patent boxes basically provide a reduced effective tax rate on income associated with eligible intellectual property. Some patent box regimes *exempt income* (royalty income, and, in some cases gains from disposal) from qualifying intellectual property, which has the effect of reducing the effective corporate tax rate on that intellectual property. Exemption rates vary – for example, 80 percent in Belgium

---

[103] In the United States, to the extent a credit is taken under section 41, deductions under section 174 must be reduced. 26 U.S.C. § 280C. A taxpayer can elect to claim a reduced research credit under section 41 and thereby avoid a reduction of the section 174 deduction. 26 U.S.C. § 280C(c)(1)–(3).

[104] Ireland's R&D tax credit (25 percent) and the corporate tax deduction available for qualifying R&D (12.5 percent) provide an overall effective rate of 37.5 percent on certain R&D expenditure. "Tax Facts 2015," PricewaterhouseCoopers, accessed October 20, 2016, *available at* http://download.pwc.com/ie/pubs/2015-pwc-ireland-tax-facts.pdf.

[105] Microsoft Part I, *supra* note 18, at 20.   [106] Microsoft Part I, *supra* note 18, at 20.

and Luxembourg, but 50 percent in Hungary and Spain. In contrast, some patent box regimes allow certain income from qualifying intellectual property to be taxed at *reduced rates*.[107] France, for example, does not offer an exemption rate, but does offer an effective rate of 15 percent on qualifying intellectual property.[108] Likewise, the United Kingdom allows for certain income from qualifying patents to be taxed at a reduced rate of 10 percent.[109] Malta offers an impressive zero percent rate on certain intellectual property!

Countries adopt patent box regimes for various reasons. Luxembourg, among other nations, use them to try to lure companies to relocate their highly mobile intellectual property and to capture additional tax revenues.[110] Some, like the United Kingdom, wish to improve the competitiveness of their own tax systems and discourage the shifting of intellectual property income abroad.[111] The Netherlands, and those like it, adopt them for nontax reasons. They wish to attract R&D activities along with all the positive spillover benefits, within their borders.[112]

European countries have begun implementing these patent boxes. The United Kingdom's became effective in 2013.[113] And Italy introduced for

[107] *See generally* Jason M. Brown, "Patent Box Taxation: A Comparison of Four Recent European Patent Box Tax Regimes and an Analytical Consideration of If and How the United States Should Implement Its Own Patent Box," *The International Lawyer* 46 (2012): 913–37, *available at* www.jstor.org/stable/23827422?seq=1#page_scan_tab_con tents; Nick Pantaleo, Finn Poschmann, & Scott Wilkie, "Improving the Tax Treatment of Intellectual Property in Canada" (Institut C.D. Howe Institute Commentary No. 379, April 25, 2013), *available at* https://papers.ssrn.com/sol3/papers.cfm? abstract_id=2303819.

[108] KPMG, "France Country Profile," *supra* note 55, at 2.

[109] KPMG, "United Kingdom Country Profile," *supra* note 50, at 6.

[110] Graetz & Doud, *supra* note 47, at 405 (stating patent boxes "seem to have been enacted by various European nations in an effort to capture a share of mobile innovative activity or at least some revenue from such especially mobile income").

[111] The United Kingdom noted that "some patent-rich UK businesses face a higher overall effective tax rate than their foreign competitors," and the patent box is explicitly intended to "improve the competiveness of the UK corporate tax regime." HM Treasury, "Corporate Tax Reform: Delivering a More Competitive System," 51, November 2010, *available at* www.hm-treasury.gov.uk/d/corporate_tax_reform_com plete_document.pdf. The UK patent box also appears to be at least partially a response to the plans of some prominent MNEs to move to Ireland. Lee A. Sheppard, "What Hath Britain Wrought?," *Worldwide Tax Daily* (December 30, 2010): 7–8, available at LexisNexis, 2010 WTD 250–2.

[112] Graetz & Doud, *supra* note 47, at Part II.D (summarizing data on benefits of R&D tax incentives). *See, e.g.*, HM Treasury, *supra* note 111, at 47 (indicating aim of UK patent box is to provide incentive for companies to locate high-value jobs in the United Kingdom and to maintain United Kingdom's positon as world leader in patented technologies).

[113] Finance Act of 2012, c. 14, sch. 2 (UK), *available at* www.legislation.gov.uk/ukpga/20 12/14/contents/enacted.

the first time in 2015 a patent box providing a 50 percent exemption on income from the exploitation of certain qualifying intellectual property.[114] Ireland's history with patent boxes is interesting. Ireland adopted the first patent box in 1973.[115] It was repealed in 2010,[116] only for a new one to be enacted in 2016. It provides a low tax rate (6.25 percent, which is half of the country's already low corporate tax rate) on revenue generated from patents and other intellectual property held in Ireland.

China is the only non-European country to adopt a patent box regime thus far.[117] The United States has not adopted a patent box yet, although there

[114] Carlo Maria Paolella, Andrea Tempestini, & Federico Bortolameazzi, "The Upcoming Implementation of the Italian Patent Box Regime," July 31, 2015, www.mwe.com/The-Upcoming-Implementation-of-the-Italian-Patent-Box-Regime-07-31-2015/.

[115] See Robert D. Atkinson & Scott Andes, "Patent Boxes: Innovation in Tax Policy and Tax Policy for Innovation," 3, 5, (The Information Technology & Innovation Foundation, October 2011), available at www.itif.org/files/2011-patent-box-final.pdf.

[116] Ireland originally exempted patent income of Irish residents only if R&D was carried out in Ireland. Wim Eynatten, "European R&D and IP Tax Regimes: A Comparative Study," Intertax 36 (2008): 512. The European Commission determined that the required underlying R&D that took place in Ireland violated E.C. Treaty rules. Press Release IP/07/408, European Commissioner, Direct Taxation: Commission Requests Ireland to End Discriminatory Rules on Tax Treatment of Patent Royalties (March 23, 2007), available at http://europa.eu/rapid/press-release_IP-07-408_en.htm#PR_metaP ressRelease_bottom. In response, Ireland extended its exemption as long as underlying R&D took placed in the European Economic Area. Eynatten, at 512. But Ireland later abolished its patent box in 2011. "The Irish Budget 2011 and Recent Tax Developments," Taxand (January 17, 2011), www.taxand.com/news/newsletters/The_ Irish_Budget_2011_and_Recent_Tax_Developments. It has been suggested that the patent box was not stimulating innovation in Ireland and did not result in increased R&D in Ireland. Graetz & Doud, supra note 47, at 372 (citing 730 No. 2, Dáil Deb., Written Answers – Tax Code, at 296 [April 14, 2011], http://debates.oireachtas.ie/dail/ 2011/04/14/unrevised2.pdf).

[117] Following the lead of the European model, China defines qualifying intellectual property broadly: including both registered patents and unregistered forms of intellectual property, such as commercial know-how and trade secrets. Also included in China's definition of qualifying intellectual property are "inventions, utility models, certain designs, software copyrights, integrated circuit layout design proprietary rights, and new plant varieties. . . . To qualify for China's patent box, three requirements must be met: (1) expenses related to R&D must meet a specific threshold amount; (2) R&D expenses must be maintained over a three-year period; and (3) at least sixty percent of the expenses related to R&D must be incurred within China. The amount of expenses that must be attributable to R&D vary based on the company's overall revenue. Unlike the European countries with patent boxes, China is unique in that it is the only country that requires R&D to be conducted within China to qualify for the lower patent box rate. The applicable corporate tax rate on qualifying profits ranges from zero to 12.5 percent. Qualifying income is also exempt if it is below five million Chinese Yuan. Amounts in excess of this five million Chinese Yuan threshold are taxed at half of the corporate income tax rate." W. Wesley Hill & J. Sims Rhyne, III, "Opening Pandora's Patent Box: Global Intellectual Property Tax Incentives and Their Implications for the United States," Idea 53 (2013): 371–408, available at http://heinonline.org/HOL/Page?handle= hein.journals/idea53&div=20&g_sent=1&collection=journals.

have been congressional proposals for one.[118] As discussed above, the United States already subsidizes technological innovation through front-ended channels (i.e., a 100 percent tax deduction for research and experimentation and a 20 percent tax credit on incremental increases in qualified research).

The following chart shows countries with existing or proposed patent boxes, and the effective rates on qualifying income for many of the countries:

Countries with Existing or Proposed Patent Boxes[119]
Belgium (6.8%)
China
Colombia
Cyprus (2.5%)
France
Hungary
Ireland (6.25%)
Israel
Italy
Korea
Liechtenstein (2.5%)
Luxembourg (5.76%)
Malta (0%)
Netherlands (5%)
Portugal
Spain
Switzerland
Turkey

[118] In the United States, there have been calls for a patent box. Former House Committee on Ways and Means Chairman David Camp has proposed a 15 percent rate on certain intellectual property income. *See* "Technical Explanation of the Ways and Means Discussion Draft Provisions to Establish a Participation Exemption System for the Taxation of Foreign Income" (House Committee On Ways & Means, 112th Congress, 2011) 34, *available at* http://waysandmeans.house.gov/UploadedFiles/FINAL_TE_-_Ways_and_Means_Participation_Exemption_Discussion_Draft.pdf.

[119] Lilian V. Faulhaber, "Taxation of Intellectual Property in the United States and Abroad," at *Taxation of Intellectual Property in a Global Economy*, Georgetown Law, March 11, 2016 (noting some of these countries may not think they have patent boxes but all offer reduced rates on intellectual property income). For other sources comparing patent box regimes, see Nick Pantaleo, Finn Poschmann, & Scott Wilkie, "Improving the Tax Treatment of Intellectual Property Income in Canada," C.D. Howe Institute Commentary No. 379, April 2013; Jason M. Brown, "Patent Box Taxation: A Comparison of Four Recent European Patent Box Tax Regimes and an Analytical Consideration of If and How the United States Should Implement Its Own Patent Box," *International Lawyer*, Fall 2012, Vol. 46: 913–937; Peter R. Merrill et al., "Is It Time for the United States to Consider the Patent Box?," *Tax Notes* (March 26, 2012): 1665.

The design of patent boxes (qualification requirements and operational mechanics) varies significantly from one country to the next.[120] As shown above, patent box effective tax rates vary. Patent boxes differ in several other important respects. First, they differ in the *types of intellectual property* eligible for special tax rate treatment. The Netherlands provides a low rate on technology assets such as patents and intellectual property from approved R&D projects, but not to copyrights or trademarks.[121] Some, however, including Hungary, Luxembourg, and Switzerland, include a broader range of intellectual property. This can entail software copyrights and trademarks in the preferential regime.[122] The Cyprus regime, for instance, covers all intellectual property assets, including patents, trademarks, copyrights, formulas, designs, know-how, and processes.

Second, patent box regimes differ in the *scope of qualifying income* (i.e., the base of income that qualifies for preferential tax treatment). Spain targets gross income from qualifying intellectual property for special treatment. Belgium and the Netherlands target net income from qualifying intellectual property differing in the expenses that reduce qualified income. Some target royalties and license income, while others include gains on the sale of intellectual property. Others include embedded royalty income. In the Netherlands and other countries, the special low rate is not limited to royalties or capital gains, but instead applies broadly to income that is reliability linked with the intellectual property.

Third, patent box regimes also differ in the *degree of external contribution* permitted. In many, only self-developed intellectual property qualifies for special rate treatment. But other countries include income from outsourced intellectual property or purchased intellectual property.[123] In

---

[120] For charts comparing the patent box regimes among different countries, *see* Pantaleo et al., *supra* note 119, at 14–15.

[121] The Dutch Innovation Box scheme is open to Dutch-issued patents and to equivalent patents issued in other countries. Although the Dutch Innovation Box does not apply to trademarks, logos, and equivalent assets, it does apply to software and nonpatentable assets such as trade secrets. Hendrik Van Duijn, "The Dutch Innovation Box," *Duijn's Tax Solutions* (December 2014), *available at* www.duijntax.com/uploads/The%20Dutch%20Innovation%20Box.pdf. *See also* Merrill et al., *supra* note 119, at 1669.

[122] Merrill et al., *supra* note 119, at 1668 (noting Luxembourg's patent box applies to software copyrights, patents, trademarks, brands, design, models, and domain names).

[123] In the Netherlands, purchased intellectual property must be further developed. Merrill et al., *supra* note 119, at 1669. Pourgoura & Aspri LLC "Cyprus and Netherlands: Tax Efficient IP Jurisdictions in Europe" (October 17, 2013), http://cypruslawyers.blogspot.com/2013/10/cyprus-and-netherlands-tax-efficient-ip.html. The Dutch Innovation Box can apply to intangibles for which the taxpayer has obtained either (1) a Dutch or foreign patent or (2) an R&D Certificate from the Netherlands Enterprise Agency. The Innovation Box applies to self-developed intangibles, including patented intangibles developed by another (affiliated or nonaffiliated) company, provided the development has taken place at the taxpayer's risk (e.g., contract R&D). Contract R&D does not have

Belgium and the Netherlands, acquired intellectual property is included but only if further developed (e.g., Belgium resident companies can deduct 80 percent of patent income earned from qualifying patents developed or improved in its own R&D center).[124] Spain does not include acquired intellectual property. The Cyprus regime, on the other hand, applies to both self-developed and acquired intellectual property.

******

While the design of front-ended and back-ended incentives varies amongst countries, the reality is that many countries are relying on them to achieve set goals. And some, even shortly after adopting incentives, modify them to make them more attractive. The United Kingdom, for example, started with a super deduction for small companies. It later created a super deduction for large companies, and later increased the super deduction for both small and large companies, thus increasing their tax deductions for R&D several times.[125] Some countries have enhanced their tax credits for R&D. Ireland did so from 20 percent to 25 percent.[126] France's incremental to volume-based rate is another example.[127] The United States made its credit permanent in 2015.[128]

In summary, there are many features of international tax that induce multinational companies with intellectual property portfolios to shift income to foreign subsidiaries: (1) varying statutory corporate tax rates; (2) countries' conflicting bases of jurisdiction to tax cross-border income (and dividend tax policies); (3) conflicting standards for determining corporate residency; (4) availability of "hybrid entity" structures; (5) countries' competing R&D incentives; and (6) "patent boxes." Chapter 7 illustrates how these features are utilized by several key multinational companies.

to take place in the Netherlands, so long as R&D coordination and management are performed in the Netherlands. Lodewijk Berger & Lyda Stone, "Netherlands: Dutch Innovation Box Regime for Intangibles Is Clarified in Decree," *Mondaq* (October 10, 2014), www.mondaq.com/x/345566/Corporate+Tax/Dutch+Innovation+Box+Regime+For+Intangibles+Is+Clarified+In+Decree.

[124] Global Tax Chart, *supra* note 4.

[125] PricewaterhouseCoopers, "Global Research & Development Incentives Group," *supra* note 96.

[126] Sporken & Gommers, "Tax Treatment of R&D Expenses in Ireland," *supra* note 102, at 28–30; IDA Ireland, Taxation in Ireland 2016, *available at* http://www.idaireland.com/docs/publications/Taxation_2016.pdf.

[127] Eparvier, *supra* note 102; PricewaterhouseCoopers, *supra* note 96, at 15; Sporken & Gommers, "Tax Treatment of R&D Expenses in France," *supra* note 102, at 18.

[128] Protecting Americans from Tax Hikes Act of 2015, P.L. 114–113, § 121(a)(1) (amending § 41).

7 International Structures Used by Apple and Other Multinational Companies

As shown in Chapter 6 the divergent tax policies of different nations drive multinationals to shift the location of their intellectual property from high-tax jurisdictions to low-tax (or no-tax) jurisdictions. The US tax system, in particular, has maintained several features that are harsh for domestic multinationals. The 35 percent corporate income tax rate in the United States is one of the highest in the world, and US companies are subject to that 35 percent rate on their *worldwide income* simply because they were organized in the United States. In addition, the earnings of a controlled foreign subsidiary of a US parent company are subject to US tax if, and when, those earnings are repatriated to the United States. Because of these US tax features and the fact that other countries offer more attractive tax regimes, many US multinational companies have formed foreign IP Holding Companies and other offshore affiliates. There is nothing illegal about this. This strategy is used by many US multinational entities for two main objectives: to avoid current US taxation on offshore profits, and to subject those offshore profits to as low of a foreign tax as possible.

These objectives can be realized by setting up just one foreign subsidiary company. For example, a US parent company could set up a foreign subsidiary company in Ireland. That subsidiary, through a license or a joint R&D development agreement, could be given economic rights to develop and exploit all of the US parent company's intellectual property outside of the US. All foreign profits would be taxed to the Irish subsidiary company at Ireland's 12.5 percent tax rate instead of to the US parent company at the US's 35 percent tax rate. And as long as those foreign profits stayed in Ireland, they would escape US taxation.

Additional tax savings can be achieved if a multinational utilizes two foreign subsidiaries. A US parent company could create two companies in Ireland. The first is treated, with the aid of either Ireland's residency rules or a relevant treaty provision, as a tax resident of a

176

tax-haven country (such as Bermuda) that offers a 0 percent tax rate.[1] This company is merely an IP Holding Company that owns and licenses the non-US rights to intellectual property to the second Irish company. The second Irish company, which is a subsidiary of the first, is a tax resident of Ireland. This second Irish company pays substantial royalties for, and receives income from, the use of the licensed intellectual property outside the United States. The profits of the first Irish company (royalties) are taxed at 0 percent, and the profits of the second Irish company (income less royalty payments) are taxed at the Irish rate of 12.5 percent. The income will be subject to US tax only if, and when, that income is repatriated to the United States. Therefore, we have not only shifted offshore profits from the United States to Ireland, but here we have also diverted profits from a low-tax foreign country to a zero tax-haven country. This is the popular technique known as the "Double Irish" structure, variations of which are used by Google, Facebook, Pfizer, Adobe, Johnson & Johnson, Yahoo, and many other multinational companies. It is illustrated below.

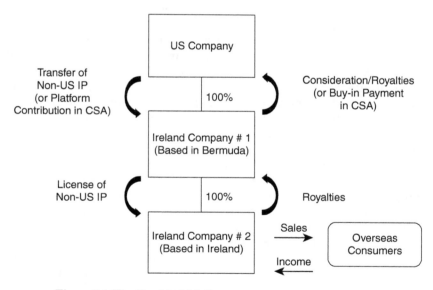

Figure 7.1 The Double Irish Structure

---

[1] Joseph P. Brothers, "From the Double Irish to the Bermuda Triangle," *Tax Notes International* 76 (November 2014): 687.

Naturally, and not surprisingly, a third foreign subsidiary can be created within the Double Irish chain of subsidiaries to further reduce tax liabilities. How can adding a so-called "Dutch Sandwich" to the "Double Irish" structure do this? As we saw above, royalty payments from the second Irish subsidiary (resident of Ireland) to the first Irish subsidiary (resident of zero-tax country) are deductible in Ireland. However, they may be subject to Irish withholding taxes (because Ireland does not have a treaty with Bermuda). To avoid this, the US parent company sets up a third subsidiary in the Netherlands, sandwiched between its two Irish subsidiaries. It then channels payments to the tax-haven country through the Dutch subsidiary. The first Irish subsidiary, paying 0 percent tax, licenses intellectual property to the Dutch subsidiary (incorporated and tax resident in the Netherlands), which then sublicenses that intellectual property to the second Irish subsidiary, paying Ireland's 12.5 percent rate. Because of agreements between Ireland and other European Union countries, Ireland does not tax money being moved among European Union countries (the money is exempt from the withholding tax). Furthermore, the Netherlands has generous tax laws as it does not impose a withholding tax (i.e., it does not have an outbound royalty withholding tax) and only collects a small fee for the use of its tax system. This creates a scheme where most of the Dutch subsidiary's revenues are transmitted to the tax-haven country virtually tax free.[2]

As illustrated above, a multinational company located in a high-tax country can reduce or even often avoid taxes on offshore profits by setting up one or more foreign subsidiaries. While one controlled foreign subsidiary can produce significant tax savings, multiple foreign affiliates typically produce the best tax results. In fact, the standard tax planning structure for many multinationals is to have one or more top-level controlled foreign corporations that hold the non-US rights to intellectual property in tax-favored jurisdictions, and then to have chains of additional foreign subsidiaries in higher-tax foreign jurisdictions. For foreign tax purposes, the royalties flowing from the subsidiaries (in the higher-taxed countries) to the IP Holding Companies (in the lower-taxed countries) are deductible in the high-tax countries. In addition, these royalties typically are not subject to the high-tax countries' withholding taxes under relevant treaties (e.g., treaties that follow the OECD model). In the end, most offshore profits of multinationals can be sent to top-level

---

[2] See Netherlands Foreign Investment Agency, "Why Invest in Holland?: Tax Treaties and Withholding Taxes," 8, accessed October 22, 2016, *available at* http://docplayer.net/555 2694-Why-invest-in-holland-tax-treaties-and-withholding-taxes.html.

foreign IP Holding Companies located in a few low-tax jurisdictions.[3] And as long as they stay there, they avoid US taxation.

With this basic background, we can look at the actual international tax planning structures used by several US multinational companies. It should be noted that the tax planning techniques of multinationals are not readily transparent because of government privacy rules regarding corporate tax matters. Much of what is reported here has been gathered from congressional hearings,[4] investigative reporting,[5] and writings of international tax experts.[6] In Chapter 8, we will look closely at government safeguards designed to target tax avoidance or deferral. We will learn there how multinationals have avoided those safeguards with careful planning, referencing back to this chapter for specific strategies.

Apple Case Study

While few may recall the Apple I first introduced in 1976, or the Macintosh computer first introduced in 1984, most of us are familiar with the more recent high-tech products of Apple, Inc. – iMac (1998), iPod (2001), iPhone (2007), and iPad (2010). These products, with their

---

[3] Hearing Before the Permanent Subcommittee on Investigations, Offshore Profit Shifting and the US Tax Code – Part I (Microsoft & Hewlett-Packard), 12, September 20, 2012, *available at* www.gpo.gov/fdsys/pkg/CHRG-112shrg76071/pdf/CHRG-112shrg76071.p df [hereinafter Microsoft Part I] (providing testimony of Reuven S. Avi-Yonah).

[4] *See* Hearing Before the Permanent Subcommittee on Investigations, Offshore Profit Shifting and the US Tax Code – Part II (Apple Inc.), 35–37, 152–91, May 21, 2013, *available at* www.gpo.gov/fdsys/pkg/CHRG-113shrg81657/pdf/CHRG-113shrg81657.p df [hereinafter Senate Apple Hearing]; Microsoft Part I, *supra* note 3, at 28–40, 160–86. *See also* Joint Committee on Taxation, "Present Law and Background Related to Possible Income Shifting and Transfer Pricing," JCX-37-10 (July 20, 2010), *available at* www.jct .gov/publications.html?func=startdown&id=3692 [hereinafter JCX-37-10 Report] (containing memorandum prepared for Hearing on Transfer Pricing Issues Before the House Committee On Ways & Means of the 11th Congress (2010)).

[5] *See* Jesse Drucker's investigative reporting has been most revealing. *See, e.g.,* Jesse Drucker, "Biggest Tax Avoiders Win Most Gaming $1 Trillion US Tax Break," *Bloomberg News,* June 28, 2011, www.bloomberg.com/news/2011-06-2/biggest-tax-avoi ders-with-most-gaming-1-trillion-u-s-tax-break.html (noting Cisco Systems, Inc. has cut its income taxes by $7 billion since 2005 by shifting half of its profits to a foreign subsidiary, cutting its effective tax rate on international income to approximately 5 percent). *See* Jesse Druker, " 'Dutch Sandwich' Saves Google Billions in Taxes: Internet Giant Uses Complex Structure to Keep Its Overseas Tax Rate at 2.4 percent," *Bloomberg Businessweek,* October 22, 2010, www.nbcnews.com/id/39784907/ns/business-us_busi ness/t/dutch-sandwich-saves-google-billions-taxes/#.Uu75D3lfVQs; Jesse Drucker, "Google 2.4 percent Rate Shows How $60 Billion Lost to Tax Loopholes," *Bloomberg News,* October 21, 2010, www.bloomberg.com/news/2010-10-21/google-2-4-rate-show s-how-60-billion-u-s-revenue-lost-to-tax-loopholes.html.

[6] *See, e.g.,* Joseph B. Darby III and Kelsey Lemaster, "Double Irish More Than Doubles the Tax Saving: Hybrid Structure Reduces Irish, US and Worldwide Taxation," *Practical US/ International Tax Strategies* 11, no. 9 (May 2007): 2.

cool and sophisticated aesthetics, have brought technology to the people through attractive design and user interface. They have boosted Apple to the top ranks as one of the most valuable companies in the world.

Apple's most valuable asset is its brand, which, with a value of $128 billion, was the most valuable global brand of 2015. The figure reflects a 23 percent increase from its $105 billion valuation in 2014.[7] In addition to the iconic brand, Apple's aesthetics in designing its products influence how electronics are and will be designed, making them deceptively simplistic and stunningly beautiful.[8]

Apple has amassed a large and valuable patent portfolio. The company owns 10,942 patents and the portfolio is the envy of all companies for the commanding value each patent generates. Each of Apple's patents enjoys the highest revenue, at $16.7 million, leading all tech companies worldwide.[9]

Apple was founded the same way most tech start-ups are, in someone's personal garage. That is where, in 1976, Steve Jobs and Steve Wozniak launched the computer revolution.[10] Although founded in 1976, Apple was not incorporated in the United States until January 3, 1977.[11] Forty years later, Apple not only designs and sells personal computers, mobile phones, and portable digital music players, but also provides a variety of software and services, including access to third-party digital content and applications.[12] Apple is now headquartered in California, where central management and control exist.

Although Apple is US-based, it is also very much a global company. Apple's products and services are sold worldwide – with international

[7] John Hahn, "Apple and Samsung Are the Most Valuable Global Brands of 2015," March 7, 2015, accessed November 9, 2016, *available at* www.digitaltrends.com/mobile/apple-is-the-most-valuable-global-brand-in-2015-followed-by-samsung-and-google/.

[8] Jonathan Jones, "How Steve Jobs Made the World More Beautiful, The Apple Aesthetic has Transformed How We See Our Lives – And the Future," *The Guardian*, October 6, 2011, *available at* www.theguardian.com/technology/2011/oct/06/steve-jobs-world-more-beautiful; Walter Isaacson, "How Steve Jobs' Love of Simplicity Fueled a Design Revolution," *Smithsonian Magazine*, September 2012, *available at* www.smithsonianmag.com/arts-culture/how-steve-jobs-love-of-simplicity-fueled-a-design-revolution-23868877/?no-ist

[9] Richard Lloyd, "Apple's Revenue Per Patent Leaves the Other Big US Portfolio Owners in the Shade," *IAM*, June 23, 2015, accessed November 9, 2016, www.iam-media.com/blog/detail.aspx?g=d37195bc-4870-406d-81cc-f9e74c6e17b8.

[10] Lev Grossman, "80 Days that Changed the Word: Apple Boots Up," *Time*, March 31, 2003, http://content.time.com/time/specials/packages/article/0,28804,1977881_1977891_1978542,00.html. *See* Testimony of Apple Inc. Before the Permanent Subcommittee on Investigations, US Senate, May 21, 2013, 3, *available at* www.apple.com/pr/pdf/Apple_Testimony_to_PSI.pdf [hereinafter Testimony of Apple Inc.].

[11] "Apple Inc. (AAPL.O)," Reuters, accessed October 21, 2016, www.reuters.com/finance/stocks/companyProfile?symbol=AAPL.O.

[12] Testimony of Apple Inc., *supra* note 10, at 3–4.

operations accounting for more than 60 percent of Apple's total revenue.[13] The materials and components for many of Apple's products are sourced globally[14] but most of Apple's research and development takes place in the United States. Apple employs 80,000 people worldwide, with 28,000 of those employees outside of the United States.[15]

For its offshore operations, Apple uses a web of controlled foreign subsidiary companies. If they didn't, sales in the United States as well as sales abroad would be subject to the US tax rate of 35 percent. But, as with many US multinational companies, Apple does not conduct foreign business operations directly through its branches. Rather, it utilizes a network of controlled foreign subsidiary corporations for its operations in Europe, the Middle East, India, Africa, Asia, and the Pacific[16] (North and South American operations are headquartered in California). Apple relies on these foreign subsidiaries around the world to perform a variety of functions such as manufacturing, distribution, sales, and support. Apple also relies on these subsidiaries to shield foreign sales from current US taxation in order to save them billions.

The chart on the following page, supplied during recent congressional hearings, shows Apple's web of offshore subsidiaries responsible for operations outside of the Americas.

As illustrated in the chart that follows, Apple does not rely on one foreign subsidiary company that might license foreign rights to intellectual property, manufacturing Apple products based on those rights, and then selling the finished products directly to Apple retail stores or third-party retailers and internet customers. Instead, Apple relies on an international network of subsidiaries located in a number of nations. Its key subsidiaries, however, are incorporated in Ireland, where Apple began its international operations.[17] Apple began these operations in 1980, merely four years after Apple was founded. At that time, Apple was manufacturing products in Ireland for sale in Europe. In fact, during the 1980s and 1990s, Apple's products were manufactured in both California and Cork, Ireland. In October 1980,

---

[13] Testimony of Apple Inc., *supra* note 10, at 2. *See* Nelson D. Schwartz and Charles Duhigg, "Apple's Web of Tax Shelters Saved It Billions, Panel Finds," *The New York Times*, May 20, 2013, www.nytimes.com/2013/05/21/business/apple-avoided-billions-in-taxes-congressional-panel-says.html?pagewanted=all.

[14] *See* Senate Apple Hearing, *supra* note 4, at 169 (citing "Memorandum RE: Offshore Profit Shifting and the US Tax Code – Part 2 [Apple Inc.]," 18).

[15] *Ibid.* at 168 (citing "Memorandum RE: Offshore Profit Shifting and the US Tax Code – Part 2 [Apple Inc.]," 17).

[16] *Ibid.* at 169 (citing "Memorandum RE: Offshore Profit Shifting and the US Tax Code – Part 2 [Apple Inc.]," 18).

[17] The five key Irish subsidiaries include the following: Apple Operations International (AOI), Apple Operations (AO), Apple Operations Europe (AOE), Apple Sales International (ASI), and Apple Distribution International (DI).

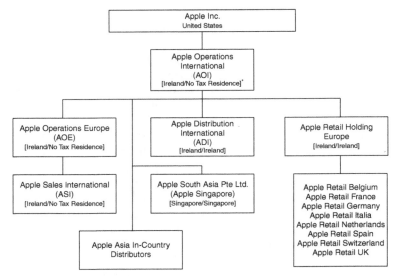

*Listed countries indicate country of incorporation and country of tax residence, respectively.

Figure 7.2 Apple's Offshore Organizational Structure
Prepared by the Permanent Subcommittee on Investigations, May
2013. Source: Materials received from Apple Inc.

Apple opened a factory in Cork, Ireland with sixty employees. But by the late
1990s, manufacturing had moved to China. Nevertheless, foreign profits
remained funneled through the original Irish subsidiaries.

Apple's main foreign subsidiary for its foreign activity is Apple
Operations International (AOI).[18] Interestingly, AOI is not engaged in
any economic activity, such as research, manufacturing, sales, or distribution. Rather, it is a mere holding company for Apple's offshore
corporate structure. AOI was originally incorporated in Cork, Ireland in
1980, but it is not clear why.[19] According to Apple, any early documents

---

[18] "Apple Inc. directly owns 97 percent of AOI and holds the remaining shares through two
affiliates, Apple UK which owns 3 percent of AOI shares, and Baldwin Holdings
Unlimited, a nominee shareholder formed in the British Virgin Islands, which holds a
fractional share of AOI, on behalf of Apple Inc." Senate Apple Hearing, *supra* note 4, at
172 (citing "Memorandum RE: Offshore Profit Shifting and the US Tax Code – Part 2
(Apple Inc.)," 21 n. 75).

[19] According to Apple, it is unable to locate the historical records regarding the business
purpose for AOI's formation, or the purpose for its incorporating in Ireland.

that indicate as to why AOI was set up in Ireland cannot be found. It has no physical presence at any address. It has never had any employees. Two of its three directors are Apple, Inc. employees who live in California. The other director is an Irish resident who seldom participates in meetings. Despite all of this, AOI is the ultimate owner of most of Apple's offshore network and, as such, it receives dividends from many of its own foreign subsidiaries – and a lot of them. If AOI performs any function at all, it is the centralized cash and investment management of this dividend income. According to Apple, AOI also "permits Apple to mitigate legal and financial risks by providing consolidated, efficient control of its global flow of funds."[20]

AOI (the first-tier subsidiary of Apple, Inc.) itself owns a number of foreign subsidiaries (second-tier subsidiaries), some of which in turn own one or more of their own foreign subsidiaries (third-tier subsidiaries). For example, AOI owns the foreign subsidiary Apple Operations Europe (AOE),[21] which in turn owns the foreign subsidiary Apple Sales International (ASI). In 1980, Apple entered into a cost sharing agreement with both AOE and ASI. Under the terms of this agreement, AOE and ASI share Apple's research and development costs, and in exchange they are granted the economic rights to use the resulting intellectual property outside the Americas. Of the two subsidiaries, ASI is the primary repository for Apple's offshore intellectual property rights[22] and it books most (84 percent) of Apple's nonoperating income.

And as the primary holder of Apple's offshore intellectual property rights, ASI contracts with third-party manufacturers in China to make Apple products. Then ASI sells those products at a substantial mark-up to one of two other foreign subsidiaries: (1) Apple Distribution International (ADI), a second-tier subsidiary of AOI, for sales in Europe, the Middle East, Africa, and India; or (2) Apple Singapore, another second-tier subsidiary of AOI, for sales in Asia and the Pacific

---

[20] Testimony of Apple Inc., *supra* note 10, at 3.

[21] Prior to a 2012 restructuring of its foreign affiliates, all of Apple's Irish employees were employed by AOE. In 2012, Apple re-distributed those employees across five different Irish affiliates, with the majority now employed by ADI. Senate Apple Hearing, *supra* note 4, at 176 (citing "Memorandum RE: Offshore Profit Shifting and the US Tax Code – Part 2 [Apple Inc.]," 25 n.103). As of 2012, AOE had about 400 employees and conducted a small of amount of manufacturing in Cork, Ireland involving a line of specialty computers for sale in Europe.

[22] Also as of 2012, ASI moved from zero to about 250 employees who manage Apple's other manufacturing activities as well as its product-line sales. *Ibid.* at 176 (citing "Memorandum RE: Offshore Profit Shifting and the US Tax Code – Part 2 [Apple Inc.]," 25).

region.[23] These two distribution subsidiaries (ADI and Apple Singapore) then manage all sales of finished products to Apple retail subsidiaries and to third-party retailers and internet customers.[24] The figure on the next page illustrates Apple's offshore distribution structure.

These key subsidiaries in the chain earn substantial foreign profits attributable to foreign sales. ASI, which booked 84 percent of Apple's non-US operating income in 2011, is responsible for the *offshore manufacturing functions* – its contracts with Chinese manufacturers to assemble Apple products – and acts as the initial buyer of those finished goods, then selling the finished products to ADI or Apple Singapore.[25] ASI receives substantial income because it charges ADI and Apple Singapore a much higher price than what it pays for the goods assembled in China. ADI and Apple Singapore are responsible for the *offshore sales functions* – that is, they purchase goods from ASI and then sell them at a markup to Apple retail subsidiaries located around the world, to third-party resellers, or directly to internet customers. These and some other lower-tier subsidiaries take most of their foreign profits and distribute them up the chain in the form of dividends to their parent or in the form of royalties for the licensing of intellectual property rights. Ultimately, dividends are sent back to AOI, the primary holding company for Apple's international structure.

Despite earning substantial foreign profits, these key foreign subsidiaries pay very little in worldwide taxes.[26] In 2011, ASI paid only $10

---

[23] For sales to China, however, the third-party contract manufacturer sells the finished products direct to ADI (not ASI), which then sells the finished products to Chinese retailers. To facilitate this arrangement, ADI sublicenses the rights to distribute Apple products in China for a substantial sum (e.g., $5.9 billion in 2012). Senate Apple Hearing, *supra* note 4, at 178 (citing "Memorandum RE: Offshore Profit Shifting and the US Tax Code – Part 2 [Apple Inc.]," 27 n.114).

[24] As a historical note, Apple has restructured its offshore operations on a couple occasions. In the 1980s and 1990s, Apple's products were manufactured in the United States and Ireland. But in the late 1990s, when Apple experienced severe financial difficulties, it began to outsource much of its manufacturing to third-party manufacturers in China. In addition, prior to 2012, ASI contracted with third-party manufacturers, bought finished Apple products, and then sold them to Apple retail affiliates and to third-party retailers and internet customers. In 2012, Apple split the manufacturing and sales functions so that ASI now sells Apple goods that it buys from third-party manufacturers to subsidiaries (ADI or Apple Singapore) that manage all sales. As part of this restructuring, Apple moved some employees from AOE to ASI and ADI. Prior to 2012, ASI operated without any employees and carried out activities through a US based Board of Directors. *Ibid.* at 176–77 (citing "Memorandum RE: Offshore Profit Shifting and the US Tax Code – Part 2 [Apple Inc.]," 25–26 n.105).

[25] Interestingly, title is transferred between the Chinese manufacturers and ASI, but the finished products themselves are shipped directly to the eventual country of sale. A very small percentage of finished products ever enter Ireland.

[26] Lower-tier subsidiaries record much lower foreign profits than the key Irish subsidiaries, and they pay minimal taxes in their high-tax countries. For example, Apple booked no tax

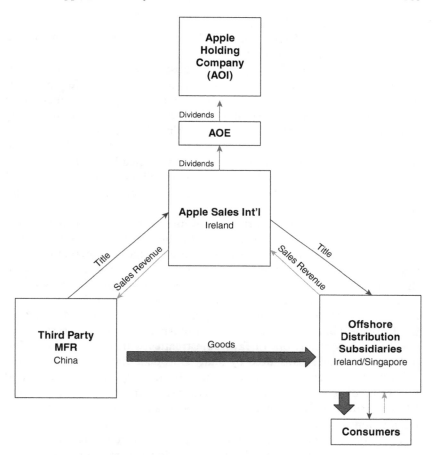

Figure 7.3 Apple's Offshore Distribution Structure
Source: Prepared by Permanent Subcommittee on Investigations
based on interviews with Apple employees

million in global taxes despite having $22 billion in foreign income, for an
effective rate of .05 percent. AOI, Apple's top-level holding subsidiary,
fared even better with a 0 percent rate. From 2009 to 2011, AOI

liability in France or Germany in 2011. It recorded less than 1 percent for Apple's
Japanese subsidiaries even though Japan is one of Apple's strongest markets. Senate
Apple Hearing, *supra* note 4, at 185 (citing "Memorandum RE: Offshore Profit
Shifting and the US Tax Code – Part 2 [Apple Inc.]," 34). This is most likely because
they send the bulk of their profits in the form of deductible payments up the chain of
subsidiaries.

received $30 billion in dividends from lower-tiered Apple subsidiaries, but paid $0 in taxes. How have Apple's foreign subsidiaries been able to pay minimal or even no taxes?

A number of Apple's key foreign subsidiaries are incorporated in Ireland. It is hard to identify "nontax" reasons for Apple's foreign affiliates to be in Ireland. The country is not integral in Apple's manufacturing functions, and it hasn't been since the 1990s when ASI started using third-party contract manufacturers in China. Ireland is not integral to Apple's distribution or sales functions either. Ireland-based ASI does not sell finished Apple products to customers but instead sells them to other affiliates who sell them to other affiliates who sell them to customers. ASI doesn't even take physical possession of the goods bought from China and sold to affiliates.

ASI also holds the foreign rights to Apple's intellectual property, pursuant to a cost sharing agreement with the US parent. But it is not essential that Ireland be the location of the foreign intellectual property rights. Those rights could be located in any jurisdiction, or even remain in the United States where actual research and development takes place. Granted, Ireland might be touted as a great location for intellectual property investment and foreign operations because of its educated English speaking workforce or its sophisticated banking system, or because it has a network of favorable treaties with other nations. But today these virtues are shared by many European nations in our rapidly evolving and emerging global economy. If anything, it could be argued that Ireland's small size, lack of infrastructure, and distance from other EU countries would seem to put it at a disadvantage relative to other jurisdictions in Europe.

The more plausible explanation for Apple's choice to maintain its key offshore subsidiaries in Ireland has more to do with *Ireland's tax-favorable policies*.[27] Ireland has long been considered tax-friendly to multinational companies, particularly high-tech and pharmaceutical companies. Indeed, it was the first country to introduce a patent box. Today, Ireland offers a number of specific tax incentives for intellectual property investment. It offers generous tax write-offs for expenditures in acquiring or developing "specified intangible assets." It offers a generous tax credit

---

[27] For summaries of Ireland's current intellectual property tax regime, see Walkers, Ireland's Intellectual Property Tax Regime, January 2016, *available at* www.walkersglo bal.com/images/Publications/Advisory/2016/01.08.201_Walkers_Ireland_Intellectual_ Property_Tax_Regime.pdf; AuthorCox, Ireland as a Location for Your Intellectual Property Trading Company, April 2015, *available at* www.arthurcox.com/wp-content/ uploads/2015/04/Arthur-Cox-Ireland-as-a-location-for-your-IP-Trading-Company-Ap ril-20152.pdf.

for research and development expenditures incurred within the European Economic Area. And recently Ireland enacted a "knowledge development box" with a 6.25 percent effective rate on income from patents and copyrighted software. Ireland is most often known, however, for its 12.5 percent tax rate on active business income. While this statutory rate is already the lowest among developed nations, as mentioned in Chapter 6 Ireland is also known to negotiate even lower rates for certain multi-nationals. Indeed, Apple revealed in US congressional hearings that it was able to negotiate a special 2 percent rate in Ireland.[28]

Even though Apple says it negotiated a special 2 percent rate with Ireland, the European Commission's (EC's) recent state aid investigation shows that Ireland issued two favorable tax rulings to Apple (1991 and 2007, terminated in 2015). These rulings concerned the internal allocation of profits within ASI, and produced better results than 2 percent. These agreements endorsed a split of the profits for tax purposes in Ireland – most profits were internally allocated away from Ireland to a "head office" within ASI, which was not based in any country and did not have employees and did not own premises. Only a fraction of the profits of ASI were allocated to its Irish branch and subject to tax in Ireland. The EC concluded that the allocation gave Apple an unfair advantage that was illegal under EU state aid rules.[29] Some question whether Ireland looks more like a legitimate low-tax country or a tax-haven country in light of the deals it has cut with firms such as Apple.[30]

While Apple has enjoyed special tax rates with Ireland, it also has been able to *exploit the difference between US and Irish tax residency rules*. We

---

[28] *Ibid.* at 171 (citing "Memorandum RE: Offshore Profit Shifting and the US Tax Code – Part 2 [Apple Inc.]," 20). ("Since the early 1990's, the Government of Ireland has calculated Apple's taxable income in such a way as to produce an effective rate in the low single digits. . . . The rate has varied from year to year, but since 2003 has been 2 percent or less.")

[29] European Commission, Press Release, State Aid: Ireland Gives Illegal Tax Benefits to Apple Worth Up to 13 Billion Euros, August 30, 2016, *available at* http://europa.eu/rap id/press-release_IP-16-2923_en.htm. The EC acknowledged that tax rulings as such are perfectly legal. They are comfort letters issued by tax authorities to give a company clarity on how its corporate tax will be calculated or on the use of special tax provisions. In a response by Apple, it has over the years received guidance from Irish tax authorities on how to comply with Irish tax laws. Apple vehemently opposes the EC's conclusion that Ireland gave a special deal on its taxes. Moreover, Ireland has decided to appeal to defend the integrity of its tax system, provide tax certainty to businesses, and challenge the use of state aid rules to curtail national sovereignty over tax matters. *See* J. Clifton Fleming, Jr., "The EU Apple Case: Who Has a Dog in the Fight?," *Tax Notes* 154 (2017): 251.

[30] "If Ireland were a legitimate low-tax country, all of Apple's Irish affiliates would be paying the statutory 12.5 percent rate on their income. Instead, those Apple affiliates that do pay Irish tax appear to be paying a lower rate due to a special income calculation." Lee Sheppard, "How Does Apple Avoid Taxes?," *Forbes*, May 28, 2013, www.forbes.com/ sites/leesheppard/2013/05/28/how-does-apple-avoid-taxes/#34f845a2d6f7.

mentioned before that, under Ireland's general rule for determining residency, a company incorporated in Ireland is subject to Irish taxes regardless of where it is managed and controlled. But an important exception exists for existing corporations, at least until it expires the end of 2020. Under this exception, an Irish-incorporated company is deemed a resident of the country where it is managed or controlled.[31] Apple's key foreign subsidiaries that are incorporated in Ireland (AOI, AOE, and ASI) seemingly qualify for this exception. Thus, for Irish tax purposes, they are deemed to be residents of the country where they are managed or controlled.

Apple's position has been that its key foreign subsidiaries are not incorporated in the United States, so they are not subject to current US taxation, and they are not managed in Ireland, so they are not subject to Irish taxation. In essence, neither country (the United States or Ireland) regards the subsidiaries as residents for domestic tax purposes. And, interestingly, there are no treaty mechanisms that assign tax residence to one of the countries. Since these subsidiaries are not tax residents of any country, they have not filed tax returns or paid taxes to any government. They are phantoms.

It should be noted that in response to pressure from the international community, Ireland recently changed its tax residency rules, which were essentially based on a corporation's principal place of business, to one which is based on the status of incorporation, similar to the rule in the United States.[32] In short, a company incorporated in Ireland shall be regarded for Irish tax purposes as a resident of Ireland. For new corporations, the rule became effective January 1, 2015. However, for existing corporations, like Apple's foreign subsidiaries, the rule takes effect in 2021.

It will be interesting to see if Apple modifies its international structure before then. It seems as if Apple has two options. First, Apple could do nothing, in which case the foreign profits of Apple's Irish subsidiaries will become subject to Irish taxes starting in 2021. But who cares, as Apple's increased taxes would be minimal since it has negotiated a very low rate

---

[31] As noted in Chapter 6, the exception applies if the Irish-incorporated company is controlled by a parent company in an EU or tax treaty country, like the United States, and if the company is engaged in a trade in Ireland or related to a company engaged in a trade in Ireland. Several of Apple's key foreign subsidiaries, such as AOI, AOE, and ASI, meet the exception's requirements. Thus for these entities, Ireland determines residency based on where central management and control is exercised.

[32] Reuters, "Ireland to End 'Double Irish' Tax Loophole," *The Telegraph*, October 14, 2014, www.telegraph.co.uk/finance/economics/11162122/Ireland-to-end-Double-Irish-tax-loopbhole.html.

with Ireland.[33] Alternatively, Apple could take advantage of an important treaty-based exclusion to Ireland's new residency rule by making some modifications to its current international structure. Ireland has entered into treaties with a number of tax-friendly countries. These treaties contain a tiebreaker in the event a company is a resident of both Ireland and the treaty country, and determine residency based on the principal place of business. So, with a few minor changes to its existing structure, Apple could move the managerial headquarters of its Irish-incorporated subsidiaries into a low-tax or zero-tax country that has a treaty with Ireland and continue to avoid paying little or no foreign taxes on its foreign income. For example, if Apple's Irish-incorporated subsidiaries were to have their principal place of business in Malta, they would not be considered a tax resident of Ireland. Malta does not impose tax on royalty income derived from trademarks, copyrights, or patents.[34]

In addition to refusing to declare a tax residency in any country for its key foreign subsidiaries, Apple has also utilized another tool to avoid taxes – a so-called *cost sharing agreement*. For Apple's foreign subsidiaries – AOE and ASI – to make and sell Apple products overseas, or to hire third parties to assemble Apple products and sell them to foreign distribution affiliates, they need intellectual property rights. AOE and ASI do not necessarily need all legal rights to Apple's intellectual property, but they do need at least the economic rights for products sold outside the Americas. Apple could have sold or licensed intellectual property rights directly to its foreign subsidiaries, but then it would have to receive and be taxed on arm's-length consideration received (or deemed received under relevant transfer pricing rules). In order to avoid having to send foreign profits back to the United States in the form of license royalties, Apple has cleverly utilized a cost sharing agreement to facilitate the shifting of intellectual property and income therefrom. Generally speaking, a cost sharing arrangement is an agreement under which two or more related parties agree to share the costs and risks of developing intellectual property in exchange for a certain interest in that intellectual property. For US tax purposes, the companies are considered to be the co-owners of any intellectual property developed under the cost sharing arrangement. As

---

[33] *Ibid. See* Leonid Bershidsky, "Goodbye Double Irish, Hello Knowledge Box," *BloombergView*, October 15, 2014, *available at* www.bloomberg.com/view/articles/201 4-10-15/goodbye-double-irish-hello-knowledge-box (noting "companies could theoretically just keep their Irish structures. Losses from increased taxes would be minimal; nothing as horrible as paying Ireland's full 12.5 percent tax rate, let alone repatriating to the US where the headline corporate tax rate is 35 percent").

[34] Deloitte Touche Tohmatsu, "Taxation and Investment in Malta 2014: Reach, Relevance and Reliability," 10, 2014, *available at* www2.deloitte.com/content/dam/Deloitte/global/ Documents/Tax/dttl-tax-maltaguide-2014.pdf.

co-owners for tax purposes, the participants can exploit any intellectual property developed under the cost sharing arrangement without having to pay arm's-length royalty payments to the other participant(s).

Apple (the US parent) entered into its cost sharing agreement with both AOE and ASI in 1980 – when Apple's foreign operations began. Most foreign profits flow to ASI, so we will focus more on the agreement between Apple and ASI. Under the terms of the cost sharing agreement, Apple and ASI agree to share in the development of Apple's products and to divide the resulting intellectual property economic rights. Apple owns the economic rights to Apple's intellectual property for goods sold in the Americas, whereas ASI owns the economic rights to intellectual property for goods sold in the rest of the world (Europe, the Middle East, Africa, India, and Asia).[35]

In theory, a cost sharing agreement works to shift intellectual property offshore if the US parent company and the foreign subsidiary company share in development costs appropriately. According to Apple, it and ASI pay an appropriate portion of worldwide research and development costs based on the portion of product sales that occur in their respective regions. In 2011, for example, 40 percent of Apple's worldwide sales occurred in the Americas, with the remaining 60 percent occurring offshore. Accordingly, Apple paid 40 percent ($1 billion) and ASI paid 60 percent ($1.4 billion) of Apple's $2.4 billion worldwide R&D costs. According to congressional reports, however, respective shares of costs have not always been in proportion to respective shares of sales. It was reported that from 2009 to 2012, Apple allocated about half of global R&D costs to Apple ($4 billion) and about half to ASI ($4.9 billion). One would expect that each would be allocated about half of the total profits from R&D, but that was not the case. Apple was allocated only $29 billion in profits, a ratio of 7 to 1 when comparing income to costs, that were subject to US taxation. ASI, in contrast, was allocated $74 billion in profits, a ratio of more than 15 to 1, which were not subject to US taxation, nor were they subject to Irish taxation because, as noted earlier, Apple declares that ASI has no tax residency. In essence, ASI profited more than twice as much as Apple under the cost sharing agreement. Interestingly, almost all of the research activity covered under the cost sharing agreement was performed in the United States. In fact, the vast

---

[35] Senate Apple Hearing, *supra* note 4, at 170 (citing "Memorandum RE: Offshore Profit Shifting and the US Tax Code – Part 2 [Apple Inc.]," 19). The Amended & Restated Cost Sharing Agreement Between Apple Inc., Apple Operations Europe, and Apple Sales International, APL-PSI-000020 is listed as a "Sealed Exhibit." *Ibid.* at 170 (citing "Memorandum RE: Offshore Profit Shifting and the US Tax Code – Part 2 [Apple Inc.]," 19 n.72).

majority of Apple's R&D (95 percent in 2011) is conducted by Apple's employees in the United States. Less than 1 percent is conducted in Ireland by ASI employees. In light of this, some question whether there is really any economic reason for the agreement, which looks more like a cost reimbursement relationship rather than a co-development relationship.[36] Nevertheless, Apple reports that its cost sharing agreement is regularly audited by the IRS and complies fully with all applicable US laws.[37]

It surprises many to learn that Apple has paid minimal taxes (even minimal US taxes) on its foreign income. After all, Apple is widely known as a very successful US-based global company. Its key management is in the United States, the majority of its worldwide employees are in the United States, and most all of its R&D takes place in the United States. But as we learned in Chapter 6 the foreign profits of the foreign subsidiaries are not subject to current US taxation.[38] Foreign subsidiaries are subject to current US taxation on any US source income. But Apple's subsidiaries, such as AOI, ASI, ADI, and Apple Singapore, all have foreign-source income. If these foreign earnings were passed on up the chain to the US parent company in California, in the form of either a royalty from ASI to the US parent or a dividend from AOI to the US parent, the earnings would be subject to current US taxation. But that does not happen. ASI has no need to pay a royalty to the US parent for foreign rights to Apple's intellectual property because ASI is a co-developer with the US parent under a cost sharing agreement. In addition, AOI does not pay dividends to the US parent. In short, most of the profits of these subsidiaries and other foreign affiliates in the international structure get passed up the chain to AOI, and remain there indefinitely.

It is estimated (in 2014) that Apple accumulated over $180 billion in foreign profits, and is saving $59 billion in US taxes by keeping profits offshore.[39] Most of this untaxed foreign income will not be subject to any US tax in the near future; Apple stated it has no plans to bring these

---

[36] *Ibid.* at 179 (citing "Memorandum RE: Offshore Profit Shifting and the US Tax Code – Part 2 [Apple Inc.]," 28).

[37] Testimony of Apple, Inc., *supra* note 10, at 10. As noted by one commentator, "Apple may be claiming the benefit of the older, more permissive rules." Lee Sheppard, "How Does Apple Avoid Taxes?," *Forbes*, May 28, 2013, www.forbes.com/sites/leesheppard/2013/05/28/how-does-apple-avoid-taxes/#37113ee7d6f7.

[38] In Chapter 8, we will see how Apple avoids the US anti-deferral rules, which impose current US taxation on certain foreign earnings.

[39] Citizens for Tax Justice, "Offshore Shell Games 2015: The Use of Offshore Tax Havens by Fortune 500 Companies," 2, October 5, 2015, http://ctj.org/pdf/offshore shell2015.pdf.

profits back stateside in the form of taxable dividends.[40] Much of the accumulated foreign earnings that are allegedly parked overseas are actually invested in US financial institutions.[41] In fact, as of 2011, Apple held between 75 percent and 100 percent of its offshore cash assets in accounts at US financial institutions.[42] According to Apple, AOI's cash is held in US banks to have the opportunity to earn higher returns, which are subject to US income tax, and are held in US dollars to protect against currency fluctuations.[43] Although Apple holds these offshore earnings in US banks, Apple is severally limited in the use of these nonrepatriated earnings.[44] It cannot, for example, use the money in its US business operations to pay US employees or make capital investments in the United States. Nor can it use these funds to repurchase shares or pay dividends to its shareholders.

[40] *Ibid.* at 156 (citing "Memorandum RE: Offshore Profit Shifting and the US Tax Code – Part 2 [Apple Inc.]," 5) (citing the April 29, 2013 Subcommittee interview of Apple Chief Executive Officer Tim Cook in which Apple indicated that it had "no intention of returning those funds to the United States unless and until there is a more favorable environment, emphasizing a lower corporate tax rate and simplified tax code").

[41] *See* Kitty Richards & John Craig, "Offshore Corporate Profits: The Only Thing 'Trapped' Is Tax Revenue," Center for American Progress, January 9, 2014, www.ame ricanprogress.org/issues/tax-reform/report/2014/01/09/81681/offshore-corporate-prof its-the-only-thing-trapped-is-tax-revenue/. *See also* Senate Permanent Subcommittee on Investigations, "Offshore Funds Located On Shore Majority Staff Report Addendum December 14, 2011 to Repatriating Offshore Funds: 2004 Tax Windfall for Select Multinationals Majority Staff Reprot October 11, 2011," December 14, 2011, 1, *available at* www.hsgac.senate.gov/download/report-addendum_-psi-majority-staff-report-of fshore-funds-located-onshore+&cd=1&hl=en&ct=clnk&gl=us [hereinafter Offshore Staff Report Addendum] (showing that of $538 billion in undistributed accumulated foreign earnings that US multinational corporations had earned at the end of FY2010, nearly half (46 percent) of the funds that the corporations had identified as offshore and for which US taxes had been deferred, were actually in the United States at US financial institutions).

[42] Offshore Staff Report Addendum, *supra* note 41, at 5.

[43] Testimony of Apple, Inc., *supra* note 10, at 13. It has been reported that Apple any many other multinationals buy Treasuries and other US securities with their overseas cash. Apple, for example, allegedly purchased US government bonds, and, in return, the government paid Apple at least $600 million or more in interest over a recent five-year period. 26 USC. § 956(c)(2) (allowing multinationals to use overseas cash tax free to buy US securities). Andrea Wong, "Americans Are Paying Apple Millions to Shelter Overseas Profits," *Bloomberg*, December 7, 2016, *available at* www.bloomberg.com/gra phics/2016-apple-profits/.

[44] The United States has rules that restrict the use of a controlled foreign subsidiary's offshore earnings for the benefit of the US parent company. 26 USC. § 956 (treating a controlled foreign corporation's offshore earnings that are invested in a broad range of US investments, including loans, as taxable dividends to the US parent). But these rules do not prevent the holding of US portfolio investments (e.g., US bank deposits, US debt and equity securities of unrelated issuers). Senate Apple Hearing, *supra* note 4, at 110 (citing "Testimony of Stephen E. Shay Before the US Senate Permanent Subcommittee on Investigations of the Committee on Homeland Security and Governmental Affairs Hearing on Offshore Profit Shifting and the Internal Revenue Code," May 21, 2013, 4).

Restrictions on the use of untaxed foreign earnings in US business make sense as multinationals with low-tax foreign earnings would have a competitive advantage over domestic US businesses that do not have access to the same low-taxed offshore earnings.[45] But such restrictions also tend to distort behavior. For instance, in 2013 Apple returned capital to its shareholders through a combination of stock repurchases and dividends. It could have used its billions in cash supposedly "parked" overseas to fund this return of capital, but the repatriated funds would have been subject to the US 35 percent corporate income tax rate. So, instead of repatriating foreign earnings, Apple borrowed $17 billion at a very low interest rate (less than 2 percent) to fund the stock repurchase.[46] Those interest payments are tax deductible. So, basically, Apple borrowed money to avoid paying taxes, and was able to reduce its tax bill even further through interest deductions.[47] Apple defended the decision to use debt, rather than repatriate foreign earnings, arguing that it was in their shareholder's best interest.[48]

We have seen how Apple has utilized foreign subsidiaries to avoid current US taxation on foreign sales. Apple does not, however, utilize its foreign subsidiaries to avoid US tax on US sales (sales of products back into the United States). This is in contrast to Microsoft. Microsoft uses a similar structure to Apple's for minimizing US tax on foreign sales. In contrast to Apple, however, Microsoft also utilizes foreign subsidiaries to minimize US tax on US sales to its US customers.

Microsoft Case Study

The second global tech company we feature is Microsoft. [49] Microsoft is a leading technology firm that develops, licenses, and supports a wide range

---

[45] Senate Apple Hearing, *supra* note 4, at 110–17 (citing "Testimony of Stephen E. Shay Before the US Senate Permanent Subcommittee on Investigations of the Committee on Homeland Security and Governmental Affairs Hearing on Offshore Profit Shifting and the Internal Revenue Code," May 21, 2013, 4–11).

[46] In practice, offshore earnings can be used as implied collateral to borrow money at low rates. Floyd Norris, "Apple's Move Keeps Profit Out of Reach of Taxes," *The New York Times*, May 2, 2013, www.nytimes.com/2013/05/03/business/how-apple-and-other-corporations-move-profit-to-avoid-taxes.html?_r=0.

[47] *Ibid.*

[48] Testimony of Apple, Inc., *supra* note 10, at 15 ("Indeed, the Company's largest investors and financial analysts urged Apple to engage in borrowing to add leverage to its capital structure").

[49] Much of we have learned about Microsoft was revealed in congressional hearings. *See* Microsoft Part I, *supra* note 3, at 29–38, 160–86. *See also* Martin A. Sullivan, "Microsoft Moving Profits, Not Jobs, Out of the US," *Tax Notes*, October 18, 2010; Glenn Simpson, "Irish Subsidiary Lets Microsoft Slash Taxes in US and Europe," *Tax Notes*, November 7, 2005.

of computer products and services. Most of its revenues are attributable to its highly valuable, highly mobile intellectual property, namely copyrights and patents related to Microsoft Windows and Microsoft Office.

Microsoft has an arsenal of 28,130 patents and each of its patents commands $3 million in revenue.[50] The company's Chief Patent Counsel informed the public that in 2015 Microsoft formed Microsoft Technology Licensing, LLC, to manage the company's patents.[51] In 2015, Microsoft received 2,845 US and 2,577 international patents for both design and utility patents. The company touts that its portfolio contains "world-class" patents, the products of its annual research and development budget of $11.4 billion.[52] It vouches to continue to be the top patent owner in the world.[53]

The Microsoft brand was ranked as the second most valuable brand in the world in 2015 (behind Apple's brand as noted above). The brand was worth $69.3 billion, an increase of 10 percent from the prior year. The company's Windows and other products captured $94 billion in sales in 2015. With the increase in sales and new release of Window 10, the company targets one billion Windows 10 users by 2018.[54]

Microsoft relies heavily on copyright and trade secret laws to protect its software. The company is a member of the BSA Software Alliance, which advocates for the global software industry and seeks to stop copyright infringement of software developed by its members.[55]

Microsoft was founded in 1975, a year before Apple. It was incorporated six years later, in 1981, in the Washington state. Like Apple, Microsoft is a global company. Although it does the bulk (85 percent) of its research and development in the United States, Microsoft employs people all over the world. Of their 90,000 people employed worldwide, 36,000 are outside the United States.

Beginning in the 1990s, Microsoft began establishing foreign subsidiaries in low-tax jurisdictions to facilitate international sales and reduce US and foreign tax. Like Apple, several of Microsoft's key subsidiaries are incorporated in Ireland. But unlike Apple, Microsoft does not declare

---

[50] Richard Lloyd, "Apple's Revenue Per Patent Leaves the Other Big US Portfolio Owners in the Shade," *IAM*, June 23, 2015, accessed November 9, 2016, www.iam-media.com/blog/detail.aspx?g=d37195bc-4870-406d-81cc-f9e74c6e17b8.

[51] Micky Minhas, "Our Growing Patent Portfolio," January 15, 2016, accessed November 9, 2016, *available at* http://blogs.microsoft.com/on-the-issues/2016/01/15/our-growing-patent-portfolio/#sm.000019o2q5dz46cr4z169jl889pmw.

[52] *Ibid.*   [53] *Ibid.*

[54] Kurt Badenhausen, "Apple and Microsoft Head the World's Most Valuable Brands 2015," *Forbes*, *available at* www.forbes.com/sites/kurtbadenhausen/2015/05/13/apple-and-microsoft-head-the-worlds-most-valuable-brands-2015/#63c47762875b.

[55] www.bsa.org/.

that any of its Irish-incorporated subsidiaries have no tax residency in any country.

Microsoft's main foreign subsidiary is Round Island One (RIO), which is incorporated in Ireland but headquartered in Bermuda. The United States views RIO as an Irish corporation since it was incorporated in Ireland. Under grandfathered tax residence rules, Ireland views RIO as a Bermuda corporation since it is managed in Bermuda. As a result, RIO is not subject to either US or Irish taxes. Instead, it is subject to pay Bermuda's 0 percent rate.[56]

RIO (first-tier subsidiary of Microsoft, Inc.) itself owns Microsoft Ireland Research (MIR) (second-tier), which in turn owns Microsoft Ireland Operations Limited (MIOL) (third-tier). Both MIR and MIOL are incorporated and headquartered in Ireland, which subjects them to Irish taxes. MIR, which has about 390 employees in Dublin, has entered into a cost sharing agreement with Microsoft US to produce and sell Microsoft products in Europe, the Middle East, and Africa, sharing 30 percent of Microsoft's worldwide R&D expenses. MIR licenses its foreign intellectual property rights to MIOL, which, with its 650 Irish employees, manufactures copies of products and sells them to distributors in foreign countries. These distributors are affiliated third-party entities who then sell finished products to customers.

Both MIR and MIOL earn substantial foreign profits, but have low effective tax rates on those earnings. In 2011, for example, MIR reported $4.3 billion of profits, with an effective tax rate of 7.2 percent. MIOL reported profits of $2.2 billion, with an effective tax rate of 7.3 percent – all well below Ireland's statutory rate of 12.5 percent.

Additionally, Microsoft does not utilize MIR and MIOL for sales throughout Asia. Instead, Microsoft has a group of entities located in Singapore. Specifically, Microsoft owns Microsoft Singapore Holdings Pte. Ltd (first-tier subsidiary), which in turn owns Microsoft Asia Island Ltd Bermuda (MAIL) (second-tier subsidiary). MAIL, a Bermuda IP Holding Company with no employees, entered into a cost sharing

---

[56] As noted earlier, Ireland recently changed its corporate residency rules. Under a grand-fathering exception, Microsoft's key holding subsidiary (RIO), which was incorporated in Ireland before January 1, 2015, but managed and controlled in a nontreaty based country, Bermuda, will be deemed a tax resident in Bermuda and will be exempt from Irish taxes until January 2, 2021. At that point RIO will be deemed a tax resident of Ireland subject to Irish taxes. There is, however, a treaty-based exception to the new Irish tax residency rules. Under this exception, if RIO were to move its management and control to a treaty-based country, like Malta or Hong Kong, the treaty tie-breaker rule would kick in and RIO would be a resident and taxable only in the treaty country, not Ireland. So with some changes to Microsoft's structure, similar tax results are still achievable.

agreement with Microsoft US, sharing 10 percent of the costs of global R&D expenses in exchange for the right to sell products throughout Asia. MAIL doesn't manufacture anything; instead, it licenses its rights for a substantial amount to Microsoft Operations Pte. Ltd (MOPL), another second-tier subsidiary, in Singapore. MOPL, which has 687 employees, duplicates products and sells them to distributors around Asia.[57] Both MAIL and MOPL have substantial income, albeit less than what the Ireland operations produce. In 2011, MAIL reported $1.8 billion in foreign earnings, with an effective rate of 0.3 percent. MOPL reported a profit of $592 million, with an effective rate of 10.6 percent.

Microsoft's foreign operations look remarkably similar to Apple's, and their similar tax planning devices have helped them avoid current US taxation of foreign profits and subjected those foreign profits to low foreign taxes. Both Microsoft and Apple conduct the bulk of their research and development in the United States (95 percent for Apple and 85 percent for Microsoft). For both, intellectual property resulting from that US-based R&D generates substantial foreign profits. Both conduct foreign operations through foreign subsidiaries. Both utilize top-level controlled foreign subsidiaries that are incorporated in Ireland but that are not deemed under grandfathered residency rules to be resident of Ireland for Irish tax purposes.[58] Below the top-level controlled foreign corporations are other foreign subsidiaries that serve varying functions, and their foreign profits flow up the chain to the top-level controlled foreign subsidiaries. These profits generally stay parked offshore in these top-level controlled foreign subsidiaries and are not repatriated to the United States in the form of dividends subject to US taxes.

To help shift intellectual property income offshore, both Microsoft and Apple transfer their intellectual property rights to key foreign subsidiaries through cost sharing agreements, under which the subsidiaries share in the costs of the US-based research in exchange for the rights to exploit the intellectual property in their respective regions of the world. For both Apple and Microsoft, only the intellectual property's economic rights (the

---

[57] Due to restrictions in local laws, Microsoft Korea, Inc. and Microsoft China Company license intellectual property rights to Microsoft products directly from the US parent, paying hefty fees ($228 million and $178 million, respectively in 2011). Microsoft Part I, *supra* note 3, at 182 (citing "Memorandum RE: Offshore Profit Shifting and the US Tax Code," 23 n.71).

[58] For instance, Apple's key Irish-incorporated subsidiaries (AOI, AOE, ASI) are managed out of the United States, so they are not viewed presently by Ireland as tax residents of Ireland. Microsoft's key Irish-incorporated subsidiary (RIO) is managed out of Bermuda so it is not viewed presently by Ireland as a tax resident of Ireland. Instead, it is viewed as a tax resident of Bermuda. But this is a distinction with no effect, as in both cases, Ireland does not view any of them as tax residents of Ireland.

right to profit from the intellectual property) are transferred offshore. Legal ownership of the intellectual property, including legal enforcement rights, remains in the United States.[59] The foreign subsidiaries obtaining the intellectual property rights (in Ireland or Singapore) do not directly sell products. Instead, the economic rights are licensed at a substantial mark up to different subsidiaries, which in turn, either manufactures, distributes, or sells products.

There are some differences in the two multinational companies' approaches. For one, Apple has negotiated a special 2 percent tax rate with Ireland, but there is no public evidence Microsoft has done the same. Further, Apple declares that its key Irish-incorporated subsidiaries (AOI, AOE, ASI) are not tax residences of any country. Microsoft, on the other hand, maintains that its key Irish-incorporated subsidiary (RIO) is a Bermuda corporation for Irish tax purposes. But this is really a distinction of form over substance, as Bermuda does not levy a corporate tax. At the end of the day, neither multinational pays much in the way of effective rates to Ireland.

A more significant difference is in how each multinational handles its Asian sales. For Apple, an Irish-incorporated subsidiary (ASI) holds the intellectual property rights supporting the sale of Apple products in Asia. ASI contracts with third-party manufacturers in China to make Apple products and then sells those products to Apple Singapore, a subsidiary located in Singapore, for sales in Asia. Microsoft, on the other hand, has MAIL hold the intellectual property rights supporting product sales throughout Asia. MAIL licenses its intellectual property rights to MOPL, which duplicates products and sells them to distribution entities around Asia.

Again, the differences here are relatively minor and contain little substance. Notice that, for each, the intellectual property rights are held by "no-tax" subsidiaries. Singapore, a low-tax jurisdiction, is involved in the chain. Therefore, each company has achieved creating low effective rates for its Asian sales.

Although Apple and Microsoft have similar tax devices to minimize taxes on foreign profits, their approach differs with respect to US sales. Apple retains the intellectual property rights for North and South America. And, although it contracts with third-party manufacturers in China for product assembly, it is responsible for sales in the United States and pays US taxes on those sales. In stark contrast, Microsoft shifts substantial profits on its US sales to US customers to Puerto Rico,

[59] Microsoft Part I, *supra* note 3, at 179 (citing "Memorandum RE: Offshore Profit Shifting and the US Tax Code," 20 n.68).

which happens to be an offshore tax haven. As noted above, Microsoft owns Round Island One (RIO), a first-tier subsidiary incorporated in Ireland but headquartered in Bermuda. RIO, in turn, owns Microsoft Operations Puerto Rico (MOPR), a second-tier subsidiary. MOPR entered into a cost sharing agreement with Microsoft paying 25 percent of Microsoft's global R&D expenses (based on a percentage of global sales in the Americas) in exchange for the intellectual property rights to produce and sell products in the United States and the rest of North and South America. With those rights, MOPR makes digital and physical copies of products, in a small production facility with 177 employees, and sells them to other Microsoft subsidiaries in the United States, which then sell them to US consumers. Under the distribution agreement, the US subsidiaries retain about half of the gross profits and send the other half to MOPR in Puerto Rico. Interestingly, Puerto Rico is not subject to US tax laws, and it levies a low 1–2 percent prenegotiated rate on Microsoft. As a result of this simple strategy of forming a company in Puerto Rico and setting up a tiny factory, Microsoft has been able to save billions in US taxes on sales in the US – an estimated $4.5 billion over a recent three-year period.[60]

Both Apple and Microsoft have come under scrutiny for their tax minimization techniques. Microsoft's ability to shift US profits from US sales in the United States raises particular concerns, and has been the focus of congressional hearings.[61]

Uber Case Study

The third global tech company we feature is Uber Technologies, Inc.[62] Unlike Apple and Microsoft, Uber is a private company. It is also a much younger company, having only begun operations in 2009. But like Apple and Microsoft, Uber is a tech company that relies largely on its high value intellectual property – a technology platform or Smartphone application that connects drivers and ride-seekers to arrange and schedule transportation. Uber has wasted no time in becoming a global company, operating now in more than 70 countries worldwide.

---

[60] *Ibid.* at 181 (citing "Memorandum RE: Offshore Profit Shifting and the US Tax Code," 22).

[61] *See generally* Microsoft Part I, *supra* note 3.

[62] Much of what we know about Uber, and summarized here, has been uncovered by investigative reporting conducted by Fortune and reported in 2015. Fortune investigated the financial statements of Uber subsidiaries and court documents in more than 100 jurisdictions worldwide. Brian O'Keefe & Marty Jones, "How Uber Plays the Tax Shell Game," *Fortune*, October 22, 2015, http://fortune.com/2015/10/22/uber-tax-shell/.

As a technology company in the ride-sharing industry, Uber disrupts the taxi industry and the automobile industry with its omnipresent of on-demand car services across the world. Uber was valued at $70 billion in September 2016 while crushing many competitors to capture the market with massive growth.[63] In 2016 alone, Uber enjoyed $4 billion in net revenues, doubling its revenue in 2015![64] Uber counts on many important companies as investors for its quest to obtain competitive technology to stay ahead of the competition.

With respect to intellectual property protection for its technology, Uber owns a number of utility patents, design patents for its user interfaces, trade secrets, and copyrights for its software. The company also owns trademarks, logos, app icons, and designs.[65] Uber's most valuable asset is its data, as Uber uses the data to improve the Uber experience for drivers, ride-seekers, and users of the Uber platform. Also, in 2015, Uber began to make deals with other companies to monetize its data.[66]

Uber Technologies, Inc. (the US parent company) is incorporated in Delaware and headquartered in San Francisco. Similar to Apple and Microsoft, Uber relies on a network of offshore subsidiaries to minimize US taxes on foreign income; its profit coming from ride-share income earned abroad. The legal structures are similar to those of Apple and Microsoft, except that Uber has set up many of its key subsidiaries in the Netherlands as opposed to Ireland. It has ten Dutch subsidiaries in total, seven of which have no employees. Only the key Dutch subsidiaries are discussed below.

As noted in Chapter 6, the Netherlands is a tax-favored jurisdiction for many multinational companies. Although it has a corporate tax rate of 25 percent, much higher than Ireland's, the use of foreign subsidiaries in the Netherlands can produce effective rates much less than that. According to one study, the Netherlands, with an effective tax rate of less than 5 percent, is the top location for foreign profits, accounting for more foreign income earned by affiliates of US multinational companies than any other country.[67] The Netherlands is particularly attractive for intellectual

---

[63] "From Zero to Seventy (Billion), The Accelerated Life and Times of the World's Most Valuable Startup," *The Economist*, September 3, 2016, *available at* www.economist.com/news/briefing/21706249-accelerated-life-and-times-worlds-most-valuable-startup-zero-seventy.

[64] *Ibid.*

[65] Audrey Ogurchak, "Uber IP: A Primer on the Patents, Trademarks and Copyrights Owned by Uber," July 23, 2016, accessed November 9, 2016, *available at* www.ipwatchdog.com/2016/07/23/uber-ip-patents-trademarks-copyrights/id=71167/.

[66] www.fastcompany.com/company/uber.

[67] Kimberly A. Clausing, "The Effect of Profit Shifting on the Corporate Tax Base in the United States and Beyond," 7, 12, June 17, 2016, *available at* https://papers.ssrn.com/sol3/papers.cfm?abstract_id=2685442.

property activities. It has a very generous patent box or innovation box regime that provides an effective rate of 5 percent to technology assets such as self-developed (and sometimes acquired) patents.[68] Its extensive treaty network generally reduces and sometimes eliminates the foreign withholding tax on royalties paid to a Dutch company. In addition, the Netherlands does not impose any withholding tax at the source on royalties paid to non-Dutch companies.[69] Among the many other attractive incentive programs, the Netherlands offers the possibility of obtaining an advance tax ruling or an advance pricing agreement. According to the Netherlands Foreign Investment Agency (NFIA), an operational unit of the Dutch Ministry of Economic Affairs, this "is one of the most attractive features of Dutch tax law."[70]

As reported by *Fortune*, Uber's main foreign subsidiary for its offshore operations is Uber International C.V. (first-tier subsidiary), which was incorporated in the Netherlands in 2013 and is headquartered in Bermuda. The United States views this main subsidiary as a Dutch corporation because it is incorporated in the Netherlands. The Netherlands, however, views it as a Bermuda corporation because it is managed and controlled in Bermuda. So neither the United States nor the Netherlands imposes its corporate income tax on Uber International C. V., and Bermuda does not impose a corporate income tax. Thus, income that flows to this main foreign subsidiary is not subject to foreign taxes. As long as the income stays parked there, and is not distributed to the US parent in the form of dividend or royalty payments, it is not subject to US taxes.

---

[68] Pourgoura & Aspri LLC "Cyprus and Netherlands: Tax Efficient IP Jurisdictions in Europe" (October 17, 2013), http://cypruslawyers.blogspot.com/2013/10/cyprus-and-netherlands-tax-efficient-ip.html. "The Dutch Innovation Box scheme is open to Dutch-issued patents and to equivalent patents issued in other countries. . . . Patent Assets are. . . required to a significant degree (30 percent or over) to be patent-dependent where their expected income are concerned." Hendrik Van Duijn, "The Dutch Innovation Box," 2, (*Duijn's Tax Solutions*, December 2014), *available at* www.duijntax.com/uploads/The%2 0Dutch%20Innovation%20Box.pdf. "Although the Dutch Innovation Box does not apply to trade marks, logos and equivalent assets it does apply to software and non-patentable Assets such as trade secrets." *Ibid.* at 4.

[69] "In order to benefit from the tax treaty network, the IP company must comply with certain specific substance requirements (both from an operational and economic perspective) in order to avoid the automatic exchange of information with other states. This new legislation aims to avoid the improper use of Dutch Licensing Companies (and Financing Companies) for treaty shopping by offering the involved Treaty Partners/EU Partners full transparency about Dutch Group Financing and/or Licensing Companies which have no or only little substance in the Netherlands." Netherlands Foreign Investment Agency, *supra* note 2, at 8.

[70] Netherlands Foreign Investment Agency (NFIA), "Why Invest in Holland?: Because Holland Offers a Highly Competitive Fiscal Climate," *available at* http://investinholland .com/nfia_media/2015/06/WiH_fiscal_8March2016.pdf.

With most multinational companies, the top-level controlled foreign corporation, which is in no-tax land, owns the intellectual property rights supporting offshore operations. This is true with Uber. *Fortune* reported that Uber entered into a couple agreements with Uber International C.V. shortly after Uber International C.V. was formed in order to shift intellectual property, and the income generated from it, offshore. First, Uber International C.V. agreed to pay $1 million plus a royalty of 1.45 percent of future net revenues for the right to use Uber's *existing intellectual property* outside the United States (it should be noted that this one-time lump sum payment and the future royalty payments are subject to US taxes upon receipt by Uber). One could argue such amounts are relatively small considering how valuable Uber is. Indeed, it was reported that weeks later Uber negotiated a new round of venture capital financing that increased the company's private valuation from $330 million to $3.5 billion. In the second and more significant cost sharing agreement, Uber and Uber International C.V. agreed that each would share in the cost of developing *future intellectual property* in return for rights to newly developed intellectual property in their respective geographical regions. Under this agreement, Uber International C.V. would not need to pay taxable royalties to the US parent for future intellectual property outside the United States.

According to *Fortune*, Uber International C.V., which is really an IP Holding Company, licenses its intellectual property rights to another key foreign subsidiary, Uber B.V. Uber B.V. is incorporated and headquartered in the Netherlands and operates with about 50 employees. In return, Uber B.V. pays a royalty to Uber International C.V. for the use of the intellectual property (ride sharing app). The fee for the royalty is large. Basically, it is whatever is left after giving Uber B.V. an operating margin of only 1 percent, and after subtracting Uber B.V.'s operation costs (payments for marketing and support services made to other foreign subsidiaries in foreign countries where Uber operates). To put it simply, Uber B.V keeps 1 percent of its revenue for itself, deducts operating costs, and sends whatever percentage remains, their royalty fee, to Uber International C.V.

Fortune reports that Uber drivers typically receive 80 percent of ride payments (80 percent of ride payments received by Uber B.V. are processed and returned to drivers via another Dutch subsidiary). The other 20 percent of ride payments go to Uber B.V. But, as noted above, Uber B. V. sends most of that in the form of a deductible royalty payments to Uber International C.V, keeping only 1 percent. Because Uber B.V. is a tax resident of the Netherlands, that 1 percent is subject to the Netherlands corporate tax rate of 25 percent. The 1 percent of revenue taxed at 25 percent results in a very low effective rate on total foreign ride share income. The large royalty sent to Uber International C.V. (based in Bermuda) is not subject to Dutch taxation because the Netherlands does not view it as a tax resident of the Netherlands. Further, as noted above, the Netherlands does not impose a withholding tax on the large royalty payments made to Uber International C.V. None of this foreign ride share income is subject to current US taxation except for the small royalty payment (1.45 percent of net revenues) that Uber International C.V. agreed in 2013 to pay to the US parent for rights to use existing intellectual property.

******

To summarize, the three case studies reveal remarkably similar tax planning structures that allow companies to achieve their objective of avoiding current US taxation of foreign earnings (and in some cases avoiding current US taxation of some US earnings) and subjecting those earnings to as low a foreign tax as possible. To do this, it is necessary for multinational companies to shift intellectual property offshore. This is often accomplished by utilizing cost sharing agreements with controlled foreign corporations located in zero-tax countries. As we have seen, multinationals transfer intellectual property to one or more top-level controlled foreign subsidiaries via cost sharing agreements. These IP Holding Companies then typically license the rights to the intellectual property to lower-tier foreign subsidiaries responsible for manufacturing and or sales functions. Usually these lower-tier subsidiaries are in low-tax jurisdictions such as Ireland, the Netherlands, and Singapore. Deductible payments flow from the lower-tier subsidiaries in low-tax countries to the top-level subsidiaries in zero-tax countries. Multinationals defer US taxation of those foreign profits by keeping those profits offshore.

In Chapter 8, we look at many government responses targeting the tax strategies of multinationals. Also, we will show how it is possible for multinationals to side step these government safeguards to continue deflecting operating income to low-tax or no-tax jurisdictions.

8 Government Barriers to Intellectual Property Income Shifting and Their (In)Effectiveness

The Apple, Microsoft, and Uber case studies in Chapter 7 demonstrate how US multinational companies that rely heavily on intellectual property utilize foreign subsidiary companies to minimize worldwide taxes on foreign earnings. These controlled subsidiaries are typically set up in low-tax foreign countries to subject foreign profits to as low of a foreign tax as possible. Perhaps more significantly, foreign subsidiaries are set up to avoid current US taxation of foreign profits. US taxation of active foreign profits is generally imposed only when the subsidiaries remit the profits (typically in the form of taxable dividends) to their US parent corporations. This delay in recognition of income, and therefore, payment of US taxes until a later time, is known as *deferral*.[1]

Benefits of Deferral

For US multinational corporations with massive earnings from the use of intellectual property portfolios, the benefits of deferral can be great. Delaying payment of US taxes that would otherwise be due allows foreign income of multinationals to be taxed currently at a lower effective rate, leaving more money in the corporate coffers. If those foreign earnings (already subject to low or no foreign taxation) are not remitted to the US parent, they may be invested. Earnings from the investment of those foreign profits may also be subject to low or no foreign taxation, which means these foreign earnings compound at a higher after-tax return than they would if brought home.[2] Using accounting jargon, multinationals

---

[1] Neal Frankle, "What is Tax Deferral?," *Wealth Pilgrim*, accessed October 23, 2016, www .wealthpilgrim.com/what-is-tax-deferral/.

[2] Rosanne Altshuler, Stephen Shay, & Eric Toder, "Lessons the United States Can Learn from Other Countries' Territorial Systems for Taxing Income of Multinational Corporations," 12 (Tax Policy Center: Urban Institute and Brookings Institution, January 21, 2015), *available at* www.taxpolicycenter.org/sites/default/files/alfresco/publi cation-pdfs/2000077-lessons-the-us-can-learn-from-other-countries.pdf (citing Alvin C. Warren, Jr., "Deferral and Exemption of the Income of Foreign Subsidiaries: A Review of the Basic Analytics," *Harvard Public Law Working Paper* 14–18 (2014);

can capitalize on the time value of money by reinvesting US taxes that would have been due if foreign profits had been repatriated. If invested long enough, the return on investment may actually exceed the amount of tax liability.[3] One commentator compared the use of foreign subsidiaries to Individual Retirement Accounts.[4] Foreign income is subject to no tax (or little tax) as it is earned and it can continue to grow virtually tax free. The foreign income will be subject to tax upon "withdrawal" (repatriated in the form of dividends). But, if a multinational waits long enough before bringing that income home, the present discount value of its total tax bill can be significantly reduced.

Another advantage of deferring US tax on foreign source income is that current US taxes do not have to be accounted for on the multinational company's financial statements, which helps keep earnings high. There is a financial accounting standard that requires US multinationals to account for future taxes they will face when they repatriate foreign profits currently held by their offshore subsidiaries.[5] However, to avoid the hit to corporate earnings, multinationals can assert that their foreign earnings are permanently or indefinitely reinvested offshore. And "[m]ultinationals routinely make such an assertion to investors and the Securities and Exchange Commission on their financial reports."[6]

Harmful Effects of Deferral

While deferral provides several advantages to the taxpayer, from the government's prospective it has several harmful effects. Deferral has the ability to (1) negatively impact the government's tax revenue; (2) encourage multinationals to accumulate foreign earnings offshore; (3) induce multinationals to make distorted and inefficient business decisions;

Daniel I. Halperin and Alvin C. Warren, Jr., "Understanding Income Tax Deferral," *Tax Law Review* 67 (2014): 317–34.

[3] Office of Tax Policy, US Department of Treasury, "The Deferral of Income Earned through US Controlled Foreign Corporations," *12*, December 2000, *available at* www.treasury.gov/resource-center/tax-policy/Documents/Report-SubpartF-2000.pdf [hereinafter Subpart F Study].

[4] Chris William Sanchirico, "As American As Apple Inc.: International Tax and Ownership Nationality," *Tax Law Review* 68 (2014): 214.

[5] Accounting Principles Board (APB) Opinion No. 23: Accounting for Income Taxes – Special Areas (April 1972), *available at* www.fasb.org/cs/BlobServer?blobcol=urldata&bl obtable=MungoBlobs&blobkey=id&blobwhere=1175820901676&blobheader=applicat ion%2Fpdf.

[6] *See* Hearing Before the Permanent Subcommittee on Investigations, Offshore Profit Shifting and the US Tax Code – Part I (Microsoft & Hewlett-Packard), 6, September 20, 2012, *available at* www.gpo.gov/fdsys/pkg/CHRG-112shrg76071/pdf/CHRG-112shr g76071.pdf [hereinafter Microsoft Part I] (providing Opening Statement of Senator Carl Levin [D-Mich.]).

(4) encourage multinationals to engage in aggressive transfer pricing strategies; and (5) encourage multinationals to actually relocate their tax residence. Each of these harmful effects is worthy of some attention in order to better understand the government's desire to impose barriers to this practice.

First, deferral negatively impacts the revenue base. Because of deferral, the US government collects little corporate tax revenue on the foreign income of US multinational companies (less than four percent of all foreign income of US multinationals in 2006).[7] As revealed in Chapter 6, income shifting by US multinational companies drains more than $100 billion in corporate revenue from the United States every year.[8] Less tax revenue, in turn, amounts to cuts in vital government services, increased budget deficits, or higher tax burdens on other taxpayers such as individuals and smaller businesses.[9] The reduced tax liability of US multinational companies also gives them a significant, unfair, competitive advantage over smaller US companies that cannot utilize overseas operations and offshore tax gimmicks to lower their effective corporate rate.[10]

Second, deferral encourages the "lock out" of foreign earnings – the accumulation of foreign earnings offshore to avoid US tax due on repatriation.[11] It is estimated that US multinationals have now

---

[7] Altshuler et al., *supra* note 2, at 17 (citing Harry Grubert and Rosanne Altshuler, "Fixing the System: An Analysis of Proposals for Reform of International Taxation," *National Tax Journal* 66 (2013): 671–712).

[8] For varying estimates, see Joint Committee on Taxation, "Estimates of Federal Tax Expenditure," *JCX-141R-15* (December 7, 2015), 29, *available at* www.jct.gov/publications .html?func=select&id=5 (estimating the loss for FY2016 to be $108.9 billion); Kimberly A. Clausing, "The Effect of Profit Shifting on the Corporate Tax Base in the United States and Beyond," 7,12, June 17, 2016, *available at* https://papers.ssrn.com/sol3/papers.cfm?ab stract_id=2685442; Gabriel Zucman, "Taxing Across Borders: Tracking Personal Wealth and Corporate Profits," *Journal of Economic Perspectives* 28 (2014): 121–48.

[9] It has been estimated, for example, that small business owners each would have had to pay $3,244 in additional taxes in 2014 if they had been obligated to pick up the full tab for offshore tax avoidance by multinational companies. Dan Smith & Jaimie Woo, "Picking up the Tab 2015: Small Businesses Pay the Price for Offshore Tax Havens," *US PIRG*, April 2015, *available at* www.uspirg.org/sites/pirg/files/reports/US%20PIRG%20Ed%2 0Fund%20-%20Picking%20Up%20The%20Tab%202015_0.pdf.

[10] These concerns have been raised by many, including members of Congress. *See* Microsoft Part I, *supra* note 6, at 1–8 (citing Opening Statement of Senator Carl Levin [D-Mich.]); Hearing Before the Permanent Subcommittee on Investigations, Offshore Profit Shifting and the US Tax Code – Part II (Apple Inc.), 8–10, May 21, 2013, *available at* www.gpo.gov/fdsys/pkg/CHRG-113shrg81657/pdf/CHRG-113shrg81657 .pdf [hereinafter Senate Apple Hearing] (citing Opening Statement by Senator John McCain).

[11] Some multinationals might be waiting for the government to introduce a special tax rate on repatriated profits (i.e., something much lower than the 35 percent statutory rate that

accumulated well over $2 trillion of un-repatriated earnings.[12] Just thirty companies account for sixty-five percent of these offshore profits, with Apple booking $181.1 billion in 2014 – more than any other company.[13] This lock out creates certain efficiency costs. By keeping foreign profits offshore for tax reasons, US multinationals forego domestic investment opportunities. If foreign profits were brought home, they could be used by US multinationals at home to invest in enhanced research and development, new jobs, expansion, and better worker benefits.[14]

The third disadvantage is that deferral induces multinational corporations to engage in inefficient behavior by making choices they would not otherwise make just to avoid US tax on repatriation.[15] Examples of harmful economic distortions abound. Deferral causes multinational companies to waste resources by engaging in costly tax planning instead of productive investment.[16] To the extent multinationals invest, deferral encourages them to invest and grow business activities in foreign countries (with low tax or no tax) rather than in the United States (or other

currently applies to dividends). President Trump has proposed a special, one-time opportunity for multinationals to repatriate offshore profits, but has not indicated how low that special rate would be.

[12] "Untaxed Foreign Earnings Top $2.3 Trillion in 2014," *Audit Analytics*, April 30, 2015, www.auditanalytics.com/blog/untaxed-foreign-earnings-top-2-3-trillion-in-20 14/. *See* Edward D. Kleinbard, "Why Corporate Tax Reform Can Happen," *Tax Notes* 146 (2015): 91, *available at* https://papers.ssrn.com/sol3/papers.cfm?abstrac t_id=2563358; Maxwell Murphy, "Indefinitely Reinvested Foreign Earnings on the Rise," *The Wall Street Journal*, May 7, 2013, http://blogs.wsj.com/cfo/2013/05/07/ind efinitely-reinvested-foreign-earnings-on-the-rise/. These funds are often held in US financial institutions, and, thus, are available to US capital markets; but US multinational corporations are constrained in their use of these funds. Although they may increase the firms' credit worthiness, they cannot be used to pay dividends or buy back shares without incurring US corporate tax liabilities upon repatriation.

[13] "Offshore Shell Games 2015: The Use of Offshore Tax Havens by Fortune 500 Companies," Citizens for Tax Justice, 2, October 5, 2015, http://ctj.org/pdf/offshore shell2015.pdf.

[14] Claire Buchan Parker, "The Path to Jobs and Prosperity: Tax Reform," *Roll Call*, January 26, 2014, www.rollcall.com/news/the_path_to_jobs_and_prosperity_tax_re form_commentary-230384-1.html?zkPrintable=true.

[15] Altshuler et al., *supra* note 2, at 12; Jason J. Fichtner and Adam N. Michel, "The OECD's Conquest of the United States: Understanding the Costs and Consequences of the BEPS Project and Tax Harmonization," Mercatus Center George Mason University, March 2016, *available at* www.mercatus.org/system/files/Fichtner-BEPS-Initiative-v1 .pdf. ("Unless every country has exactly the same tax system and tax rates there will always be tax distortions to investment.") *But see* Erik Cederwall, "Reconciling the Profit-Shifting Debate," *Tax Notes Today*, February 10, 2016 (arguing "the real economic implications and distortions of profit shifting are largely unknown," and calling for more research on the effect of income shifting on economic decisions and the economy).

[16] The White House and Department of the Treasury, "The President's Framework for Business Tax Reform: An Update," 11, April 2016, *available at* www.treasury.gov/reso urce-center/tax-policy/Documents/The-Presidents-Framework-for-Business-Tax-Refor m-An-Update-04-04-2016.pdf [hereinafter President Obama's Framework].

high-tax foreign countries).[17] Further, if a multinational needs to raise capital for domestic uses (operations, capital projects, stock buy backs, etc.), it may choose to borrow money instead of repatriating stashed offshore earnings to avoid being forced to pay taxes.[18] As noted in Chapter 7, Apple did just that in 2013. It borrowed $17 billion to return capital to its shareholders (buy back shares and issue dividends) even though it had billions of un-repatriated dollars available to it.[19]

Fourth, deferral encourages multinationals to use inappropriate transfer prices or pay inadequate royalties.[20] In fact, the value of deferral can be maximized with aggressive intercompany transfer pricing strategies that shift much of a multinational entity's profits to low-tax, or no-tax, foreign jurisdictions. To illustrate how multinational companies can direct the bulk of their profits from one country to another by underpricing or overpricing transactions with foreign subsidiaries, consider the following example. Assume US Parent Co., a major manufacturer of soft contact lenses, formed a subsidiary corporation in Ireland (Foreign Sub). US Parent granted Foreign Sub a nonexclusive license to manufacture and sell contact lenses outside the United States using US Parent's technology, in exchange for an annual royalty payment. To maximize the amount of foreign profits taxed at Ireland's low rate, and to minimize the amount of those profits sent back to the United States, the parties have an incentive to set the royalty rate as low as possible. Now, in contrast, assume that US Parent jointly develops intellectual property under a cost sharing agreement with its controlled foreign subsidiary in Bermuda (which has a zero percent tax rate), which then sublicenses the intellectual property to Foreign Sub in Ireland (which has a 12.5 percent tax rate). To maximize the amount of foreign profits taxed at Bermuda's zero percent rate, the parties have an incentive to set the royalty payment from Foreign Sub to Bermuda as high as possible.

Finally, deferral encourages inversions. Inversions are transactions in which multinationals merge with foreign corporations to relocate their tax

---

[17] These concerns have been raised by many, including the former Obama administration. *See* President Obama's Framework, *supra* note 16, at 11.

[18] Altshuler et al., *supra* note 2, at 12 (discussing implicit costs of deferring income, which likely increase as offshore retentions grow) (citing Harry Grubert & Rosanne Altshuler, "Fixing the System: An Analysis of Proposals for Reform of International Taxation," *National Tax Journal* 66 (2013): 671–712 (estimating that the implicit cost of the tax on foreign profits is about 7 percentage points)).

[19] Senate Apple Hearing, *supra* note 10, at 40. *See also* Floyd Norris, "Apple's Move Keeps Profit Out of Reach of Taxes," *The New York Times*, May 2, 2013, www.nytimes.com/2013/05/03/business/how-apple-and-other-corporations-move-profit-to-avoid-taxes.html?_r=0.

[20] Altshuler et al., *supra* note 2, at 17.

residence.[21] Deferral can cause multinationals to reconsider whether they want to keep their US tax residence. As the amount of un-repatriated profits continues to grow, so too has the number of US-based multinationals that have moved their domicile to a foreign jurisdiction. Of course that jurisdiction must be one that adopts a territorial rather than a worldwide approach to taxation.[22]

Anti-Deferral Regimes

As we have discussed, countries that have implemented worldwide tax systems, such as the United States, generally allow deferral of domestic tax on foreign income until it is repatriated to the taxpayer, and this deferral creates an irresistible incentive to shift income to low-tax or no-tax foreign locations. To reduce such incentives, and to counter the harmful effects outlined above, governments have responded with various anti-deferral mechanisms. Many of these mechanisms target highly mobile income from easily moveable intellectual property of domestic multinational companies. Indeed, most barriers are aimed at multinational companies that perform research and development domestically, but then shift ownership (and related functions) of developed intellectual property to low-tax or no-tax foreign countries where profitable operations occur, and then engage in advantageous transfer pricing practices. Highlighted below are two anti-deferral regimes applicable to US companies that use foreign corporations to avoid or defer US tax. The first is the controlled foreign corporation rules of Subpart F of the Internal Revenue Code. The second involves the transfer pricing rules under section 482. Many countries have adopted similar anti-deferral regimes, but because many of the largest multinationals that engage in intellectual property income shifting are US based, US tax rules are featured more predominately here. The chapter ends by summarizing recent anti-inversion laws adopted in the United States to prevent the ultimate deferral technique: movement of corporate residency from the United States to another jurisdiction.

Controlled Foreign Corporation Rules

So-called "controlled foreign corporation" (CFC) rules target resident-based multinationals that place assets in controlled foreign subsidiaries to

---

[21] President Obama's Framework, *supra* note 16, at 11 ("The US system for taxing multinational corporations... encourages inversions").

[22] *See* Donald J. Marples & Jane G. Gravelle, *Corporate Expatriation, Inversions, and Mergers: Tax Issues* (CRS Report No. R43568) (Washington, DC: Congressional Research Service, 2016), 3.

defer payment of domestic tax on income from those assets. These rules require domestic parent companies to pay an *immediate* corporate income tax on certain types of foreign income earned abroad by their CFCs, even if the parent companies did not actually receive any of that income. In other words, they tax currently domestic companies as if they received certain earnings from CFCs, treating the parent corporations as if they had constructively received dividends from their foreign subsidiaries.

Most developed countries have enacted CFC regimes, some consisting of looser rules than others.[23] Countries differ in how they define a CFC, which is typically by reference to how much influence a domestic shareholder has over a foreign subsidiary company. In the United Kingdom, the CFC rules apply when UK corporate shareholders have an interest of twenty-five percent or more in the foreign subsidiary.[24] In Japan, the CFC rules apply when Japanese shareholders own more than fifty percent of a foreign company,[25] and the same rule applies in Germany. Countries also have exemptions and threshold requirements, which vary based on how privileged that foreign tax regime is (i.e., the subsidiary's effective foreign tax rate). In France, for example, the CFC rules kick into play if the CFC's effective tax is fifty percent lower than the tax that would be paid in France.[26] In Japan, the CFC rules apply only if

---

[23] *See* Joint Committee on Taxation, Background, Summary, and Implications of the OECD/G20 Base Erosion and Profit Shifting Project, November 30, 2015, at 15 (noting that all thirty countries participating in the OECD's recent Base Erosion and Profit Shifting Project have CFC rules). *See also* Michael J. Graetz & Rachel Doud, "Technological Innovation, International Competition, and the Challenges of International Income Taxation," *Columbia Law Review* 113 (2013): 342 (noting Australia as one country having looser CFC rules than others); Stephanie Berrong, "News Analysis: How Much Would Territoriality Cost?," *Tax Notes Today*, April 20, 2011 (noting Japan has stringent CFC rules). *See also* Reuven S. Avi-Yonah, "Three Steps Forward, One Step Back? Reflections on 'Google Taxes,' BEPS, and the DBCT," *Univ. of Mich. Public Law and Legal Theory Research Paper Series Paper* No. 516, May, 2016, *available at* https://papers.ssrn.com/sol3/papers.cfm?abstract_id=2783858 (noting if the US had CFC rules like Germany, France, or Japan, the extent of low-taxed income of US multinationals would have been significantly reduced).

[24] KPMG, "United Kingdom Country Profile," 4, *EU Tax Centre* (March 2013), *available at* www.kpmg.com/Global/en/services/Tax/regional-tax-centers/european-union-tax-centre/Documents/eu-country-profiles/2013-uk.pdf.

[25] Althsuler et al., *supra* note 2, at 26.

[26] If a French company subject to French corporation taxation holds an interest of at least 50 percent (5 percent if more than half of the foreign entity is held by French companies acting in concert or by entities controlled by the French company) in any type of structure benefiting from a privileged tax regime in its home country (effective tax is 50 percent lower than the tax that would be paid in France in similar situations), the profits of the foreign entity are subject to France's corporate income tax. *See* KPMG, "France Country Profile," 3, *EU Tax Centre* (March 2013), *available at* www.kpmg.com/global/en/services/tax/regional-tax-centers/european-union-tax-centre/documents/eu-country-profiles/2013-france.pdf; Bloomberg BNA, Tax and Accounting Center, *Global Tax Guide*, 27,

the CFC is subject to an effective tax rate of 20 percent or less.[27] In Germany, the CFC rules apply if the CFC's income is subject to a foreign tax rate of less than 25 percent.[28] Countries also take different approaches in defining the type of CFC income subject to current domestic taxation. Most nations include passive income, which is highly mobile and most easily shifted to low-tax jurisdictions.[29] Some countries' CFC regimes tax certain active income as well.[30]

The United States enacted its CFC rules in the 1960s, a time when the country faced a large deficit and slow economic growth relative to other industrialized nations.[31] The Kennedy Administration, concerned about the potential for perpetual deferral of US tax on foreign earnings, wanted to completely end deferral, and proposed to tax all the current foreign income, both passive and active, of subsidiaries of US multinational companies.[32] Big business pushed back, and a compromise was struck with the enactment in 1962 of what is known as Subpart F of the Internal Revenue Code.[33] Under the compromise, the CFC rules would currently tax only certain income earned by controlled foreign subsidiaries. Namely, the rules would tax income from passive investments and not earnings from active business investments abroad. Thus, US multinationals would be allowed to defer US taxation on active business income earned by their subsidiaries and thus remain competitive in the emerging global economy. However, they would not be allowed to defer taxation on passive income earned by their subsidiaries, such as interest, dividends, and royalties, since this income is easily moveable to low-tax or no-tax jurisdictions.

The US CFC rules are subject to a number of complexities beyond the scope of this book. But, to best understand how multinationals maneuver around them, it is worth spending some time in the weeds. The US CFC rules provide that if a foreign subsidiary corporation is a "controlled

---

July 31, 2014, *available at* http://taxandaccounting.bna.com/bta/display/batch_print_dis play.adp [hereinafter Global Tax Guide].

[27] Altshuler et al., *supra* note 2, at 26.   [28] *Ibid.*

[29] Germany's CFC rules apply to passive income unless the CFC is a resident in a European Economic Area (EEA) country, "It carries on genuine business activity, the passive income is connected to the activity, and the EU Mutual Assistance Directive or a similar agreement is available in the EEA country." Altshuler et al., *supra* note 2, at 29.

[30] Japan's CFC rules apply to active income unless the CFC maintains a place of business sufficient to carry on its business, carries on business with its own management, and meets a certain test for dealing with unrelated parties. Altshuler et al., *supra* note 2, at 26.

[31] Paul W. Oosterhuis, "The Evolution of International Tax Policy-What Would Larry Say?" *Ohio Northern University Law Review* 33 (2006): 2.

[32] *Ibid.* (citing John F. Kennedy, President of the US, "Annual Message to Congress on the State of the Union" (January 11, 2962), in *Published Papers* 1 (1963): 13–14).

[33] 26 U.S.C. §§ 951–964. Oosterhuis, *supra* note 31, at 3.

foreign corporation" (as defined in the statute) for an uninterrupted period of thirty days or more during the taxable year, each "US shareholder" who owns stock on the last day in such a year shall pay tax on its share of the subsidiary's "Subpart F income."[34] Therefore, if a US parent corporation owns 100 percent of a foreign subsidiary company, the US parent's share of the subsidiary's Subpart F income will be 100 percent and will be subject to current US taxation regardless of whether any foreign earnings were actually distributed.

There are several categories of Subpart F income.[35] The categories generally target income that is easily shifted overseas and subject to low rates of foreign tax. This includes passive investment income and sales or services income from related party transactions.[36] These categories contain exceptions that can be supported on policy grounds but that have been exploited by tax planners in ways never contemplated by legislators.[37]

A major category of Subpart F income (foreign personal holding company income) consists of passive income of a CFC, such as interests, dividends, and royalties.[38] To illustrate, assume a US parent company wholly owns a CFC in a low-tax foreign country, which in turn wholly owns a subsidiary in a high-tax foreign country. The lower-tiered subsidiary may have substantial foreign earnings from manufacturing and sales functions and it passes those earnings up to the higher-tiered CFC in

---

[34] 26 U.S.C. § 951(a). A foreign corporation is a "controlled foreign corporation" (CFC) if the US shareholders, in the aggregate, own more than 50 percent by vote or value of the foreign corporation. 26 U.S.C. § 957(a). A "US shareholder" for CFC purposes is any US person who owns "10 percent or more of the total combined voting power of all classes of stock entitled to vote." 26 U.S.C. § 951(b). Typically, CFCs are wholly owned subsidiaries of a US parent company.

[35] A major category of Subpart F income is "foreign base company income." 26 U.S.C. § 954. Foreign base company income is divided into three main categories: (1) foreign personal holding company income, (2) foreign base company sales income, and (3) foreign base company services income. We focus on the first two categories. Under the third category, services income is treated as Subpart F income when a CFC (1) performs services for, or on behalf of, a related person, and (2) performs such services outside its country of organization. 26 U.S.C. § 954(a)(3), (e). Services include technical, managerial, engineering, architectural, scientific, skilled, industrial, commercial, or like services.

[36] Subpart F Study, *supra* note 3, at xii ("[S]ubpart F generally targets passive income and income that is split off from the activities that produced the value in the goods or services generating the income").

[37] It should be noted that there are other exceptions to Subpart F income in addition to those noted above. There is a *de minimis* rule, under which a CFC's foreign base company income will be deemed to be zero if it is less than 5 percent of the CFC's gross income or $1,000,000 (whichever is less). 26 U.S.C. § 954(b)(3)(A); Treas. Reg. § 1.954–1(b)(1)(i). Also, there is a *high-tax exception*, under which an item of income is excluded if the effective rate of tax imposed on the income by a foreign country is greater than 90 percent of the maximum rate of US tax. 26 U.S.C. § 954(b)(4); Treas. Reg. § 1.954–1(d).

[38] 26 U.S.C. § 954(c).

the form of dividend payments or royalty payments for the use of the CFC's intellectual property. Under Subpart F, both types of passive income (dividends and royalties) would be subject to current US taxation even if the CFC did not actually pass that income up to the US parent company.[39]

There are two important exceptions to personal holding company income. The first exception applies to royalties derived from the active conduct of a CFC's trade or business and received from an unrelated party.[40] This exception, commonly referred to as the *active business rents and royalty exception*, is based on the theory that if a CFC is engaged in activity, then economic reasons, not tax reasons explain location of the subsidiary in that country. The second exception applies to dividends, interest, and royalties received by a CFC where the payor is organized and operating in the same foreign country as the CFC recipient.[41] This exception, referred to as the *same country exception*, is based on the theory that little incentive to avoid US taxes exists if both the payor and payee corporations are in the same country and subject to the same foreign tax regime.[42]

A second major category of Subpart F income (foreign base company sales income) consists of income received by a CFC attributable to goods purchased from or sold to a related party where the CFC's country of organization is not the origin or destination of the goods, and the CFC has not "manufactured" the goods itself.[43] More specifically, (1) the CFC purchases property from or sells property to a related person, (2) the property is manufactured, produced, grown, or extracted outside the CFC's country of incorporation by someone other than the CFC, and (3) the property is sold for use, consumption, or disposition outside the CFC's country of incorporation.[44] This category targets income from a CFC (which typically sits in a tax haven) set up as a distribution center through which goods produced outside the CFC's country of organization are distributed or sold for use outside the CFC's country of organization.

To illustrate, consider the following example: USCo, a US multinational company, sells computer software to both US and non-US customers around the world. USCo creates a wholly owned subsidiary in Ireland that will purchase prepacked software from USCo and then package and

---

[39] Senate Apple Hearing, *supra* note 10, at 15.

[40] 26 U.S.C. § 954(c)(2)(A). Recent regulations narrow the application of the active rents and royalties exception. Treas. Reg. § 1.954–2T (excluding activities performed by persons other than employees and officers of the CFC).

[41] 26 U.S.C. § 954(c)(3)(A), (d)(3) (defining related corporation for these purposes).

[42] Senate Apple Hearing, *supra* note 10, at 15.   [43] 26 U.S.C. § 954((a)(2), (d).

[44] Treas. Reg. § 1.954–3(a)(4)(i).

resell it to customers outside the United States. The CFC's sales income is Subpart F income that must be included in USCo's gross income. Consider another example: USCo creates a wholly owned subsidiary in Ireland that buys finished goods from a third-party manufacturer in another country, and then sells the finished goods to a related distribution subsidiary for sales abroad. The CFC's sales income is Subpart F income subject to current US taxation. In this example, USCo has split the manufacturing function from the sales function to deflect sales income to Ireland, a low-tax jurisdiction, something Congress wanted to discourage.[45]

An important exception for foreign base company sales income, mentioned above, is the so-called *manufacturing exception*. It exists if the CFC itself manufactures the goods it sells. In other words, the CFC can sell products to any country without generating foreign base company sales income if those products are manufactured by the CFC in the CFC's country of incorporation.[46] The rationale for this exception is that if a CFC is engaged in manufacturing efforts, then economic reasons, not tax reasons, explain location of the subsidiary in that country.

Multinational companies often have one or more top-level CFCs that, in turn, wholly own lower-tier subsidiaries, which often own their own subsidiaries. Foreign income of all the lower-tier subsidiaries typically gets funneled up the chain of subsidiaries to the top-level CFCs in the form of dividends or royalties. We saw this with all three case studies presented in Chapter 7. And it is the exact technique that the CFC rules of Subpart F were designed to address.

In reality, the CFC rules have been quite ineffective at eliminating deferral of taxation on a subsidiary's foreign income. Statistics reveal that most foreign income of CFCs is still deferred from current US taxation. In fact, only 12 percent of CFC earnings are currently taxed under Subpart F.[47] And, believe it or not, some of that Subpart

---

[45] Senate Apple Hearing, *supra* note 10, at 16. It should be noted that the foreign base company sales income provisions contain a *branch rule* under which the foreign base company sales income rules may apply if manufacturing and sales activities are conducted in different countries by the CFC and the effective tax rate on sales income is significantly lower than the tax rate that would be imposed on such income if the sales were taxed in the country where the manufacturing activities occurred. 26 U.S.C. § 954(d)(2); Treas. Reg. § 1.954–3(b)(1)(ii)(B) (establishing when a substantial tax rate disparity exists between the sales branch country and the CFC country). The branch rule is designed to target CFCs that establish manufacturing functions in a high-tax country and sales activities in a low-tax country to take advantage of the fact that the United States does not treat a branch as a separate entity and reduce tax on the sale of the manufactured item.

[46] 26 U.S.C. § 954(d)(1)(A); Treas. Reg. § 1.954–3(a)(4).

[47] Microsoft Part I, *supra* note 6, at 89 (citing "Testimony of Stephen E. Shay Before the US Senate Permanent Subcommittee on Investigations of the Committee on Homeland Security and Governmental Affairs Hearing on Offshore Profit Shifting and the Internal Revenue Code," September 20, 2012, 3 n.10). *See also* Lee Mahoney & Randy Miller,

F income is generated intentionally by multinationals for tax advantages – for example, to use foreign tax credits to offset US taxes on other income without paying foreign withholding taxes that typically would be due on an actual dividend distribution of non-Subpart F income.[48]

US multinationals have been able to avoid having their offshore income taxed under Subpart F by taking advantage of various statutory and regulatory provisions that undermine the intended application of the CFC rules. The three main loopholes are: (1) the check-the-box regulations; (2) the temporary CFC "look through" rule; and (3) the "same country" and "manufacturing" statutory exceptions that are built into the CFC rules. These loopholes sometimes overlap providing bulletproof layers of protection against the imposition of current US taxation on foreign profits.

Elaborating on our discussion from Chapter 6, the first important loophole technique used by many US multinationals is utilization of the check-the-box entity classification regulations issued by the Treasury Department in 1997. To review, in the 1990s the Treasury thought it would be a good idea to simplify, for US tax purposes, the classification of entities – whether they would be treated for US tax purposes as corporations, partnerships, branches, etc. At that time, entity classification was based on a cumbersome multifactor test, and international entity classification was generally dependent upon foreign law. To eliminate uncertainties and complexities inherent in this classification approach, the Treasury adopted a simplified, elective classification approach in regulations known as "check-the-box" regulations. Under the check-the-box regulations, still in force today, a US parent can elect to treat a controlled foreign subsidiary either as a *corporation* or as *disregarded* (transparent) for US tax purposes. If a CFC is checked as a corporation, US tax law recognizes payments to and from it; conversely, if a CFC is checked as disregarded, US tax law will ignore payments to and from it.

The Treasury's goal to simplify international entity classification was laudable. Its regulations, however, have had unintended consequences and have been used by multinationals to undermine the application of Subpart F. Many US multinationals elected to have their top-level CFC, which is often in a tax-haven country, treated as a foreign corporation (recognizable legal entity), but in turn elected to have their lower-tier CFCs disregarded or ignored for US tax purposes (transparent entities).

"Controlled Foreign Corporations, 2006," *Statistics of Income Bulletin* (2011): 202, *available at* www.irs.gov/pub/irs-soi/11coforeign06winbull.pdf (Figure C).

[48] *See also* Microsoft Part I, *supra* note 6, at 89 (citing "Testimony of Stephen E. Shay Before the U.S. Senate Permanent Subcommittee on Investigations of the Committee on Homeland Security and Governmental Affairs Hearing on Offshore Profit Shifting and the Internal Revenue Code," September 20, 2012, 3).

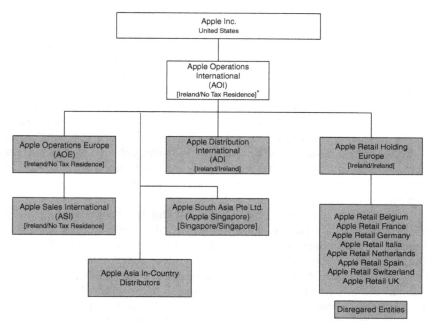

*Listed countries indicate country of incorporation and country of tax residence, respectively.

Figure 8.1 Effect of Check-the-Box
Prepared by the Permanent Subcommittee on Investigations,
May 2013. Source: Materials received from Apple Inc.

The chart above shows Apple's offshore corporate structure. As can be seen, its top-level CFC (AOI) is recognized as a legal foreign corporation, but many of its lower tier subsidiaries are disregarded under check-the-box regulations.

For US tax purposes, the lower-tiered CFCs are not treated as separate legal entities, but rather as part of the upper-tier CFC. US tax law does not recognize payments an entity makes to itself. Thus, since all are treated as one corporation, any passive income (dividends or royalties) paid by the lower-tiered CFCs to the upper-tier CFC are ignored and do not fall under Subpart F. Clearly, if the upper- and lower-tiered CFCs were viewed as separate legal entities, royalties and dividends that go up to the top-level CFC from the lower-level CFCs would be regarded as Subpart F income. However, if the lower-tiered CFCs have been "checked" and are disregarded, payments the top-level CFC receives from them are disregarded as well.

The Treasury realized it made a huge mistake soon after it finalized the check-the-box entity classification system, but pressure from taxpayers and members of Congress precluded any administrative fix. Surprisingly, in 2006 proponents of check-the-box convinced Congress to enact supporting legislation.[49] The temporary legislation, known as the CFC "look through" rule, excludes from Subpart F related-party passive income. Specifically, it excludes payments (dividends, interest, rents, and royalties) received by one CFC from a related CFC.[50] Under the look through rule, payments from one CFC to another are disregarded regardless of check-the-box regulations. Because the look through rule is a temporary rule that periodically expires and is renewed, multinationals continue to rely on check-the-box regulations to avoid such payments from inclusion in Subpart F income.[51]

Clearly, the check-the-box regulations and the temporary statutory look through rule (which wrote the effect of the regulations into law) reduce the effectiveness of the antideferral rules of Subpart F. To make matters worse, the Subpart F rules themselves contain certain statutory exceptions that reduce the effectiveness of Subpart F, even without the check-the-box regulations or the statutory look through rule.

As noted above, Subpart F income includes certain passive income (dividends and royalties) received by a CFC. But under the *same country exception*, introduced earlier, payments received by a CFC from a related CFC in the same country are exempt. The same country exception can be supported on policy grounds in that a payment is not likely to be tax motivated if both the payor and payee are subject to the same foreign tax regime. In its application, the exception can be manipulated quite easily and can have the same effect as the check-the-box regulations and the look through rule, which have been the source of much government consternation. Looking back to the case studies in Chapter 7, a multinational company's top-level CFC and its lower-level CFCs are often incorporated in the same low-tax foreign country (although often managed in different jurisdictions) – hence, the names "Double Irish" or "Double Dutch" often ascribed to such structures. Because the United States looks to the place of incorporation and not to the place of management, any passive income payments made by lower tier CFCs to the top-level CFC would qualify for the same country statutory exception

---

[49] 26 U.S.C. § 954(c)(6), added by Tax Increase Prevention and Reconciliation Act of 2005, Pub. L. No. 109–222, § 103(b)(1) (2006). At the time of this writing, the look through rule has been extended through 2019.

[50] David R. Sicular, "The New Look-Through Rule: W(h)ither Subpart F?," *Tax Notes* (2007): 359, *available at* www.paulweiss.com/media/104725/SubPartF04-May-07.pdf.

[51] Microsoft Part I, *supra* note 6, at 12 (providing testimony of Reuven S. Avi-Yonah).

contained in Subpart F without regard to the check-the-box regulations or the temporary statutory look through rule.

Also mentioned above, Subpart F income includes certain active income – certain sales income from related parties specifically derived by a CFC in connection with the sale of products purchased from a related party and sold outside the CFC's country of organization. Built into the rules, however, is a *manufacturing exception* under which income retained by a CFC will not be subject to current US taxation if the CFC itself is a manufacturer. The level of CFC manufacturing necessary to qualify for this exception has be liberalized by regulations; thus it is quite easy for a multinational to achieve. To qualify, a CFC must meet one of three tests. The first two are physical manufacturing tests: (1) the substantial transformation test, under which property is considered manufactured if it is substantially transformed prior to sale;[52] and (2) the substantial activity test, under which property is considered manufactured if the assembly or conversion of the purchased component parts into the final product involves activities that "are substantial in nature and generally considered to constitute the manufacture, production, or construction of property."[53] Under a safe harbor rule, operations are deemed to constitute manufacturing if the direct labor and overhead costs to convert the purchased components into the final product account for 20 percent or more of the total costs of goods sold.

In 2008, the Treasury added a third alternative test, a substantial contribution test, under which a CFC may qualify for the manufacturing exception if it makes a substantial contribution through the activities of its employees to the manufacture, production, or construction of personal property.[54] It has been argued that moving from the requirement that the CFC demonstrate it performed a manufacturing activity to a requirement where the CFC must demonstrate it made a "substantial contribution" to the goods being sold has transformed this exception into another possible loophole for multinationals to shield offshore income from Subpart F taxation.[55]

Transfer Pricing Rules

The controlled foreign corporation rules were designed to prevent US companies from utilizing foreign subsidiaries to defer US taxes on their foreign income. As shown above, a number of loopholes, such as the

---

[52] Treas. Reg. § 1.954–3(a)(4)(ii).
[53] Treas. Reg. § 1.954–3(a)(4)(iii) and Example 3 (noting packaging, labeling, or minor assembly are insufficient).
[54] Treas. Reg. § 1.954–3(a)(4)(iv).   [55] Senate Apple Hearing, *supra* note 10, at 16.

check-the-box regulations, temporary statutory changes, and certain statutory exceptions exist to shield foreign income from the CFC rules. Thus,
deferral is still available in many cases, and the value of deferral can be
maximized with aggressive intercompany transfer pricing strategies that
shift much of a US multinational entity's profits to low-tax, or no-tax,
foreign jurisdictions.

In order for a foreign subsidiary to earn income from the manufacturing
and sale of products, it must possess rights to the intellectual property on
which those products are based. Assuming a foreign subsidiary does not
develop and own its own, it typically receives intellectual property rights
from its US parent company. There are several ways a US parent company can transfer its intellectual property to an offshore subsidiary. A US
parent may make an outright *sale* of all substantial rights to its controlled
foreign subsidiary. Alternatively, the US parent may *license* the rights to its
foreign subsidiary.[56] Licensing of specified rights is more popular than
outright sale. This is because US multinationals wish to take advantage of
intellectual property protections offered by the US legal system, and thus,
do not transfer legal ownership outside the United States.[57] Regardless,
under either approach (sale or license), the US parent must pay tax on the
consideration it receives from its foreign subsidiary.[58]

There is an incentive for the foreign subsidiary to pay an artificially low
price for the intellectual property. Setting license royalties as low as
possible will maximize the amount of the foreign subsidiary's profits
taxed at the low foreign tax rate and maximize the amount of US tax
deferral, assuming those profits will not be distributed to the US parent.
Consider an example: US Parent, a major manufacturer of soft contact
lenses, formed a subsidiary corporation, Europe Co, in low-tax foreign

---

[56] A US parent may also transfer intellectual property to its foreign subsidiary in exchange
for stock in the foreign subsidiarity. In contrast to the sale and license options, no royalties
actually flow from the foreign subsidiary to the US parent. Under 26 U.S.C. § 367(d),
special rules are provided for the transfer of IP (including patents, know-how, inventions,
formulas, processes, copyrights, trademarks, and trade names) to a foreign corporation in
exchange for stock. In such foreign outbound transfers, the transferor US corporation is
treated as receiving income (deemed royalty payments) over the useful life of the IP in an
amount reflecting reasonable payments contingent upon the productivity, use, or disposition of the IP. Such US corporation, over the useful life of the property, must
annually include in gross income an amount that represents an appropriate arm's-length
charge for the use of the property, even if payments are not actually made. This implicates
the transfer pricing rules of section 482, discussed more fully below.
[57] Senate Apple Hearing, *supra* note 10, at 8–9.
[58] The US parent will be subject to US tax on the consideration it receives. In the case of
a license, the royalties will be classified as "foreign source income" because royalty
income is sourced according to where the intellectual property is located, not where it
was developed. The US tax due on this foreign source income, however, can be offset by
foreign tax credits.

country. US Parent granted Europe Co a nonexclusive license to manufacture and sell contact lenses using US Parent's technology, in exchange for a royalty of 1 percent of Europe Co's net contact lens sales. The active foreign sales income of Europe Co will not be subject to current US taxation because it is not considered Subpart F income. However, the royalty that Europe Co pays to US Parent will be. Notice how setting the royalty fee extremely low allows more profit from contact lens sales to be realized in the low-tax foreign country, rather than in the high-tax United States.

This incentive to manipulate the royalty payments between a domestic multinational and its related foreign subsidiaries brings us to another significant barrier to intellectual property income shifting: transfer pricing rules. The approach taken by many foreign governments to transfer pricing concerns has been to treat transactions between related parties, such as a domestic parent company and its controlled foreign subsidiary, the same as if the transactions were between unrelated parties. Thus, related parties must be dealing with each other at arm's length, and the transactions and transfers of property between them must reflect arm's-length consideration. Foregoing this requirement, the related parties risk that the government may make arm's-length transfer pricing adjustments to ensure that such transactions clearly reflect income. In the example above, the royalty payment from Europe Co to US Parent was set extremely low so more profit from contact lens sales would be earned in the low-tax foreign country, rather than in the high-tax United States. Under section 482, however, the Service would argue that the 1 percent royalty rate is unreasonable and should be higher to reflect an arm's-length consideration.[59] A correlative adjustment may or may not be made by the foreign taxing authority, which could result in double taxation. Many tax treaties, however, attempt to provide relief in some form.

Many countries use the arm's-length method.[60] Determining an appropriate arm's-length transfer price between related parties is a challenge because it is difficult to determine what price uncontrolled parties

---

[59] Section 482 authorizes the Service to "distribute, apportion, or allocate gross income, deductions, credits or allowances" among controlled businesses where "such distribution, apportionment or allocation is necessary in order to prevent evasion of taxes or clearly to reflect the income" of such controlled businesses. 26 U.S.C. § 482; Treas. Reg. § 1.482–1 (describing broadly the "controlled" taxpayers and transactions to which section 482 applies).

[60] For the historical development of the arm's length standard in the US, see Reuven S. Avi-Yonah, "The Rise and Fall of Arm's Length: A Study in the Evolution of US International Taxation," *Va. Tax. Rev.* 15 (1995): 89.

would have set in similar transactions under similar circumstances.[61] This is especially true with respect to transfers and licenses of unique and difficult-to-value intangible assets, such as patents, copyrights, trademarks, and other similar property. Some countries have developed specific transfer pricing methodologies that are deemed acceptable. Many employ the methodologies stated in the OECD guidelines.[62] Multinational companies typically hire appraisers and economists to determine arm's-length transfer prices.

The United States basically provides three methods for determining an arm's-length price for the transfer or use of intangible property between related parties: (1) the comparable uncontrolled transaction method; (2) the comparable profits method; and (3) the profit split method.[63] Under the "best method" rule in the regulations, a taxpayer should use whichever method provides the most reliable measure of an arm's-length result.[64] The reliability of a pricing method is determined by the degree of comparability between similar controlled and uncontrolled transactions, and the quality of the data and assumptions used in the analysis.[65] Factors to consider in assessing the comparability of controlled and uncontrolled transactions include: functions performed, risks assumed, contractual terms, economic conditions and markets, and nature of the property or services transferred in the transaction.[66] Taxpayers often conduct detailed-oriented economic analysis of relevant data and information regarding comparable companies and transactions to determine the best method for intercompany transactions. In reality economists, not lawyers, perform much of the transfer pricing work.

Although we do not attempt here to provide detailed treatment of the transfer pricing methods, we offer a brief summary of the US options. Under the *comparable uncontrolled transaction* (CUT) method, the

---

[61] *See* Treas. Reg. § 1.482–1(b) (acknowledging that "identical transactions can rarely be located" and that controlled transactions generally will be analyzed by reference to "the results of comparable transactions under comparable circumstances"); Treas. Reg. § 1.482–1(b)(1), (d) (elaborating on the standard of comparability).

[62] *See* Global Tax Guide, *supra* note 26, at 27. *See* OECD "Transfer Pricing Guidelines for Multinational Enterprises and Tax Administrations" (OECD Publishing, 2010).

[63] Treas. Reg. § 1.482–4(a) (referring to Treas. Reg. §§ 1.482–4(c), -5, -6). The first two are considered "one-sided" in that one party is the test party (with the untested party entitled to residual profits by default). The third is considered "two-sided" in that both affiliates are tested parties in allocating multinational combined income. *See* Bret Wells & Cym Lowell, "Tax Base Erosion: Reformation of Section 482's Arm's Length Standard," *University of Houston Public Law and Legal Theory Series* 2013-W-6, August 13, 2013, *available at* http://isites.harvard.edu/fs/docs/icb.topic1321119.files/September%2018%20Readings-%20Articles%20Mentioned%20in%20Class%20Last%20Evening/Erosion_Tax_Base.pdf.

[64] Treas. Reg. § 1.482–1(c).   [65] Treas. Reg. § 1.482–1(d)(1).

[66] Treas. Reg. § 1.482–1(d)(2).

arm's-length price for the transfer of an intangible, in a controlled (related party) transaction, is the amount charged for the same or comparable intangibles in transactions between uncontrolled (unrelated) parties, adjusted for material differences that exist between the controlled and uncontrolled transactions.[67] Of course, an uncontrolled transaction in which the transferor transferred the *same* intangible to an unrelated party under the *same or substantially similar* circumstances is generally the most reliable measure of the arm's-length result for the controlled transaction. But, if an exact comparable transaction cannot be identified, the regulations permit the use of an uncontrolled transaction that involves the transfer of a *comparable* intangible under *comparable* circumstances. In order to be considered comparable, both intangibles must be used in connection with similar products or processes within the same general industry or market, and have similar profit potential.[68] The regulations provide a number of factors that must be considered in evaluating the comparability of the circumstances of the controlled and uncontrolled transactions.[69]

In determining an arm's-length royalty between related parties, the *comparable profits method* (CPM) compares the profitability of a "tested party" (one of the participants in the controlled transaction) with the profitability of unrelated taxpayers engaged in similar business activities under similar circumstances.[70] If profitability of the tested party differs materially from the profitability of the similar uncontrolled taxpayer, the IRS can adjust the intercompany royalty to bring the tested party's retained profit more in line with the uncontrolled taxpayer's profit.[71]

---

[67] Treas. Reg. § 1.482–4(c)(1).   [68] Treas. Reg. § 1.482–4(c)(2)(iii)(B)(1).
[69] *See* Treas. Reg. § 1.482–4(c)(2)(iii)(B)(2).
[70] Treas. Reg. § 1.482–5(a). The "tested party" is that "participant in the controlled transaction whose operating profit attributable to the controlled transactions can be verified using the most reliable data and requiring the fewest and most reliable adjustments, and for which reliable data regarding uncontrolled comparables can be located." Treas. Reg. § 1.482–5(b)(2)(i). In many cases, the tested party is the intellectual property licensee, such as a foreign subsidiary that is licensing intellectual property from its US parent company. The licensee is typically the least complex of the controlled taxpayers; it typically does not own valuable intangibles or unique assets that distinguish it from potential uncontrolled comparables.
[71] Treas. Reg. § 1.482–5(b)(1). "The tested party's reported operating profit is compared to comparable operating profits." Comparable operating profits are calculated by determining "profit level indicators" of uncontrolled comparables (ratios that measure relationships between profits and costs incurred or resources employed over a reasonable period of time), and applying the indicators to the tested party's financial data that is related to controlled transactions. *See* Treas. Reg. § 1.482–5(b)(4) (listing profit level indicators that may provide a reliable basis for comparing a tested party's operating profits and uncontrolled comparables). If the tested party's actual operating profit is not within a certain range of comparable operating profits, the IRS can adjust the intercompany royalties to achieve that result.

In some controlled groups, each related party owns valuable intangibles that contribute to the group's combined operating profit or loss. The *profit split method* evaluates whether the allocation of the combined profit or loss attributable to one or more related party transactions is arm's length by reference to the relative value of each related party's contribution.[72] The allocation between the related parties should correspond to the division of profit or loss that would result from an arrangement between uncontrolled taxpayers. The regulations under section 482 provide two profit split methods: (1) the "comparable profit split method"[73] and (2) the "residual profit split method."[74]

Related-party transfers (that expand several years) of intellectual property that have *high profit potential* present unique issues. A US multinational company and its related foreign subsidiary may use comparable transfers to originally set a reasonable, albeit low, royalty rate. But that rate may not reflect the actual income that the intangible ultimately produces in the market. Indeed, before 1986, it was common practice for US multinationals to deduct the costs of research and development in the United States and transfer, at a reasonable but low royalty rate, the resulting intellectual property to tax haven jurisdictions such as Puerto Rico. As the intellectual property became more valuable, no adjustment would be made to the initial royalty rate, and huge profits attributable to the highly valuable intellectual property accumulated in the tax-haven

---

[72] Treas. Reg. § 1.482–6(a), (b) (noting the appropriate share of profits and losses must reflect functions performed, risks assumed, and resources employed by each party in the relevant business activity consistent with the comparability provisions of Treas. Reg. § 1.482–1[d][3]).

[73] Under the comparable profit split method, the combined operating profit or loss from the relevant business activity is allocated between related parties in the same proportion as profits and losses are allocated between unrelated parties engaged in similar transactions and activities. Treas. Reg. § 1.482-6(c)(2). This method is seldom used because it depends upon reliable external market data, which is often unavailable. *See* Treas. Reg. § 1.482-6(c)(2)(ii) (describing comparability and reliability considerations).

[74] Under the residual profit split method, the combined operating profit or loss from the relevant business activity is allocated between related parties using a two-step process. The first step allocates profits based on a market return for each party's "routine" contributions to the relevant business activity (e.g., contributions of tangible property, services, and intangible property similarly made by uncontrolled taxpayers involved in similar activities). Treas. Reg. §1.482-6(c)(3)(i)(A). The second step allocates remaining (residual) profit based on the relative value of each party's "non-routine" contributions to the relevant business activity. Treas. Reg. §1.482-6(c)(3)(i)(B). In most cases, nonroutine contributions include contributions of intangible property, the relative value of which may be measured by (1) external market benchmarks that reflect the value of such property, (2) capitalized costs of developing the property and all improvements and updates, less amortization allowances based on useful life, or (3) actual development expenditures if such expenditures are relatively constant over time. Treas. Reg. §1.482-6(c)(3)(i)(B)(2).

country, escaping current US taxation.[75] In 1986, Congress tried to close this loophole by adopting a rule that said, "In the case of any transfer (or license) of intangible property . . . the income with respect to such transfer or license shall be *commensurate with the income* attributable to the intangible."[76] This provision, which emphasizes income actually generated by the intangible subsequent to the transfer, allows the IRS to make periodic royalty adjustments in subsequent years to ensure the arm's-length standard is satisfied. This is so even if the initial royalty was completely reasonable at that time it was set.[77]

Transfer pricing rules, such as the commensurate with income standard that was designed to transfer foreign income back to the United States, have largely failed. The United States, as with many countries, has struggled with transfer pricing enforcement despite devoting substantial resources to it. To help enforce arm's-length transfer pricing rules, many nations impose information reporting requirements.[78] Some governments impose penalties for improper pricing to encourage voluntary compliance with the arm's-length standard.[79] In general, efforts to

---

[75] Microsoft Part I, *supra* note 6, at 12 (providing testimony of Reuven S. Avi-Yonah).

[76] 26 U.S.C. § 482.

[77] Treas. Reg. § 1.482-4(f)(2)(i). The regulations provide some important exceptions. For example, no adjustment will be made in a subsequent year if the initial royalty was set under the CUT method based on a transaction involving the same intangible. Treas. Reg. § 1.482-4(f)(2)(ii)(A). Also no adjustment will be made if the initial royalty rate was set under any acceptable method (CUT, CPM, or profit split) based on transactions involving a comparable intangible under comparable circumstances, but only if the controlled taxpayer's actual profits or cost savings from exploitation of the intangible are not less than 80 percent nor more than 120 percent of the prospective profits or cost savings that were originally foreseeable. Treas. Reg. § 1.482-4(f)(2)(ii)(B).

[78] In the United States, certain US corporations that own stock in foreign subsidiaries and certain US corporations whose stock is owned by foreign companies must file appropriate forms. Specifically, a US parent company that owns more than 50 percent of the stock of a foreign subsidiary company must file IRS Form 5471 (Information Return of US Persons with Respect to Certain Foreign Corporations). 26 U.S.C. § 6038; Treas. Reg. § 1.6038-2(a)-(b). In addition, a US subsidiary company, 25 percent of the stock of which is owned by a foreign company, must file IRS Form 5472 (Information Return of a 25 percent Foreign-Owned US Corporation). 26 U.S.C. § 6038A; Treas. Reg. § 1.6038A-1(c). Both of these forms require certain information regarding the foreign related party, as well as dollar amounts of transactions entered into with the related party. Treas. Reg. §§ 1.6038-2(f); 1.6038A-2(b). Both forms are often used by the IRS as a starting point for conducting transfer pricing examinations.

[79] The United States has enacted two special transfer pricing penalties: (1) the transactional penalty and (2) the net adjustment penalty. The *transactional penalty* is 20 percent of the tax underpayment related to a section 482 adjustment made by the IRS. It is raised when the IRS determines under section 482 that the transfer price used on the return is 200 percent more or 50 percent less than the correct price. The penalty rate is increased to 40 percent when the price claimed on the return is 400 percent more or 25 percent less than the correct price. *See* 26 U.S.C. § 6662(a), (e)(1)(B)(i), (h); Treas. Reg. § 1.6662-6(b). The *net adjustment penalty* is also 20 percent of the tax underpayment related to a transfer pricing adjustment by the IRS. *See* 26 U.S.C. § 6662(b)(3), (e)(1)

improve transfer pricing rules have been ongoing on a multilateral basis at the OECD. And, as noted above, some countries are responding and introducing transfer pricing rules in accordance with the OECD guidelines.

Efforts to improve transfer pricing rules, however, continue to prove ineffective. A main reason is that transfer pricing rules can be avoided if a US parent company that would sell or license the rights in a transaction where arm's-length consideration must be received, instead uses a cost sharing agreement to transfer the economic rights to its intellectual property to an offshore affiliate or foreign subsidiary.

In the United States, taxpayers are generally immune from section 482's effects if intellectual property is developed under a bona fide *cost sharing agreement*. A bona fide cost sharing arrangement is an agreement between a US parent company and its foreign subsidiary to share the costs and risks of developing one or more intangible assets in exchange for a certain interest in the intangible property developed. For tax purposes, the US parent and the foreign subsidiary are considered to be the owners of any intellectual property developed under the cost sharing arrangement. As owners for tax purposes, the participants can exploit any IP developed under the cost sharing agreement without having to pay arm's-length royalty payments to the other participants. As the Joint Committee on Taxation explained: "The arrangement provides that the US company owns legal title to, and all US marketing and production rights in, the developed property, and that the other party (or parties) owns rights to all marketing and production for the rest of the world. Reflecting the split economic ownership of the newly developed asset, no royalties are paid between cost sharing participants when the product is ultimately marketed and sold to customers."[80]

(B)(ii), (e)(3)(A), (h); Treas. Reg. § 1.6662-6(c). It is raised when the IRS determines that the net of adjustments made under section 482 exceeds the lesser of $5 million or 10 percent of the taxpayer's gross receipts for the year. The penalty is increased to 40 percent when the net of adjustments made under section 482 exceeds the lesser of $20 million or 20 percent of the taxpayer gross receipts for the year. There are important safe harbor exceptions for the transfer pricing penalties in the United States. For example, the transactional penalty will not be imposed if the taxpayer can demonstrate that it had reasonable cause and acted in good faith. Treas. Reg. §§ 1.6662-6(b)(3), 1.6664-4(a). With respect to the net adjustment penalty, the reasonable cause and good faith exception applies only if the taxpayer maintains contemporaneous documentation (i.e., documentation in existence when a timely tax return is filed) to show adherence and compliance with the arm's-length standard. 26 U.S.C. § 6662(e)(3)(B)(i); Treas. Reg. § 1.6662-6(d)(2)(iii)(A). For a list of supporting transfer pricing documentation, *see* Treas. Reg. § 1.6662-6(d)(2)(iii)(B).

[80] Joint Committee on Taxation, "Present Law and Background Related to Possible Income Shifting and Transfer Pricing," 21, JCX-37-10 (July 20, 2010), *available at* www.jct.gov/publications.html?func=startdown&id=3692.

Cost sharing agreements were sanctioned by the US Congress in 1986 and are expressly authorized by US Treasury regulations.[81] The regulations provide detailed rules for evaluating the compensation received by each participant for its contribution to the agreement. Specifically, the participants must share "intangible development costs" in proportion to their "reasonably anticipated benefits" from the developed intangible.[82] As we saw in Chapter 7, Apple, the US parent company, and ASI, its foreign subsidiary, allegedly share research and development costs based on the portion of product sales that occur in their respective regions. Of the $2.4 billion in worldwide research and development costs in one year studied, Apple paid 40 percent (representative of worldwide sales occurring in the Americas), and ASI paid 60 percent (percentage of worldwide sales occurring offshore). Microsoft similarly alleges to share costs of developing intellectual property with its subsidiaries based on the portion of sales that occur in their respective regions. For example, Microsoft's Puerto Rico subsidiary pays 25 percent of Microsoft's global R&D expenses because 25 percent of global sales occur in the Americas.

In a typical cost sharing arrangement, the US parent company owns and brings to the agreement existing intangibles, which are used as platforms for the development of new intangibles. The US parent is treated as having transferred interests in such property and thus must be compensated an arm's-length amount through buy-in payments from the other participant(s). The final regulations refer to these buy-in payments as "platform contribution transaction" (PCT) payments.[83]

The determination of what is considered a platform contribution for which a buy-in payment is required, and the determination of arm's-length payment for such contribution, has been the source of much contention between US multinational entities and the IRS in recent years. In a familiar scheme, a US parent company conducts R&D and then contributes the

---

[81] Treas. Reg. § 1.482-7.

[82] Treas. Reg. § 1.482-7(a)(1), (b)(1)(i). "Intangible development costs" that must be shared include all costs directly identified with or reasonably allocable to the intangible development activity under the cost sharing arrangement. *See* Treas. Reg. § 1.482-4(d). A controlled participant's share of reasonably anticipated benefits is equal to its reasonably anticipated benefits divided by the sum of the reasonably anticipated benefits of all controlled participants. Treas. Reg. § 1.482-7(e)(1)(i). Such "shares" must be updated to account for changes in economic conditions, the business operations and practices of the participants, and the ongoing development of intangibles under the cost sharing arrangement. For purposes of determining such shares at any given time, reasonably anticipated benefits must be estimated over the entire period (past and future) of exploitation of the developed intangible, updated to take into account the most reliable data regarding past and projected future results available at such time. *Ibid.*

[83] Treas. Reg. § 1.482-7(b)(1)(ii), (c).

new technology (e.g., software) to a cost sharing arrangement for further joint development with its low-tax foreign subsidiary. The participants set the PCT payment for the technology low to maximize the amount of profits taxed to the foreign subsidiary, similar to the previous scheme involving royalties. The IRS challenges the PCT payment as too low since (1) the US parent also contributed certain workforce to the arrangement for which no PCT payment was received, and (2) the foreign subsidiary earned substantial profits from the cost sharing arrangement. In response to these controversial scenarios, the Treasury finalized, in 2011, regulations related to cost sharing arrangements; these include guidance for identifying and valuing platform contributions.

The government has attempted to tighten the cost sharing regulations. For example, a foreign subsidiary's reasonably anticipated benefits, which dictate the foreign subsidiary's share of development costs, must be estimated over the entire period, past and future, of exploitation of the developed intangible, and must be updated to take into account the most reliable data regarding the entire period available at that time.[84] According to congressional reports, however, respective shares of costs have not always been in proportion to reasonable shares of sales. Over a period of years (2009–2012), Apple and its foreign subsidiary ASI each paid about half of worldwide research and development costs; yet over that period, Apple was allocated $29 billion in profits and ASI was allocated $74 billion in profits. Further, regulations relating to cost sharing arrangements included guidance for identifying and valuing platform contributions. However, often there are transitional grandfathering rules for cost sharing agreements entered into prior to regulatory changes. It has been suggested that multinationals have worked to preserve the grandfathered status of their cost sharing arrangements.[85]

Anti-Inversion Measures

In perhaps the most drastic measure to avoid US taxation of current, accumulated, and future earnings of a foreign subsidiary, some US-based multinationals may attempt to give up their US residency through a corporate inversion. A corporate inversion is a transaction in which a US multinational company merges with a foreign company, typically a smaller company located in a low-tax country such as Ireland, and then the merged group adopts the foreign country as its domicile (i.e., the new foreign corporation replaces the existing US parent as the parent of the

---

[84] *Ibid.*   [85] Senate Apple Hearing, *supra* note 10, at 21.

group of subsidiaries).[86] In a common scenario, a foreign company acquires either the assets or the stock of the US-based multinational, and some or all of the shareholders of the US company become shareholders of the new foreign company. Even if the former US company remains under the new foreign parent (and former foreign subsidiaries remain under the former US parent), new foreign intellectual property rights and new foreign subsidiaries can be directly under the new foreign parent, thus providing an opportunity to escape US taxation. In addition, profits repatriated to the new foreign parent may qualify for the foreign country's tax exemption, in which case they escape corporate taxation altogether rather than merely deferring it.

There is nothing illegal about corporate inversions. Indeed, a number of US-based multinationals have pursued inversions in recent years to avoid paying US tax on foreign earnings.[87] In 2014, for example, Burger King (US multinational) merged with Tim Hortons in Canada and moved its residence from the United States to Canada to become Restaurant Brands, International. Although profits from the United States will still be subject to the US rate of 35 percent, the profits in Canada will be subject to Canadian taxation at 15 percent – which may save $275 million per year.[88] Many other examples exist.[89]

Because inversions are the ultimate deferral technique, however, many governments have attempted to crack down on the practice in recent years. In 2004, the US Congress passed an anti-inversion statute.[90] The legislation provides that for an inversion to work, the foreign merger partner has to be of a certain size relative to the US company. In terms of stock ownership, an inversion will not work (i.e., US law will disregard the transaction for purposes of determining the residency of the combined entity) if the shareholders of the foreign company own less than 20 percent of the combined entity after the merger. In other words, an inversion would work only if the US company has a value of less than 80 percent and the foreign company

---

[86] Office of Tax Policy, Department of the Treasury, "Corporate Inversion Transactions: Tax Policy Implications," May 2002, *available at* https://web.law.columbia.edu/sites/defa ult/files/microsites/millstein-center/panel_1_001_office_to_tax_policy.pdf. The foreign company acquires either the assets or the stock of the domestic target. Some or all of the shareholders of the domestic target may become shareholders of the new foreign parent company.

[87] *See* Marples and Gravelle, *supra* note 22.

[88] Kevin Drawbaugh, "Burger King's Move to Canada Could Save It $275 Million in Taxes," *Huffpost Business*, February 10, 2015, *available at* www.hffingtonpost.com/201 4/12/11burger-king-inversion-deal-millions_n_6306206.html.

[89] *See* Liz Hoffman, "The Tax Inversion Wave Keeps Rolling," *Wall St. Journal*, July 8, 2015, at C1.

[90] 26 U.S.C. § 7874.

acquiring them has a value of greater than 20 percent in the inverted company, or, it will work (US company could invert) only if the US shareholders subsequently own less than 80 percent of stock of the new firm (there are additional restrictions if the US shareholders subsequently own between 60 percent and 80 percent). An exception exists if the foreign company conducts "substantial business" activities in the foreign jurisdiction and meets certain other requirements.[91] Under new rules, substantial business is defined as a minimum of 25 percent of an inverting company's business – which must be met in three different ways as measured a year before the inversion.[92] The anti-inversion law basically took away the tax benefits of the inversion if ownership of the group was not significantly affected by the transaction (e.g., the US company is very large relative to the foreign acquirer and most of the foreign company's stock ends up being held by shareholders of the preinversion US company) or if the restructuring results in only minimal presence in a foreign country.[93]

US multinational companies have, not surprisingly, found creative ways to bypass the anti-inversion law.[94] Under the statutory hurdles, the foreign merger company has to be of a certain size relative to the US-based company for the inversion to work (i.e., greater than 20 percent with the US company's value at less than 80 percent). In fact, to gain full tax benefits to an inversion, the foreign company has to be almost as large as the US company. To circumvent the statutory hurdles, multinationals would "skinny down" the US company or "fatten up" the foreign acquirer prior to the inversion so that shareholders of the foreign acquiring company own enough of the newly merged company. One way to fatten them up is to have the foreign company acquire other companies in stock-based transactions to increase its size. The size/value of the foreign acquiring company increases to the extent it issues its stock in connection with acquisitions of each company. Sometimes a foreign acquiring company would engage in successive acquisitions over a short period of time,

---

[91] T.D. 9592 (June 12, 2012). *See* Latham and Watkins LLP, "IRS Tightens Rules on Corporate Expatriations – New Regulations Require High Threshold of Foreign Business Activity," *Lexology*, June 12, 2012, www.lexology.com/library/detail.aspx?g=82 d4ade8-fa4f-4b7b-b8ed-10623e8f8ed1.

[92] *See* Treas. Reg. § 1.7874-3(a), (b)(1)-(3).

[93] For a review, *see* Jefferson P. VanderWolk, "Inversions Under Section 7874 of the Internal Revenue Code: Flawed Legislation, Flawed Guidance," *Northwestern Journal of International Law & Business* 30 (2010): 699.

[94] Zachary R. Mider, "Here's How American CEOs Flee Taxes While Staying in U.S.," *Bloomberg News*, May 5, 2015, www.bloomberg.com/news/articles/2014-05-04/u-s-firm s-with-irish-addresses-criticized-for-the-moves.

such that a large portion of its size would be attributable to assets of recently acquired companies.[95]

The US Treasury responded to such maneuvers. It issued administrative pronouncements in 2014 and 2015, and new regulations in 2016.[96] For purposes of the 80/20 percent requirement, the 2014 rules disregarded large dividend payments made by the US company prior to inversion out of concern that such payments were made to skinny it down below the 80 percent threshold. The 2014 rules also disregarded stock of the foreign merger partner that was attributable to passive assets not used for daily business, such as cash or marketable securities, out of concern that a foreign acquirer could be fattened up by being stuffed with assets not used for business to rise above the 20 percent threshold.

The response in 2015 was even tougher. The Treasury applied anti-stuffing rules not just to passive assets but also to any assets acquired by the foreign acquiring company with the principle purpose of rising above the 20 percent threshold. The 2015 rules also took action on postinversion transactions designed to remove income from foreign operations from US taxation. After an inversion, the former US parent may transfer stock in its CFCs or other property to the new foreign parent. If it does so, the gain upon that transfer (called inversion gain) must be recognized.[97]

The 2014 and 2015 guidance only partly succeeded in limiting tax inversions. The Treasury responded forcefully in 2016 with its third set of new rules in three years.[98] The 2016 regulations adopted and implemented the 2014 and 2015 administrative actions. But more significantly, they adopted a new approach to serial acquisitions preceding an inversion transaction. The regulations limited inversions by ignoring the stock of the foreign company attributable to recent acquisitions (assets acquired from another company within the past three years). By ignoring preinversion transactions, the foreign acquirers appear smaller than they actually

---

[95] "Fact Sheet: Treasury Issues Inversion Regulations and Proposed Earnings Stripping Regulations," U.S. Department of Treasury, April 4, 2016, www.treasury.gov/press-center/press-releases/Pages/jl0404.aspx [hereinafter Inversion Regulations Fact Sheet].

[96] IRS Notice 2014-52, IRB 2014 2014–42, 712 (October 14, 2014); IRS Notice 2015–79, IRB 2015–49, 775 (November 19, 2015); T.D. 9761. For a summary of anti-inversion efforts, see Victor Fleischer, "On Inversions, the Treasury Department Drops the Gloves," The New York Times, April 5, 2016, www.nytimes.com/2016/04/06/business/dealbook/on-inversions-the-treasury-department-drops-the-gloves.html.

[97] "Fact Sheet: Treasury Actions to Rein in Corporate Tax Inversions," US Department of the Treasury, September 22, 2014, www.treasury.gov/press-center/press-releases/Pages/jl2645.aspx.

[98] Inversion Regulations Fact Sheet, supra note 95.

are and run afoul of the statutory inversion thresholds, thus becoming subject to more stringent statutory rules.

Many believe that the 2016 regulations targeted a proposed merger of drug makers Pfizer and Allergan. In one of the biggest deals of its kind, Pfizer (US based) wanted to merge with Allergan (Irish based) and move its residency to Ireland. Allergan, however, was too small of an inversion partner. So, over a three-year period, Allergan acquired and took over several other companies to bulk up its size prior to the merger to meet the statutory inversion thresholds. Using the 2016 regulations, which cracked down on serial acquirers/inverters, the Treasury killed the deal.[99]

It should also be noted that the 2016 regulations adopted a new approach to so-called earnings stripping, a technique which uses interest payments to shift US income to low-tax jurisdictions. Following an inversion, the former US parent may borrow money from the new foreign parent (which can in turn transfer the debt to a low-tax foreign subsidiary) and use the interest deduction to offset US earnings. The regulations make it more difficult for a new foreign parent to load up its US subsidiary with debt by treating related party debt not used to fund actual business investment as equity (stock). Classifying the transactions as equity and not debt eliminates the interest deduction for the US subsidiary of the foreign acquirer.

Although the Treasury has taken much action in recent years to limit inversions, most agree that a complete solution requires Congressional action.

---

[99] Jonathan D. Rockoff, Liz Hoffman, & Richard Rubin, "Pfizer Walks Away from Allergan Deal," *The Wall Street Journal*, April 6, 2016, www.wsj.com/articles/pfizer-walks-away-from-allergan-deal-1459939739; Michael J. de la Merced & Leslie Picker, "Pfizer and Allergan Are Said to End Merger as Tax Rules Tighten," *The New York Times*, April 5, 2016, www.nytimes.com/2016/04/06/business/dealbook/tax-inversion-obama-treasury.html?_r=0. Kristen Hallam, Cynthia Koons, & Zachary Tracer, "Pfizer Confirms Termination of Proposed $160 Billion Allergan Merger," *Bloomberg News*, April 6, 2016, www.bloomberg.com/news/articles/2016-04-06/pfizer-allergan-end-160-billion-merger-amid-new-tax-rules. Leslie Picker & Michael J. de la Merced, "U.S. Moves to Thwart Use of Foreign Inversions as Tax Dodge," *The New York Times*, April 4, 2016, www.nytimes.com/2016/04/05/business/dealbook/us-acts-to-end-use-of-foreign-acquisitions-to-dodge-taxes.html?_r=0.

9 Foreign Tax Havens: Exploring Solutions to Intellectual Property Income Shifting Offshore

A nation's tax system should contain certain features.[1] First, the system should levy taxes commensurately with one's *ability to pay* those taxes. Second, the system should be *fair* in the sense that persons or entities that are similarly situated should be taxed in a similar fashion. And third, the system should be *efficient* in seeking a balance between maximizing tax revenues and minimizing the social costs of taxation (i.e., the tax system should generate enough money for the government to do its job without stifling beneficial economic activity).

The current tax system governing intellectual property arguably violates each of these tenants. As to the ability to pay, some of the largest and most successful global companies have been able to sidestep billions of dollars in taxes with intellectual property shifting techniques, and have been able to achieve low effective tax rates not commensurate with their ability to pay. As to fairness, large multinational companies with intellectual property income can, and do, avail themselves of complex loopholes to reduce taxes, whereas large multinationals that do not rely on intellectual property (or even multinationals with intellectual property that do not utilize foreign subsidiaries) have to bear a heavier burden.[2] As to efficiency, present tax rules distort the decisions multinational companies make regarding where to conduct research and development and where to hold their intellectual property rights; as well as whether and when to repatriate foreign profits generated from

---

[1] *See* John A. Miller & Jeffrey A. Maine, *The Fundamentals of Federal Taxation* (North Carolina: Carolina Academic Press 3d ed., 2017), 4–5.

[2] *See* J. Clifton Fleming, Jr., Robert J. Peroni, & Stephen E. Shay, "Worse Than Exemption," *Emory Law Journal* 59 (2009): 84–85 (noting the present US tax system inequitably permits residents who earn foreign-source income to avoid the tax burden borne by their fellow residents). According to the Joint Committee on Taxation, the effective tax rates paid by large multinational companies are about 4 to 8.5 percentage points lower than similar companies with only domestic operations. Joint Committee on Taxation, "Background, Summary, and Implications of the OECD/G20 Base Erosion and Profit Shifting Project," 28, *JCX-139–15* (November 30, 2015), *available at* www.jct .gov/publications.html?func=startdown&id=4853 [hereinafter JCX-139–15 Report].

the use of intellectual property.[3] They also encourage such entities to devote substantial resources to tax planning rather than productive investment.

Concededly, these principles may sometimes run counter to one another. Governments, for example, may choose to deliberately tolerate inequities to achieve certain efficiencies. It may be more efficient to permit domestic multinationals with large portfolios of intellectual property to achieve lower taxation on foreign earnings rather than allowing domestic multinationals that do not rely on intellectual property to do the same in order to keep the former from moving their residency offshore and to keep beneficial economic activity (R&D) at home.[4] But this violates notions of fairness if one accepts the two groups of multinationals are similar and, thus, should face similar tax burdens.

When viewed in light of these principles (ability to pay, tax fairness, and efficiency), the techniques used by many multinational entities with intellectual property income prove to be more negative than positive for our tax base, and reforms are necessary to close existing loopholes.[5] Some of the large multinationals accused of income shifting themselves have recognized this. Apple, for instance, has called upon Congress to simplify the US tax system by lowering the corporate income tax rate, eliminating tax expenditures, and imposing reasonable tax on foreign earnings that will permit capital to flow back to the United States.[6]

Fixing the problem will be no easy task, especially since tax planners always seem to be one step ahead of policy makers. Although the world has become more interconnected, each country has its own tax policies. So, action by some sovereign countries but inaction (our counter action) by other sovereign countries could maintain present income shifting incentives and prevent any meaningful change. Even if sovereign nations agreed on a uniform approach to income shifting, lack of enforcement by some could also prevent meaningful change. Indeed, tax collection is a domestic activity carried out by sovereign nations, and history is replete

---

[3] *See* Fleming et al., *supra* note 2, at 84–85; Edward D. Kleinbard, "Stateless Income," *Florida Tax Review* 11 (2011): 706 (arguing that stateless income "distorts the investment decisions of multinational firms, and... distorts a US multinational firm's decision whether to repatriate that stateless income back to the United States").

[4] *See* Noam Noked, "Integrated Tax Policy Approach to Designing Research & Development Tax Benefits," *Virginia Tax Review* 34 (2014): 132–33 (justifying lower taxation on mobile capital and higher taxation on immobile capital).

[5] *See* Stephen C. Loomis, "The Double Irish Sandwich: Reforming Overseas Tax Havens," *Saint Mary's Law Journal* 43 (2012): 845.

[6] Testimony of Apple Inc. Before the Permanent Subcommittee on Investigations, US Senate, May 21, 2013, 3, *available at* www.apple.com/pr/pdf/Apple_Testimony_to_PSI.pdf (noting Apple supports comprehensive corporate tax reform even though it would likely result in Apply paying more US taxes).

with examples of varying enforcement policies and practices among nations.

Enough concern has been raised about income shifting that many developed and emerging economies now seem intent on addressing the problem. In recent years, there has been a growing level of public outrage at tax avoidance techniques used by Apple, Starbucks, Hewlett-Packard, Caterpillar, Microsoft, and many other large multinational companies. This public attention has pressured high-tax governments to start taking action, such as conducting high profile investigations[7] and considering various tax reform proposals.[8] Another example are the high-tax country governments with a significant erosion of their domestic tax bases putting pressure on low-tax country governments to change tax policies that encourage income shifting from the former to the latter.[9] Because of this, meaningful reform seems within reach now more than ever – in countries hurt by income shifting and countries benefitting from it alike. The real challenge, however, is figuring out the best approach. This chapter examines possible approaches.

---

[7] In the United States, a number of US multinational companies have come under scrutiny and have been the subject of high-profile congressional hearings. *See* Hearing Before the Permanent Subcommittee on Investigations, Offshore Profit Shifting and the US Tax Code – Part II (Apple Inc.), 35–37, 152–91, May 21, 2013, *available at* www.gpo.gov/fdsys/pkg/CHRG-113shrg81657/pdf/CHRG-113shrg81657.pdf [hereinafter Senate Apple Hearing]; Hearing Before the Permanent Subcommittee on Investigations, Offshore Profit Shifting and the US Tax Code – Part I (Microsoft & Hewlett-Packard), 6, September 20, 2012, *available at* www.gpo.gov/fdsys/pkg/CHRG-112shrg76071/pdf/CHRG-112shrg76071.pdf [hereinafter Microsoft Part I]. *See also* Joint Committee on Taxation, "Present Law and Background Related to Possible Income Shifting and Transfer Pricing," *JCX-37-10* (July 20, 2010), *available at* www.jct.gov/publications.html?func=startdown&id=3692 [hereinafter JCX-37-10 Report] (containing memorandum prepared for Hearing on Transfer Pricing Issues Before the House Committee On Ways & Means, 111th Congress [2010]). *See also* Nelson D. Schwartz & Charles Duhigg, "Apple's Web of Tax Shelters Saved It Billions, Panel Finds," *The New York Times*, May 20, 2013, www.nytimes.com/2013/05/21/business/apple-avoided-billions-in-taxes-congressional-panel-says.html.

[8] Members of Congress from both parties have put forth various tax reform proposals. In particular, House Speaker Paul Ryan's blueprint for fundamental tax reform, which involves a destination-based cash flow type business tax, has gain much attention. Under the proposal, imports are not deductible to purchasers and exports are exempt from tax. *See* http://abetterway.speaker.gov/_assets/pdf/ABetterWay-Tax-PolicyPaper.pdf. Although the Trump Administration has yet to offer a comprehensive plan, the Obama Administration targeted income shifting in "The President's Framework for Business Tax Reform." *See* The White House & Department of the Treasury, "The President's Framework for Business Tax Reform: An Update," 11, April 2016, *available at* www.treasury.gov/resource-center/tax-policy/Documents/The-Presidents-Framework-for-Business-Tax-Reform-An-Update-04-04-2016.pdf [hereinafter President Obama's Framework].

[9] As we saw in Chapter 7, European Union governments recently pressured the Irish government to make changes to its tax code that may impact a popular tax planning structured used by multinational companies.

Tax Reform Options to Limit Intellectual Property Income Shifting – Sticks and Carrots

Proposals to address intellectual property income shifting often are described in terms of *sticks* and *carrots*.[10] Some countries could adopt a "stick" approach to prevent domestic companies from shifting income offshore. This compulsory approach may include strengthening transfer pricing rules, expanding controlled foreign corporation (CFC) rules, enacting a minimum tax on foreign income, restricting the use of hybrid entities, or adopting formulary apportionment (allocating a multinational company's worldwide income based on some combination of sales, payroll, and/or physical assets). Alternatively, countries could adopt a "carrot" approach to attract and retain intellectual property and related income and, thus, achieve a similar goal. Examples may be moving to a dividend exemption system, lowering the statutory corporate income tax rate, enacting a so-called "patent box," and expanding and simplifying the research and development tax credit. Each of these "tax" options receives treatment below. It should be noted, however, that "nontax" options may be available as well.[11]

Sticks

1   Strengthen Transfer Pricing Rules

Many countries have transfer pricing rules which are often based on the OECD's *Transfer Pricing Guidelines for Multinational Enterprises and Tax Administrations*.[12] These rules attempt to ensure arm's-length pricing of

---

[10] *See, e.g.*, Jane Gravelle, "Policy Options to Address Corporate Profit Shifting: Carrots or Sticks?," New York University School of Law Colloquium on Tax Policy and Public Finance, April 26, 2016, *available at* www.law.nyu.edu/sites/default/files/upload_docu ments/Jane%20Gravelle.pdf. Although we group proposals in terms of carrots and sticks, another approach is to group proposals in terms of efforts to either: (1) fix gaps in "source-based" taxation (e.g., tightening transfer pricing rules or adopting formulary apportionment); or (2) expand "residence-based" taxation (e.g., expanding controlled foreign corporation rules). *See* Michael J. Graetz & Rachel Doud, "Technological Innovation, International Competition, and the Challenges of International Income Taxation," *Columbia Law Review* 113 (2013): 414.

[11] *See, e.g.*, Andrew Blair-Stanek, "Intellectual Property Law Solutions to Tax Avoidance," *UCLA Law Review* 62 (2015): 2. *See also* Andrew Blair-Stanek, "Just Compensation as Transfer Prices," *Arizona Law Review* 58 (2016): 1077.

[12] The OECD's Transfer Pricing Guidelines were first published in 1979 (Report on Transfer Pricing and Multinational Enterprises); they were revised in 1995 (Transfer Pricing Guidelines for Multinational Enterprises and Tax Administrations), and updated again in 2010 (Transfer Pricing Guidelines for Multinational Enterprises and Tax Administrations). In 2012, the OECD released a discussion draft on the transfer pricing treatment of intangibles (Discussion Draft: Revision of the Special Considerations for Intangibles in Chapter VI of the OECD Transfer Pricing Guidelines and Related

transactions between related companies (e.g., between a domestic parent and its controlled foreign subsidiary, or between a top-level foreign subsidiary in a low-tax country and a lower-level foreign subsidiary in a high-tax country). The arm's-length principle has a long history. It is found in several treaties and both the OECD and UN Model Tax Conventions. To date, however, transfer pricing rules and their reliance on the arm's-length principle have been largely ineffective at evaluating transfer prices between related parties and limiting intellectual property income shifting.[13]

One stick approach would be to strengthen existing transfer pricing rules. This could be done in two ways: (1) reduce the number of available transfer pricing methods and revise rules so that intellectual property income is allocated to the economic activities that generate them; and (2) require substantial participation by a controlled foreign company in a cost sharing arrangement.[14] Prior efforts to strengthen transfer pricing rules have failed for varying reasons.[15] In fact, over that past three decades, the United States has attempted to strengthen its transfer pricing rules to no avail. Congress amended its transfer pricing statute in 1986 to provide that payment for the transfer of intellectual property should be "commensurate with the income" attributable to the intellectual property.[16] This provision, which emphasizes income actually generated

Provisions). *See* "Transfer Pricing," OECD, accessed November 2, 2016, www.oecd.org/ctp/transferpricing.

[13] *See* Graetz & Doud, *supra* note 10; Edward D. Kleinbard, "Stateless Income's Challenge to Tax Policy, Part 2," *Tax Notes* (2012): 1431, *available at* http://gould.usc.edu/centers/class/class-workshops/cleo-working-papers/documents/C12_14_paper.pdf; George Mundstock, "The Borders of E.U. Tax Policy and US Competitiveness," *University of Miami Law Review* 66 (2012): 737; Lee A. Sheppard, "Reflections on the Death of Transfer Pricing," *Tax Notes* (2008): 1112. *See also* Reuven S. Avi-Yonah, Kimberly A. Clausing, & Michael C. Durst, "Allocating Business Profits for Tax Purposes: A Proposal to Adopt a Formulary Profit Split," *Florida Tax Review* 9 (2009): 510–23.

[14] *See* Bret Wells & Cym Lowell, "Tax Base Erosion: Reformation of Section 482's Arm's Length Standard," *University of Houston Public Law and Legal Theory Series* 2012-W-6, 13–14, August 13, 2013, *available at* http://isites.harvard.edu/fs/docs/icb.topic1321119.files/September%2018%20Readings-%20Articles%20Mentioned%20in%20Class%20Last%20Evening/Erosion_Tax_Base.pdf (arguing a section 482-based solution is preferable "because it would create the least conflict with our existing treaty partners who in turn largely endorse the arm's-length standard," and it would minimize "the risk of international double taxation whereas other policy responses... are unilateral acts that create a significant risk of creating an anticompetitive tax environment").

[15] Graetz & Doud, *supra* note 10, at 415–16 (arguing "success remains elusive" because transfer pricing rules continue to apply an arm's-length pricing standard even though multinationals shift intellectual property assets, along with associated risks and rewards, among related companies "to an extent and in a manner they would never do with unrelated parties").

[16] Tax Reform Act of 1986, Pub. L. No. 99–514, 1231(e)(1), 100 Stat. 2085, 562–63 (amending IRC § 482) ("super royalty" provision).

by the intellectual property subsequent to the transfer, allows the IRS to make periodic royalty adjustments in subsequent years even if the initial royalty was reasonable at the time it was set.[17] Congress also enacted transfer pricing penalty statutes, imposing penalties of 20 percent (40 percent in some cases) on tax underpayments related to transfer pricing adjustments.[18] The US Treasury Department has adopted hundreds of pages of regulations dealing with transfer pricing that provide various ways to determine appropriate arm's-length pricing for related party transactions.[19] Despite these efforts, US multinationals have successfully found ways around the transfer pricing rules and penalties to shift intellectual property income offshore.[20]

One thing that could be done is to reduce the number of available transfer pricing methods and revise rules so that intellectual property income is allocated to the economic activities that generate them. Currently, there are too many pricing alternatives. The several methods listed in the Treasury Department's regulations require only that the "best method" be used.[21] Finding relevant data and information regarding comparable companies and transactions to determine the best method for intercompany transactions is nearly impossible, especially with respect to transfers and licenses of unique and difficult-to-value intellectual property assets.[22] To make matters worse, multinational

---

[17] Treas. Reg. § 1.482–4(f)(2)(i).

[18] *See* Omnibus Budget Reconciliation Act of 1990, Pub. L. No. 101–508, 11312, 104 Stat. 1388, 1388–454 to -455 (amending IRC § 6662(e), (h) (amending tax code to penalize misstatements, rather than just overstatements, and lowering threshold from 400 percent to 200 percent overvaluation). *See* 26 USC. § 6662(a), (b)(3), (e)(1)(B)(i)-(ii), (e)(3)(A), (h); Treas. Reg. § 1.6662–6.

[19] Treas. Reg. §§ 1.482-1 (allocation of income and deductions among taxpayers); -2 (determination of taxable income in specific situations); -3 (methods to determine taxable income in connection with a transfer of tangible property); -4 (methods to determine taxable income in connection with a transfer of intangible property); -5 (comparable profits method); -6 (profit split method); -7 (methods to determine taxable income in connection with a cost sharing arrangement); -8 (examples of the best method rule); -9 (methods to determine taxable income in connection with a controlled services transaction). *See* PricewaterhouseCoopers LLP, "International Transfer Pricing 2012," 792–95, 2012, *available at* http://download.pwc.com/ie/pubs/2012_international_trans fer_pricing.pdf.

[20] Graetz & Doud, *supra* note 10, at 417 ("[G]iven the failures of two decades of efforts, it is difficult to be optimistic that looking solely to improved transfer pricing rules as a solution to [intellectual property] income shifting will prove successful").

[21] Treas. Reg. § 1.482-1(e) (allowing a multinational to select a price that falls within a range of alternative methods).

[22] *See* Floyd Norris, "Apple's Move Keeps Profit Out of Reach of Taxes," *The New York Times*, May 2, 2013, www.nytimes.com/2013/05/03/business/how-apple-and-other-cor porations-move-profit-to-avoid-taxes.html (Governments can try "but it is especially hard for countries to monitor prices on intellectual property, like patents and copyrights. There is unlikely to be a real market for that information, so challenging a company's

companies can manage much of the information used in assessing the comparability of controlled and uncontrolled transactions (e.g., functions performed, risks assumed, contractual terms, etc.), placing the government at a distinct disadvantage.[23] Under the arm's-length principle, emphasis is placed on how related parties have contractually allocated functions, assets, and risks. But this is vulnerable to manipulation, which can lead to outcomes that are not tied to value creation. Thus, a major "stick" would be to revise transfer pricing rules so that intellectual property income is allocated to the economic activities that generate them – not based on related party contractual allocations but instead on conduct, for example. Indeed, some governments have recognized this stick approach, as discussed at the end of the chapter.

Multinational companies have cleverly used cost sharing agreements to avoid the transfer pricing rules altogether.[24] So a necessary second step would be to address their use. As explained in earlier chapters, if a US parent company and a related foreign subsidiary company in a low-tax jurisdiction agree to jointly develop intellectual property, they are generally immune from the effects of the transfer pricing rules. How? If they agree to share the costs and risks of developing intellectual property assets in exchange for certain interests in the intellectual property developed, they can, in turn, exploit their economic rights in their respective regions of the world without having to pay arm's-length royalty payments to the

pricing is difficult."); Patrick Temple-West, "IRS Forms 'SWAT Team' for Tax Dodge Crackdown," *Reuters*, March 20, 2012, www.reuters.com/article/us-usa-tax-irs-transfer-idUSBRE82J10W20120320 (Certain tax experts, who had previously served in senior government tax positions, have described the valuation problems as "insurmountable"). *See also Eli Lilly & Co. v. United States*, 372 F.2d 990 (Fed. Cir. 1967) (quoting Oxenfeldt, "Multistage Approach to Pricing," *Harvard Business Review* 38 [1960]: 125) ("Of all the areas of executive decision, pricing is perhaps the most fuzzy. Whenever a price problem is discussed..., divergent figures are likely to be recommended without a semblance of consensus").

[23] Microsoft Part I, *supra* note 7, at 91 (citing "Testimony of Stephen E. Shay Before the US Senate Permanent Subcommittee on Investigations of the Committee on Homeland Security and Governmental Affairs Hearing on Offshore Profit Shifting and the Internal Revenue Code," September 20, 2012, 5) ("The problems are exacerbated by the taxpayer's control over information and procedural advantage"). One commentator noted several disadvantages of the IRS: "First, a multinational hires the appraisers, who naturally 'tend to agree with their paymasters'.... Second, a multinational inherently knows far more about the characteristics, potential, and value of its IP than do IRS employees or appraisers. Third, the transfers tend to occur soon after the IP is developed, before its value has become apparent." Andrew Blair-Stanek, "IP Law Solutions to Transfer Pricing Abuse," *Tax Notes* 143 (2014): 1538.

[24] *See, e.g.*, "Avi-Yonah Testimony for Hearing on Profit Shifting US Senate Permanent Subcommittee on Investigation," Homeland Security & Governmental Affairs Permanent Subcommittee on Investigations, September 20, 2012, 3, *available at* www.hsgac.senate .gov/subcommittees/investigations/hearings/offshore-profit-shifting-and-the-us-tax-code [hereinafter Testimony of Avi-Yonah, Microsoft Part I].

other party. In essence, because the related foreign subsidiary has all foreign rights to the intellectual property, it has the right to all the foreign income generated by exploitation of that intellectual property.

The use of cost sharing agreements to shift economic rights in intellectual property offshore undermines the transfer pricing rules, especially the "commensurate with income" standard described above.[25] This is because cost sharing agreements are technically not needed – that is, it is not necessary that the economic intellectual property rights to sell products in a given country be located in that country. For example, why is it necessary for an Irish subsidiary to acquire Apple intellectual property economic rights in order for Apple to conduct foreign business?[26] Moreover, the cost sharing agreement looks more like a cost reimbursement agreement in which the foreign subsidiary writes a check to the US parent for R&D conducted by the US parent in the United States.[27] Arguably, there is no increased risk for the US parent company that enters into an agreement with a controlled foreign subsidiary. True, the US parent company gives up some R&D tax deductions for the costs borne by the foreign subsidiary, but typically the US parent is able to, in turn, shield much more money in foreign profits from US taxation.[28] Likewise,

[25] Testimony of Avi-Yonah, Microsoft Part I, *supra* note 24, at 2–4 (arguing the congressional intent behind the 1986 amendment to section 482 has been completely undermined and arguing "cost-sharing has been an expensive mistake" and should be overridden by Congress). In a congressional hearing, Senator Carl Levin questioned how Apple's cost sharing agreement could be considered an arm's-length transaction: "All the money supposedly changing hands belongs to Apple and all the signatories were Apple employees. The agreement on its face allocates the costs to be shared among the Apple companies; but since all of these costs ultimately come out of the same pocket, in reality, the agreement is about shifting profits." "Statement of Senator Carl Levin (D-MICH) Before US Senate Permanent Subcommittee on Investigations on Offshore Profit Shifting and the US Tax Code – Part 2 (Apple Inc.)," Homeland Security & Governmental Affairs Permanent Subcommittee on Investigations, May 21, 2013, 3, *available at* www.hsgac.senate.gov/subcommittees/investigations/hearings/offshore-prof it-shifting-and-the-us-tax-code_-part-2 [hereinafter Statement of Levin, Apple Part 2].

[26] Apple has argued that cost sharing arrangements play an important role in encouraging US multinationals to keep up R&D efforts, and that eliminating cost sharing arrangements "would harm American workers and the broader US economy." Testimony of Apple Inc., *supra* note 6, at 11–12 ("If cost sharing agreements were no longer available, many US multinational companies would likely move high-paying American R&D jobs overseas").

[27] Senate Apple Hearing, *supra* note 7, at, 179 (citing "Memorandum RE: Offshore Profit Shifting and the US Tax Code – Part 2 (Apple Inc.)," 28) (noting employees of Apple's key Irish subsidiaries conduct less than 1 percent of Apple's R&D, making Apple's cost sharing arrangement "closer to a cost reimbursement than a codevelopment relationship, where both parties contribute to the intrinsic value of the intellectual property being developed").

[28] Testimony of Avi-Yonah, Microsoft Part I, *supra* note 24, at 3. Payments made by a foreign subsidiary to a US parent under cost sharing are typically a very low percentage compared to the very significant profits that result from the codeveloped intellectual

there is little risk for the related foreign subsidiary, as the US parent will arguably enter into a cost sharing agreement only if the R&D will be successful, and the US parent is in the best position to know that.[29] For these reasons, cost sharing arrangements fail to pass a common sense reality test.[30] As a necessary stick measure, the government should take steps to ensure that cost sharing arrangements do not undermine a real analysis of functions performed, risks assumed, and resources deployed. The fact that a controlled foreign subsidiary might own economic rights to intellectual property under the special agreement should not necessarily be determinant of its rights to intellectual property income. Substantial participation by the CFC could be required.[31]

2 Expand Controlled Foreign Corporation (CFC) Rules

A second stick option would be to expand existing CFC rules to tax currently more foreign intellectual property income. As noted in Chapter 8, several countries have enacted CFC rules (antideferral rules) that currently tax domestic companies at the home country rate on certain foreign income of their controlled foreign corporations. This is true for countries that have worldwide systems of taxation (those that tax domestic companies on income earned at home and abroad) and territorial systems of taxation (those that tax domestic companies on income earned at home). They typically target domestic companies that place intellectual property assets in a controlled foreign corporation to avoid paying current domestic tax on income earned from those assets. Thus, they typically target mobile passive income earned abroad (although some also target certain sales income earned on goods manufactured and used outside the country of incorporation).

---

property. Even with buy-in payments (i.e., platform contribution payments), cost sharing cannot achieve results intended by the transfer pricing rules of section 482, as amended in 1986. *Ibid.* at 3–4.

[29] Microsoft Part I, *supra* note 7, at 13. As argued by Professor Avi-Yonah, multinational companies do know that the development will be successful: "They enter into these agreements at the point where the intangible is, in fact, on the verge of being profitable, and they are the only ones that have this information. It is very hard for outsiders to get that information". *Ibid.*

[30] Microsoft Part I, *supra* note 7, at 94 (citing "Testimony of Stephen E. Shay Before the US Senate Permanent Subcommittee on Investigations of the Committee on Homeland Security and Governmental Affairs Hearing on Offshore Profit Shifting and the Internal Revenue Code," September 20, 2012, 8).

[31] "Testimony of Professor Reuven S. Avi-Yonah Hearing on Transfer Pricing Issues, Committee on Ways and Means," 9, July 22, 2010 [hereinafter Testimony of Avi-Yonah, Transfer Pricing Issues].

With respect to foreign intellectual property income, countries may consider expanding their CFC rules to reduce the level of deferral achieved.[32] The United States, which has less "robust" CFC rules than many other countries,[33] might move in this direction. Former House Ways and Means Committee Chairman Dave Camp proposed several options to expand the US CFC rules. One option, similar to one that was proposed earlier by former President Obama, is to tax currently, at the US rate, income associated with intellectual property transferred off-shore (to a foreign-related entity) if the income is not taxed at a foreign rate of greater than 15 percent. Camp would treat profits in excess of 150 percent of costs ("excess returns") as attributable to intellectual property.[34] A second, and simpler, option proposed by Camp is to currently tax all nonactive income of a CFC that is not otherwise taxed at a foreign rate of at least 10 percent.[35] And another option is similar to the first (specifically, tax foreign intellectual property income that is subject to a foreign rate of less a certain threshhold), but includes a preferential US "patent box" rate (15 percent) for intellectual property income from serving foreign markets.[36] These three are similar in that

---

[32] *See, e.g.*, Kleinbard, "Stateless Income's Challenge to Tax Policy, Part 2," *supra* note 13; Edward D. Kleinbard, "Stateless Income's Challenge to Tax Policy," *Tax Notes* 132 (2011): 1021, *available at* https://papers.ssrn.com/sol3/papers.cfm?abstract_id=1875077; Edward D. Kleinbard, "The Lessons of Stateless Income," *Tax Law Review* 65 (2011): 99, *available at* https://papers.ssrn.com/sol3/papers.cfm?abstract_id=1791783. Some scholars have advocated for ending deferral entirely. *See, e.g.*, Jasper L. Cummings, Jr., "Consolidating Foreign Affiliates," *Florida Tax Review* 11 (2011): 143; Jeffrey M. Kadet, "US Reform: Full-Inclusion Over Territorial System Compelling," *Tax Notes* 139 (2013): 295, *available at* https://papers.ssrn.com/sol3/papers.cfm?abstract_id=2275488; Robert J. Peroni, J. Clifton Fleming, Jr., & Stephen E. Shay, "Getting Serious About Curtailing Deferral of US Tax on Foreign Source Income," *SMU Law Review* 52 (1999): 455. As an alternative to indirect taxation under the CFC rules, direct taxation could be considered – that is, imposition of US tax on the "effectively connected income" of application foreign subsidiaries. *See* Jeffery M. Kadet, "Attacking Profit Shifting: The Approach Everyone Forgets," *Tax Notes* (2015): 193, *available at* https://papers.ssrn.com/sol3/papers.cfm?abstract_id=2636073.

[33] *See* Reuven S. Avi-Yonah, "Three Steps Forward, One Step Back?: Reflections on 'Google Taxes,' BEPS, and DBCT," *University of Michigan Public Law and Legal Theory Research Paper Series Paper* No. 516 (May 2016), *available at* https://papers.ssrn.com/sol3/papers.cfm?abstract_id=2783858 (citing the 1997 check-the-box rules and the 2006 temporary look-through rule as making US CFC rules essentially "toothless").

[34] *See* House Committee On Ways & Means, 112th Congress, "Technical Explanation of the Ways and Means Discussion Draft Provisions to Establish a Participation Exemption System for the Taxation of Foreign Income," 32–33, October 26, 2011, *available at* http://waysandmeans.house.gov/UploadedFiles/FINAL_TE_-_Ways_and_Means_Participation_Exemption_Discussion_Draft.pdf [hereinafter Technical Explanation] (detailing option A).

[35] *See* Technical Explanation, *supra* note 34, at 33–34 (detailing option B).

[36] *Ibid.* (detailing option C). Camp would lower the US corporate tax rate to 25 percent, and provide a 40 percent deduction for foreign intangible income of a domestic company, producing an effective "patent box" rate of 15 percent. *Ibid.* at 1, 34.

they focus on low-taxed foreign income – they all target currently foreign income taxed below a threshold foreign rate and tax it in the US. But they differ in the income to be covered – for example, whether the foreign income is linked to intellectual property or not. The third option is unique in that it incorporates a patent box. For reasons articulated later, the United States is not likely to adopt a patent box any time soon.

In expanding the CFC rules to reach more foreign income, existing statutory exceptions built into the CFC rules should be tightened.[37] One exception is the so-called *manufacturing exception*, mentioned in Chapter 8, which provides that income retained by a CFC will not be subject to current taxation at the US rate if the CFC itself is a manufacturer. Remember that it is easy for a multinational to claim this exception as the degree of manufacturing necessary has been liberalized.[38] Today, a CFC does not have to necessarily demonstrate that it performed a manufacturing activity; it instead can demonstrate that it made a "substantial contribution" to the goods being sold. This means reform to limit intellectual property income shifting would have to revisit the definition of manufacturing, and enhanced efforts to enforce the exception would have to be made. In addition to tightening statutory exceptions built into the CFC rules, the check-the-box regulations would have to be limited or repealed as discussed below.

3 Restrict the Use of Hybrid Entities

As illustrated in earlier chapters, multinationals have been able to utilize hybrid entities – entities classified differently under the tax laws of one country than under the laws of another – to purposefully avoid the home country's CFC rules. One way US multinationals can create hybrid entities is to take advantage of a quirky tax regulation promulgated in the 1990s that allows US multinationals to declare what type of entity their foreign subsidiaries are for US tax purposes. By simply checking a box on a tax form, a US multinational can declare that a foreign subsidiary is disregarded as a separate entity. That means a "checked" foreign IP Holding Company of a US parent could be viewed as fiscally transparent (disregarded as a separate entity) by the United States, yet treated as a real corporation by foreign countries. As can be seen, hybrid structures can result in a deduction in one country with no corresponding

---

[37] For the history of the US CFC rules, *see* Paul W. Oosterhuis, "The Evolution of International Tax Policy-What Would Larry Say?," *Ohio Northern University Law Review* 33 (2006): 3.

[38] Treas. Reg. § 1.954-3(a)(4).

income in another. Eliminating check-the-box elective classification would help restrict the use of hybrid entities.

Getting rid of check-the-box, however, would also require repeal of the "same country exception" that is currently built into the CFC rules. The reason why is that differing residency standards between countries can also allow hybrid entities to be created, without regard to check-the-box regulations. Here is an illustration of the same country exception and how multinationals can achieve the same result as check-the-box: US parent company forms two affiliated foreign subsidiaries. Sub #1 is incorporated in High Tax Country but managed in Zero Tax Country; Sub #2 is incorporated in High Tax Country and managed in High Tax Country. The United States determines corporate residency by looking to where a company is incorporated. Assume High Tax Country, in contrast, looks to where a company is managed. Under these dual residency standards, the United States would view Sub #1 and Sub #2 as both being in High Tax Country, because they were both incorporated there. Under the "same country exception" to the US CFC rules (discussed in Chapter 8) royalty payments received by Sub #1 from Sub #2 would escape current US taxation regardless of check-the box regulations. They would also escape foreign taxation because of Zero Tax Country's 0 percent rate. High Tax Country, however, would view Sub #1 as being in Zero Tax Country and thus would permit Sub #2 a deduction for payments made to Sub #1. This is another example of a deduction allowed in one country (High Tax Country) with no corresponding income in another country (neither the United States nor Zero Tax Country).

4   Enact a Minimum Tax on Foreign Income

In addition to strengthening a government's existing conventional tools, new "stick" approaches could be considered. A minimum tax could be designed to target all income from a controlled foreign subsidiary. Presumably, passive income from the intellectual property of a CFC is already subject to the current US rates under existing CFC rules, so a minimum tax would likely target all active CFC income, thus eliminating deferral of US taxation all together. The minimum tax rate could be the present statutory rate (35 percent) or some lower rate, such as 19 percent, which has been proposed. The White House and the Treasury Department, under the Obama administration, released "The President's Framework for Business Tax Reform," which, among other things, targets income shifting by including a new minimum tax on foreign income.[39] The proposal would introduce a 19 percent minimum tax, and it would target all the income of offshore subsidiaries (not just intellectual property income).[40] The framework states that a minimum tax would help prevent a "race to the bottom," and would help keep US companies on a level playing field with competitors when engaged in activities, which, by necessity, must occur in a foreign country.[41] Jane Gravelle, with the Congressional Research Service, has argued that a minimum tax "should apply country by country with a per country limit on the foreign tax credit (otherwise, the lower rate would probably be swamped by foreign tax credits)."[42]

5 Adopt Formulary Apportionment

The last stick approach to address foreign income shifting is formulary apportionment. Historically, countries have adopted *separate reporting*, or *separate accounting*, to allocate profits among the countries. Separate reporting sources income to the country in which it is earned, which encourages multinational companies to create separate corporations throughout the world. With separate corporations throughout the world, multinationals then have to transfer, through a license or cost sharing arrangement, their intellectual property assets to those foreign corporations to justify those countries as the source of profits. These transfers of intellectual property from one country to another implicate the arm's-length transfer pricing rules of nations. The flexibility of the arm's-length standard, as described above, is what makes it possible for multinational companies to avoid domestic taxes and minimize foreign taxes. In short, the adoption of separate reporting explains why many

---

[39] President Obama's Framework, *supra* note 8. For explanations of former President Obama's proposals, *see* "Administration's Fiscal Year Revenue Proposals," US Department of the Treasury, accessed November 3, 2016, www.treasury.gov/resource-center/tax-policy/Pages/general_explanation.aspx.

[40] President Obama's Framework, *supra* note 8, at 24 ("Foreign earnings would be subject to current US taxation at a rate of 19 percent less a foreign tax credit equal to 85 percent of the per-country average foreign effective tax rate. The minimum tax would be imposed on foreign earnings regardless of whether they are repatriated to the United States, and all foreign earnings could be repatriated without further US tax. Thus, under the proposal, all active earnings of foreign subsidiaries of US firms (controlled foreign corporations, or CFCs) would be subject to tax either immediately or not at all. Passive or highly mobile income such as dividends, interest, rents, and royalties would continue to be subject to full US tax on a current basis under the existing 'Subpart F' rules").

[41] *Ibid.* at 23–24 ("The minimum tax on foreign earnings would ensure that no matter what tax planning techniques a US firm engages in, and no matter where it reports its profits, it would still face a tax rate of at least 19 percent. Unlike the current system, there would be no 'deferral' of tax – the minimum tax would apply to profits in the year they are earned").

[42] Gravelle, *supra* note 10, at 21–22.

multinationals have dozens, sometimes hundreds, of foreign subsidiaries and why they engage in aggressive transfer pricing practices.

To reduce intellectual property income shifting, countries should consider adopting so-called *formulary apportionment*, which is on the opposite end (from separate reporting) of the spectrum of profit allocation methods.[43] Formulary apportionment would allocate a multinational company's income based on some combination of factors. To illustrate, assume that the United States has a three-factor formula – sales, payroll, and physical assets – and gives equal weight to each factor. Now assume that a multinational company earned $1 billion worldwide. Thirty percent of the multinational's payroll and assets are in the United States, but 60 percent of the multinational's sales are in the United States. Under these facts, the US's share of that worldwide profit would be $400 million, determined as follows:

$$\$1 \text{ billion earnings} \times \frac{(30\% \text{ payroll factor} + 30\% \text{ assets factor} + 60\% \text{ sales factor})}{3 \text{ equally weighted factors}}$$

$$= \$400 \text{ million}$$

Now assume that the United States has adopted a sales-only formula. Under the same facts above, the United States's share of the $1 billion of worldwide income would be $600 million, determined as follows:

$$\$1 \text{ billion earnings} \times (60\% \text{ sales–only factor}) = \$600 \text{ million}$$

With formulary apportionment, income shifting would be reduced because profit allocation would be based on factors that reflect real economic activity, and tax revenues would be raised.[44] Profit allocation

---

[43] *See* Avi-Yonah, Clausing & Durst, *supra* note 13; Kimberly A. Clausing & Reuven S. Avi-Yonah, "Reforming Corporate Taxation in a Global Economy: A Proposal to Adopt Formulary Apportionment," *The Hamilton Project Discussion Paper* 2007–08, The Brookings Institute (June 2007), *available at* www.brookings.edu/wp-content/uploads/2 016/06/200706clausing_aviyonah.pdf; Susan C. Morse, "Revisiting Global Formulary Apportionment," *Virginia Tax Review* 29 (2010):593, *available at* http://repository.ucha stings.edu/faculty_scholarship/554. It has been said that formulary apportionment is a "second best" alternative to taxing income (i.e., it is most useful when income cannot be traced to its source). "When we can readily identify the geographic location or source of income – or the taxpayer that earned the income – by focusing directly on the transactions that produce the income, there is no warrant, as a matter of principle, for resorting to the second-best approach of formulary apportionment." Walter Hellerstein, "Designing the Limits of Formulary Income Attribution Regimes," *Tax Analysts* (2014): 51–52, *available at* www.taxanalysts.com/www/freefiles.nsf/Files/U.S.%20State%20Tax%20Consid erations.pdf/$file/U.S.%20State%20Tax%20Considerations.pdf.

[44] *See* Douglas Shackelford & Joel Slemrod, "The Revenue Consequences of Using Formulary Apportionment to Calculate US and Foreign-Source Income: A firm-Level Analysis," *International Tax and Public Finance* 5 (1998): 42 (estimating a 38 percent revenue increase from an equally weighted three-factor formula system). *See also*

would not be sensitive to countries' varying tax policies regarding tax rates, standards for determining corporate residency, and approaches to transfer pricing enforcement. It would not be beholden to arbitrary behavior of multinational companies, such as the number and residency of foreign subsidiaries, or which transfer pricing methods they use. In fact, with formulary apportionment, there would be no need for multinationals to form foreign subsidiaries *for tax reasons* and no need for transfers of intellectual property which create transfer pricing concerns.[45] In theory, it would place all companies on a level playing field.

In some countries, such as Canada and the United States, formulary apportionment is already used to allocate income among states or territories within the country,[46] and there is some evidence of reduced income shifting under this domestic formulary apportionment.[47] Commentators, however, have identified conceptual and practical difficulties with applying formulary apportionment in the global context.[48] It may prove difficult for countries to coordinate and agree on how to measure the tax base, something that is easier for US states to do since they exist within a common federal system. In addition, it might be challenging for countries

---

Clausing & Avi-Yonah, *supra* note 43 (estimating a sales-based formula system would raise approximately 35 percent of added revenue). *See also* Michael Udell & Aditi Vashist, "Sales-Factor Apportionment of Profits to Broaden the Tax Base," *Tax Notes Today* (2014): 2 (showing that a single-sales-factor apportionment of global profits could result in a US corporate income tax base up to 97 percent larger than the current base).

[45] *But see* Testimony of Avi-Yonah, Transfer Pricing Issues, *supra* note 31, at 8 ("I would propose that in hard transfer pricing cases, in which no comparables can be found beyond the return on routine functions, the US should adopt and the OECD should encores using the traditional three factor state formula to allocate the residual under the Profit Split method").

[46] "Multistate Tax Compact, 1967, art IV, § 9," accessed November 4, 2016, *available at* www.mtc.gov/The-Commission/Multistate-Tax-Compact. *See* Hellerstein, *supra* note 43 (noting formulas are used in Canada).

[47] Jack Mintz & Michael Smart, "Income Shifting, Investment, and Tax Competition: Theory and Evidence from Provincial Taxation in Canada," *Journal of Public Economics* 88 (2004): 1149–1168, *available at* www.sciencedirect.com/science/article/pii/S0047272703000604.

[48] *See* Gravelle, *supra* note 10, at 31–32 (summarizing barriers to formulary apportionment); Julie Roin, "Can the Income Tax Be Saved?: The Promise and Pitfalls of Adopting Worldwide Formulary Apportionment," *Tax Law Review* 61 (2008): 169, *available at* https://litigation-essentials.lexisnexis.com/webcd/app?action=DocumentDisplay&crawlid=1&srctype=smi&srcid=3B15&doctype=cite&docid=61+Tax+L.+Rev.+169&key=fe7783fe38ab9e9f17ca6e54bd3168ac (noting political realities); James R. Hines, Jr., "Income Misattribution Under Formula Apportionment," *European Economic Review* 54 (2010): 108; Rosanne Altshuler & Harry Grubert, "Formula Apportionment: Is It Better Than the Current System and Are There Better Alternatives?," *National Tax Journal* 63 (2010): 1145; Morse, *supra* note 43. *See also* Hellerstein, *supra* note 43.

to agree on the formula factors.[49] In the United States, different states use different formulas, although many states now place greater weight on the "sales" factor over employees or capital. Countries with large markets would likely want to place greater weight on the "sales" factor over employees or capital; countries with small markets would likely resist.[50] Additionally, it might be difficult to get countries to require their resident multinationals to account for all related entities. In the United States, some states have adopted so-called "combined reporting," which effectively eliminates income shifting. Some states, however, maintain "separate reporting," which allows for profit shifting to low-tax (or no-tax) states through transfer pricing. As shown in the first half of this book, transfer pricing problems and income shifting still exists between states where formulas are not uniform and where combined reporting is not adopted (or where companies are not required to account for all income).[51]

Even if countries could agree on all of the challenges listed above, formulary apportionment might encourage multinationals to move formula factors, such as jobs and factories, to low-tax jurisdictions in order to reduce their tax burden.[52] Evidence based on the United States suggests,

---

[49] Advocates of formulary apportionment typically leave intangibles out of the formula because if they were included, "the same problems of attributing income to a location under transfer pricing would arise." Jason J. Fichtner & Adam N. Michel, "The OECD's Conquest of the United States: Understanding the Costs and Consequences of the BEPS Project and Tax Harmonization," Mercatus Research, Mercatus Center at George Mason University (March 2016), *available at* www.mercatus.org/system/files/Fichtner-BEPS-Initiative-v1.pdf (citing Charles E. McLure, "US Federal Use of Formula Apportionment to Tax Income from Intangibles," *Tax Notes Today* (1997)). *See also* Testimony of Avi-Yonah, Transfer Pricing Issues, *supra* note 31, at 8 ("Intangibles are excluded, but in my opinion that is appropriate because (a) their value results from physical and human capital and from the market and those elements are included [in the traditional three factor formula of payroll, sales, and tangible assets], and (b) you cannot allocate their value and trying to include them invites manipulation").

[50] *See* Udell & Vashist, *supra* note 44. China may benefit from formulary apportionment because of its large employment footprint. Fichtner & Michel, *supra* note 49, at 31. Tax haven countries typically employ relatively few employees of multinationals. In 2011, for example, Microsoft had only 177 employees in Puerto Rico, even though Puerto Rico accounted for over $4 billion of earnings. Testimony of Avi-Yonah, Microsoft Part I, *supra* note 24, at 3.

[51] Fichtner & Michel, *supra* note 49, at 18 ("The benefits of apportionment persist only if all jurisdictions account for all profits and are uniform in all other rules. In practice, different jurisdictions end up using different apportionment formulas and do not require comprehensive accounting for all related entity profits. If a company is not required to account for all related entities, transfer pricing is still an avenue for profit shifting and additional complexity").

[52] *Ibid.* at 21 (arguing that with formulary apportionment real profit shifting will replace artificial profit shifting) (citing David Ernick, Hardeo Bissoondial, & Jack Kramer, "You Look Familiar: The OECD Looks to US State Tax Policy for BEPS Solutions," *in US State Tax Considerations for International Tax Reform* (Tax Analysts, 2014: 116)). Currently, the top employment countries for the foreign affiliates of US multinational

however, that formulary apportionment reduces income shifting from one US state to the next without encouraging the movement of economic activity (jobs and capital).[53] Perhaps this is because many US states have increased the weight of the "sales" factor in the formula.[54] Indeed, some US states have moved to a sales-only factor in the formula, most likely to avoid incentives to shift jobs and investment to low-tax states. As noted above, a sales-only factor would appeal to countries with large markets while other smaller market countries would resist the sales only approach.

In short, international coordination is critical for formulary apportionment to work. It is needed to reduce the potential for double taxation and reduce tax competition pressures. International cooperation, however, may prove difficult as noted above. In 2016, in the Common Consolidated Corporate Tax Base, the European Union proposed (for the second time) a version of formulary apportionment for dividing profits among member countries.[55] But that proposal is still pending, and some observers suggest it could be a hard sell to member countries. In addition, the OECD seems firmly committed to separate entity accounting and adherence to the arm's-length transfer pricing approach, as evidenced by its recent action plans to address base erosion and profit shifting, which are discussed later.

6   Tax Existing Profits Held Offshore and Close Inversion Loopholes

Some multinational companies have found ways (through creative short term loans from their own CFCs) to bring home profits "trapped" overseas without incurring US tax, even though profits brought home are

---

companies are large economies with large markets (China, United Kingdom, Canada, Mexico, India, Germany, Brazil, France, Japan, and Australia). Kimberly A. Clausing, "The Effect of Profit Shifting on the Corporate Tax Base in the United States and Beyond," 8, 32, June 17, 2016, *available at* https://papers.ssrn.com/sol3/papers.cfm?abstract_id=2685442.

[53] Clausing, *supra* note 52.   [54] *Ibid.*

[55] The CCCTB was first proposed in 2011. European Commissioner, Proposal for a Council Directive on a Common Consolidated Corporate Tax Base (CCCTB), March 16, 2011. But it stalled. The European Commission reintroduced it in 2016. European Commissioner, Proposal for a Council Directive on a Common Consolidated Corporate Tax Base (CCCTB), October 25, 2016. The CCCTB would favor larger consumer-based economies, such as France, over smaller exporting ones like Ireland. In fact, it is estimated that Ireland could lose up to 50 percent of its corporate tax base if CCCTB comes to fruition. *See* http://www.irishtimes.com/business/economy/ireland-could-lose-4bn-in-revenue-if-eu-tax-plans-go-ahead-says-ibec-1.3058505.

supposed to be taxed as dividends.[56] By and large, however, a massive amount of untaxed foreign income is parked offshore by many multinationals including those studied in this book – Apple, Microsoft and Uber. In fact, it is estimated that US multinationals have now accumulated between $2.4 million and $2.6 million of un-repatriated earnings, which will be subject to over $600 billion in US taxes when repatriated in the form of dividends.[57] The real question is "when" to tax this income – now, or wait until dividends (or deemed dividends) are paid? Governments could take stick measures to tax now the existing profits held offshore. Indeed, it has been proposed that the US government should tax that offshore money now (a "deemed repatriation") at the full corporate tax rate while it is trying to figure out a permanent solution to income shifting.[58]

The above stick approaches to limit foreign income shifting may introduce new incentives for corporate inversions by multinationals. Ironically, the ultimate income shifting technique is a corporate inversion,

---

[56] As a general rule, if a CFC loans money to its US parent company, that money is subject to US taxes (treated as dividends). But there are a number of exclusions and limitations. For example, offshore profits can be used for short-term lending. It was revealed in recent congressional hearings that Hewlett-Packard used a short-term loan program (a series of back to back to back to back loans to the US) to get between $6 billion and $9 billion of offshore profits to the US in 2010 without paying US taxes). *See* "Statement of Senator Carl Levin (D-MICH) Before US Senate Permanent Subcommittee on Investigations on Offshore Profit Shifting and the US Tax Code," Homeland Security & Governmental Affairs Permanent Subcommittee on Investigations, September 20, 2012, 4–5, *available at* www.hsgac.senate.gov/subcommittees/investigations/hearings/offshore-profit-shift ing-and-the-us-tax-code [hereinafter Statement of Levin, Microsoft]; Microsoft Part I, *supra* note 7, at 94–95_ (citing "Testimony of Stephen E. Shay Before the US Senate Permanent Subcommittee on Investigations of the Committee on Homeland Security and Governmental Affairs Hearing on Offshore Profit Shifting and the Internal Revenue Code," September 20, 2012, 8–9).

[57] Press Release, "Brady, Neal Highlight Another Reason for Pro-Growth Tax Reform: Joint Committee on Taxation Estimates Even More Foreign Earnings from US Companies Stranded Overseas," September 29, 2016, *available at* http://waysand means.house.gov/brady-neal-highlight-another-reason-pro-growth-tax-reform/ (providing two separate estimates, one based on the most recent tax return data and the other based on financial statement data from Audit Analytics).

[58] *See* Daniel Shaviro, "Pfizer-Allergan," *Daniel Shaviro Blogspot*, April 7, 2016, http://dan shaviro.blogspot.com/2016/04/pfizer-allergan.html. *See also* "Offshore Shell Games 2016: The Use of Offshore Tax Havens by Fortune 500 Companies," Citizens for Tax Justice, 21, October 2016, *available at* http://ctj.org/pdf/offshoreshellgames2016.pdf [hereinafter Offshore Shell Games 2016] ("The best way to deal with existing profits being held offshore would be to tax them through a deemed repatriation at the full 35 percent rate [minus foreign taxes paid]"). Of course, the long-term solution of ending deferral completely could raise significant revenue – nearly $900 billion over ten years according to both the Congressional Joint Committee on Taxation and the US Treasury Department. Office of Management and Budget, *Fiscal Year 2016: Analytical Perspectives of the US Government*, Washington, DC: US Government Printing Office, 2015, 228, *available at* www.whitehouse.gov/sites/default/files/omb/budget/fy2016/assets/spec.pdf.

which involves a multinational giving up its domestic residency to avoid domestic taxation of current and future earnings of foreign subsidiaries.[59] Governments can, and have in recent years, taken steps to crack down on inversions while they are trying to find a solution to income shifting.[60] Germany has a strong "exit tax" to curb inversions.[61] The United States has administratively taken actions in recent years to limit the benefits of tax inversions, although most agree congressional action is still needed.[62]

Carrots

Alternatively, countries could decrease taxation and adopt a "carrot" approach to attract and retain intellectual property and related income, which has the same effect as limiting the shifting of income. Examples to be discussed below include moving to a dividend exemption system, lowering the statutory corporate income tax rate, enacting a "patent box," and expanding and simplifying the research and development tax credit.

1   Move to a Pure Territorial or Dividend Exemption System

The United States and only a handful of other countries still have a worldwide system of taxation with relief (tax credit) for foreign taxes paid.[63] This approach encourages the use of foreign subsidiaries to

---

[59] As noted by the Treasury, "the primary purpose of an inversion is not to grow the underlying business, maximize synergies, or pursue other commercial benefits. Rather the primary purpose of the transaction is to reduce taxes, often substantially." "Fact Sheet: Treasury Issues Inversion Regulations and Proposed Earnings Stripping Regulations," *US Department of the Treasury*, April 4, 2016, www.treasury.gov/press-ce nter/press-releases/Pages/jl0404.aspx [hereinafter Fact Sheet Treasury Issues].

[60] President Obama's Framework, *supra* note 8, at 2 (noting "inversions are a particularly prominent symptom of a broken system... and should be addressed immediately even absent broader business tax reform").

[61] Rosanne Altshuler, Stephen Shay, & Eric Toder, "Lessons the United States Can Learn from Other Countries' Territorial Systems for Taxing Income of Multinational Corporations," 28 (Tax Policy Center: Urban Institute & Brookings Institution, January 21, 2015), *available at* www.taxpolicycenter.org/sites/default/files/alfresco/publi cation-pdfs/2000077-lessons-the-us-can-learn-from-other-countries.pdf (noting that a German corporation that moves its legal seat or place of management outside of the European Union is deemed liquidated, resulting in a deemed disposition of its assets and taxation of unrealized built-in gains); *see also* Klaus Sieker, *Business Operations in Germany* (Amsterdam: International Bureau of Fiscal Documentation V.B.4.b(5), V.B.2.d(2)(c), 2014).

[62] For a summary of government actions to limit inversions, *see* Chapter 8.

[63] Scott A. Hodge et al., *Business in America Illustrated* (Washington, DC, Tax Foundation, 2014), http://taxfoundation.org/sites/taxfoundation.org/files/docs/BIA 2 0Chartbook.pdf.

achieve deferral – for example, the ability of US multinationals to shift income to foreign subsidiaries in low-tax countries to avoid current US taxation of foreign earnings (until brought home in the form of dividends to the US parent) and to increase their current after-tax profits.[64] Indeed, many US multinational companies delay paying themselves dividends to avoid the US tax hit. Thus, worldwide taxation is partly to blame for the large sum of foreign profits stashed overseas.[65]

The ultimate carrot for multinationals to repatriate foreign profits would be to move to a territorial system of taxation, which would exempt overseas profits repatriated to the United States as dividends (thus, all active foreign income would be subject to zero or nominal US tax).[66] Recall that countries with a territorial system of taxation collect tax only on income earned within their territorial borders. They generally do not seek to tax foreign income earned directly abroad or indirectly abroad through foreign subsidiaries. Tax exemption is achieved in the latter case by exempting dividends received by a domestic multinational company from its foreign subsidiary company. That is why territorial systems are often referred to as dividend exemption systems.

Some countries such as Australia and Germany have had long-standing territorial systems, while others, such as Japan and the UK, have recently moved to a territorial approach to international taxation.[67] Former House

---

[64] *See* Office of Tax Policy, US Department of Treasury, "The Deferral of Income Earned through US Controlled Foreign Corporations," 12, December 2000, *available at* www.treasury.gov/resource-center/tax-policy/Documents/Report-SubpartF-2000.pdf. *See also* President Obama's Framework, *supra* note 8, at 11–12 ("Because of deferral, US corporations have a significant opportunity to reduce overall taxes paid by shifting profits to low-tax jurisdictions").

[65] Danny Yadron, Kate Linebaugh, & Jessica E. Lessin, "Apple Avoided Taxes on Overseas Billions, Senate Panel Finds," *The Wall Street Journal*, May 20, 2013, www.wsj.com/articles/SB10001424127887324787004578495250424727708 (citing Harvard Business School Professor Mihir Desai).

[66] *See* Edward D. Kleinbard, *We Are Better Than This: How Government Should Spend Our Money* (New York, New York: Oxford University Press, 2015) (proposing, as one tax reform option, a territorial tax system with teeth); Wells & Lowell, *supra* note 14, at 61 (noting congressional willingness in 2011 to consider a territorial regime). *But see* Altshuler et al., *supra* note 61, at 18 (noting that even under dividend exemption, "[a]n incentive would remain to reinvest earnings offshore in active business operations if the effective rate of tax on reinvestment earnings were lower than the US effective tax rate" and "[a]n incentive would also continue to exist for some US firms to change domicile if US tax rules limiting the scope of the exemption were stronger than similar rules in the competitor countries and residence rules were not modified to address these incentives").

[67] The United Kingdom adopted its 100 percent dividend exemption in 2009. *See* Altshuler et al., *supra* note 61, at 21 (providing summary of United Kingdom taxation); Barbara Angus, Tom Neubig, Eric Solomon, & Mark Weinberger, "The US International System at a Crossroads," *Tax Notes* (2010): 45, 54 Table 3, *available at* http://taxprof.typepad.com/files/angus.pdf. For discussion of Japan's shift to dividend exemption in 2009, *see* Altshuler et al., *supra* note 61, at 25 (citing Yoshihiro Masui, "Taxation of Foreign

Ways and Means Committee Chairman Dave Camp has proposed, among other measures, allowing a 95 percent exemption for repatriated earnings of foreign subsidiaries of US parent corporations, and President Trump more recently has argued for a move to a territorial system.[68] There are several arguments in favor of the United States moving in the direction of territoriality. Worldwide taxation emphasizes corporate residence, which "is not a particularly meaningful concept," and which "provides an impetus for inversions."[69] The current system distorts corporate behavior while collecting little revenue. A move to a territorial system would limit incentives to shifting income because our rules would finally align with those of the rest of the world.[70]

Most likely the United States would see the move to territoriality as too costly,[71] and as aggravating, rather than fixing, problems (e.g., US multinationals would have even greater incentive to locate operations abroad, shift income offshore, or invert to low-tax jurisdictions).[72] Ironically,

---

Subsidiaries: Japan's Tax Reform 2009/10," *Bulletin for International Taxation* 64 (2010): 242–48).

[68] For Camp's proposal, *see* "H.R.1 – Tax Reform Act of 2014," 113th Congress, Congress. gov, accessed October 30, 2016, www.congress.gov/bill/113th-congress/house-bill/1. *See* Technical Explanation, *supra* note 34, at 32–36. *See also* Press Release, "Camp Releases International Tax Reform Discussion Draft Effort," October 26, 2011, *available at* http:// waysandmeans.house.gov/news/documentsingle.aspx?DocumentID=266168. *See* Joint Committee on Taxation, "Technical Explanation of the Senate Committee on Finance Chairman's Staff Discussion Draft of Provisions to Reform International Business Taxation," *JCX-15-13* (November 19, 2013), *available at* www.jct.gov/publications.ht ml?func=startdown&id=4530. *See* Technical Explanation, *supra* note 34, at 18 (discussing Camp's proposed dividends-received deduction).

[69] *See* Testimony of Avi-Yonah, Transfer Pricing Issues, *supra* note 31, at 2.   [70] *Ibid.*

[71] The Joint Committee on Taxation estimates that switching to a territorial tax system could add almost $300 billion to the deficit over ten years. "A 'Patent Box' Would Be a Huge Step Back for Corporate Tax Reform," Citizens for Tax Justice, June 4, 2015, *available at* http://ctj.org/pdf/patentboxstepback.pdf. *See* Testimony of Avi-Yonah, Transfer Pricing Issues, *supra* note 31 (suggesting without transfer pricing reform, "the move to territoriality will lead to an even stronger incentive to shift profits overseas, and to further revenue losses and erosion of the US corporate tax base").

[72] President Obama's Framework, *supra* note 8, at 23 (outlining problems if the US switched to a pure territorial system); Stephanie Berrong, "News Analysis: How Much Would Territoriality Cost?," *Tax Notes Today*, April 20, 2011, www.taxnotes.com/docu ment-list/contributors-authors/berrong-stephanie. *See also* "A 'Patent Box' Would Be a Huge Step Back for Corporate Tax Reform," *supra* note 71 (arguing that moving toward a territorial system would make tax haven abuse worse: "Companies could shift profits to tax haven countries, pay minimal or no tax under those countries' tax laws, and then freely use the profits in the United States without paying any US taxes."); Norris, *supra* note 22 (arguing that a territorial system "would simply be a recipe for giving up on collecting tax revenue"). In the 1990s, the US Treasury Department proposed corporate integration through a dividend exemption, but Congress chose to lower the rate on dividends instead. Department of the Treasury, "Integration of the Individual and Corporate Tax Systems: Taxing Business Income Once," January 1992, *available at* www.treasury.gov/resource-center/tax-policy/Documents/Report-Integration-1992.pdf.

however, many US multinationals purposefully keep their foreign subsidiaries' profits overseas instead of having them distributed in the form of dividends. Because of this, the US's worldwide system already looks a lot more like a de facto or do-it-yourself territorial system – one in which taxes are never paid on foreign income.[73] Formally moving from a worldwide system to a territorial (or dividend exemption) system may have little effect other than allowing trillions of dollars of foreign profits to come back home – which wouldn't be a bad thing.[74]

Australia's dividend integration system is worth pointing out because it may limit incentives to shift income offshore. In Australia, a resident shareholder who receives a dividend from an Australian multinational corporation receives a tax credit for only domestic and not foreign taxes paid on taxable profits underlying the dividend. That resident shareholder, however, receives no credit if the dividend is with respect to foreign profits that are exempt from domestic taxes (e.g., foreign income earned directly or a dividend from a foreign subsidiary). Australian companies like to distribute tax-free dividends to their shareholders. But that is not possible if the Australian corporation distributes foreign profits that have not been subject to domestic corporate taxation. Thus, there may be less incentive to shift income. As suggested by some commentators, Australian's dividend integration system (really an imputation credit system) may reduce the tendency of Australian companies to shift intellectual property and income overseas because Australian shareholders cannot get tax credits if domestic taxes have not been paid.[75]

2   Lower the Statutory Corporate Income Tax Rate

There is no doubt that corporate tax rates have played a major role in income shifting. Economists have shown that income is very sensitive to tax rates – that is, significant rate differentials between a home country and a foreign country encourage income shifting.[76] The greater the difference between corporate tax rates, the greater the incentive to shift

---

[73] Berrong, *supra* note 72.

[74] H. David Rosenbloom & Joseph P. Brothers, "Reflections on the Intersection of US Tax Treaty Policy, US Tax Reform, and BEPS," *Tax Notes International* 78 (2015): 759 (noting a global movement toward territorial regimes arguably reduces the need for treaties).

[75] Altshuler et al., *supra* note 61, at 34; Graetz & Doud, *supra* note 10, at 432–33 ("Australia's lack of concern with income shifting may be due to its integrated system of corporate taxation. . . . Because Australian companies want to pay tax-free or low-taxed dividends to their shareholders, [Australian companies] have much less incentive than US companies to erode their domestic tax base").

[76] Clausing, *supra* note 52. For further evidence that multinationals' decisions about where to invest are sensitive to tax rates in foreign jurisdictions, *see* Rosanne Altshuler & Harry

income. Indeed, a handful of countries offering low tax rates account for the bulk of foreign income earned by foreign subsidiaries of multinational companies showing a statistically significant negative relationship between profits and tax rates. To counter this, a high-tax country could lower its corporate income tax rate, narrowing the gap between its rate and other countries' low foreign rates.[77]

The United States has the third highest corporate tax rate in the world (35 percent, or 39 percent when considering state income taxes), explaining why much of the income shifting occurs with respect to US multinational companies. The United States acknowledges that the reduction in tax rates abroad has increased the incentive to shift income offshore,[78] and there now is general consensus that the US statutory rate should be reduced,[79] or that the corporate income tax should be repealed.[80] There have been proposals to lower the statutory rate. The Obama administration proposed lowering it to 28 percent, whereas the Trump

Grubert, "Taxpayer Responses to Competitive Tax Policies and Tax Policy Responses to Competitive Taxpayers: Recent Evidence," *Tax Notes International: Special Reports* (2004), *available at* https://ideas.repec.org/p/rut/rutres/200406.html; Harry Grubert & John Mutti, "Taxes, Tariffs and Transfer Pricing in Multinational Corporation Decision Making," *The Review of Economics and Statistics* 73 (1991): 285.

[77] *But see* Gravelle, *supra* note 10, at 10 (arguing that cutting the corporate statutory rate is an "undesirable step (in a revenue neutral environment) for encouraging real investment" and "it is also a relatively fruitless endeavor for discouraging profit shifting": "cutting the statutory tax rate to entice firms to reduce profit shifting appears to be throwing the baby out with the bath water").

[78] President Obama's Framework, *supra* note 8, at 14.

[79] *See, e.g.*, Karen C. Burke, "Is the Corporate Tax System 'Broken' "? *Virginia Tax Review* 28 (2008): 341; Robert Carroll & Thomas Neubig, Ernst & Young, "The Economic Benefits of Reducing the US Corporate Income Tax Rate," September 2011, *available at* http://ra tecoalition.com/wp-content/uploads/2013/04/ey-report-economic-benefits-of-a-lower-cor porate-tax-rate-2011-09-17.pdf. For proposals to lower the statutory corporate tax rate (while at the same time eliminating tax expenditures), *see, e.g.*, Mark P. Keightley & Molly F. Sherlock, *The Corporate Income Tax System: Overview and Options for Reform* (CRS Report No. R42726) (Washington, DC: Congressional Research Service, 2014), 23–25, 28–31; Staff of US House Ways & Means Comm., 113th Cong., Tax Reform Act of 2014 (Comm. Print 2014) (Discussion Draft) [hereinafter Tax Reform Act of 2014 Discussion Draft], *available at* http://waysandmeans.house.gov/UploadedFiles/Statutory_Text_ Tax_ Reform_Act_of_2014_Discussion_Draft__022614.pdf; President Obama's Framework, *supra* note 8; Joint Committee on Taxation, Technical Explanation of the Tax Reform Act of 2014, "A Discussion Draft of the Chairman of the House Committee on Ways and Means to Reform the Internal Revenue Code: Title III – Business Tax Reform," JCX-14-14 (February 26, 2014), *available at* www.jct.gov/publications.html?func=startdow n&id=4556; Jane G. Gravelle, "Reducing Depreciation Allowances to Finance a Lower Corporate Tax Rate," *National Tax Journal* 64 (2011): 1039.

[80] *See* Noel B. Cunningham & Mitchell L. Engler, "Prescription for Corporate Income Tax Reform: A Corporate Consumption Tax," *New York University Tax Law Review* 66 (2013): 445; *see also* Hans Fehr et al., "Simulating the Elimination of the US Corporate Income Tax," *National Bureau of Economic Research Working Paper* No. 19757 (2013), *available at* www.nber.org/data-appendix/w19757/CorporateTaxPaper.pdf.

administration has recently proposed lower it to 15 percent.[81] Dave Camp proposed lowering it to 25 percent. Lowering the US corporate tax rate would achieve a number of goals including reducing the incentive for income shifting.[82] It would also help put the United States in line with other major competitor countries and encourage greater investment in the United States. The United Kingdom has already reduced its statutory rate to 20 percent as a carrot to achieve these goals, and there is movement to slash it to less than 15 percent (which is President Trump's proposed US rate).

Cutting corporate tax rates is often accompanied by measures to maintain the same amount of revenue. But usually there is wide disagreement over most details. The Obama administration proposed three measures: (1) scaling back tax depreciation allowances, an approach taken by other large countries that have reduced their statutory rates; (2) limiting interest deductibility; and (3) eliminating special tax breaks for specific industries, such as tax preferences that are currently available for the fossil fuel industries, and reforming the treatment of capital gains.[83] Professor Graetz has suggested that the US enact a Value Added Tax (VAT) to help pay for a lower US corporate income tax rate.[84] Jane Gravelle, with the Congressional Research Service, questions the ability to reduce the corporate tax rate without losing revenues.[85] Indeed, it is anticipated that Trump's proposal would cause significant loss of revenues.

3   Enact a Patent Box

In addition to reducing its general corporate income tax rate, a country could offer an even lower effective tax rate on income associated with

---

[81] For Obama's proposal, see President Obama's Framework, *supra* note 8, at 4. For Trump's proposal, see https://www.nytimes.com/2017/04/26/us/politics/trump-tax-cut-plan.html.

[82] *See, e.g.,* Testimony of Avi-Yonah, Microsoft Part I, *supra* note 24, at 5 (noting there would be less incentive to shift profits out of the US especially if the US corporate tax rate is reduced to a level commensurate with the OECD average).

[83] President Obama's Framework, *supra* note 8, at 19. For details of specific proposals, see Department of the Treasury, "General Explanations of the Administration's Fiscal Year 2017 Revenue Proposals," February 2016, *available at* www.treasury.gov/resource-cen ter/tax- policy/Documents/General-Explanations-FY2017.pdf. For other countries' approaches, see Alan J. Auerbach, Michael P. Devereux, & Helen Simpson, "Taxing Corporate Income," *National Bureau of Economic Research Working Paper Series* (2008), *available at* www.nber.org/papers/w14494.pdf.

[84] *See* Michael J. Graetz, *100 Million Unnecessary Returns: A Simple, Fair, and Competitive Tax Plan for the United States* (2008), 108–09 (suggesting decrease in corporate income tax rate to 15 percent would "dramatically improve the competitive position of the American economy and reduce tax sheltering behavior").

[85] Gravelle, *supra* note 10, at 10.

intellectual property. As noted in Chapter 6, many countries have in recent years enacted so-called "patent boxes" or "innovation boxes" to discourage the shifting of intellectual property income abroad and/or to lure other multinational companies to relocate their highly mobile intellectual property to their jurisdiction and to capture additional tax revenues.[86] We have seen widespread adoption of patent boxes particularly in Europe in recent years. In the United States, House Representatives Charles Boustany and Richard Neal offered a patent box proposal that allows (by means of a 71.4 percent deduction) a 10 percent US tax rate for certain intellectual property income that has a US link.[87] The effect of any patent box, of course, really depends on its design, and, as shown in Chapter 6, existing patent box regimes vary.

While patent boxes arguably influence intellectual property location decisions and improve international competitiveness of multinationals by reducing their taxes,[88] they are not without flaws.[89] First, patent boxes

[86] *See* Graetz & Doud, *supra* note 10, at 405–406 (describing reasons for adopting patent boxes).

[87] For details, *see* Press Release, "Ryan Welcomes Boustany-Neal Innovation Box Discussion Draft," July 29, 2015, *available at* https://waysandmeans.house.gov/ryan-welcomes-boustany-neal-innovation-box-discussion-draft/. For further details, *see* "US Representatives Boustany and Neil Release Innovation Box Draft as Part of International Tax Reform Deliberations," Ernst & Young (July 31, 2015), *available at* www.ey.com/Publication/vwLUAssets/US_Representatives_Boustany_and_Neal_release_innovation_box_draft_as_part_of_international_tax_reform_deliberations/$FILE/2015G_CM5649_US%20Reps%20Boustany%20and%20Neal%20release%20innovation%20box%20draft%20as%20part%20of%20intl%20tax%20reform%20delibs.pdf. For commentary on whether the United Should consider a patent box, *see* Peter R. Merrill et al., "Is It Time for the United States to Consider the Patent Box?," *Tax Notes* (2012): 1665, *available at* www.pwc.com/us/en/washington-national-tax/assets/merrill0326.pdf; Martin A. Sulllivan, "Time for a US Patent Box?," *Tax Notes* (2011): 1304. For the case that Canada should adopt one, see Nick Pantaleo, Finn Poschmann & Scott Wilkie, "Improving the Tax Treatment of Intellectual Property Income in Canada," *C.D. Howe Institute Commentary* No. 379 (April 25, 2013), *available at* https://papers.ssrn.com/sol3/papers.cfm?abstract_id=2303819.

[88] Ike Brannon & Michelle Hanlon, "How a Patent Box Would Affect the US Biopharmaceutical Sector," *Tax Notes Today* (2015), *available at* www.taxnotes.com/tax-notes-today/corporate-taxation/how-patent-box-would-affect-us-biopharmaceutical-sector/2015/02/03/9512776 (using data obtained from a survey of biotech and pharma companies to estimate the potential effects of implementing a patent box in the United States).

[89] President Obama's Framework, *supra* note 8, at 22 ("Measured by the criterion of economic efficiency, the innovation box comes up short as a desirable tax policy tool"). *See* Jason Furman, "Encouraging Innovation and the Role of Tax Policy" (speech, Joint International Tax Policy Forum & Georgetown University Law Center, March 11, 2016), *available at* www.whitehouse.gov/sites/default/files/docs/20160311_innovation_and_tax_policy_itpf.pdf *See also* Jason J. Fichtner & Adam N. Michel, "Don't Put American Innovation in a Patent Box: Tax Policy, Intellectual Property, and the Future of R&D," Mercatus Center, George Mason University (December 2015), *available at* www.mercatus.org/system/files/Fichtner-Patent-Boxes-MOP.pdf.

provide tax benefits for intellectual property already in existence, and research suggests they are less effective than R&D credits in encouraging new innovation. R&D deductions and credits do a better job of encouraging new research, which results in positive spillover effects like attracting high value workers as well as luring capital essential for intellectual property.[90] Second, patent boxes are costly.[91] The United Kingdom, for example, saw a reduction in corporate revenues with its patent box even though additional innovation was reported.[92] If the United States adopted a patent box, the large size of its market could mean a significant loss of revenue.[93] Third, patent boxes require new rules and compliance checks that would only further complicate the tax system.[94] Finally, patent boxes can result in a "race to the bottom" wherein countries compete to have the lowest rate on intellectual property income.[95] This could have a negative impact on funding of goods and services the government provides.

4   Expand R&D Tax Deductions and Credits

Front-ended tax incentives, such as R&D tax deductions and credits, have proven effective in encouraging new R&D. As with patent boxes, R&D tax deductions and credits can also reduce the effective tax rate on intellectual property income and encourage the shifting of intellectual property income offshore.

As a carrot tool, countries could expand and simplify their R&D deductions and credits. For example, the United States has a 100 percent tax deduction for qualified R&D spending. It could, in contrast, offer an enhanced deduction greater than 100 percent for qualifying spending, as many other countries do. The United States also has a tax credit for R&D, which is 20 percent of qualified research spending above the firm's normal level of R&D investment. This too could be enhanced in a number of ways. The United States could increase the credit to greater than 20 percent, in line with what some other nations offer (e.g., 25 percent in Spain and Ireland; 30 percent in France). It could change

---

[90] President Obama's Framework, *supra* note 8, at 22 ("Compared to the R&E credit, an innovation box is less effective in encouraging innovation."); Graetz & Doud, *supra* note 10, at Part II.D (summarizing data on benefits of R&D tax incentives).

[91] President Obama's Framework, *supra* note 8, at 22.

[92] Rachel Griffith, Helen Miller, & Martin O'Connell, "Ownership of Intellectual Property and Corporate Taxation," *Journal of Public Economics* 112 (2014): 12.

[93] *See* Luca Gattoni-Celli, "Ryan Eyeing Research Cost Recovery to Pay for Innovation Box," *Tax Notes* (2015): 824 (proposing five-year amortization of R&D costs to make up tax revenue loss).

[94] President Obama's Framework, *supra* note 8, at 22.   [95] *Ibid.*

the nature of the credit from one that is incremental (applicable only if the firm increases its R&D over time) to one that is volume based (applicable simply on the volume or amount of qualified R&D spending). Some countries, such as Ireland and France, have recently made such a move.[96] Finally, the R&D deductions and credits could be expanded to cover all or some capital expenditures on buildings or structures used in carrying on R&D activities. It should be noted that in December 2015, the US made permanent its R&D tax credit, perhaps the most significant enhancement to the credit since its enactment. Further reforms, however, could be considered along the lines just described.[97]

Regardless of enhancements chosen, it would be important for countries to ensure that the intellectual property receiving the benefits of R&D deductions or credits remain in its home country. Currently, a multinational can conduct R&D in the United States, claim tax credits for the R&D, and then shift profits attributable to the R&D offshore. Thus, modifications to R&D credits could involve a combination of carrots in the form of enhancements described above, along with a stick in the form of a mechanism to ensure profits attributable to R&D in the United States stay in the United States.

5   Enact a Repatriation Holiday for Existing Profits Offshore

While examining options to deal permanently with intellectual property income shifting, governments can enact carrot incentives to encourage multinational companies to bring home accumulated profits that are being held offshore. One approach, lobbied by multinational companies, would be to enact a special low tax rate on these existing profits when

---

[96] See Louise Kelly, "Looking to the future: Life after the 'Double Irish,'" *International Tax Review*, February 24, 2015, www.internationaltaxreview.com/Article/3430276/Looking-to-the-future-Life-after-the-Double-Irish.html. Patrick Eparvier, "Monitoring and Analysis of Policies and Public Financing Instruments Conducive to Higher Levels of R&D Investment – The 'POLICY MIX' Project – Country Review FRANCE," 19, March 2007, *available at* http://ec.europa.eu/invest-in-research/pdf/download_en/france.pdf; PricewaterhouseCoopers, "Global Research & Development Incentives Group," *PricewaterhouseCoopers* (November 1, 2012), *available at* www.pwc.com/gx/en/tax/assets/pwc-global-research-development-incentives-group-november-2012-pdf.pdf; Eduard Sporken & Edwin Gommers revised by Alan Katiya, Nathalie Cordier-Deltour, & Vincent Berger, "Tax Treatment of R&D Expenses in France," *International Transfer Pricing Journal* 14 (2007): 14–18.

[97] The President Obama's Framework, released by the Obama administration, acknowledges that further reforms should be made to make the R&D tax credit more effective. President Obama's Framework would, for instance, simplify the credit by repealing the outdated formula and enhance the credit for pass-through businesses. President Obama's Framework, *supra* note 8, at 21.

brought home.[98] The United States did this in 2005 by providing a special 5.25 percent effective tax rate on foreign profits repatriated to the United States. In response, multinational companies brought home $362 billion, almost half of what multinationals had stashed offshore.[99] If history repeats itself, a similar repatriation holiday now would bring home close to $1 trillion of foreign earnings parked offshore. It should be noted that the Obama administration proposed a mandatory one-time tax at 14 percent, and the Trump administration recently hinted at a reduced tax rate to bring offshore profits home but provided no details.[100] Former House Ways and Means Committee Chair Dave Camp has proposed a similar tax at 8.75 percent.[101] These rates are not as low at the 2005 special rate, but they are lower than the current 35 percent corporate income tax rate.

Multinational companies may use repatriated funds for a variety of purposes, such as conducting additional R&D, expanding operations, hiring new employees, paying bonuses to executives, repurchasing stock from shareholders, and paying dividends to individual shareholders, some of whom are US residents and some of whom are not.[102] In designing a repatriation holiday, the government should consider likely uses and appropriate restrictions. It has been suggested that the 2005 repatriation holiday that brought home $362 billion was used mostly for stock repurchases and executive compensation, and not for R&D, expansion, or employees.[103]

[98] Apple has asked the government to change the law so that it could pay no tax if it brought home its earnings booked offshore. Lee Sheppard, "How Does Apple Avoid Taxes?," *Forbes*, May 28, 2013, www.forbes.com/sites/leesheppard/2013/05/28/how-does-apple-avoid-taxes/#34f845a2d6f7. Ironically, multinationals that have launched a lobbying effort and promised to bring home billions of offshore dollars, have declared these amounts "permanently reinvested offshore" for financial reporting purposes. *See* Statement of Levin, Microsoft, *supra* note 56, at 5.

[99] *See* Melissa Redmiles, "The One-Time Dividends Received Deduction," *IRS Statistics Income Bulletin* (Spring 2008), 102–103, *available at* www.irs.gov/pub/irs-soi/08codivde ductbul.pdf.

[100] President Obama's Framework, *supra* note 8, at 24 (allowing a proportional credit for foreign taxes associated with such earnings).

[101] "Offshore Shell Games 2016: *supra* note 58 (noting President Obama's proposal would allow multinational companies to avoid around $500 billion in taxes they owe, and Camp's proposal would allow multinational companies to avoid around $550 billion in taxes that they owe).

[102] Claire Buchan Parket, "The Path to Jobs and Prosperity: Tax Reform," *Roll Call*, January 26, 2014, www.rollcall.com/news/the_path_to_jobs_and_prosperity_tax_re form_commentary-230384-1.html?zkPrintable=true.

[103] *See* "Repatriating Offshore Funds: 2004 Tax Windfall for Select Multinationals Majority Staff Report," Permanent Subcommittee on Investigations of the Committee on Homeland Security and Governmental Affairs of the United States Senate, 3, 22–23, October 11, 2011, *available at* www.gpo.gov/fdsys/pkg/CPRT-112SPRT70710/pdf/C PRT-112SPRT70710.pdf [hereinafter 2004 Tax Windfall Report].

The government should address additional questions. First, to what extent are unrepatriated foreign earnings of multinationals already sitting in US bank accounts or investments by US multinationals? Evidence suggests that "the vast majority of the unrepatriated foreign earnings of companies like Apple, Cisco, and Google already reside in US bank accounts or other US investments."[104] Second, if repatriated earnings are paid out to the shareholders of US parents instead of going toward R&D, employees, and suppliers, what will the shareholders likely do with the funds (i.e., will the funds exit the US or be spent in the US economy on US goods and services)? As argued by Professor Sanchirco, the answer to this question requires an understanding of who these shareholders are. This underscores the importance of understanding ownership nationality in the current debate over international tax policy: "When we speak of 'US multinationals,' what do we mean by 'US'? More specifically, to what extent are these 'US' companies owned by non-US investors?"[105]

A Framework for International Tax Reform: Intellectual Property Income Shifting

As we just saw, there are many different ways to deal with intellectual property income shifting, and there are pros and cons with each international tax reform approach. Numerous factors can influence the direction a nation takes, and numerous considerations can influence the design of new rules. The following is a framework of questions that should be considered in designing new cross-border tax policy.

1   What Are the Goals for Setting Cross-Border Tax Policy?

The particular goals of a country, or how they prioritize tax policy objectives, can influence the reform path chosen – in particular, the carrot or

---

[104] Chris William Sanchirico, "As American As Apple Inc.: International Tax and Ownership Nationality," *Tax Law Review* 68 (2015): 216 (citing Majority Staff of S. Permanent Subcomm. on Investigations, 112th Cong., Offshore Funds Located Onshore: Addendum to Repatriating Offshore Funds 5 (Comm. Print 2011) (showing percentage of undistributed foreign earnings held in US bank accounts or investments by various large US multinationals)). In many instances, the shifted income is deposited in the names of CFCs in accounts in US banks. *See, e.g.,* 2004 Tax Windfall Report, *supra* note 103, at 57 (showing that of $538 billion in undistributed accumulated foreign earnings at the end of FY2010, nearly half [46 percent] of the funds that the corporations had identified as offshore and for which US taxes had been deferred, were actually in the United States at US financial institutions).

[105] Sanchirico, *supra* note 104, at 210.

stick approach.[106] Some countries may wish, as their primary goal, to provide a more positive business environment for domestic companies, make domestic companies more competitive, attract new intellectual property to increase economic activity, or encourage companies to repatriate earnings to improve the economy. These goals generally favor a carrot approach, especially if the country has a small market, struggling economy, or harsh tax climate. Indeed, we have seen in recent years some countries, such as Japan, moving to a dividend exemption system to make its companies more competitive, to encourage them to repatriate offshore earnings without further tax, and to trigger domestic economic growth.[107] The United Kingdom has also adopted a territorial tax system and lowered its corporate income tax rate to attract and retain investment.[108] And several other European countries have created enhanced deductions and credits for research and development activity, and also patent boxes to attract intellectual property to their jurisdictions.[109]

Some countries, in contrast, may have, as their primary goal, the reduction or elimination of income shifting by large multinational companies and the making up of lost tax revenue. Most of these countries are concerned primarily about domestic-to-foreign income shifting (i.e., the shifting of income out of the home country to another jurisdiction). But some may also be concerned about foreign-to-foreign income shifting (the shifting of income from another high-tax country to another zero-tax jurisdiction).[110] Such goals generally favor a stick approach, especially if the country already has a large market or is already the location of large multinational companies and substantial research and development activity.[111] The United States, concerned chiefly with erosion of its tax revenue base, has shown a propensity for this approach in addressing income shifting. For years, the US has focused on strengthening its transfer pricing rules through layers of new legislation and regulation. In

---

[106] The primary tax policy objectives should be identified. A problem with recent reform efforts is that nations have tried to balance multiple goals including protecting the base and encouraging economic activity. JCX-139-15 Report, *supra* note 2, at 41 (referring to past US cross-border tax policy).

[107] Altshuler et al., *supra* note 61, at 25 (citing Yoshihiro Masui, "Taxation of Foreign Subsidiaries: Japan's Tax Reform 2009/10," *Bulletin for International Taxation* 64 (2010): 242–48); *see ibid.* at 34–35.

[108] *See* Angus et al., *supra* note 67, at 45, 54 Table 3.   [109] For a review, *see* Chapter 6.

[110] If other countries permit foreign to foreign income shifting and the United States does not, US multinationals might suffer a competitive disadvantage versus foreign multinationals, which might in turn encourage US multinationals to move their residency. Graetz & Doud, *supra* note 10, at 424.

[111] Gravelle, *supra* note 10, at 33 (suggesting that US policy "needs to employ sticks, rather than carrots, to address the concerns with profit shifting").

the past, there has been talk in the United States about expanding the controlled foreign corporation (CFC) rules,[112] enacting a minimum tax,[113] and restricting the use of hybrid entities – all sticks.[114] Under the Trump administration, there has been some talk about substantially lowering the statutory corporate tax rate and moving to a territorial approach to taxation (both carrot approaches). But such measures would be quite drastic for the United States and likely face political hurdles. In light of its historical approach to tax policy (and considering the size of the US market and the fact that it is already home to large multinational companies with unique intellectual property assets), the US may remain content with stick approaches to limit tax avoidance by its multinationals.

Concededly, some of the same goals can be achieved with *either a carrot or stick* approach. Assume, for example, that a country wishes to prevent domestic multinational companies from moving their corporate headquarters out of the country. That country could adopt favorable tax incentives to keep multinational companies onshore; alternatively, the country could adopt severe penalties on the relocation of corporate headquarters, or even rules that effectively eliminate any tax benefit of such maneuvering. Both approaches have been utilized in recent years. In response to the recent wave of corporate inversions, the United Kingdom, which is in close proximity to countries with lower tax rates and which is subject to EU restrictions on adopting inversion rules, has lowered its statutory rate and adopted a patent box.[115] In contrast, the United States adopted new regulations that eliminate the tax benefits of corporate inversions.[116]

Some goals can also be achieved with a *combination of both carrot and stick* approaches. The United Kingdom, in particular, has been quite aggressive in addressing income shifting with both carrots and sticks. While lowering its corporate tax rate and adopting a patent box to keep

---

[112] *See, e.g.*, Technical Explanation, *supra* note 34.

[113] *See, e.g.*, President Obama's Framework, *supra* note 8.

[114] *See, e.g.*, Testimony of Avi-Yonah, Microsoft Part I, *supra* note 24, at 4–8.

[115] The UK's patent box, which applies a reduced tax rate of 10 percent to profits from patents, became effective in 2013. Finance Act of 2012, c. 14, sch. 2 (UK). HM Revenue & Customs, "*The Patent Box: Technical Note and Guide to the Finance Bill 2012 Clauses,*" 8, November 2012, *available at* www.hmrc.gov.uk/budget-updates/mar ch2012/patent-box-tech-note.pdf. The United Kingdom noted that some patent-rich UK businesses faced higher taxes than their foreign competitors. HM Treasury, "Corporate Tax Reform: Delivering a More Competitive System," 51, November 2010, *available at* www.hm-treasury.gov.uk/d/corporate_tax_reform_complete_docu ment.pdf. The patent box appears to have been, at least partially, in response to the plans of some prominent multinational companies to move to Ireland. Lee A. Sheppard, "What Hath Britain Wrought?," *Worldwide Tax Daily* (December 30, 2010): 7–8, *available at* LexisNexis, 2010 WTD 250–2.

[116] *See* Fact Sheet Treasury Issues, *supra* note 59.

domestic companies and their intellectual property home, it has also adopted strict measures, such as its diverted profits tax, to penalize the shifting of assets and income offshore.[117] In the United States, the Obama administration (in the President's Framework) proposed a combination of carrots and sticks. Specifically, while reducing the corporate tax rate to reduce incentives for shifting assets and income overseas, the President's plan also would tighten the rules governing cross-border transfers of intellectual property, expand the CFC rules, and restrict the use of "hybrid" arrangements that generate stateless income.[118] And as noted earlier, a legislative proposal would combine the carrot of a patent box with the stick of expanded CFC rules. While the Trump administration has shown an interest in utilizing carrots, a combination of carrots and sticks may be a necessary political compromise.

2   What Are Constraints in Setting Cross-Border Tax Policy?

Nations face different fiscal, economic, legal, and political constraints that might influence tax reform policy choices.

Fiscal constraints can limit a country's options for dealing with income shifting. Some countries have large budget deficits and, thus, are limited in their ability to lower tax rates on intellectual property income (e.g., adopt "patent boxes"), or to move to a pure territorial system unless they find ways to raise other revenues.[119] Countries without structural deficit problems, on the other hand, are not so limited.

The size of a country's economy and the level of trade and capital flows can also limit tax policy options. Some countries that have a net outbound investment, such as Japan, may be inclined to adopt different measures than countries that have a net inbound investment, such as Australia.[120] Countries in the European Union are exposed to free internal movement of people and capital and may be hesitant to adopt tax policies that might encourage multinationals to change their headquarters.[121] The United

---

[117] See HM Treasury, supra note 115, at 23–44 (discussing United Kingdom's plan for reform of CFC rules to target artificially diverted UK profits).

[118] President Obama's Framework, supra note 8, at 25.

[119] Altshuler et al., supra note 61.

[120] Altshuler et al., supra note 61, at 5. (citing "Inward and Outbound FDI from OECD Factbook 2014," Outward and Inward FDI Stocks Table, OECD Library, available at www.oecd-ilibrary.org/economics/oecd-factbook-2014/outward-and-inward-fdi-stock s_factbook-2014-table77-en; portfolio investment from International Monetary Fund, Coordinated Portfolio Investment Survey (CPIS), available at http://ellibrary-data.imf .org/DataReport.aspx?c=26593551&d=33061&e=169309/).

[121] Altshuler et al., supra note 61, at 5.

States, in contrast, is less exposed to trade and capital movements, and with the size of its economy may be inclined to maintain higher tax rates.[122]

Legal constraints also affect a country's tax policy options. European Union member countries, in particular, are constrained by EU law in the design of tax rules. A member country generally cannot apply different tax rules to its residents and EU residents.[123] An EU-member country cannot strengthen its CFC rules in relation to EU CFC regimes.[124] EU-member countries are also not permitted to design a patent box that only applies if the R&D took place in that country (as opposed to the European Economic Area).[125] In contrast, the United States is not limited by such legal constraints.

Politics can also restrict a country's options in dealing with intellectual property income shifting. Countries that are the headquarters for large multinationals typically face tremendous political pressure from multinationals. In the 1990s, the Internal Revenue Service attempted to restrict the use of foreign hybrid entities with the check-the-box regulations.[126] US multinationals resisted, Congress got involved, and the IRS pulled back.[127] Eventually, multinationals got Congress to

---

[122] *Ibid.*

[123] *Ibid.* at 21 (noting The European Court of Justice's interpretation of the EU treaty's single market provision restricts the ability of member countries to apply different tax rules to residents and EU residents).

[124] *Ibid.* (citing *Cadbury Schweppes v. Commissioners of Inland Revenue* (European Court of Justice, September 12, 2006) (limiting "the application of EU CFC regimes to... wholly artificial arrangements," which means that a EU country's CFC regime can apply, if at all, only to obvious tax avoidance schemes)).

[125] Graetz & Doud, *supra* note 10, at 366 (citing Press Release IP/07/408, "European Commissioner, Direct Taxation: Commission Requests Ireland to End Discriminatory Rules on Tax Treatment of Patent Royalties," March 23, 2007, *available at* http://europa.eu/rapid/press-release_IP-07-408_en.htm#PR_metaPressRelease_bottom (The EC notified Ireland in 2006 that its requirement that R&D be carried out in Ireland was incompatible with the EC treaty rules regarding freedom of establishment and free movement of services).

[126] IRS Notice 98–11, Internal Revenue Services (January 16, 1998), 2, *available at* www.irs.gov/pub/irs-drop/n-98-11.pdf ("Treasury and the Service have concluded that the use of certain hybrid branch arrangements [disregarded entities] is contrary to the policies and rules of subpart F. This notice announces that Treasury and the Service will issue regulations to address such arrangements"). A couple months after issuing the Notice, the Treasury and the IRS proposed regulations to prevent check the box undermining subpart f. "Guidance Under Subpart F Relating to Partnerships and Branches," 26 CFR Parts 1 and 301 [TD 8767], 2, March 26, 1998, *available at* ftp://pmstax.com/intl/td8767.pdf.

[127] IRS Notice 98–35, Internal Revenue Services (June 19, 1998), *available at* www.irs.gov/pub/irs-drop/n-98-35.pdf. JCX-37-10 Report, *supra* note 7, at 49 (noting the "issuance of Notice 98-11 and the temporary and proposed regulations provoked controversy among taxpayers and members of Congress"). *See* Sheppard, "How Does Apple Avoid Taxes?," *supra* note 98.

actually codify the result of check-the-box regulations by enacting a temporary statutory rule.[128] As another example, the United Kingdom wanted to impose stronger CFC rules. UK multinationals threatened to expatriate and move their headquarters elsewhere, and the UK pulled back and settled with less drastic changes. The political climate itself varies from country to country, which also affects the possibility of reform. Notably, in the United States, there is intense partisanship making it hard for the United States to address its biggest issues.[129]

3   What Is the Scope of Entities, and Nature and Scope of Foreign Income, That Would be Targeted?

In designing new rules to limit foreign income shifting, decisions would have to be made as to the scope of entities whose income would be targeted, and those decisions could dictate the reform options available. A country looking to target only domestic multinational companies might, for example, focus on revising its controlled foreign corporation rules, which apply only to domestic multinationals and not foreign multinationals doing business in the country. In contrast, a country wishing to target all multinational entities (domestic multinationals as well as foreign multinationals doing business in the country) might instead focus on revising its transfer pricing rules, which apply to both.[130] In contrast to the CFC rules and the transfer pricing rules, certain reform measures, such as a minimum tax on a multinational's foreign income, could target either just domestic multinationals or all multinationals.[131] The United States has a long history of focusing on outbound investment and on the taxation of US multinationals. However, observers have suggested that it may be time to consider more reforms targeted at inbound investment

---

[128] 26 USC. § 954(c)(6) (the "look-through" rule for related CFCs. Tax Increase Prevention and Reconciliation Act of 2005, Pub. L. No. 109–222, § 103(b)(1) (2006)). David R. Sicular, "The New Look-Through [R]ule: W(h)ither Subpart F?," *Tax Notes* (2007): 359, *available at* www.paulweiss.com/media/104725/SubPartF04-May-07.pdf.

[129] *See* Altshuler et al., *supra* note 61, at 35 (noting intense and growing partisanship makes enacting complex fiscal reforms harder for the US); Clausing, *supra* note 52, at 23 ("[O]ne wonders if the requisite political will can be mustard to close the loopholes that enable pervasive profit shifting"); Gravelle, *supra* note 10, at 34 ("The sticks that might work best for addressing profit shifting... probably face some significant political barriers"). For the political difficulties of enacting a value-added tax (VAT) in the United States, which many countries have, *see* Michael J. Graetz, *supra* note 84, at 70–77.

[130] Graetz & Doud, *supra* note 10, at 415 (summarizing which proposals would apply to all multinational companies doing business within the country and which ones would impact only domestic multinational companies).

[131] Gravelle, *supra* note 10, at 23 (noting a minimum tax "would have effects only on US multinationals... and not US subsidiaries of foreign multinationals").

and raising taxation of foreign companies.[132] A general move in that direction could affect how the government approaches intellectual property income shifting.

To the extent reform measures target the income of foreign subsidiaries (controlled foreign corporations), a decision would need to be made regarding whether to cover all controlled foreign subsidiaries or only those subsidiaries located in low-tax foreign jurisdictions. For instance, a minimum tax could be imposed on the foreign income of all controlled foreign corporations, or it could be imposed just on the foreign income of those corporations located in designated tax haven jurisdictions offering the lowest rates.[133]

In addition to defining which entities will\be targeted, a country would also need to determine the nature and scope of the foreign source income being targeted.[134] A country could choose to go after all the foreign income of a multinational. Alternatively, a country could choose to target just foreign income attributable to intellectual property. The latter approach may contain "measurement and definitional" hurdles, however, as it is not easy to define income attributable to intellectual property.[135] One method, such as that adopted by the United Kingdom's new patent box, is to subtract some level of "normal" return for production, distribution, and marketing costs, with "excess" return deemed attributable to intellectual property.[136]

Under either approach a country could carve out exceptions. It could, for instance, adopt a different rule for active business income. Or it could impose its new measure only on income taxed at a low foreign rate. These exceptions would not come without their own definitional problems. What type of income should be considered active? What should be the

---

[132] Shaviro, *supra* note 58 (arguing that the US should "rely relatively more on approaches that affect foreign as well as domestic multinationals, and relatively less on approaches that only hit US companies [i.e., via our CFC rules]"). *See also* Wells & Lowell, *supra* note 14, at 57 (criticizing reform proposals that only address US multinationals and that ignore strategies of non-US multinationals).

[133] Graetz & Doud, *supra* note 10.

[134] Graetz & Doud, *supra* note 10, at 422 ("The most fundamental issue is determining what income will be covered.... [F]irst, whether the income to be covered is linked to [intellectual property] and, if so, how that is link is defined; second, whether there is a different rule for sales or active business income earned abroad; and third, whether the US tax turns on the rate of foreign tax and, if so, how").

[135] Graetz & Doud, *supra* note 10, at 425 ("Because of the difficulties of identifying income attributable to [intellectual property], any effort to calculate and apply a special regime only to [intellectual property] income creates measurement and definitional difficulties that are fraught with both policy risks and opportunities for political mischief").

[136] *Ibid.* at 409 (summarizing Camp's proposal to treat profits in excess of 50 percent of costs as attributable to intellectual property and the UK's proposal to treat profits in excess of 10 percent of costs as attributable to intellectual property).

minimum threshold effective foreign rate? Ultimately, many of these questions over the scope of income to be targeted come down to the simple question: What is the desired level of tax rate imposed on foreign earnings? The United States currently imposes a 35 percent statutory rate. What lower US rate on foreign earnings is reasonable?

4   Should Countries Utilize Narrow Measures (a Piecemeal Approach) or Broad Measures (a Comprehensive Approach) to Effectuate Tax Reforms?

First, a country could choose to address the problem of intellectual property income shifting by adopting a narrow or piecemeal approach. It is estimated that the bulk of income shifting is conducted by a relatively small group of large multinationals. In fact, just thirty companies account for 65 percent of profits parked offshore.[137] Multinationals with the most money held offshore include Apple, General Electric, Microsoft, and Pfizer. Therefore, the government could audit specific multinational companies within this group and challenge their tax strategies using current rules already in place.[138] The US government has relied heavily upon its current transfer pricing rules in going after specific multinationals, but it has been losing a number of key cases in recent years and might achieve better results using a different tool.

A different tool already in existence but only used sparingly is the "piercing the corporate veil" doctrine which might be used to target CFCs that are under the management and control of US parent companies. This is a common (court-created) law concept. We generally view corporations like a US parent company and its foreign subsidiary as independent companies. That view is questionable when a wholly owned foreign subsidiary is a mere instrumentality of the parent

---

[137] Citizens for Justice, "Offshore Shell Games 2015: The Use of Offshore Tax Havens by Fortune 500 Companies," *Citizens for Tax Justice*, October 5, 2015, http://ctj.org/ctjre ports/2015/10/offshore_shell_games_2015.php#.Vv6bncf6X8s.

[138] The IRS went after Caterpillar Inc., imposing current US tax on certain income earned by a Swiss subsidiary, not by applying transfer pricing rules or the CFC rules, but by applying substance over form or assignment of income doctrines. Kadet, "Attacking Profit Shifting: The Approach Everyone Forgets," *supra* note 32. *See, e.g.*, 26 USC. § 7701(l) (codifying the economic substance doctrine). *See* Microsoft Part I, *supra* note 7, at 95 (citing "Testimony of Stephen E. Shay Before the US Senate Permanent Subcommittee on Investigations of the Committee on Homeland Security and Governmental Affairs Hearing on Offshore Profit Shifting and the Internal Revenue Code," September 20, 2012, 9) (noting section 7701(l) as designed to give the Treasury Department authority to combat certain abuses without a need for new legislation).

company.[139] Some, albeit few, courts have applied the piercing-the-corporate-veil doctrine when determining whether to disregard the separateness of two related entities, and to attribute the activities of a subsidiary to its parent for tax purposes.[140] Under a fact-specific analysis, courts have looked at such factors as: the financial support of the subsidiary's operations by the parent; the lack of substantial business contracts between the subsidiary and anyone except the parent; and whether the property of the entity is used by each as if jointly owned.[141] Review of the case studies in Chapter 7 show us that US-based multinationals often control the affairs of their key foreign subsidiaries and could be at risk if the government chose to utilize this doctrine.[142]

Adopting narrow measures to deal with income shifting has its drawbacks. Targeting specific companies requires costly and timely audits, and reliance on "fuzzy" common law doctrines, such as the piercing-the-corporate-veil doctrine, requires fact specific inquiries and analysis.[143] In addition, despite the availability of the piercing doctrine, the IRS and courts alike respect the corporate form and have been reluctant to actually use the doctrine in attributing the activities or income of a subsidiary to its parent.[144] So it is not practical to assume it would be used now. Adopting

---

[139] If a US parent "so controls the affairs of a subsidiary that it 'is merely an instrumentality of the parent,'" the subsidiary could be at risk of being disregarded for US tax purposes. George E. Constantine, "Recent IRS Determination Highlights Importance of Separation Among Affiliates," 1, February 2011, *available at* www.venable.com/recent-irs-determination-highlights-importance-of-separation-among-affiliates-02-24-2011/.

[140] Senate Apple Hearing, *supra* note 7, at 11. *See also, e.g., Moline Properties v. Commissioner of Internal Revenue*, 319 US 436, 439 (1943) (holding that, for income tax purposes, a taxpayer cannot ignore the form of the corporation that he creates for a valid business purpose or that subsequently carries on business, unless the corporation is a sham or acts as a mere agent).

[141] *Moline Properties*, 319 US at 439.

[142] Statement of Levin, Apple Part 2, *supra* note 25, at 3 (noting Apple, Inc.'s key foreign subsidiaries, AOI, AOE, and ASI, "all sure seem to fit that description").

[143] Kadet, "Attacking Profit Shifting: The Approach Everyone Forgets," *supra* note 32 (arguing the government needs a better way to attack profit shifting – an approach that relies more on statutes and less on fuzzy judicial doctrines). In congressional hearings, Apple noted that its key Irish subsidiary observes corporate formalities. Apple also noted nontax functions (e.g., AOI consolidates and manages a substantial portion of Apple's foreign, posttax income), which creates certain economies of scale that allow AOI to obtain better rates of return with money management firms, better control cash and redeploy funds to meet international operational needs. Testimony of Apple Inc., *supra* note 6, at 12–13.

[144] Kadet, "Attacking Profit Shifting: The Approach Everyone Forgets," *supra* note 32. *See also Bass v. Commissioner of Internal Revenue*, 50 T.C. 595, 600 (1968) ("[A] taxpayer may adopt any form he desires for the conduct of his business, and . . . the chosen form cannot be ignored merely because it results in a tax savings." However, the form the taxpayer chooses for conducting business that results in tax-avoidance "must be a viable business entity, that is, it must have been formed for a substantial business purpose or actually engage in substantive business activity").

new rules (piecemeal legislation or administrative regulations) targeted at specific transactions of select companies, like the new regulations targeting the Pfizer inversion, could be viewed as unfair and could erode trust in the government.[145] Thus, adopting more broad measures is preferred.

Comprehensive intellectual property tax reform could have numerous benefits. First, it would allow the government to step back and consider all necessary changes that would need to be made to prevent multinationals from shielding foreign intellectual property income from taxation. As noted in Chapter 8, the present system contains overlapping layers of loopholes. Specifically, US multinational companies have been able to avoid having their foreign income taxed under the controlled foreign corporation (CFC) rules by taking advantage of a panoply of statutory and regulatory loopholes – the check-the-box regulations, the temporary CFC "look-through" rule, and various statutory exceptions that are built into the CFC rules. These loopholes sometimes overlap providing multiple layers of protection. Piecemeal legislation targeting a particular loophole might overlook other loopholes that provide similar tax savings. The Treasury's withdrawal of the check-the-box regulations, by itself, would be fruitless unless Congress also repealed the temporary look-through rule and modified the statutory exceptions built into the CFC. A comprehensive approach would consider all law changes necessary to address the problem.[146]

Importantly, comprehensive tax reform to address intellectual property income shifting by corporations would have to take into account likely impact on unincorporated businesses, such as partnerships, limited liability companies, and other pass-through entities.[147] For example, if the United States were to lower its corporate tax rate, it might decide to maintain revenues by eliminating certain tax preferences. Many tax preferences available to corporations, however, are also available to these unincorporated businesses. Thus a reduction of these tax preference items for multinational corporations could adversely affect pass-through

---

[145] *See* Diana Furchtgott-Roth, "Free Pfizer! Why Inversions Are Good for the US," *The New York Times*, April 7, 2016, www.nytimes.com/2016/04/08/opinion/free-pfizer-why-inversions-are-good-for-the-us.html?_r=0 ("[A] targeted rule like that erodes trust in government. 'It's like King John going after the peasants' money hidden in haystacks. . . . That's what led to the Magna Carta' ").

[146] Microsoft Part I, *supra* note 7, at 12–14 (providing Testimony of Reuven S. Avi-Yonah) (arguing this need for comprehensive reform because of multiple exceptions and loopholes that form overlapping layers of protection against offshore income being taxed under the CFC rules).

[147] *See* Martin J. McMahon, Jr., "Rethinking Taxation of Privately Held Businesses," *Tax Lawyer* 69 (2016): 347–48 (arguing "corporate tax reform that involves broadening the base and reducing the rates cannot thoughtfully be addressed without also reconsidering the taxation of unincorporated businesses").

entities.[148] In addition, if the United States reduced its corporate income tax rate but not the personal income tax rate, many pass-through entities might decide to incorporate to benefit from the lower corporate rate.[149] More corporations would mean more corporate tax revenue, but fewer pass through entities could mean a greater reduction in personal income tax revenues.[150] A comprehensive approach would consider the likely impact of corporate tax law changes on other revenue bases.

5   Should Unilateral Actions or a Multilateral Approach Be Adopted?

On the one hand, nations could adopt at home, unilaterally, new tax policies to deal with intellectual property income shifting. This has been the US approach, by far. On the other, nations could choose to cooperate with other nations in order to harmonize tax policies to achieve the same goal.

A unilateral approach to intellectual property corporate tax reform has the advantage of expediency. Trying to get agreement among nations on a unified response to intellectual property income shifting could take time, although the OECD's BEPS project has moved rather quickly.

Another significant advantage to a unilateral approach is that it permits a nation to design its own tax policies by taking into account its own unique constraints. As discussed earlier, countries face different fiscal, economic, legal, and political constraints in designing tax policy. And a unilateral approach allows countries to adopt specific approaches that suit their particular climates.

---

[148] See Karen C. Burke, "Passthrough Entities: The Missing Element in Business Tax Reform," *Pepperdine Law Review* 40 (2013): 1334 ("If corporate tax cuts are financed by reducing business tax preferences, pass-throughs would be adversely affected, since most tax preference items used by corporations are also used extensively by pass-throughs"); Edward D. Kleinbard, "Why Corporate Tax Reform Can Happen," *Tax Notes* 146 (2015): 93 ("The question is made difficult by the fact that most business tax reforms that broaden the tax base by eliminating business tax expenditures would affect both the corporate and unincorporated business sectors").

[149] See Bret Wells, "Pass-Through Entity Taxation: A Tempest in the Tax Reform Teapot," *Houston Business & Law Journal* 2 (2014): 3–4 ("[L]owering corporate tax rates to 28 percent while maintaining the top individual rate at 39.6 percent, and maintaining a tax rate on capital gains and qualified dividends at 20 percent, should cause a broad cross-section of closely-held businesses to decide on their own to exit their pass-through entity structures and to opt for reincorporating their businesses back into C corporation form").

[150] Altshuler et al., *supra* note 61, at 8–9 (citing Daniel I. Halperin, "Mitigating the Potential Inequity of Reducing Corporate Rates," *Tax Policy Working Paper* (July 29, 2009) (discussing the "consequences of setting the top corporate rate below the top personal rate and possible policy responses to prevent individuals from using the corporate form to shelter their personal income from tax").

While a unilateral approach to intellectual property income shifting would allow countries to adopt rules tailored to their specific goals and constraints, it does come with risks. Invariably, countries would adopt different measures to deal with intellectual property income shifting, and the severity of such measures would differ. The ramifications of disparate tax measures would be great considering that the effects of a country's tax policies stretch beyond its borders in today's global economy. Consider, for example, what would happen if the United States decided unilaterally to adopt new source rules or a sales-only formulary apportionment of income. Bilateral and multilateral agreements with other nations would undoubtedly come unglued.[151] Other nations would be disadvantaged and likely take retaliatory actions.[152] And multinationals would face increased uncertainty likely resulting in double taxation.[153] "Unilateral" approaches have already seen backlashes. The UK's diverted profits tax has been criticized as too broad and in conflict with EU freedom of establishment rules, as well as contradicting UK treaties.[154] Indeed, the United States has expressed concerns over the EU's unilateral approach in recent years of investigating member states that have provided special tax benefits to multinational companies – illegal under EU state aid rules.[155]

With a unilateral approach, there is also the risk that nations will one-up other nations in trying to attract and retain intellectual property investment. We have seen this already. Most countries have been lowering their statutory corporate income tax rate in response to other countries doing the same. We have seen countries adopt patent boxes in response to other countries adopting patent boxes. We are now witnessing a "race to the bottom" when it comes to tax measures designed to attract and retain

---

[151] Graetz & Doud, *supra* note 10, at 419.   [152] *Ibid.*   [153] *Ibid.*

[154] *See* Dan Neidle, "The Diverted Profits Tax: Flawed by Design?," *British Tax Review* 2015 (2015): 147; Jonathan Peacock, "UK's Diverted Profits Tax: A Regime Much, Much Broader Than its True Target?," *European Tax Service* 17 (2015): 4.

[155] *See* Dara Doyle & Stephanie Bodoni, "Apple Ordered to Pay Up to $14.5 Billion in EU Tax Clampdown," *Bloomberg*, August 30, 2016, www.bloomberg.com/news/articles/2016-08-30/apple-ordered-to-pay-up-to-14-5-billion-in-eu-tax-crackdown (noting the EU's investigations may undermine coordinated efforts to prevent erosion of the tax base and expressing concern that any actions need to be fair to US taxpayers and businesses). According to the US Treasury, the EC's Apple ruling could "undermine foreign investment, the business climate in Europe, and the important spirit of economic partnership between the US and the EU." "Apple Should Repay Ireland 13bn Euros, European Commission Rules," *BBC*, August 30, 2016, www.bbc.com/news/business-37220799; James Kanter & Mark Scott, "Apple Owes $14.5 Billion in Back Taxes to Ireland, E.U. Says," *The New York Times*, August 30, 2016, www.nytimes.com/2016/08/31/technology/apple-tax-eu-ireland.html ("Europe is overstepping its power, unfairly targeting American companies and hurting global efforts to curtail tax avoidance").

intellectual property. Indeed, some European countries have insisted that President Trump's tax plan will accelerate a "race to the bottom."[156]

In contrast to a unilateral approach to income shifting, in which nations adopt tax measures suited to their particular goals and constraints, a multilateral approach would involve nations coming together to establish a set of normative tax principles.[157] The rationale is that we have a global economy in which the economic differences among nations has narrowed. If the economic differences between different nations have narrowed, then why should significant tax differences continue to exist? Intellectual property income shifting is a global concern. As a result, it requires cohesive, cooperative efforts among nations to deal with it.

A multilateral approach would have significant advantages.[158] Unilateral actions by nations would require thousands of existing bilateral treaties to be renegotiated. But if developed nations could agree on a set of normative tax principles, they could enter into some multilateral instrument, which would have the same effect as simultaneous renegotiation of bilateral tax treaties.[159] In such a multilateral agreement, nations could agree, for example, on a unified set of transfer pricing rules, or on a set of new rules to determine the source of intellectual property income – where R&D took place, or where intellectual property is granted protection, or where products are sold. Some scholars have suggested that income should be linked better to sales, that is, income should be sourced to where products are sold.[160] Studies have shown that various tax policies impact

---

[156] Joe Kirwin, "EU Lawmakers Label Trump Tax Plan a 'Race to the Bottom,' " *available at* https://www.bna.com/eu-lawmakers-label-n57982087281/.

[157] Altshuler et al., *supra* note 61, at 33 (noting need for countries to agree on some normative tax principles).

[158] Professor Reuven Avi-Yonah-Yonah has been a staunch supporter of a multilateral approach. *See* Reuven S. Avi-Yonah-Yonah, "Hanging Together: A Multilateral Approach to Taxing Multinationals," *University of Michigan Law & Economics Workings Papers* (2015), *available at* http://repository.law.umich.edu/cgi/viewcontent.c gi?article=1226&context=law_econ_current. *See also* Manal S. Corwin, "Sense and Sensibility: The Policy and Politics of BEPS," *Tax Notes* (2014): 137, *available at* http s://kpmg-us-inst.adobecqms.net/content/dam/kpmg/taxwatch/pdf/2014/beps-corwin-ti llinghast-tn-100614.pdf (recognizing "the value, power and critical role of coordinated action over unilateral action to mitigate negative consequences and achieve sensible results" using the experience with FATCA).

[159] JCX-139-15 Report, *supra* note 2, at 32 (noting there is strong enough support to eliminate base erosion that it may be time to consider a multilateral instrument that would have the same effect as a simultaneous renegotiation of thousands of bilateral tax treaties).

[160] Graetz & Doud, *supra* note 10, at 434 (urging a much closer link between a company's level of US sales and its minimum US taxable income, and arguing that "anything less seems unlikely to succeed"). ("Aligning the source of income more closely with the location of sales suggests that income from royalties, sales of personal property, and services might be more consistently be sourced to the country where the product is sold and where services are delivered.") *Ibid.* at 426. A focus on sales could come in many

a foreign country's share of income (lower foreign rates increase foreign share of income), but tax policies have less impact on foreign share of sales.[161] A nation's unilateral steps in that direction would be difficult, but a multilateral agreement to move in that direction would stand a fighting chance.

Comprehensive agreements on how to determine the location or source of income will be controversial. A more realistic goal might aim to get countries to agree on how to achieve a fair split of multinational profits among nations. Countries might agree, for instance, to allocate multinational company income to countries by an agreed upon formula. Formulary apportionment as introduced earlier would tax multinational companies where economic activity takes place and where value is created. In theory, less income shifting would occur since tax would be based on factors in the formula, factors that reflect real economic activities.[162] A country's share of a multinational company's income would not be sensitive to that company's arbitrary behavior, such as its declared residency, its organizational structure, or its transfer pricing decisions. A nation's unilateral movement to formulary apportionment would be highly disruptive to the current order, but multilateral agreement among nations to adopt such an approach could work to reduce income shifting.

The drawbacks of a multilateral approach include the difficulty in getting nations to work together on solutions to intellectual property income shifting. Getting nations to agree to enhance transfer pricing rules is one thing, but getting them to agree on the specific transfer pricing methods or on enforcement is quite another. Likewise, the concept of formulary apportionment is one thing, but getting agreement on the formula factors, or how to measure the tax base, or how to define a consolidated business is quite another. For formulary apportionment to work, international coordination would be required. Nations would have to choose harmonized formulas to reduce the potential for double taxation and to reduce tax competition pressures. If nations used different formulas or if some nations did not require a multinational company to

---

forms, such as (1) sales-based formulary apportionment, (2) modified transfer pricing rules that reallocate profits when domestic share of sales exceeds domestic share of profits, or (3) expanded CFC rules that are based on domestic share of sales. *Ibid.* at 427. *See* Udell & Vashist, *supra* note 44. But for difficulties of allocating income based on sales, *see* Roin, *supra* note 48, at 207–09.

[161] Harry Grubert, "Foreign Taxes and the Growing Share of US Multinational Company Income Abroad: Profits, Not Sales, Are Being Globalized," *National Tax Journal* 65 (2012): 247, *available at* www.ntanet.org/NTJ/65/2/ntj-v65n02p247-81-foreign-taxes-growing-share.pdf.

[162] Mintz & Smart, *supra* note 47 (providing evidence of reduced income shifting under Canada's formulary apportionment).

account for all related entities, income shifting through transfer pricing would still be achievable. As was shown in the first half of the book, income shifting among US states is still persistent where state formulas are not uniform and combined reporting is not required. More fundamental, in order to achieve a comprehensive formulary apportionment agreement, nations would have to depart from separate entity accounting. The OECD seems firmly committed to separate entity accounting, and this may prove a significant hurdle to formulary apportionment as a multilateral solution to income shifting.

A multilateral approach also raises interesting policy questions about the role of tax competition among nations. Tax policy is at the core of national sovereignty – that is, countries should be able to design tax systems in ways they consider appropriate.[163] Some countries have taken advantage of globally integrated economies and designed preferential tax regimes to attract and retain high value activities and promote growth and prosperity.[164] Other countries have not, resulting in a misalignment of domestic tax systems. This misalignment incentivizes multinational companies to engage in income shifting, which causes base erosion and gives multinational companies a competitive advantage over those that operate domestically.[165] In short, tax competition among nations can distort and weaken the benefits (economic efficiencies) of market

[163] Angel Guria, "Taxation and Competition Policy, Brussels, France," *OECD* (February 11, 2014), *available at* www.oecd.org/tax/taxation-and-competition-policy.htm. Erik Cederwall, "Reconciling the Profit-Shifting Debate," *Tax Notes* 150 (2016): 713; OECD, "BEPS Action 11: Improving the Analysis of BEPS (Base Erosion and Profit Shifting Public Discussion Draft)," 25 (OECD, April 16, 2015), available at www.oecd .org/ctp/tax-policy/discussion-draft-action-11-data-analysis.pdf (arguing stopping legitimate tax competition is against the principles of sovereign states). Apple has argued that the European Commission's recent finding that it must retroactively pay additional taxes to Ireland is a "devastating blow to the sovereignty of EU Member states over their own tax matters." Tim Cook, "A Message to the Apple Community in Europe," Apple, August 30, 2016, www.apple.com/ie/customer-letter/. Senate Finance Committee Chairman, Orrin G. Hatch, said the recent EC's decision "encroaches on US tax jurisdiction." Kanter & Scott, *supra* note 155. Both Ireland and Apple plan to fight the EC's decision.

[164] Some observers have noted that this tax competition reflects a race to the bottom. *See, e.g.*, Graetz & Doud, *supra* note 10.

[165] Misaligned tax systems also impact international competitiveness – give foreign based companies a competitive advantage over US businesses. *See* R. Glenn Hubbard, "Tax Policy and International Competitiveness," *Taxes* 82 (2004): 219 ("If US businesses are to succeed in the global economy, the US tax system must not generate a bias against their ability to compete effectively against foreign-based companies."). *But see* Jane G. Gravelle, "Does the Concept of Competitiveness Have Meaning in Formulating Corporate Tax Policy?," *Tax Law Review* 65 (2012): 347 (It is important that public discourse move away from meaningless concepts such as international competitiveness and instead focus on what tax policies might be optimal, in that they fulfill the more appropriate objective of 'better off' ").

competition among multinational and domestic firms.[166] An interesting question is whether multilateral efforts among nations to unify domestic tax policies to combat base erosion and achieve more effective market competition would somehow weakens each country's sovereignty in terms of tax policy. In other words, in order to achieve efficient market competition, do we have to give up on healthy tax competition? The OECD has suggested that "acting together will reinforce rather than weaken each country's sovereign tax policies," as countries "have long accepted that they should set limits and that they should not engage in harmful tax practices."[167] The OECD's Base Erosion and Profit Shifting Project, discussed below, is essentially a step to get countries to practice what they have long accepted.

OECD's Base Erosion and Profit Shifting (BEPS) Project

In discussing international tax reform related to intellectual property income shifting, it is important to look at the most important development in cross-border taxation in decades: the OECD's Base Erosion and Profit Shifting (BEPS) Project. The OECD was formed by twenty countries in 1960,[168] and has since expanded to thirty-four members worldwide.[169] Member countries, which have agreed on a number of goals for the increasing interdependence of economies, are required to inform, consult, and cooperate with other members.[170] The OECD works with the Group of Twenty (G20) on a range of issues, including transparency in tax administration and exchange of information.

In 2015, the OECD delivered a number of concrete action plan recommendations to help nations address the problems of income shifting,

---

[166] Guria, *supra* note 163. *See* Graetz & Doud, *supra* note 10, at 405 ("Unfortunately, when nations compete over such tax policies, there is no governmental equivalent to Adam Smith's 'invisible hand,' which produces economic efficiency in competitive markets").

[167] Guria, *supra* note 163.

[168] Convention on the Organization for Economic Cooperation and Development, signed December 14, 1960 at Paris (effective September 30, 1961), *available at* www.oecd.org/general/conventionontheorganisationforeconomicco-operationanddevelopment.htm [hereinafter OECD Convention].

[169] Member countries include: Australia, Austria, Belgium, Canada, Chile, Czech Republic, Denmark, Estonia, Finland, Germany, Greece, Hungary, Iceland, Ireland, Israel, Italy, Japan, Korea, Luxembourg, Mexico, Netherlands, New Zealand, Norway, Poland, Portugal, Slovak Republic, Slovenia, Spain, Sweden, Switzerland, Turkey, United Kingdom, and United States. "Members and Partners," OECD, accessed November 4, 2016, www.oecd.org/about/membersandpartners. Membership is expected to increase; accession talks with Columbia, Latvia, Lithuania, and Costa Rica are ongoing. *Ibid.* A number of nations have been accorded "key partner" status. They include Brazil, India, Indonesia, China, and South Africa. *Ibid.*

[170] *See ibid.* at Article 3.

including intellectual property income shifting.[171] More specifically, the BEPS Project consists of fifteen actions, which were endorsed at the 2015 G20 Summit.[172] Many of these actions, which provide principles (minimum standards) for appropriate taxation of multinational companies, attempt to tax profits where value is added and to promote greater tax transparency with increased information exchange between tax authorities.[173] Most importantly, many of the actions attempt to tax income in the source country as opposed to the residence country.[174]

The following is a list of the actions.

BEPS 2015 Final Reports

Action 1: Addressing the Tax Challenges of the Digital Economy

Action 2: Neutralizing the Effects of Hybrid Mismatch Arrangements

Action 3: Designing Effective Controlled Foreign Company Rules

Action 4: Limiting Base Erosion Involving Interest Deductions and Other Financial Payments

Action 5: Countering Harmful Tax Practices More Effectively, Taking into Account Transparency and Substance

Action 6: Preventing the Granting of Treaty Benefits in Inappropriate Circumstances

Action 7: Preventing the Artificial Avoidance of Permanent Establishment Status

Actions 8–10: Aligning Transfer Pricing Outcomes with Value Creation

Action 11: Measuring and Monitoring BEPS

Action 12: Creating Mandatory Disclosure Rules

---

[171] *See* "BEPS 2015 Final Reports," OECD (October 5, 2015), *available at* www.oecd.org/tax/beps-2015-final-reports.htm. In 2013, the OECD released a report concluding that "the interaction of various principles and the asymmetries among tax regimes of multiple jurisdictions with which a taxpayer has contact allows base erosion and profit shifting to occur." "Addressing Base Erosion and Profit Shifting," OECD (February 12, 2013), *available at* http://dx.doi.org/10.1787/9789264192744-en. *See* JCX-139-15 Report, *supra* note 2. Later that year, the G20 approved a plan that identified fifteen action items on a variety of topics. In 2015, the G20 endorsed final reports on each of the fifteen action items.

[172] The G20 recognized the importance of widespread and consistent implementation of the project and encouraged all nations, including developing ones, to participate. *See* "G20 Leaders' Communiqué, Antayla Summit, 15–16 November 2015," paragraph 15, *available at* www.consilium.europa.eu/en/press/press-releases/2015/11/16-g20-sum mit-antalya-communique/.

[173] Robert B. Stack, "Stack Discusses Treasury's International Tax Initiatives," *Tax Notes Today* (2014), *available at* www.taxnotes.com/document-list/contributors-authors/stac k-robert-b (noting the "principal target of the BEPS project is so-called 'stateless income,' basically very low- or nontaxed income within a multinational group").

[174] *See* Rosenbloom & Brothers, *supra* note 74, 764 (noting many of the BEPS actions "point clearly in the direction of greater source-basis taxation").

Action 13: Providing Guidance on Transfer Pricing Documentation
and Country-by-Country Reporting

Action 14: Making Dispute Resolution Mechanisms More Effective

Action 15: Developing a Multilateral Instrument to Modify Bilateral
Tax Treaties

We do not set out to discuss each of these BEPS actions.[175] We do, however, highlight a few of the actions relevant to intellectual property income shifting and IP Holding Companies.

As we saw in Chapters 7–8, multinational companies can create foreign IP Holding Companies to make income magically disappear. In response, BEPS Action 2 neutralizes the effects of hybrid arrangements and entities by recommending "internal law rules to stop taxpayers from achieving favorable tax outcomes through hybrid mismatch arrangements." Action 2 addresses a number of mismatch arrangements, such as those that result in a deduction in one country but no income inclusion in another. It recommends including in the OECD Model Tax Convention "a new provision to ensure that an entity that is a hybrid entity under the tax laws of two treaty countries is eligible for treaty benefits in appropriate circumstances but that treaty benefits are not allowed for income that neither treaty country treats as income of one of its residence."[176] This change could have a significant impact on existing tax structures used by many multinationals that currently achieve double nontaxation of foreign income.

As we also saw in Chapter 8, multinational companies with a lot of intellectual property have been able to successfully sidestep their country's domestic CFC rules in ways unanticipated by government. Action 3 recognizes that the CFC rules of many countries are not effective at tackling profit shifting and deferral of taxation.[177] It thus sets forth recommendations in the form of six building blocks for the design of better and more effective rules. For example, it sets forward recommendations on how to determine which foreign-controlled subsidiaries should be subject to CFC rules, it sets out approaches for defining income of a CFC that should be subject to current taxation at home, and it

---

[175] For a summary of the actions, see JCX-139-15 Report, *supra* note 2.

[176] JCX-139-15 Report, *supra* note 2, at 14–15.

[177] As argued in this book, the US CFC rules are undermined by various statutory exceptions, the check-the-box regulations, and the temporary statutory look-through rule. The United Kingdom revised its CFC rules in 2013, applying to arrangements a main purpose of which is to reduce or eliminate the liability of any person for UK tax or duty. But undermining these rules are various exceptions (e.g., for active business income and much financing income) and carve outs for CFCs that are in a long list of good countries.

recommends steps to prevent double taxation.[178] It remains to be seen whether the recommendations, if implemented, will result in current domestic taxation of more foreign income.

In recent years the European Commission has uncovered that some low-tax countries, including Ireland, Luxembourg, and the Netherlands, have been issuing favorable tax rulings to multinational companies, such as Apple, Fiat, and Starbucks, that have given them a competitive advantage.[179] Action 5 establishes a framework for improving transparency in relation to tax rulings that may give rise to income shifting concerns – a framework for compulsory spontaneous information exchange between governments in respect of taxpayer-specific rulings. Under Action 5, when a country has provided a ruling, which is subject to the obligation of spontaneous exchange, it must exchange the relevant information on that ruling with any affected country as quickly as possible.[180]

As noted in Chapter 6, many countries have enacted patent boxes to lure intellectual property to their jurisdiction. Unfortunately, patent boxes can "unfairly erode the tax bases of other countries, potentially distorting the location of capital and services," especially when they are offered to entities that engage in no substantial activity.[181] Action 5 requires "substantial activity" by a multinational company in order for the multinational to benefit from the patent box's lower rate on intellectual property income. It uses R&D expenditures as a proxy for substantial activity. Thus, there must be a link or appropriate nexus between a multinational company's R&D expenditures and intellectual property income receiving the low rate. If a multinational incurred 100 percent of the costs to develop an intellectual property asset in a country with a patent box regime, then 100 percent of the overall income from the intellectual property asset would be eligible for the regime's preferential

---

[178] *See* OECD "OECD/G20 Base Erosion and Profit Shifting Project 2015 Final Reports Executive Summaries," 12–13, October 5, 2015, *available at* www.oecd.org/ctp/beps-reports-2015-executive-summaries.pdf [hereinafter OECD BEPS Executive Summaries].

[179] It was reported that Luxembourg granted favorable tax treatment to Fiat via a transfer pricing agreement, and that the Netherlands artificially lowered tax paid by Starbucks through a favorable tax ruling. JCX-139-15 Report, *supra* note 2, at 20 n.33. A number of multinational companies have been part of investigations by the European Commission into the ways that member countries tax multinationals. For a recent example, *see* European Commission Press Release, "State Aid: Ireland Gave Illegal Tax Benefits to Apple Worth up to 13 Billion Euros," August 30, 2016, *available at* http://europa.eu/rapid/press-release_IP-16-2923_en.htm.

[180] JCX-139-15 Report, *supra* note 2, at 20.

[181] OECD, "Countering Harmful Tax Practices More Effectively, Taking into Account Transparency and Substance," 7, September 16, 2014, *available at* www.oecd-ilibrary.org/taxation/countering-harmful-tax-practices-more-effectively-taking-into-account-transparency-and-substance_9789264218970-en.

rate. However, if the multinational outsourced all R&D to related parties, then none of the income from the intellectual property asset would receive tax benefits. The following formula illustrates how Action 5 determines intellectual property income that is eligible for preferential tax rate treatment:

$$\frac{\text{Qualifying expenditures}*\text{ to develop IP asset}}{\text{Overall expenditures}**\text{ to develop IP asset}} \times \text{Overall income from IP asset}$$

$$= \text{Income receiving tax benefits}$$

*Qualifying expenditures = 1.3 x (expenditures incurred by the tax-payer + expenditures for outsourcing to *unrelated* parties)

**Overall expenditures = qualifying expenditures + expenditures for outsourcing to related parties + acquisition costs

In should be noted that Action 5 defines *qualifying intellectual assets* as patents and their functional equivalents, copyrighted software, and other intellectual property in the case of certain smaller companies.[182] *Qualifying expenditures* are those that are directly connected to the intellectual property asset – that is, R&D expenditures that would typically qualify for R&D credits in most jurisdictions.[183] Costs related to acquisition of intellectual property or outsourcing of intellectual property development to related parties are not considered qualifying expenditures, but countries may permit taxpayers to increase qualifying expenditures by up to 30 percent to account for such costs. Members countries will have to revise their patent boxes to meet the nexus requirement, which can limit the objectives they were designed to achieve.[184]

As noted earlier, a major theme of the BEPS Project is linking intellectual property income with value creation. The action plans dealing with *transfer pricing* attempt to achieve just that. As shown in earlier chapters, existing transfer pricing rules have proven ineffective at limiting intellectual property income shifting. Current transfer pricing rules rely on the

---

[182] Qualifying intellectual property income includes embedded royalties, linked through tracking/tracing.

[183] These include "salary and wages, direct costs, overhead costs directly associated with R&D facilities, and the cost of supplies, incurred from the performance of activities undertaken to advance the understanding of scientific relations or technologies, address known scientific or technological obstacles, or otherwise increase knowledge or develop new applications." JCX-139-15 Report, *supra* note 2, at 19.

[184] *See, e.g.*, Lily Faulhaber, "Tax Incentives for Innovation: Designing R&D Credits and Patent Boxes in the Age of BEPS" (presentation, Northwestern University, April 5, 2016) (concluding that the nexus approach will limit the policy objectives that innovation boxes can be designed to achieve).

arm's-length principle. The principle looks at which of the related companies are performing important functions, contributing assets, and controlling risks. With its emphasis on contractual allocations of functions, assets, and risks, however, the arm's-length principle can easily be manipulated by multinational companies, resulting in intellectual property income not aligning with the economic activity that produced it.

Actions 8, 9, and 10 of the BEPS Project target transfer pricing problems and recommend several changes to ensure that income is allocated to the country *where value is created.*

First, in revised guidelines (in the form of amendments to the OECD's Transfer Pricing Guidelines), BEPS attempts to replace or supplement the *contractual arrangements* between the related parties with the *conduct* of the parties if the contracts are incomplete or are not supported by the conduct. This will lead to the allocation of intellectual property income to locations where contributions are made and to where business activities are conducted.[185]

Second, the BEPS Actions provide clarification relating to *risks.* Because higher risks warrant higher returns, multinational companies would contractually reallocate risks to shift income even though there was no change in business operations and the company assuming the risk could not control the risk, nor have the financial capacity to assume the risk. BEPS clarified that risk will be allocated to the party that does exercise control over risks and has financial capacity to assume them. BEPS also provides clarification with respect to intangibles. Specifically, it clarifies that "legal ownership alone does not necessarily generate a right to all (or indeed any) of the return that is generated by the exploitation of the intangible."[186] Specific guidance will ensure that the analysis of functions performed, resources employed, and risks assumed will not be weakened by cost sharing agreements and other special contractual agreements.[187]

Third, the BEPS Actions ensure that a capital-rich, low functioning company in the group, for example, a "cash box" foreign subsidiary that performs few activities and is located in a low-tax country, that provides funding but does not control risks associated with its funding, will not be allocated income associated with the financial risks (other than a risk-free return).[188]

Finally, the BEPS Actions ensure that pricing methods will allocate profits to the most important economic activities – that is, allocate income to those members of an integrated global value chain that are actually

---

[185] OECD BEPS Executive Summaries, *supra* note 178, at 28.   [186] *Ibid.* at 29.
[187] *Ibid.*   [188] *Ibid.*

contributing to the synergistic benefits of operating as a group.[189] Follow-up work is expected on the so-called transactional profit split method (to be carried out during 2016 and finalized in 2017).[190]

In short, Actions 8–10 maintain the arm's-length principle but ensure that transfer-pricing outcomes are more in sync with value creation. The actions will not eliminate the use of cash-rich, low-functioning foreign subsidiaries, but they are designed to make their role less relevant in income shifting tax planning.

For Actions 8–10 to work, however, we must have transparency since government enforcement depends on access to information. Action 13 fulfills that need by providing new transparency requirements. Action 13 contains one of the most controversial recommendations of the BEPS Project.[191] It increases automatic exchanges of taxpayer information through a new country-by-country (CBC) reporting requirement. Under this requirement, multinational companies must report annually their activities in each country where they do business. More specifically, they must provide a jurisdictional breakdown of their global revenue, profits, taxes, retained profits, employment, capital, tangible assets, and business activities.[192] In theory, CBC reporting will force multinational companies to take consistent cross-border transfer pricing positions, and will provide countries the additional information they need to uncover income shifting and make effective audit decisions. It should be noted that, in 2016, the European Union proposed rules that would require many multinationals to *publicly* disclose more data and to share information about their offshore operations, rules that some multinationals and

---

[189] *Ibid.*

[190] For the promise of profit split methods, *see* Hugh J. Ault, "Recent Developments in the OECD Work on Transfer Pricing: Increasing Sophistication and Increasing Simplification," 1–2, 10–11 (2012), cited in Graetz & Doud, *supra* note 10, at 416 n.399.

[191] Although, an annual survey of CEOs supported country-by-country reporting as a way to crack down on tax avoidance. Tom Bergin, "CEOs Back Country-by-Country Tax Reporting – Survey," *Reuters*, April 23, 2014, http://uk.reuters.com/article/2014/04/23/uk-taxcompanies-idUKBREA3M18I20140423.

[192] Specifically, BEPS recommends three documents: (1) a master file that provides an overview of the multinational's group business, including information on organizational structure, intangibles, and financial and tax positions; (2) a local file that provides detailed information related to specific intercompany transactions, including amounts involved and analyses of transfer pricing determinations; and (3) a country-by-country report that shows global allocation of income, economic activity, and taxes paid among countries. JCX-139-15 Report, *supra* note 2, at 30. CBC reporting documents apply to multinationals with annual consolidated group revenue equal to or exceeding 750 million euros (about $800 million). OECD, "Transfer Pricing Documentation and Country-by-Country Reporting, Action 13–2015 Final Report," 9–10, October 5, 2015, *available at* www.oecd.org/ctp/transfer-pricing-documentation-and-country-by-country-reporting-action-13-2015-final-report-9789264241480-en.htm.

low-tax European governments will likely resist.[193] It has been suggested, however, that public disclosure of corporate tax returns may actually increase corporate tax aggressiveness, not decrease it.[194]

******

It will be interesting to see how nations respond to the OECD's BEPS recommendations. Sixty-two countries were involved in some way with the BEPS Project. But many of these countries could simply choose to ignore most of the BEPS recommendations.[195] OECD recommendations, after all, are not binding, but instead, are "minimum standards" and "best practices." Although OECD countries cooperated in developing the BEPS Action Plans, it is doubtful all will follow through and adopt BEPS compliance measures back home. The United States, in particular, has a long history of "tax exceptionalism" and does not feel bound to any international norms.[196] Some would argue that the United States does not feel bound even by its own treaties, as it has a history of making tax law changes that differ from its treaties and then later modifying those treaties.[197] Although the United States was at the table in developing the BEPS Actions, many members of Congress have already expressed reluctance to adopt all of BEPS's sweeping proposals. Senator Orrin Hatch stated: "The recommendations contained in BEPS raise a number of serious concerns."[198] House Speaker Paul Ryan also remarked: "[Regardless of BEPS] Congress will craft the tax rules that it believes work best."[199] It will be interesting to see whether countries like the

---

[193] James Kanter, "European Union Calls for Big Companies to Disclose More Tax Data," *The New York Times*, April 12, 2016, www.nytimes.com/2016/04/13/business/interna tional/european-union-corporate-taxes.html. The rules would need approval of the European Parliament and a majority of European Union governments.

[194] *See* Joshua D. Blank, "Reconsidering Corporate Tax Privacy," *New York University Journal of Law & Business* 11 (2014): 31 (arguing for continued privacy of BEPS Project disclosures, but arguing for public disclosure of certain US tax forms).

[195] Stack, *supra* note 173 (noting "failure in the BEPS project could well result in countries taking unilateral, inconsistent actions thereby increasing double taxation, the cost to the US Treasury, and the number of tax disputes").

[196] Altshuler et al., *supra* note 61, at 37 (noting the United States is the only major country with a worldwide tax system, as opposed to a territorial tax system; is the only country that does not use a national sales tax to raise revenues; and is the only major country that has not reduced its corporate tax rate).

[197] Altshuler et al., *supra* note 61, at 33. For the impact of BEPS on the future of tax treaties, see Yariv Brauner, "Treaties in the Aftermath of BEPS," *Brook. J. Int'l L.* 41 (2016): 973.

[198] "Hatch to Hold Finance Hearing on OECD BEPS Reports," United States Senate Committee on Finance, November 24, 2015, www.finance.senate.gov/chairmans-new s/hatch-to-hold-finance-hearing-on-oecd-beps-reports.

[199] Senator Orrin Hatch and Representative Paul Ryan, letter to Jacob Lew, Secretary of the Treasury, June 9, 2015.

United States will ultimately opt to relinquish some of their jurisdictional autonomy.[200]

Doing nothing, however, is not a viable option for both low-tax countries that are under scrutiny for their harmful tax practices and high-tax countries that are looking for ways to increase tax revenue.[201] Most likely countries will attempt to pass laws that are BEPS compliant. Some, such as Australia, France, the United Kingdom, and Mexico have already done so. Ireland was the first country to have its new patent box approved as BEPS compliant, since it aligns Ireland's special rate on certain intellectual property income with the carrying on of qualifying R&D activities within the European Economic Area. Despite reservations expressed by members of US Congress, there are signs that the United States intends to meet at least some of the multilateral commitment it made in the OECD's BEPS Project. The Treasury and the IRS have recently released regulations that require country-by-country reporting as recommended in BEPS Action Plan #13 (transfer pricing documentation).[202] Developing countries are also paying attention to BEPS implementation and its focus on source-based taxation.[203]

There remain several challenges ahead. For starters, it is likely we will see incomplete and uneven adoption by OECD member countries.[204] The BEPS Project recommendations (totaling nearly 2,000 pages) could be subject to differing interpretations which could lead to inconsistent laws.[205] In addition, as discussed earlier, countries have different goals

[200] Altshuler et al., *supra* note 61, at 38 (The economic differences between the United States and other countries has narrowed. The US share of world output declines. The ability of the United States to sustain US tax exceptionalism will also decline).

[201] Corwin, *supra* note 158, at 137 ("Doing nothing or making it go away are not options").

[202] T.D. 9773 Treas. Reg. § 1.6038–4 (requiring country-by-country reports from US parent companies with $850 million or more in annual revenue). The US has begun signing competent authority agreements effectively implementing country-by-country reporting. *See* Kevin A. Bell, "US Signs First Two Pacts to Exchange Global Tax Reports," Daily Tax Report, *available at* https://www.itpf.org/itpf_blog?article_id=6199. *See* Mark A. Luscombe, "BEPS Update," *Taxes* 94 (2016): 3, *available at* http://saskatoonlibrary.ca/eds/item?dbid=edsggr&an=edsgcl.450294372 (discussing CBC implementation concerns, including coordinated timing of implementation and disclosure of information to the public); Pricewaterhouse Coopers, LLC, "Proposed Regs an 'Important Step' for CBC Reporting, PWC Says," *Tax Notes Today* (2015), *available at* www.taxnotes.com/tax-notes-today/transfer-pricing/proposed-regs-important-step-cbc-reporting-pwc-says/2015/12/30/18145561.

[203] *See, e.g.,* Yariv Brauner, "What the BEPS?," *Florida Tax Review* 16 (2014): 74–75 (describing source rules as a main source of "controversy between developing countries and the OECD").

[204] Clausing, *supra* note 52, at 15.

[205] For example, some tax experts have questioned whether BEPS transfer pricing guidelines are consistent with current US transfer pricing guidance. *See* Luscombe, *supra* note 202, at 4. While the IRS's position is that they are consistent, US courts have relied less on allocation theories in transfer pricing disputes and more on "empirical evidence such

and face different constraints which could result in different types and levels of taxation.[206] Some commentators have suggested that the BEPS Project will encourage countries to move away from separate entity accounting and adopt formulary apportionment to expand their tax base.[207] To the extent countries adopt inconsistent or incoherent rules, more disputes are likely to arise.[208]

It has also been argued that the BEPS Actions will harm multinational companies. The actions will increase tax compliance costs for multinational companies, especially with respect to increased information sharing.[209] Indeed, some have suggested that the revenue gains may equal compliance expenditures.[210] With increased information disclosure, some worry as well about the increased vulnerability of proprietary data.[211] In addition, BEPS will diminish the rights of multinationals to locate their intellectual property to the physical location they choose.

Substantively, BEPS adheres to separate entity reporting and maintains reliance on transfer pricing and the arm's-length principle to limit

as market place benchmarks or contracted agreements that are in fact followed by contracting parties." *Ibid.* Well-known commentator Martin A. Sullivan notes uncertainty surrounding the BEPS Project: "The all-important details of the OECD recommendations for transfer pricing of intangibles are still up in the air. How each country will implement them is unknown. And, in any case, there will be a lot of subjectivity about what constitutes sufficient economic activity given that it will largely be a facts and circumstances determination." Martin A. Sullivan, "Economic Analysis: From Check-the-Box to a Patent Box," *Tax Notes Today* (2015), *available at* www.taxnotes.com/wo rldwide-tax-daily/intangible-assets/economic-analysis-check-box-patent-box/2015/06/ 29/14682241. David Rosenbloom has predicted: "Coordination of the BEPS actions seems unlikely. . . . The more foreseeable result is a cacophony of new rules, predicated on BEPS and tempered only by the views of individual countries regarding adverse impacts on the inflow of capital." Rosenbloom & Brothers, *supra* note 74, at 764.

[206] *See* Deloitte, "OECD's Base Erosion and Profit Shifting (BEPS) Initiative: Summary Results of Second Annual Multinational Survey," 3, May 2015, *available at* www2.del oitte.com/content/dam/Deloitte/global/Documents/Tax/dttl-tax-beps-short-summary-survey-resullts-may-2015.pdf (finding 75 percent of multinationals surveyed expect some form of double taxation as nations respond to the OECD's recommendations).

[207] *See* Fichtner & Michel, *supra* note 49, at 31 ("The availability of country-by-country tax information may pressure some countries to use a formulary apportionment standard as a mechanism to artificially expand their tax base").

[208] Action 14 makes dispute solution mechanisms more effective. This is important because many BEPS disputes are likely forthcoming.

[209] Fichtner & Michel, *supra* note 49, at 30.

[210] *Ibid.* at 32–33 (noting that OECD efforts will likely have similar cost implications as FATCA).

[211] Fichtner & Michel, *supra* note 49, at 33 ("Assembling a new, centralized database of highly sensitive corporate financial information increases the vulnerability of proprietary business data. It would take just one breach to the system in any of the party jurisdictions for all the information to be disclosed"); Stack, *supra* note 172 (noting "we must ensure that information of US-based multinationals is made available only through our treaty and information exchange networks so as to ensure its confidentiality and appropriate use by our treaty or information exchange partners").

income shifting.[212] While adhering to the arm's-length principle, BEPS provides steps to ensure that transfer pricing outcomes better align with value creation. In essence, BEPS is a move toward more robust source taxation. Aligning transfer pricing outcomes with value creation, or identifying a locatable source of income, however, is easier said than done, because it is always debatable where value is created.[213] Some have even questioned whether international income has a locatable source,[214] a reason the second-best option, formulary apportionment, might make sense. Consider a multinational company that conducts research in the United States, has goods based on that research manufactured in China, and then directly sells those manufactured goods to customers in Europe. Where is the value created? The United States would argue that much of the value lies in the intellectual property that goes into the goods. China, in turn, would argue that much of the value of the firm's products lies in their physical production.[215] And European nations would insist that the value lies in marketing and product sales to customers in Europe. The trouble identifying where value is created is magnified if the intellectual property that resulted from R&D conducted in the United States under this example is moved to a low-tax or no-tax country. The problem is magnified even further when we consider that globally integrated multinationals typically earn more profits than their component parts would have earned alone.[216]

---

[212] Indeed, the relevance of arm's-length pricing is a key component of the BEPS Project; it forms the basis of several Actions Plans as noted above. Joy Hail, "An Overview of the OECD Action Plan on BEPS," *Taxes: The Tax Magazine* 94 (2016): 47.

[213] Clausing, *supra* note 52, at 22 ("An essential difficulty lies in the problem of establishing the source of income for firms that are truly globally integrated"); Graetz & Doud, *supra* note 10, at 420 (noting that achieving multilateral consensus on where intellectual property income should be sourced – e.g., where R&D is conducted, where intellectual property is legally protected, where intellectual property is exploited, and where products created with intellectual property are consumed – will be controversial).

[214] Income "is not susceptible to characterization as to source at all. Income... attaches to someone or something that consumes and that owns assets. Income does not come from some place, even though we may construct accounts to approximate it by keeping track of payments that have identifiable and perhaps locatable sources and destinations." Graetz & Doud, *supra* note 10, at 416 (citing Hugh J. Ault & David F. Bradford, "Taxing International Income: An Analysis of the US System and Its Economic Premises, in Taxation in the Global Economy," 11, 30–31 (Assaf Razin & Joel Slemrod eds., 1990)), *available at* www.nber.org/chapters/c7203.pdf.

[215] Keith Bradsher, "China to Crack Down on Tax Collection from Multinational Companies," *The New York Times*, February 4, 2015, www.nytimes.com/2015/02/05/business/international/china-to-enforce-tax-collection-from-multinational-companies.html ("Officials in China, the world's largest manufacturer, have long contended that much of the value of a good lies in its physical production, and not in the intellectual property that went into the item, which is often created elsewhere").

[216] Clausing, *supra* note 52, at 23 ("The global integration of businesses generates profits above and beyond what would be generated if domestic businesses merely interacted at

The OECD points out the advantages of a multilateral approach to international tax reform, as has the US Joint Committee on Taxation.[217] But, as noted earlier, this approach also raises questions about the role of diversity and *tax competition*.[218] Today, nations compete with one another to attract and retain valuable activities within their borders through tax incentives, such as R&D credit incentives and patent boxes. Some have argued that the BEPS Project, designed to harmonize international tax rules, will harm tax competition by protecting high-tax countries at the expense of low-tax countries. Some fear that there is a movement toward a unified international tax system in which tax competition is eliminated completely.[219]

The OECD, however, suggests the opposite:

[T]he BEPS Project is not intended to promote the harmonization of income taxes or tax structures generally within or outside the OECD, nor is it about dictating to any country what should be the appropriate level of tax rates. Rather, the work is about reducing the distortionary influence of taxation on the location of mobile financial and services activities, thereby encouraging an environment in which free and fair tax competition can tax place.[220]

arm's length. Since multinational firms earn more than their component parts would have earned alone, it is an arbitrary exercise to figure out where the additional profit should reside").

[217] JCX-139-15 Report, *supra* note 2, at 32 (It is time for "a multilateral instrument to enable interested countries to develop and design an innovative approach to international tax matters that is in close alignment with the realities of a rapidly and continuously evolving global economy").

[218] On tax competition generally, *see* Ian Roxan, "Limits to Globalization: Some Implications for Taxation, Tax Policy, and the Developing World," *LSE Legal Studies Working Paper* No. 3/2012 (January 30, 2012), 23–24, *available at* https://papers.ssrn.com/sol3/papers.cfm?abstract_id=1995633.

[219] The Mercatus Research Center has criticized BEPS' solution to income shifting as attempting to consolidate rather than coordinate diverse systems. *See* Fichtner & Michel, *supra* note 49 (exploring the unintended and unseen consequences of consolidating international tax rules, using the BEPS Project as an example of how such centralization is costly and ultimately ineffective). *Ibid.* at 22 (arguing OECD's mission has "evolved from issues of double taxation to advocation for a unified international tax system"). The Coalition for Tax Competition has asked Congress to stop subsidizing the OECD because the BEPS Project is undermining American interests by targeting US companies. According to the group, "reducing tax competition results in an overall higher tax environment and a weaker global economy." Letter from Coalition for Tax Competition to Senators and Representatives, May 12, 2016, *available at* www.freedomandprosperity.org/files/OECD/ctc-OECDFundingBEPS-2016-05-12.pdf.

[220] *See, e.g.*, OECD, "Countering Harmful Tax Practices More Effectively, Taking into Account Transparency and Substance, Action 5–2015 Final Report," 11, October 5, 2015, *available at* www.oecd.org/ctp/countering-harmful-tax-practices-more-effectively-taking-into-account-transparency-and-substance-action-5-2015-final-report-9789264241190-en.htm [hereinafter Countering Harmful Tax Practices Final Report].

Someday we may see movement toward a completely unified international tax system.[221] Until that day comes, there is room for a combination of both unilateral action by nations to ensure a healthy level of tax competition, and multilateral efforts by nations to eliminate harmful tax practices.[222] Unilaterally, countries should be able to lower their statutory corporate tax rates to compete for economic activity (such as Germany did in response to competition within the European Union).[223] It makes sense, however, for nations multilaterally to agree not to offer special negotiated rates with multinational companies.[224] Unilaterally, countries should be able to adopt patent box regimes and other special tax preferences for targeted activities (e.g., R&D credits).[225] But, in turn, it makes sense for nations to agree multilaterally that activities be substantial, such as that there be some link between the intellectual property income receiving the benefits and the substantial activity utilizing it. In this regard, the BEPS Project is an important step in addressing intellectual property income shifting – laying "the foundations of a modern international tax framework under which profits are taxed where economic activity and value creation occurs."[226]

---

[221] The European Commission has already attempted to harmonize EU member state's corporate taxes. *See* Michael J. Graetz & Alvin C. Warren, Jr., "Income Tax Discrimination and the Political and Economic Integration of Europe," *Yale Law Journal* 115 (2006): 1186, 1228 n.143 (2006).

[222] According to the OECD, what is not fair are tax systems that encourage financial secrecy and inhibit effective information exchange, that lack transparency, and that do not require activities to be "substantial" to receive tax preferences. Organization for Economic Cooperation and Development, "Harmful Tax Competition: An Emerging Global Issue," 1998, *available at* www.oecd.org/tax/transparency/44430243.pdf.

[223] Indeed, the BEPS Project documents explicitly avoid suggesting any desired level of statutory corporate tax rates. *See, e.g.*, Countering Harmful Tax Practices Final Report, *supra* note 220, at 11.

[224] E.U. Member States, for example, cannot give tax benefits to selected companies.

[225] Indeed, the BEPS Project explicitly contemplates that countries will compete for economic activity by creating special tax preferences for targeted activities. *See, e.g.*, Countering Harmful Tax Practices Final Report, *supra* note 220, at 11.

[226] JCX-139-15 Report, *supra* note 2. *See* Clausing, *supra* note 52, at 22 ("The OECD/G20 process is commendable for pushing forward international cooperation in this area"); Brian O'Keefe & Marty Jones, "How Uber Plays the Tax Shell Game," Fortune, October 22, 2015, http://fortune.com/2015/10/22/uber-tax-shell/ (stating "The OECD's recommendations... represent the starting gun for a great tax grab by countries all over the world").

10 Final Thoughts on IP Holding Companies and Corporate Social Responsibility

In 2016, the US presidential election campaign brought tax avoidance to the forefront, exposing tax loopholes that allow individuals and corporations to avoid taxes. Years earlier people learned through news media and congressional hearings about wealthy individuals in Europe and the United States engaged in camouflage transactions to hide assets in overseas accounts to avoid taxes.[1] More recently, congressional hearings have turned attention to multinational companies, such as Apple, GE, and Microsoft, and on their offshore intellectual property shifting strategies.

While much attention has been directed to offshore IP Holding Companies, little has been paid to domestic tax havens and the use of domestic IP Holding Companies. The news media does not devote its time to Delaware's secrecy as it has with Swiss secrecy. The faraway shores seem to cast a glamorous spell on journalists and the public alike. However, the striking similarities between the domestic and foreign IP Holding Company tax avoidance schemes are difficult to dismiss. Both schemes begin with the recognition that there is enormous value in intellectual property assets. The assets are intangible, yet omnipresent, as the transfers and licensing of the assets are almost invisible and seamless. Corporate structures can be easily designed to facilitate the transfers and licenses of intellectual property assets among related companies without arousing suspicion. Shell companies, IP Holding Companies, are used to hold the intellectual property assets.

In both domestic and foreign schemes, multistate and multinational companies similarly seek to identify no-tax or low-tax jurisdictions where they can maximize benefits from their intellectual property portfolios. They locate the IP Holding Companies in those jurisdictions to ensure that the profits generated from the intellectual property assets are pretty much tax free. Both schemes exploit the intangible nature of intellectual

---

[1] "Offshore Tax Evasion: The Effort to Collect Unpaid Taxes on Billions in Hidden Offshore Account, Majority and Minority Staff Report," US Senate Permanent Subcommittee on Investigation, February 26, 2014.

property assets by creating a mailbox existence for IP Holding Companies. The obscure mailbox existence allows the related companies to create income deductible in one jurisdiction but not taxable in others. At the same time, the obscure mailbox existence allows for business as usual; the intellectual property assets are still within the control of and are used by the related companies. Business as usual continues, also, because outside competitors are kept out of the intellectual property assets. Both domestic and foreign IP Holding Companies accumulate vast amounts of income. Related affiliates devise strategies to allow them to use the accumulated wealth in ways that continue to avoid taxation. The familiar schemes continue year after year without attracting much attention.

Both schemes, ironically, involve companies that we the public admire for their product innovations, aesthetic designs, and attractive brands. We rely on Microsoft every day when we go to the office and turn on the operating system at our computers. We rely on GE for its equipment used in our offices and hospitals. We do not dare to deny that we love the Apple stores across the nation, bewitching us with their cool products and turning some of us into cultish fans bracing harsh weather to stand in line for hours to be the first to caress the latest design release. We admit that the Victoria's Secret lingerie is alluringly sexy, and its models have become household names. When winter comes, we want nothing except Gore-Tex products. The kid in us loves toys whenever we shop at Toys "R" Us or online. And we linger at buildings and houses that are freshly painted with Sherwin-Williams paint products.

Despite the important role these companies play in the economy, should governments – both national and subnational – stop them from utilizing their tax avoidance schemes? On the *domestic front*, some US states have tried. Some states, for example, have passed legislation requiring "combined reporting" of income of all affiliated companies. Other states have attempted in different ways to prevent a parent company from deducting royalties paid to controlled IP Holding Companies for the licensing of intellectual property – most recently through enactment of so-called "addback" statutes. On the *international front*, national governments have also tried to prevent the shifting of intellectual property income to low-tax jurisdictions. Some have tried, for example, to tighten their transfer pricing rules when related companies transfer or license intellectual property to one another. Some have adopted rules, specifically controlled foreign corporation (CFC) rules, that attempt to impose current domestic taxation on foreign IP Holding Company income even if that foreign income is not sent home right away.

These domestic and international "stick" approaches to prevent intellectual property income shifting have not worked so well. With respect to domestic IP Holding Companies, "combined reporting" and "addback" legislative measures have not solved the problem completely because of definitional problems and various built-in exceptions that dilute their effectiveness. A significant hurdle is that not all states have adopted similar legislative measures. With respect to foreign IP Holding Companies, transfer pricing rules and CFC rules have been largely ineffective. Transfer pricing rules are too fuzzy, especially with respect to difficult-to-value intellectual property assets owned by multinationals that control much of the information with respect to them. CFC rules are subject to varying exceptions and statutory hurdles that undermine their effectiveness.

Some domestic and foreign governments have rejected these stick measures because they want to be competitive to encourage the use of IP Holding Companies within their jurisdictions. A few US states have created very attractive tax incentives for IP Holding Companies, while at the same time demanding little from them and protecting them through secrecy. Although these states do not collect corporate income tax from IP Holding Companies, they do obtain various registration fees from the IP Holding Companies. In addition, these states reap the benefit of job creation in connection with the legal, accounting, and office-related services utilized by the IP Holding Companies. The registration fees and job creation associated with IP Holding Companies come without the headaches of dealing with brick-and-mortar companies, ranging from physical space demands and land use issues to environmental pollution. Mailbox existence does not require much! In other words, these states understand the power and benefits of using tax policy as competition.

Globally, a number of countries have created very attractive incentives for multinational companies to form IP Holding Companies. Some countries begin by offering a very low statutory corporate income tax rate, and some go even further by negotiating with select multinationals much lower rates than the statutory rate. Some countries offer attractive tax deductions and credits for R&D spending, and then offer a special low rate on intellectual property income resulting from R&D. While all of these incentives reduce the effective tax rate on intellectual property income and result in little corporate income tax revenues for the government, the incentives can work to lure intellectual property to the countries' borders. This in turn can enhance economic growth in the country, including increased jobs and a resulting increase in personal income tax revenues.

Governments have been using tax policy as a means to compete with other governments for years. Each US state or each country develops strategies to enhance its competitiveness in order to ensure economic growth, as each government has its own responsibilities to its own citizens. Attracting companies to invest and do business in a particular state or country is a priority for many governments, as they routinely engage in efforts to maneuver against one another. Tax incentives are often used by governments to encourage new companies to be created within their borders and to encourage existing foreign companies to uproot themselves, leaving one state to come to another state, or leaving one country to come to another. The perfect union of the United States does not prevent states from engaging in tax competition, as long as what states are doing is not in violation of the US Constitution. Likewise, shared global goals, such as those recognized by the Organization for Economic Cooperation and Development (OECD), to improve international economies do not prevent nations from developing different tax policies to attract and retain valuable activities within their borders.

But it seems that some governments (including some states within the United States, and some countries across the globe) have taken tax competition to another level in attracting intellectual property to their jurisdictions. Take Delaware for an example – a domestic tax haven that was the subject of the first half of this book. That state has shown that it has long anticipated and appreciated the "evolving nature of the American economy" to now become highly dependent on the development of new technology in every sector. Delaware understands that many corporations will spend enormous resources to develop their intellectual property assets. If corporations cannot develop the intellectual property assets in-house, they will acquire them from target companies in order to remain competitive in the marketplace. Unlike physical assets, the intellectual property assets require proper maintenance, strategic monetization, protection, and enforcement in order for the corporations to obtain the maximum value from the assets. Delaware's "key component" for its "economic development strategy" is none other than its "corporate tax policy" squarely aimed at corporations with intellectual property portfolios that have products or services dependent on the use of intellectual property rights in many states.[2] These corporations are the multistate corporations – prized targets for Delaware. As the nature of the American economy has become more innovative and tech dependent, the number of Delaware's targeted corporations has grown, and will continue to grow. Delaware has carefully considered its math: It will come out ahead by *not* imposing corporate tax on multistate corporations with intellectual property assets.

---

[2] Brief of the State of Delaware as Amicus Curiae in Support of Petitioner, *VFJ Ventures, Inc. v. Surtees*, 2009 WL 481241, at *3 (February 23, 2009).

Here is how. Delaware banks on the corporate fees, lots of fees.[3] The more companies that are incorporated in Delaware, the more fees it will generate.[4] Delaware also collects a franchise tax at the rate of $350 per $1,000,000 of assumed par value capital. The maximum amount of franchise tax a corporate taxpayer will pay is $180,000. With the fees and franchise taxes that Delaware receives annually for its general fund revenue, according to Chancellor William B. Chandler, Delaware Court of Chancery, Delaware can "avoid" imposing "other taxes" including corporate tax on multistate corporations with intellectual property assets.[5] Intellectual property assets generate large income from licensing arrangements. Delaware, however, purposefully forgoes taxing the corporate income stemming from the licensing of intellectual property assets received by multistate corporations. In other words, Delaware strategically encourages the multistate corporations to form more corporations (think more fees) to hold intellectual property assets separately in Delaware.

Also, Delaware shifts the tax focus from corporations to its individual citizens. As a tradeoff, by luring multistate corporations to form tax-free IP Holding Companies in Delaware, the state creates new jobs relating to serving these companies. Multistate companies need lawyers, accountants, business entity agents, and specialized administrative support personnel to service the needs of their IP Holding Companies. These are the types of jobs that offer competitive compensation for Delaware citizens. The state in turn collects tax on the personal income of the employees of the IP Holding Companies and their service providers, not the income of the IP Holding Companies themselves. This is a policy choice that Delaware has made, and it is the way Delaware competes with other states. Indeed, Delaware derives only 3.7 percent of its tax revenue from the corporate income tax, compared to 32.9 percent from the

---

[3] "Delaware Department of State Division of Corporations Fee Schedule," revised August 1, 2016, *available at* https://corp.delaware.gov/Julyfee2016.pdf.

[4] In addition to corporation-related fees, Delaware also collects UCC filing fees whenever businesses engage in borrowing or financing transactions. *See* "UCC Filing & Expedited Fees," State of Delaware, accessed October 30, 2016, https://corp.delaware.gov/uccfees Sept09.shtml.

[5] William B. Chandler III & Anthony A. Rickey, "Manufacturing Mystery: A Response to Professors Carney and Shepherd's 'The Mystery of Delaware Law's Continuing Success,'" *University of Illinois Law Review* 2009 (2009): 99 ("As of April 2008, over 63 percent of Fortune 500 companies were incorporated in Delaware, and the state had captured about 75 percent of all U.S. initial public offerings since January 2003, despite being one of the nation's smallest and least populous states. Delaware has every incentive to maintain its advantage in this area; the franchise taxes and chartering fees procured from this dominance constitute a significant portion of the state's general fund revenue and allow the General Assembly to avoid imposing other taxes").

personal income tax in 2016.[6] With this tax policy choice, Delaware has edged out other states in business recruitment. Indeed, Delaware's tax policy has been successful, and it touts that it has become the "leading intellectual property center" and the home of domestic IP Holding Companies.[7]

Another benefit of Delaware's tax policy decision is that it has become the leading intellectual property center *without* environmental and infra-structure problems suffered by other states with companies that are actually *producing* intellectual property. California tech workers, from software to biotech, cannot afford housing. They face daily traffic congestion and pay a high cost of living. Urban cities like Seattle and Boston, producers of intellectual property, encounter similar problems. Delaware and its cities are not known as producers of intellectual property, and yet there are more intellectual property assets held in Delaware than in any other state. This anomaly can only happen due to the nature of intellectual property assets. The value of the intellectual property assets are the rights granted by law. The intellectual property rights are separate from the physical embodiments of patents, copyrights, trade secrets, trademarks, and the like. The rights can be transferred and licensed without the attending physical assets. Billions in value can be transferred and licensed with ease. That is how Delaware IP Holding Companies so easily receive the intellectual property rights from their affiliates and then so easily license them back without the need for trucks, trains, or aircraft for the actual transactions.

The effortless transactions between multistate companies and their IP Holding Companies happen daily without attracting attention from any pairs of prying eyes. Delaware makes the transactions much easier by adding a layer of corporate secrecy. The transactions are private. Delaware protects corporate privacy; it is difficult to break through to take a peek at private corporate filings. Also, because Delaware does not tax IP Holding Companies, it does not need to know much about how these companies make money, and, therefore, it does not need these companies to file much of anything.

There is no question that Delaware is the poster child for multistate tax competition. What Delaware has been doing – making itself a domestic tax haven for multistate corporations with intellectual property portfolios – is legitimate. Other states are free to do exactly what

---

[6] "State General Fund: Revenue By Category (F.Y. 2014 – F.Y. 2016)," accessed October 30, 2016, *available at* http://finance.delaware.gov/publications/fiscal_notebook_15/Secti on02/sec2page30.pdf.

[7] Brief of the State of Delaware as Amicus Curiae in Support of Petitioner, *VFJ Ventures, Inc. v. Surtees*, 2009 WL 481241, at *5.

Delaware does. Yet few states have tried, because none can really match the almighty Delaware. Delaware already has a significant head start through its existing dominance in all things corporation. Indeed, the majority of Fortune 500 companies are incorporated there, and two-thirds of all US initial public offerings occur in Delaware.

Delaware has every incentive to maintain its advantage. It does not want to work with other states to destroy its status as the leading intellectual property center and home of IP Holding Companies. It does not want to change the tax policy that it has carefully calibrated but which other states for years have ignored. The tax competition works well for its citizens and allows Delaware, as a whole, to survive, to compete, and to thrive. In fact, any approach or reform by other states relating to IP Holding Companies is a threat to Delaware, a kiss of death to its tax advantage.

Here is why. If other states find a bulletproof way to prevent multistate companies from deducting royalties payments that they make to their IP Holding Companies, then there would be no need to form the IP Holding Companies in Delaware! Put another way, if states prohibit multistate companies from taking royalty deductions, then intellectual property income would not be shifted tax free to Delaware but instead would effectively be subject to taxation in all the states in which the multistate companies do business. Without the royalty deductions, there would be no incentive for multistate companies to form the IP Holding Companies in the first place. And without tons of IP Holding Companies, Delaware would collect no fees. Moreover, Delaware jobs would disappear, and the personal income tax base that Delaware has relied upon so heavily would be eroded. The snowball effect would be significant. But there would be little that Delaware could do other than abandon its corporate tax exemption for IP Holding Companies. That may not be a bad thing.

Tax havens (domestic ones like Delaware, or international ones like Ireland, Singapore, Luxembourg, and the Netherlands) have allowed multistate and multinational corporations to aggressively create schemes and engage in transactions inconsistent with the notion of corporate social responsibility.[8] Under the banner of maximizing profits for its shareholders, corporations have passed social responsibility obligations onto the state. As states need funding to meet their obligations, they run into the layers of tax strategies in connection with a corporation's most valuable intellectual property assets to prevent them from raising necessary revenue. They face the tax competition policies carefully crafted by other

---

[8] Reuven S. Avi-Yonah, "Corporate Taxation and Corporate Social Responsibility," *NYU Journal of Law & Business* 11 (2014): 1.

states or nations. They react and chase after the income imbued in circuitous movements. The governments cannot win in this chase, and individuals continue to pay the lion's share of the tax burden.

Finding a "government" solution may be too hard. A number of "stick" measures have already been tried to no avail, and most new ideas have conceptual and practical challenges.[9] This is especially apparent when comparing government approaches in the domestic context (first half of this book) and in the international context (second half of the book). For example, it has been suggested that US states look to international tax sourcing rules as a solution to prevent the shifting of intellectual property income among states. Ironically, existing international source rules are not doing so well to prevent the extensive shifting of intellectual property income among nations that we see today. To combat global shifting of intellectual property income, it has been suggested that countries could adopt formulary apportionment to allocate multinational income among countries. Ironically, the United States already uses that approach to allocate multistate income among individual states, and, as we saw in the first half of the book that approach does not eliminate the shifting of intellectual property and related income. Interestingly, the European Commission has proposed a version of formulary apportionment for dividing profits among member countries, but the proposal has met with resistance from some European countries and many European companies.

Many governments are shifting to "carrot" measures to compete for intellectual property and related income, such as lowering the statutory tax rate on corporate income in general and offering a special low rate on intellectual property income. The Trump administration has trumpeted the idea of a "tax repatriation holiday" to encourage US multinational companies to bring home the trillions in cash they have stashed offshore (much of which is attributable to untaxed profits from intellectual property). But that would not "fix" the underlying problem; moreover, there is no guarantee that the money coming back would benefit the US economy. As a more permanent solution to income shifting, the Trump administration has proposed lowering the US corporate income tax rate from 35 percent to 15 percent, following corporate rate reductions by

---

[9] In 2016, the U.S. House GOP released a tax reform proposal that would replace the current corporate income tax with what is called a Destination Based Cash Flow Tax (DBCFT). The tax, which would be somewhat similar to a value added tax, would attempt to tax goods where sold and, as such, might reduce tax advantages of shifting intellectual property to low tax countries. But the proposal has a long list of "known unknowns" and its passage is uncertain. *See* Michael J. Graetz, *The Known Unknowns of the Business Tax Reforms Proposed in the House Republican Blueprint*, February 2, 2017, *available at* https://papers.ssrn.com/sol3/papers2.cfm?abstract_id=2910569.

many other nations. While such change would seemingly bring US companies close to a level playing field with competitors, it would not be the lowest rate among nations considering the special rate deals some countries give multinationals and the many newly created "patent boxes" that offer low statutory rates on income from intellectual property. Moreover, it would likely be followed by further rate reductions by other nations. We clearly would see a new "race to the bottom." Indeed, the Ontario government has said recently that it is prepared to lower corporate taxes, if necessary, to keep the province competitive with the United States.

Efforts by both state and national governments to curtail the use of IP Holding Companies to avoid taxes are unlikely to be completely effective for a couple key reasons. Consider a spectrum of profit allocation methods that might be adopted. On one end of the spectrum, there is *separate reporting* (or separate accounting), which sources income to the jurisdiction in which it is earned. On the other end, there is *formulary apportionment*, which allocates income based on some combination of factors such as sales, employees, and physical assets. Separate reporting is currently adopted in the international context to allocate profits among countries. Formulary apportionment, in contrast, is currently adopted in the domestic context to allocate profits among US states. As seen in this book, neither approach, as currently designed, works to prevent intellectual property income shifting. For either approach to be completely effective, the unachievable would have to be achieved. For separate reporting to be effective, cost sharing agreements would have to be eliminated and the arm's-length transfer pricing rules would have to be fixed. These measures would seemingly be impossible in light of failed efforts over the past three decades to fix transfer pricing. For formulary apportionment to be effective, jurisdictions would have to agree on the tax base and the formula factors; in addition, they would have to require their residents to account for all related entities. These measures have not fully been achieved in the US states (explaining income shifting domestically), and would be nearly impossible to achieve globally as international coordination would be difficult. Any profit allocation methods adopted somewhere between separate reporting and formulary apportionment would be "second best" approaches.

With a lack of viable options by governments to control the use of IP Holding Companies to shift intellectual property income, now may be a good time to push for voluntary self-regulation by multistate and multinational companies with valuable intellectual property assets. Indeed, the best approach to reduce the number of tax-motivated, aggressive corporate tax transactions, like the IP Holding Company schemes, may not be a government approach at all, but rather a shift in the corporate culture of multistate and multinational corporations: rejecting such schemes as inconsistent with corporate social responsibility.[10] Companies often defend their aggressive tax strategies as in the best interest of their stakeholders. They claim that they have a fiduciary duty to maximize corporate profits for the benefit of shareholders, and, therefore, are legally required to engage in tax strategies to minimize corporate taxes. But basing aggressive tax strategies upon the fiduciary duties owed to stockholders is wrong. Corporate governors satisfy their legal obligations if they run the corporation "*primarily* for the profit of the stockholders,' which leaves room for other secondary considerations."[11] Doctrines other than the fiduciary duty doctrine, such as the "corporate social responsibility" doctrine come into play when necessary "to protect society from the damage that tax avoidance can create."[12]

Corporate governance scholars have observed that in today's modern, dynamic, viral social media world, companies have shown that they take corporate social responsibility on a much broader and meaningful level than in the past. Issues once thought to be outside the core business functions are now included in corporate missions and business models to create shared value for both business and society. In the environmental efforts area, many companies today do not just only donate to charities for natural disasters, they embed sustainability into the core of their missions and business functions. They take steps to reduce their own carbon footprints. In the information privacy front, they have carefully drafted privacy policy and taken steps to address unauthorized disclosure. After all, companies do not exist in isolation. Their employees, customers, communities, vendors, distributors, suppliers, creditors, and governments are all affected by companies and their activities. The internet and social media force companies to be increasingly transparent. Companies can no longer sit back while pictures, video clips, and Twitter messages that are negative about them and

---

[10] Avi-Yonah, *supra* note 8, at 26 (arguing that aggressive tax-motivated transactions are inconsistent with the notion of corporate social responsibility, and that maximizing profits for shareholders requires social responsibility obligations to fall onto the government); *but see* Manal S. Corwin, "Sense and Sensibility: The Policy and Politics of BEPS," *Tax Notes* (2014): 136, *available at* https://kpmg-us-inst.adobecqms.net/content/dam/kpmg/tax watch/pdf/2014/beps-corwin-tillinghast-tn-100614.pdf (arguing "morality cannot serve as a guiding principle for establishing, implementing, or enforcing complex international tax rules and standards in a global world").

[11] Eric C. Chaffee & Karie Davis-Nozemack, "Corporate Tax Avoidance and Honoring the Fiduciary Duties Owed to Corporation and Its Stockholders," *Boston College L. Rev.* 59 (forthcoming 2017).

[12] *Ibid.* (concluding "that while some minimal amount of tax avoidance may be acceptable that very aggressive forms of tax avoidance should be avoided").

their activities go viral. Their credibility, trust, and associated brands and goodwill are at stake in the incredibly dynamic world where what was permissible yesterday may not be tomorrow. In some cases, compliance with the laws is no longer good enough, as we have seen with Nike and its child labor practices in international locations. Nike could not hide behind local laws when its factories used child labor. Outcries from communities ensure that companies have integrity and adhere to certain values.

Take a look at Starbucks. Since 1998, the Starbucks Coffee Company Limited has been serving its latte and coffees in posh stores across the UK. Starbucks, however, reported that in fourteen out of the fifteen years in operation there, the company recorded losses. It achieved losses by utilizing a scheme involving its intellectual property assets, paying substantial sums to related group companies through "(1) royalties and license fees paid to a Dutch affiliate, (2) markups on coffee purchased via another Dutch affiliate and Swiss affiliate, and (3) interest paid on a loan from the US parent company."[13] While Starbucks claimed losses on its UK financial statements, the Company bragged that "Canada, the UK, China and Japan are our largest international markets and drive the majority of the segment's revenue and operating profits. Each of these markets is profitable to Starbucks. Each is a priority for future investment, and each is a key component of future growth."[14] The public expressed outrage at Starbucks for stashing its profits in tax havens through the use of intellectual property schemes in order to avoid paying corporate tax in the UK[15] There is no doubt that Starbucks was law-abiding, but in the eyes of the public and communities, what it did was just not right. A few months after the public outrage, in June 2013, Starbucks decided to voluntarily pay over 5 million pounds in UK taxes and promised to pay 15 million pounds of tax in 2014.[16] Starbucks

---

[13] Edward D. Kleinbard, "Through a Latte Darkly: Starbucks's Stateless Income Planning," *Tax Notes* (2013): 1520, *available at* www.law.usc.edu/centers/class/class-workshops/usc-legal-studies-working-papers/documents/c13_9_paper.pdf.

[14] Lisa Pollack, "Media Said, Starbucks Said," *Financial Times Alphaville Blog*, December 12, 2012, http://ftalphaville.ft.com/2012/12/12/1304442/media-said-starbucks-said/.

[15] *See* Margaret Hodge & Jeff Jarvis, "Should We Boycott Google, Starbucks and Amazon?," *The Guardian*, November 17, 2012, www.theguardian.com/commentisfree/2012/nov/17/should-boycott-google-starbucks-amazon ("Of course it is up to the government to act, both in the UK and internationally, to ensure that global companies pay tax according to where they make their profit and don't stash it away in tax havens such as Luxembourg and Bermuda. But consumers can use their power too. By boycotting these companies we not only voice our anger but hit them where it hurts. And any credible government will have to respond to public outrage at unacceptable tax avoidance").

[16] Matthew Boyle, "Starbucks Pays $15.4 Million U.K. Corporation Tax Amid Backlash," *Bloomberg*, June 24, 2013, www.bloomberg.com/news/articles/2013-06-24/starbucks-pays-15-4-million-u-k-corporation-tax-amid-backlash.

stated that it "listened to [its] customers . . . and decided to forgo certain deductions."[17] Starbucks's action has been hailed as an example of corporate social responsibility. Paying corporate taxes instead of claiming tax losses from the aggressive tax avoidance scheme is Starbucks's way of showing that Starbucks is doing its part of being a citizen, a member of the community. Indeed, Starbucks and other companies are social actors and receive benefits from the security, the police departments, roads and transportation means, education, infrastructure, and labor pools provided by the community and the government. They benefit from the judicial system provided by the government to enforce business contracts. Moreover, on their own initiatives, US companies have also sought from the Supreme Court, and gained, the rights of citizens to free speech and the right to free exercise of religion. The rights of citizens include the civic obligations of sharing the costs of social policies funded by governments through taxes.

Starbucks's voluntary action is laudable. Starbucks is just one company, however, and its voluntary payment of additional taxes was an isolated act. And, it may be difficult for companies to follow Starbucks's lead especially if they feel that they will lose a competitive tax edge if many other companies do not follow suit. To the extent we hope multistate and multinational companies will act voluntarily in response to social pressures, it might be more useful to encourage entire industries that rely on intellectual property to work together so that no one company loses a competitive edge. There is precedent for this type of collaboration on social issues other than tax (e.g., labour and environmental policies),[18] and we see no reason why similar collaboration on cross-border tax policies could not be considered as an option. In the past, changing public attitudes (and companies' vulnerability to bad publicity) have provided the context in which corporate codes of conduct have been adopted. The current wave of public resentment over the use of aggressive tax strategies should provide a similar impetus for industry self-regulation with respect to tax matters. Sectors of the economy that rely heavily on intellectual property, such as high tech and big pharma, should consider developing voluntary codes of conduct governing tax strategies. These codes could range from vague declarations of tax principles to more substantive self-regulation tax efforts.

---

[17] *Ibid.*
[18] *See* Rhys Jenkins, "Corporate Codes of Conduct: Self-Regulation in a Global Economy," Technology, Business and Society Programme Paper Number 2 (April 2001), United Nations Research Institute for Social Development, *available at* http://www.unrisd.org/80256B3C005BCCF9/search/E3B3E78BAB9A886F80256B5E00344278.

Starbucks's action is the beginning of multistate and multinational corporations doing what is right for business and society with respect to aggressive tax avoidance schemes. Hopefully, we will soon see a snowballing effect, as we have seen what corporations did in the environmental standards, working conditions, human rights, and discrimination areas. Their actions become norms, regardless of laws. They exhibit the new wisdom that today's forward-thinking corporations must be both constituency-centered and shareholder-centric.

Index

Cambridge Intellectual Property and Information Law

Titles in the series (formerly known as Cambridge Studies in Intellectual Property Rights)